SPRACHWISSENSCHAFTLICHE
STUDIENBÜCHER

*Für Katja,
herzlichst,
Martin

3.6.2002*

MANFRED GÖRLACH

A Re-view of Reviews

Universitätsverlag
C. WINTER
Heidelberg

Die Deutsche Bibliothek – CIP-Einheitsaufnahme
Ein Titeldatensatz für diese Publikation
ist bei der Deutschen Bibliothek erhältlich.

ISBN 3-8253-1319-0

Dieses Werk einschließlich aller seiner Teile ist urheberrechtlich geschützt. Jede Verwertung außerhalb der engen Grenzen des Urheberrechtsgesetzes ist ohne Zustimmung des Verlages unzulässig und strafbar. Das gilt insbesondere für Vervielfältigungen, Übersetzungen, Mikroverfilmungen und die Einspeicherung und Verarbeitung in elektronischen Systemen.

© 2002 Universitätsverlag C. Winter Heidelberg GmbH
Imprimé en Allemagne · Printed in Germany
Druck: Strauss Offsetdruck GmbH, 69509 Mörlenbach

Gedruckt auf umweltfreundlichem, chlorfrei gebleichtem
und alterungsbeständigem Papier

Den Verlag erreichen Sie im Internet unter:
www.winter-verlag-hd.de

Abbreviations

AmE	American English	NZE	New Zealand English
AusE	Australian English	OE	Old English
BrE	British English	*OED*	*Oxford English Dictionary*
CarE	Caribbean English	p.c.	personal communication
EETS	Early English Text Society	PC	Pidgin/Creole
EModE	Early Modern English	SAfE	South African English
GhPE	Ghanaian Pidgin English	ScE	Scottish English
IntE	International English	St E	Standard English
ME	Middle English		

AAA	*Arbeiten aus Anglistik und Amerikanistik*. Tübingen: Narr.
Anglia	*Anglia, Zeitschrift für englische Philologie*. Tübingen: Niemeyer.
AS	*American Speech. Journal of the American Dialect Society*. Tuscaloosa: The University of Alabama Press.
AUMLA	*Journal of the Australian Universities Modern Languages Association*. Melbourne: University Press.
CQ	*Colloquia Germanica*. Amsterdam: Benjamins.
ELL	*English Language and Linguistics*. Cambridge: University Press.
EWW	*English World-Wide*. Amsterdam: Benjamins.
FLH	*Folia Linguistica Historica*. The Hague: Mouton.
Germanistik	Tübingen: Niemeyer.
IF	*Indogermanische Forschungen*. Berlin: de Gruyter.
IJL	*International Journal of Lexicography*. Oxford: University Press.
JEngL	*Journal of English Linguistics*. Tuscaloosa: The University of Alabama Press.
JPCL	*Journal of Pidgin and Creole Languages*. Amsterdam: Benjamins.
Lexicographica	*International Annual for Lexicography*. Tübingen: Niemeyer.
LPLP	*Language Problems and Language Planning*. Amsterdam: Benjamins.
LSoc	*Language in Society*. Cambridge: University Press.
N&Q	*Notes and Queries*. Oxford: University Press.
PBB	*Pauls und Braunes Beiträge = Beiträge zur Geschichte der deutschen Sprache und Literatur*. Tübingen: Niemeyer.
RES	*Review of English Studies*. Oxford: Clarendon.
Sociolinguistica	*Internationales Jahrbuch für Europäische Linguistik*. Tübingen: Niemeyer.
ZAA	*Zeitschrift für Anglistik und Amerikanistik*. Tübingen: Stauffenberg.
ZCPh	*Zeitschrift für Celtische Philologie*. Tübingen: Niemeyer.
ZDL	*Zeitschrift für Dialektologie und Linguistik*. Wiesbaden: Steiner.

CONTENTS

Foreword 1

1 Medieval Studies

1   Recent facsimile editions of Middle English literary manuscripts 3
2   *The Vernon Manuscript*, ed. A.I. Doyle 29
3   *The Works of Geoffrey Chaucer,* eds. Julia Boffey and A.S.G. Edwards ... 32
4   *Studies in the Vernon Manuscript*, ed. Derek Pearsall 33
5   A Variorum Edition of the Works of Geoffrey Chaucer 36
6   *Geoffrey Chaucer, Troilus & Criseyde,* ed. B.A. Windeatt 40
7   Helen Cooper, *The Canterbury Tales* and Barry Windeatt, *Troilus and Criseyde* 43
8   William Langland, *Piers Plowman. A Parallel-Text Edition of the A, B, C and Z Versions*, ed. A. V. C. Schmidt and William Langland, *The Vision of Piers Plowman*, A Critical Edition of the B-Text, ed. A.V.C. Schmidt ... 46
9   Angus McIntosh, *et al., Middle English Dialectology* and *The English of Chaucer and his contemporaries.* 49

2 Historical Linguistics and the History of English

10 Lyle Campbell, *Historical Linguistics. An Introduction* 53
11 Recent introductory text books in (English) historical linguistics
    N.F. Blake, *A History of the English Language* 55
    J.J. Smith, *An Historical Study of English Function, Form and Change* ... 56
    R.L. Trask, *Historical Linguistics* 57
12 *The Cambridge History of the English Language.*
    Vol. 1, *The Beginnings to 1066*, ed. Richard M. Hogg
    Vol. 2, *1066-1476*, ed. Norman Blake 58
13 Vol. 4, *1779-1997*, ed. Suzanne Romaine 63
14 David Denison, *English Historical Syntax* 66
15 A *British Linguistics in the 19th Century*, ed. Roy Harris 70

3 Dialectology, Sociolinguistics and Contact Linguistics

16 William Labov, *Principles of Linguistic Change. Internal Factors* 85
    Principles of Linguistic Change. Social Factors. 88
17 Werner Besch, *et al.*, eds., *Dialektologie.* 92
18 W.N. Francis, *Dialectology. An Introduction* 94
19 Peter Trudgill, ed., *Language in the British Isles* and
    Glanville Price, *The Languages of Britain* 95
20 Peter Trudgill, *Dialects in Contact* 101
21 Charles Jones, ed., *The Edinburgh History of the Scots Language* 103

22	John Corbett, *A History of Literary Translation into Scots*.	109
23	Graham Tulloch, *A History of the Scots Bible*	111
24	John Holm, *Pidgins and Creoles*	113
25	Jean D'Costa and Barbara Lalla, eds., *Voices in Exile* and Barbara Lalla and Jean D'Costa, *Language in Exile*	116
26	Magnus Huber, *Ghanaian Pidgin English*	119
27	Stephen A. Wurm & Peter Mühlhäusler, eds., *Handbook of Tok Pisin*	121
28	Peter Mühlhäusler, *Growth and Structure of the Lexicon of New Guinea Pidgin*	124
29	Sarah Grey Thomason & Terence Kaufman, *Language Contact, Creolization, and Genetic Linguistics*	126
30	Hans Goebl, *et al.*, eds., *Contact Linguistics*.	128

4   Lexicography

31	Jane Roberts and Christian Kay, *A Thesaurus of Old English*..	133
32	Werner Hüllen, *English Dictionaries 800-1700. The Topical Tradition*	136
33	C.I. Macafee, ed., *A Concise Ulster Dictionary*	140
34	Frederic G. Cassidy, *Dictionary of American Regional English*, vols I-III	143
35	*Dictionary of Jamaican English*, ed. F. G. Cassidy and R. B. Le Page and *Dictionary of Bahamian English*, John A. Holm	148
36	Richard Allsopp, *Dictionary of Caribbean English Usage*	155
37	Jean Branford, *A Dictionary of South African English* and D.R. Beeton & Helen Dorner, *A Dictionary of English Usage in Southern Africa*	161
38	Penny Silva, ed., *A Dictionary of South African English*	165
39	W.S. Ramson ed., *The Australian National Dictionary*	168
40	H.W. Orsman, ed., *The Dictionary of New Zealand English*	171

Reviews 1972-2002: A bibliography 174

Index of persons 214

Index of topics 220

Foreword

Reviews count among the most ephemeral text types in a scholar's life. They are often excluded from lists of publications, read superficially when fresh and forgotten soon after. And yet this lack of attention is in stark contrast to the amount of care and toil that tends to go into writing reviews. There are even a few famous cases where duly critical reviews are so important for the understanding of the original work that should be best bound together with the books treated. Some reviews have substantially contributed to the (book) author's scholary career, or helped to slow it down. Much more seldom have reviews added to the nitpicking reviewer's fame.

My 750 reviews, written in the course of the past thirty years, show obvious concentrations as far as topics and journals are concerned. The fact that I was the founder-editor of *EWW* and responsible for the Shorter Notices section of condensed reviews included in the journal largely accounts for the fact that more than half of the reviews I ever wrote are on varieties of English and were written for *EWW*. However, the early phase of my reviews concentrates more on medieval studies and historical linguistics, with journals like *Anglia* and *Archiv* predominating. More recently, many reviews have been written for *AAA*, *IJL* and *Linguistics*, on topics including dictionaries/lexicography and sociolinguistics. Two graphs illustrating the share of individual journals and documenting the annual output of reviews are illustrative of such changing activities.

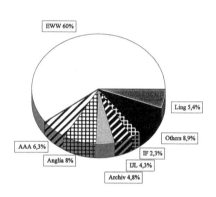

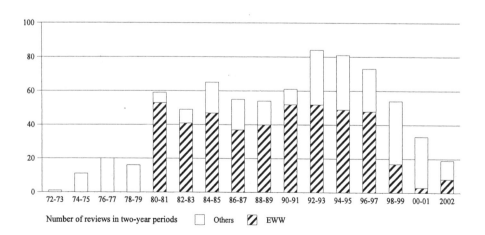

Dispersed in so many journals, some difficult to access, the reviews are not easy to find. I have therefore decided to reprint a small part of those published. For my personal selection I have chosen those that appear to have survived the sad fate of ephemerality, or (arguably) appear to be worth reprinting; I hope they contain enough material to be informative in their own right, taking up topics relating to philological and linguistic method rather than flogging dead horses. Let the benevolent reader judge whether the collection here reprinted is of sufficient interest to be re-read – and even re-open the books which in many cases have been counted amongst the classics in the scholarly literature of the past few decades.

I have arranged the texts by subject matter grouping them in four sections, neglecting the chronological sequence of their publication. The texts are printed as they were published (including instances where I may have gone astray); I have, however, inserted a few instances of updated information in [brackets] and deleted a few overlaps caused by the publication of reviews of related books in different journals.

I have included only reviews written in English (although the books reviewed are not restricted to publications in English). The fields used for the arrangement of the reviews are as follows:

1) Medieval studies
2) Historical linguistics and the history of English
3) Dialectology, sociolinguistics and contact linguistics
4) Lexicography

(There was no room to accommodate a representative selection of my reviews of books on varieties of English and world English; summaries of my most important reviews in this field is therefore included in my *Still More Englishes*. (VEAW, Amsterdam: Benjamins, 2002), where they have an appropriate place).

There is a full list of my reviews (1972-2002) towards the end of the book in which the reprints are clearly indicated. Indexes to topics refer to both reprinted texts and the unannotated section, whereas names are indexed only for the texts, the authors of reviewed books being easily available in the alphabetical list.

I would like to thank the publishers of the original reviews for their consent to let me reprint the texts, Eilert Erfling of Universitätsverlag C. Winter, who was immediately willing to accept my proposal of a slightly unusual book, Sirka Laass for the immaculate production of photoready copy – and all the helpers who read through my draft reviews before they were published, O.S. Pickering and Helen Weiss in particular. I am grateful for the permission of Loriot to reproduce two of his cartoons for the inner title.

Cologne, January 2002   Manfred Görlach

1 Medieval Studies

Since my early research was dominated by ME texts, in particular ME legends (which formed the topic of my Heidelberg 1970 doctoral thesis and has resulted in five monographs and my founding the Middle English Text series in 1975), my concern for ME philology will not come as a surprise. This is reflected in a great number of reviews from which I here reprint first those describing the potentials of ME facsimiles (an enterprise that does not appear to have been continued after the 1980s, as a consequence of the enormous costs involved). Also, reviews of editions and linguistic monographs on Chaucer and Langland have been selected for their intrinsic interest.

1 "Recent facsimile editions of Middle English literary manuscripts[1]", from *Anglia* 105 (1987), 121-51.

The Auchinleck Manuscript, National Library of Scotland, Advocates' MS. 19.2.1. With an introduction by Derek Pearsall and I.C. Cunningham. London: Scolar Press, 1977, xxvi pp. + 355 folios in facsimile.

Cambridge University Library MS Ff. 2.38. Introduction by Frances McSparran and P.R. Robinson. London: Scolar Press. 1979, xxx pp. + 247 folios in facsimile.

The Thornton Manuscript, Lincoln Cathedral MS 91. Introduction by D.S. Brewer and A.E.B. Owen. London: Scolar Press, 1975, ²1977, xxii pp. + 321 folios in facsimile.

The Findern Manuscript, Cambridge University Library Ff. 1.6. With an introduction by Richard Beadle and A.E.B. Owen. London: Scolar Press, 1977, xxxv pp. + 165 folios in facsimile.

Bodleian Library MS Fairfax 16. With an Introduction by John Norton-Smith. London: Scolar Press, 1979, xxx + 688 pp.

Geoffrey Chaucer, Troilus and Criseyde. A facsimile of Corpus Christi College Cambridge MS 61, with introductions by M.B. Parkes and Elizabeth Salter. Cambridge: D.S. Brewer, 1978, 23 + 302 pp.

The Winchester Malory. A facsimile edition, with an introduction by N.R. Ker. EETS, SS4. Oxford: Oxford University Press, 1978, xxii pp. + 473 folios in facsimile.

The Chester Mystery Cycle. A facsimile of MS Bodley 175. With an introduction by R.M. Lumiansky and David Mills. Medieval Drama Facsimiles, I. Leeds: The University, School of English, 1973, xv pp. + 176 folios in facsimile.

The Towneley Cycle. Facsimile of Huntington MS HM 1. With an introduction by A.C. Cawley and Martin Stevens. MDF, II. Leeds: The University, School of English, 1976, xix pp., one colour plate and 132 folios in facsimile.

---

[1] Many colleagues have kindly helped me with factual information and stylistic advice. I would like to thank H. Bonheim, A.I. Doyle, H. Gneuss, A. Hudson, H. Käsmann, D. Pearsall, O.S. Pickering and M.L. Samuels. For a list of earlier facsimiles of Brown (1974). The magnificent facsimiles of OE texts are quite different in aim and price, and are not considered in this survey.

The Digby Plays. Facsimiles of the plays in Bodley MSS Digby 133 and e Museo 160. With an introduction by Donald C. Baker and J.L. Murphy. MDF, III. Leeds: The University, School of English, 1976, xix pp., 2 colour plates and 89 + 33 folios in facsimile.

The N-Town Plays. A facsimile of British Library MS Cotton Vespasian D VIII. With an introduction by Peter Meredith and Stanley J. Kahrl. MDF, IV. Leeds: The University, School of English, 1977, xxiv pp., one colour plate and 225 folios in facsimile.

The Macro Plays. The Castle of Perseverance, Wisdom, Mankind. A facsimile edition with facing transcriptions edited by David Bevington, New York: Johnson Reprint Corp./Washington: The Folger Library, 1972, xxvi pp. + 306 pp. in facsimile.

1.   *Introductory*

1.1   *The scope of the present article*

The following survey is intended to provide a critical review of several facsimile editions of manuscripts of ME texts mostly published between 1973 and 1979, and to reflect on the functions that such volumes can have for philological research, apart from the obvious attraction they have for the palaeographer – and the bibliophile.

In a future history of ME philology, the 1970s and early 1980s may well be described as the period of important facsimile production, of research into the background history of the ME book (cf., e.g., Robinson 1972, Guddat-Figge 1976, Rigg 1977, Pearsall 1982 and large sections of the *festschriften* devoted to R.W. Hunt (Alexander/Gibson 1976), N.R. Ker (Parkes/Watson 1978), A. McIntosh (Benskin/Samuels 1981) and N. Davis (Gray/Stanley 1983)), and of the study of textual transmission[2]; concurrently, a start has been made in the production of new editions based on these fresh insights and changes of focus: scholarly interest has recently been moving away from critical editions in the classical sense, which were exclusively aimed at recovering a version as close to the author's original as possible.[3] The monumental editions of the *A and B Versions of Piers Plowman* (Kane 1960, Kane/Donaldson 1975; the *C* text is being edited by G.H. Russell) could well prove to be the last specimens of a scholarly tradition that has tried to apply the rigorous principles of reconstruction to medieval texts, even though the editors did not use the classical method of *recensio* which was developed to explain the transmission of Greek and Latin authors.

---

[2] For a similar activity in Medieval German studies cf. the conspectus of the main MS collections of MHG lyric poetry and their available facsimiles in Müller (1983:22-25). The wave of facsimiles finds its parallel in reproductions of early printed books, among which the series *English Linguistics 1500-1800* and *English Experience* are most representative.

[3] For such tendencies in textual editing cf. most recently B.A. Windeatt in his edition of *Troilus*, who stresses the importance of 'errors' "Scribal transcribing is a form of writing which constitutes an 'active reading', [...] which involves judgement-through-variation on the difficulties and peculiarities of what it encounters" (1984:26); and cf. 3.1. below.

1.2 Possible functions of facsimile volumes

It is obvious that facsimile editions of MSS can serve a variety of functions: they provide a safeguard against the accidental destruction of unique documents, or against their damage or deterioration as a consequence of continuous use in libraries; they make unique copies accessible world-wide, and available for comparison with other MSS or facsimile volumes[4]; and they often give rise to important research, as some of the introductions show.

These functions, however, are not in themselves sufficient to justify such costly undertakings, or even to enable one to judge *which* MSS *ought* to be reproduced, and so it comes as a surprise to find the reasons for an individual project so rarely explained. Ker's statement in the facsimile of MS Bodley 34 is an exception – but the MS is not representative and so reasons cannot be generalized:

> Stains, rubbing, the scribe's changes of intention or his careless writing can easily make it difficult to see exactly how a word is spelt. These causes of illegibility are present in Bodley 34, and editors have had an unusual amount of trouble with it. A facsimile has two principal advantages. With its aid a reader is able to range over the whole of the scribe's work and thereby gain understanding of his methods, and he is often able to see at a glance the nature of alterations and ambiguities which an editor can only convey clearly in footnotes of some length.
> (Ker 1960:x)

In the case of the facsimiles reviewed below, the following factors appear to have been important in the choice of the specific MS:

1. status of author and literary quality of contents;
2. beauty of the individual MS;
3. palaeographical, codicological, historical, or linguistic interest of the MS or of its individual texts;
4. documentation of the collection as a reflection of the taste of an individual, a group or a class, or as an illustration of its texts' development through time.
5. difficulty of access, or poor state of preservation precluding extensive use.

Most of the editors of the facsimiles reviewed here leave it to the reader to judge which of these factors weighed most heavily in the choice of the individual MS.

---

[4] Many scholars must have shared my sense of relief when first having the two Thornton MSS available for comparison in the B.L. – the facsimile of the Lincoln MS and the original Additional MS (the facsimile of which is an urgent desideratum). Also cf. the 're-unification' of the main Auchinleck MS with its disconnected fragments (2.1 below).

2. *A critical survey of recent facsimile volumes containing ME texts*
2.1 *The Auchinleck Manuscript*

The Auchinleck MS, a vellum MS now comprising 351 folios (including fragments) of 250 x 190 mm, compiled 1330-1340 probably in London, is one of the most famous ME collections, and considering the great variety of texts preserved in it, it well deserves this fame: It was thus an obvious choice for a facsimile edition, and has ample claim, not only for reasons of chronology, to first place in this review. The MS has served as the basis for innumerable editions of religious poems and romances for which it comprises the only text (for at least half of its 44 items, classification as 'unique' being questionable for rewritten versions); for others it frequently preserves the earliest and best text. It thus comes close to ranking with the Bannatyne MS which Sir Walter Scott claimed had "saved the literature of a whole nation". Apart from this literary interest, the Auchinleck MS as the main representative of M.L. Samuels' "Dialect II", the precursor of Chaucerian English, is also an important piece of linguistic evidence.

The facsimile edition is worthy of the occasion. It presents, for the first time, the Auchinleck MS together with the Edinburgh, St. Andrews and London University fragments, inserted at their appropriate places. Pearsall writes with great lucidity on the "Literary and historical significance of the manuscript" (pp. vii-xi), pointing out that the MS contains only English items, which "together with the dominantly secular provenance and unsophisticated tone of the contents, already marks the first significant emergence of a new class of readers [...]. The taste that it appeals to and is designed for is that of the aspirant middle-class citizen, perhaps a wealthy merchant" (p. viii). Pearsall admits that "In an age about which little is known it is mere supposition to assign discernible tastes to unidentifiable classes", and it could be that his assignment is too much influenced by what we believe we know about Auchinleck-style romances and their audience seen through Chaucer's eyes (in *Sir Thopas*) – fifty years later.

Pearsall accepts, in principle, the hypothesis proposed by L.H. Loomis (1942), that the MS is a commercial compilation made in a London bookshop. He carefully and cautiously summarizes the evidence for this assumption, but he is wise enough not to agree without qualification, warning against the "dangers of over-enthusiastic pursuit of the 'bookshop' theory" (p. xvii, n. 9). In fact, I myself found that Loomis' hypothesis fails to account for a plausible genesis of the portions containing saints' legends: in whatever way the scribes managed to get hold of their copy texts, there is little organization, let alone editing, visible in the legends included (Görlach 1981); and McSparran casts some doubt on the central section of Loomis' hypothesis, the editing assumed to have taken place in the romances sections, in particular in the *Guy of Warwick* items (C.U.L. Ff. 238, p. xi; cf. 2.2 below). We may also note the reservations expressed by Doyle and Parkes (1978). Moreover, the assumption of similar 'bookshops' has not been favoured recently to account for the production of, e.g., MSS of Chaucer's *Minor Poems* in the 15th century, a period (one would have thought) even more inclined towards commercial book production. Closely related issues about poems supposedly *composed* in the bookshop are even more hypothetical. Pearsall is "almost certainly" wrong when he claims (summarizing a mistaken notion of Bliss):

> the author of *St Margaret* (item 4), having learnt his craft in reworking an older copy of his poem, is almost certainly the man who went on to write an original St Katherine in the same vein. (p. xi)

The existence of an independent text of the same *Katherine* poem shows that the Auchinleck version cannot be original, and linguistic differences between the two legends indicate that they are not by the same author (cf. Görlach 1981).

Pearsall is likewise cautious about Loomis' hypothesis that "Chaucer, ... [may have] had the Auchinleck MS in his possession, and was familiar with its contents". The fact that *Horn Childe, Guy* and *Beves*, singled out for "affectionate contempt" in *Sir Thopas*, occur together only in the Auchinleck MS is striking, but though Loomis' assumption is "natural, probable and pleasing", it is not susceptible of proof – there must have been hundreds of booklets circulating in Chaucer's London, even if not many MSS were of the size of Auchinleck.

Cunningham's "Physical description" (pp. xi-xvi) supplies, succinctly and clearly, the necessary information on size, signatures, collation, the six scribes and the sections copied by them, as well as the binding. His method of describing features such as the different lay-out used by the six scribes deserves to be imitated by other writers discussing details difficult to visualize.

Pearsall's description of the "Contents of the manuscript" (pp. xix-xxiv) is both detailed and reliable. He lists titles, incipits, *Index* and *Manual* identification, related/ rephrased versions, numbers of extant MSS for each text, and existing editions. Stanza forms, metrical patterns and numbers of lines are noted.

The text is presented in impeccable reproduction. However, the fragments inserted after fols. 13, 277 and 326 are in very poor condition, and it might have been worth considering whether better legibility could not have been achieved by the use of special types of photography (cf. the *Beowulf* facsimile where ultraviolet photography has been used with success). It is also a pity that the MS's lavish decoration can only be guessed at in the half-tone reproduction; most initials have long since been cut out of the MS, but the surviving five might well have been reproduced in colour in the introduction.

2.2 *Cambridge University Library MS Ff. 2.38*

MS C.U.L. Ff. 2.38, a plain paper MS of now 247 folios, measuring 297 x 210 mm, was copied around 1500 by a single scribe into what appears to have begun as two 'booklets' (fols. 3-156, 161-261). The MS is probably best known as one of the four collections which together preserve some three quarters of the surviving corpus of romances, but it is not restricted to this genre, religious interest being prominent as well. McSparran's well-argued introduction to the "Literary and historical significance of the MS" (pp. vii-xii) is admirable in its combination of codicological evidence and socioliterary interpretation, continuing, in a sense, the path explored by Pearsall in his introduction to Auchinleck. McSparran sees the collection unified by the anonymous compiler's principles of selection which led him to combine religious material "with items stressing the domestic virtues and practical wisdom, and with popular romances which are pious, lively and full of incidents and marvels" (p. vii). Such an intention, she rightly claims, underlies other contemporary collections and can therefore be regarded as characteristic of the compiler and his class. However, in the absence of information about who owned and used the MS, it is doubtful whether all this can be asserted without falling into circular arguments. Moreover, the arrangement and textual history of individual poems in other MSS makes one doubt whether the make-up of Ff. 2.38 can have been as well-planned as McSparran thinks. The possible influence of the sources on the arrangement in Ff. 2.38 is mentioned with reference to MSS C.U.L. Ff. 5.48 and B.L. Harley 5396, which share items 27-32, whereas 1-15 are also found in MS Pepys 1584 – with divergent texts for 9 and 10, and 9-15 or 9-14 in two Harley MSS, 2339 and 1706. What we have here is very similar to the contemporary (15th-century) semi-regular transmission of Chaucer's *Minor Poems* (see Findern and Fairfax below). The "context of lay spirituality" encouraged by the tradition of the Fourth Lateran Council (1215) gave rise to literature as found in Ff. 2.38 which is "sober-religious, didactic and chastening, meditative and penitential" (p. viii) – compare the heading used to introduce items 1-15 in the related MS Pepys 1584, f. 1r: "This litill boke is compilid of full notabill and prophetabill sentencis to stir and edifie them *that* Redith in it gode conuersacion and gydyng", quoted by Robinson (p. xvi). Whether deliberate selection or the vagaries of textual transmission are the cause of the collection of romances in Ff. 2.38, it is impossible to say: the mixture of early couplet and later tail-rhyme romances (as opposed to Thornton and Caligula A II, in which the 15th-century tail-rhyme form predominates) may indicate that the compiler used what sources were available. Thus one wonders what kind of relevance there is in the fact that the last four romances were copied as a separate booklet (Robinson, p. xiii). These quibbles apart, McSparran's interpretation of the characteristic and the individual features of the MS is exemplary in her attempt to relate ME poems to the user and uses of an extant collection: in the past few years such approaches have become more frequent, and it is to be hoped that the increasing number of facsimiles will further encourage such studies (cf. McSparran, p. xii).

Robinson provides a very useful "palaeographical description and commentary" (pp. xii-xvii), discussing the date (based on script and watermarks), foliation and collation (concluding that the four romances in the second booklet were added to complement the first set), and giving a clear account of handwriting (homogeneous), abbreviations, corrections (careful throughout), decoration (plain), and binding (misbound at an early time, present binding 1972). There are also some very interesting remarks on the hypothetical history of the MS (pp. xxvif.): Robinson stresses the booklet structure of its sources, which are likely to have combined various items according to an existing sequence (a theory which reduces the responsibility of the compiler). She adduces various other instances of overlap between 15th-century manuscripts, and, like McSparran, thinks that Ff. 2.38 could have provided "appropriate reading at mealtimes in a devout and pious household". The fact that no identifiable names or other clues to early owners are found, and that we are, in fact, totally in the dark as to the history of the MS before it came into the possession of John More (1646-1714) is a particular difficulty. No dialectal study of the texts appears to have been made, and it might be useful to investigate how underlying dialect features (NE Midland for *Le Bone Florence*, the South for the *Assumption* etc.) were partly levelled out, and what conclusions this permits us to draw about the date, locality and users of the compilation.

Robinson also provides a very reliable description of the "Contents of the manuscript" (pp. xxi-xxv), the first time that they have been listed in their medieval sequence, which was restored in the rebinding of 1972. Her descriptions contain a number of well-considered features which one would like to see adopted in other volumes: she gives not only titles, incipits, *Index*, *Manual*, and *CBEL* identifications of items and best editions, but also indicates (by 'Pr' instead of 'Ed') which editions use the Ff. 2.38 version as base text, the specific nature of the revision (where applicable), the number of other MSS, the stanza forms and rhyme schemes, and the number of lines: all this takes up very little space and is eminently useful.

The text is beautifully reproduced; very few passages are difficult to read. Folio numbers are repeated in print in order to make identification easier. In terms of editorial care and assistance extended to the reader, this facsimile edition is certainly one of the best reviewed here.

2.3 *The Thornton Manuscript, Lincoln Cathedral MS 91*

The 'Lincoln' Thornton MS, a paper MS of now 315 (formerly 335) folios measuring 291 x 210 mm, was seemingly compiled and written by Robert Thornton of East Newton, North Yorkshire, ca. 1440. Together with its sister volume, B.L. MS Addit. 31042 (the definite article in the title of the facsimile is misleading), it is one of the most important medieval collections in the vernacular on various counts: The two MSS not only preserve a great number of unique texts (there is no overlap with , e.g., MS Auchinleck, although both collections contain a great number of romances), but they also illustrate in a unique way the literary tastes of a 15th-century country gentleman, and the sources available to him, somewhere 'up north'.

Since the two Thornton MSS are complementary (no single item is repeated in the other MS) and may have been intended to be thematically or otherwise different, it is disappointing that in the introduction to the present volume so little use is made of the B.L. MS. Brewer merely says, without giving further reasons: "[it] cannot be further discussed here, but its existence may be remembered as reinforcing what may be said of the generally similar compilation ..." (p. vii; cf. Stern 1976 and Thompson 1983 for such research). Brewer accepts (rightly, I think) the received opinion that both MSS were written by Thornton throughout (though his handwriting varies considerably), but there is no detailed discussion nor indeed a facsimile page of the B.L. MS, which would have facilitated comparison. Thornton's language is not treated, either, although we are told: "The dialect of all the pieces shares certain northern English characteristics which must be those of the scribe, since other evidence shows in some pieces a different underlying dialect" (p. vii). There is no mention here of A. McIntosh's finding that *Morte Arture* (53^r-98^v) and the *Previte off the Passioune* (179^r-279^r) must have been copied from the same source, a fact which permits important conclusions about Thornton's compilation practices (McIntosh 1962, cf. Thompson 1983:117).

There is much less on what may be gathered concerning Thornton's literary taste from his choices and arrangements than might have been expected from Dr Brewer's pen. In particular, the inclusion of legends and the notorious *Lyarde* among the romances is not discussed, nor is the importance that Thornton's preferences have for the transmission of Rolle's works, many of which survive only in a single copy – Thornton's.[5]

The section "Collation and handwriting" (pp. xiii-xvi) by Owen is similarly short and somewhat unsatisfactory. Shortly after publication of the first edition (1975) Owen found himself in the unpleasant situation of learning that three important corrections were necessary. These are made on p. xvi of the second edition, namely, 1) Quire i has lost one bifolium, which brings the folios of the original volume to 349; 2) Madden's account of the MS in 1839 shows that it was then in medieval, possibly original, white leather binding; and 3) the MS is likely to have reached the Cathedral Library through Daniel Brevint, Dean of Lincoln 1682-95. Whereas Owen's new collation, possible after the MS was unbound in 1974, is quite helpful, too little is said on what bearings the findings have on the hypothetical story of the manuscript's compilation. This topic is handled with greater perspicuity by Thompson (1983), whose article (which is still inconclusive in many details) advances our knowledge of Thornton's methods considerably, especially because of Thompson's perceptive interpretation of the 'problem' pieces in the romances section. He also indicates that the supply of copy texts for Thornton must have been very irregular with the result that no proper 'planning' of the eventual contents of the two MSS can have been possible. Finally, Owen includes nothing on handwriting (despite the title of his section) although the reader might have expected a detailed discussion of the arguments for and against the assumed ascription of the two MSS to Thornton; nor is there anything on watermarks, except for an unsatisfactory reference to a 1913-14 publication.

Brewer and Owen together list the "Contents of the Manuscript" on pp. xvii-xx. They provide a somewhat selective list (but do not admit to this, nor give a reason), omitting mainly shorter pieces (some in Latin) and lumping others together under one number. Since they omit references to the *Index/Supplement* and the *Manual*, and occasionally the customary titles of individual items (43 is *The Lay Folk's Catechism*) and the names of authors (45, 47, 48 are by W. Hilton, the last an extract from his *Scale*

---

[5] It would also have been interesting to learn whether Stern's characterization of the scribe as "a man of conservative, not to say old-fashioned tastes" (1976:212) is really conclusive, or whether the selection mainly reflects the compiler's *provincial* character. Stern also ventures to suggest: "It is tempting to see in Thornton a Northern literary speculator equivalent to John Shirley. As yet, however, too little is known of the background of such collections to warrant such a conclusion" (1976:213).

of Perfection), it is not always easy to identify the shorter items. Finally, only one edition is cited for each item, and this not always the most recent or most reliable one – in short, if a new edition is ever published, this section in particular needs to be expanded and updated.

The photography is impeccable. It is a pleasure to browse through a collection never before available in print in its entirety and rather difficult of access in Lincoln. Although the MS has suffered some mutilation, what remains is legible throughout in spite of a few smudges.

Moving on to the Findern anthology, one is impressed by both the similarities and the conspicuous differences in the shape, contents and style of the two collections. Though Thornton and the Derbyshire compilers and users of Findern are likely to have belonged to the same class, the more courtly selection in Findern contrasts with the predominance of romances and religious items in the two Thornton MSS.

2.4 The Findern Manuscript

The plain and irregular paper MS of 159 + 6 (formerly 188) folios measuring 205 x 148 mm was compiled, and continuously added to, between 1450 and the early 16th century by several generations of a single family living at a country house south of Derby. It has aroused a great deal of scholarly interest (cf. Harris 1983:318, n. 1), most importantly Robbins' article (1954), which, in spite of various necessary corrections, is still indispensable. (Robbins also coined the name 'Findern Anthology' for the MS).

Beadle and Owen tacitly accept the attribution of the MS to the country house at Findern, some five miles to the south-west of Derby, adding that the numerous names "scribbled in or added more formally to F [...] suggest a net-work of family and social relationships amongst a circle of north midland gentry" (p. viii). Harris, who finds that the ascription to Findern is based on tenuous evidence as regards the early history of the MS, does not question "the social 'milieu' nor the geographical area in which the manuscript was produced" (1983:307). The contents of the collection, which show some significant overlap with the Thornton MS, have been taken to comprise "the typical non-religious entertainment verse as contrasted with the practical or instructional verse found in citizens' commonplace books" (Robbins 1954:611), an interpretation accepted in principle by Beadle and Owen, who stress the 'provincial' nature of the collection and quote on p. viii Stevens' characterization (1961:224) of it as "deliberate borrowing of the courtly mode by those outside the charmed circle".

Two aspects of the contents (not sufficiently brought out by Beadle/Owen, but cf. now Harris' interpretation, especially 1983:308-12) are the nature of the unique poems not recorded from other sources and the relationship with the manuscripts of Chaucer's *Minor Poems* and related items of the 'Oxford Group' (cf. MS Fairfax 2.6 below). Among the 33 unique items love lyrics predominate, and some of these may well be drafts, entered as fillers in the blank spaces. The problem of the Chaucer texts is much more complicated since Ff. 2.38 variously agrees with Tanner 346 or Fairfax 16 and with C.U.L. Gg. 4.27; though late, the MS preserves some very good readings, and the Findern Facsimile, though not itself forming part of the Chaucer *Variorum* facsimiles, will provide an excellent opportunity for further exploration of the genesis of the early Chaucer canon.

Such questions are obviously related to the physical make-up of Findern. The reader will certainly look for a discussion of the hypothesis that the MS was bound together from independent booklets "by a compiler who was too interested in ME lyrics to risk their getting lost in loose gatherings" (Guddat-Figge 1976:93; similar views were held by Brusendorff (1925) and others) or for evidence to the contrary. Beadle/Owen provide a good survey, but the first really thorough investigation of the interrelationship of the collation, the forty (!) hands represented (thus Harris; Beadle/Owen speak of "some thirty") and of the watermarks is given in Harris' article, which is indispensable for every user of the facsimile. Only a linguistic analysis remains to be done in order to confirm, or refute, the hypotheses proposed, as Harris admits on p. 318. Her well-founded conclusions are that

> rather than separate production and collection, close analysis of the make-up of Ff. 1.6 suggests piecemeal preparation and intermittent copying of the manuscript; it suggests a process of accretion over a considerable period, extensions being made to the volume or, more properly, the loose collection of gatherings, when necessary [...]. The constant shifting of the personnel involved in making entries in the manuscript, the limited association of many of the copyists with the collection, the informality of the whole, all seem to imply that Ff. 1.6 was used in the manner of an album, a loose-leaf album by the south Derbyshire family [...].   (Harris 1983:317 f.)

She reasons that this process may have taken decades, from the mid-15th century onwards, and argues on the basis of scribes, watermarks and other physical features that originally only quire xiii (fols. 143-164) is likely to have been an independent booklet, which was not bound together with the rest until ca. 1500.

As has happened with other MSS, the Findern MS has recently been taken apart for rebinding, an occasion that gave some new information on the collation, although with an irregular paper MS of complicated history many doubts still remain (cf. Beadle & Owen's diagram, p. x, and Harris 1983:328 f.). In particular, Beadle and Owen make no mention of watermarks. Although the rebinding by Cockerell made possible the excellent photographs in the facsimile, Harris (1983:329) rightly complains: "Given the position of the watermarks in the gutter of the manuscript, it is unfortunate that they were not recorded when the volume was rebound."

Beadle and Owen provide a full description of Findern's 62 items on pp. xix-xxx, listing *Index* numbers, giving information on editions, and marking unique items with an asterisk. However, they missed the opportunity to indicate which copyists they believe responsible for which texts, thus allowing the reader to form an opinion on the discrepancy of their "some thirty" as against Harris' "forty" contributors (listed, with the sections assigned to them, 1983:331-3).

The introduction, though competently done, could have given much more information about the importance of the texts contained in the MS and about the correlation of collation, copyists and watermarks – points that could be easily taken up in a second edition which is likely to come as interest in Findern is rekindled by the Chaucer Variorum edition (cf. 36-40 below).

2.5 Chaucer: Hengwrt and Ellesmere

Chaucer's works have suffered from a neglect as regards facsimile editions that is not easy to explain. The magnificent facsimile of the Ellesmere MS is now difficult to consult even in larger libraries (the plans for a new facsimile of the MS have come to nothing). The scene changed only after the *Variorum Edition* was projected, and with the insight that the Hengwrt MS was greatly to be preferred to the Ellesmere MS (a fact established by Manly/Rickert in 1940), it was appropriate to make this the first facsimile in the Variorum series (the only volume devoted to the *Canterbury Tales*). Although Paul G. Ruggiers' magnificent edition is not itself under review here, it must be mentioned for its exemplary character and the pattern it could provide for other facsimile projects.

The textual situation and the editorial consequences arising from it are both exceptional; Hg and El both are of such outstanding quality, and have so dominated the reception of the text of the *Canterbury Tales*, that for the 'best-text method' of reference the editors decided to facsimilize only Hg (cf. pp. xviif.), but left open the vital question of the priority of Hg or El.[6] As Hg is the base text of the *Variorum Edition*, a facsimile of it has a uniquely well-defined purpose: it follows that it is accompanied by a conservative transcription on facing pages, and by variant readings (down to variant flourishes) in the sister MS El. The information is so exhaustive (there is also the full collational evidence of Manly/Rickert's edition for those who are interested) that we become aware of how preliminary a stage of investigation a facsimile edition is in most other cases: however much we welcome the availability in facsimile of manuscripts such as Auchinleck, Thornton or Vernon, the textual status of these collections has not been investigated as extensively as that of Hg/El - and it is unlikely that it ever will be.

In what follows, two non-*Variorum* Chaucer facsimiles are reviewed, one of his *Minor Poems* and one of his *Troilus & Criseyde*. In order to place these in context, the other projects in the full *Variorum* facsimile programme[7] (Norman, Oklahoma, in connection with D.S. Brewer Ltd., Cambridge) may be listed here (* published, end of 1985): Collected works: *MS C.U.L. Gg. 4.27, 3 vols.; *MS Bodl. Tanner 346; *MS Bodl. 638; MS Cambridge Pepys 2006; MS Cambridge Trinity College R. 3.19. *Troilus & Criseyde*: *MS Cambridge St John's College L. 1; MS Pierpont Morgan M 817.

---

[6] They state on p. xx, n. 4: "The arguments over whether Hg or El was copied first are so complex that the present writers [i.e. A.I. Doyle and M.B. Parkes] are not in complete agreement on this particular issue." Samuels (1983) has since proved on the basis of developments in the scribe's spelling that Hg must antedate El by anything up to a decade.

[7] Reference should also be made to facsimiles of early prints: Caxton's second edition of the *Canterbury Tales* (1484) was reproduced by Cornmarket Reprints (London, 1972). D.S. Brewer's edition of *The Works* of 1532 (London: Scolar, 1978) replicates the first attempt at collecting Chaucer's complete works in their entirety; the reprint very conveniently includes supplementary material from the editions of 1542, 1561, 1598 and 1602, thus providing a full account of the 'Renaissance Chaucer'.

2.6 Bodleian Library MS Fairfax 16

MS Fairfax 16, a professionally made paper volume of 343 folios measuring 232 x 154 mm, is one of the most important and impressive manuscripts of 15th-century "aureate collections" (Robbins 1955: xxiii), which combined Chaucerian, Lydgatian and other poems "sownynge in moral vertu". Its value is attested to by Tyrwhitt, who largely relied on Fairfax (fols. 187-206) to establish a canon of Chaucer's authentic *Minor Poems* (1798:525 ff.), by Furnivall, who used the MS in his parallel edition of the *Minor Poems* (1871-80), and, most recently, by Pace/Davis, who chose the MS as the base text for five of the 14 items of Part One of the *Variorum Edition* (1982).[8] The Fairfax poems, then, form part of a tradition whose complicated interrelationships and ascription it took generations of scholars to disentangle (for a summary see Pace and Davis 1982). The prevailing interpretation of the early textual history found its clearest expression in Hammond (1908), who hypothesized an archetypal Oxford collection of ca. 1410-20 from which closely related manuscripts such as Fairfax 16, Tanner 346 and Bodley 638 were thought to have descended. However, Brusendorff (1925) claimed that a tradition of independent booklets underlying these MSS is a much more plausible explanation to account for their complicated textual interrelationships. His view was largely vindicated by later research and it can now be tested with most of the important witnesses available in facsimile.

Norton-Smith provides a very clear introduction to all the physical, historical and literary problems of the MS. He stresses its booklet structure (fols. ii-186, 187-201, 202-305, 306-13, 314-40), arguing that these portions were put together by a bookseller according to choices offered to John Stanley of Horton, who commissioned[9] the book (viif.). The close relationship with MSS Tanner 346 and Bodley 638 is illustrated by the fact that those three MSS (together with Harley 7578) exhibit the greatest overlap in content and textual affiliation of individual poems. However, a full reconstruction of the early textual transmission is impossible because no collection of Chaucer's *Minor Poems* survives from the first half of the 15th century. This is possibly because

> the small, separate manuscript booklets of one or two quires tended to become fragile or simply become mislaid if not collected into a manuscript book of larger and more substantial proportions – and the idea of collections of Chaucer's minor poems probably arose in the mid fifteenth century.
> (p. ix)

Comparison with similar collections is, then, the only method for reconstructing the history of the textual transmission of these poems, 1400-1450. The booklet hypothesis is greatly favoured by P. Robinson (Tanner 346) who sees in her MS an earlier stage of

---

[8] He comments: „The Minor Poems manuscripts are a mixed lot. One manuscript, Fairfax 16, is outstanding, though not unvaryingly so" (1982: 22).

[9] The fact that "f. 14 is a singleton and the quality of the parchment is finer" (p. xii) makes it uncertain when the page with the Stanley arms was added to the MS. Norton-Smith fails to draw the obvious conclusion that Stanley may well not have *commissioned* the book, but bought it and then had f. 14 inserted as his ex-libris.

development, with *The Book of the Duchess* and *The Parliament of Fowls* having booklets reserved to them, and *The Legend of Good Women* and the *Temple of Glass* starting new booklets – whereas the Fairfax scribe, working from such booklets, combined them into a larger unit (items 10-13, fols. 83^r-147^v). With no MS of authority comparable to Hengwrt available, it is clear why the *Variorum Chaucer* facsimile project comprises six MSS of the *Minor Poems*, including Fairfax and Tanner 346 – although no explicit reason for the selection is given either in the facsimiles themselves or in the first volume of the edition proper (Pace and Davis 1982).

The Fairfax MS in one of the finest English MSS of the mid-15th century. (This makes Fairfax' note on the flyleaf, fol. 1^r, all the more surprising: "I bought this at Gloucester/ 8 Sept 1650 ffairfax/ intendinge to exchange itt for a better booke"). Its decoration is much more ambitious than that found in the textually related Tanner and Bodley MSS, reflecting the rank and financial capacities of John Stanley. The introduction to the facsimile does full justice to this fact, providing a detailed description of handwriting and decoration (pp. xiif.) as well as two beautiful colour reproductions of fols. 14^v and 15^r and three half-tone plates. The customary details of MS description such as binding, scribbles, heraldry and ownership are well covered. Norton-Smith's form of listing the contents (pp. xxiii-xxix) deserves special mention: it far exceeds the mere identification of the poems and information on where they are printed, introducing the reader to controversies about ascriptions, sources, and evaluations, and thus providing him with all the essential information in the minimal amount of space.

The MS is in excellent condition and thus presented no technical problems for the photographer; the text in the facsimile is eminently clear and a pleasure to read, the book format leaving wide margins all around the reproduced pages.

2.7 *Troilus and Criseyde, Corpus Christi College Cambridge MS 61*

This beautiful vellum MS of 153 folios measuring 318 x 220 mm (trimmed) has for long been regarded as containing one of the most important texts of Chaucer's *Troilus*: Root based his text on Cp, finding that it "presents the γ text with a high degree of purity, and is spelled with exceptional consistency" (Root 1926:liii). Windeatt, in what will be the definitive edition of the poem for some time to come, fully agrees; he states the Cp "is carefully and accurately written, with some feeling for the lines' metrical form" (Windeatt 1984:69). One deficiency, which the facsimile impresses upon the reader much more drastically than a text edition ever will, is that the MS is incomplete a) because of the loss of leaves (such as the first folio of quire 12), b) because some text was omitted, and the correction never made (cf. Parkes, p. 1), and c) because, as with the corrections, the illumination of the MS never proceeded beyond the famous full-page 'Troilus frontispiece'(described in a full-length essay by Salter, who places it in the context of frontispiece iconography in 14/15th-century Europe, pp. 15-23; cf. Pearsall 1977b). Parkes, who is responsible for the first part of the introduction, rightly points to the traditional two stages of medieval MS production, but admits that we cannot make even a plausible guess as to why such a lavish manuscript was never corrected (even though lacunae were marked by 'deficit' p. 7) and the spaces for 90 illustrations were left unfilled, i.e. the intended masterpiece abandoned mid-way. The same grand intention is indicated by the fine-quality vellum, by the regular quires of eight, the perfect ruling, the use by both scribes of *littera quadrata* (a 'display' script reserved for de-luxe MSS, p. 5) and a lay-out precisely calculated to accommodate five stanzas per page. Admittedly, the spaces left for initials and illustrations indicate a certain degree of scribal improvisation (p. 4). Parkes stresses that the *Troilus* "is the first work in English to be divided into books" (p. 4), and Cp the MS that most clearly emphasises this fact.

One would like to agree with Parkes, even though no conclusive proof is available, that the planned volume "was too ambitious in terms of what any other 15th-century patron in England was prepared to accept, either financially or in terms of literary and artistic taste" (p. 13). But this remains an unsatisfactory argument in connection with a text which generations of readers considered Chaucer's main work, and illustrates how defective are our means of reconstructing the sociology of literature even in a comparatively late period.

The MS is lavish in its accommodation of no more than 35 lines of text on one large page, and the facsimile manages to reflect this impression to the full, a beautiful torso. Together with another carefully written *Troilus* MS (St John's College Cambridge MS L. 1, now also available in facsimile) Cp provides a challenging stimulus to reflect on how different was the textual transmission of at least four distinct strands among Chaucer's works – the *Canterbury Tales*, *Troilus and Criseyde*, the prose *Astrolabe* and *Boethius*, and the *Minor Poems* (among which the *vers de société* have to be distinguished from the moral ballades, cf. Pace and Davis 1982:7).

2.8 *The Winchester Malory*

The Winchester Malory, a fine paper volume of 473 (formerly 492) folios measuring 185 x 285 mm, is the largest book ever published by the EETS, and one of the few facsimiles in the series: of the more than 420 EETS volumes published so far, only one OE text (*Beowulf* 1882/1959) and five ME texts (the *Pearl* MS 1923; MS Bodley 34, 1960; *Owl and Nightingale*, 1963; MS Harley 2253, 1965; and the volume under review) have been printed in facsimile, the last four all introduced by the late N.R. Ker. The editions of 1960, 1963, 1965 are referred to as members "of a new series, to be issued from time to time, or reproductions of Early English manuscripts". The Winchester facsimile is not so described, which leaves open whether the EETS, whose aim is rather to produce reliable, critical text editions, will publish any more facsimiles.

The story of the rediscovery of the Winchester Malory has frequently been told. It had never been lost sight of, but because it was fragmentary, and a complete printed version of Caxton's text was available at Winchester, it was not considered to be of great interest. Walter Oakeshott identified the text in 1934 but handed the task of editing it to Vinaver, who was at that time engaged on a new edition of Caxton's text (cf. Oakeshott's own account, 1977); Vinaver's definitive edition of *The Works of Sir Thomas Malory* came out in 1947. A comparison of the two shows how wrong the

Winchester librarians had been when content with the printed version: Caxton, as was his habit, freely edited and rephrased his copy text when he "enprysed to enprynte a book of the noble hystoryes of the sayd Kynge Arthur/and of certeyn of his knyghtes after a copye vnto me delyuerd/whyche copye Syr Thomas Malory dyd take oute of certayn bookes of frensshe and reduced it in to Englysshe". Vinaver's edition is a monumental achievement, and although his text is slightly modernised with regard to *w/v*, *yogh* and *thorn*, capitalization, punctuation and paragraphing, it is reliable throughout (discounting a few errors concerning final *-e*, etc.). Notwithstanding the existence of Vinaver's edition, the Council of the EETS for a long time pursued the plan of a facsimile edition, at least from 1949 onwards, when C.T. Onions proposed one; the volume is appropriately dedicated to his memory.

Ker provides an introduction to the physical details of the MS: he discusses collation and loss of leaves (Vinaver had to supply the missing text from Caxton), watermarks, the characteristic features of scribes A and B (and the sections copied by them), date ("'roughly contemporary with Caxton's edition' (Vinaver) is as near as palaeography can get"), decoration, marginalia, and binding, and he also gives a sketch of the history of the MS. It is a pity that the great literary-textual importance of the MS – the reason for its facsimile reproduction – is not discussed in the introduction. In addition, a hypothesis on who commissioned or used such a large MS (whose beauty is well brought out by the two colour reproductions included in the facsimile) might have been possible. (An ingenious hypothesis to account for the pre-1660 history of the MS was put forward by Oakeshott 1977).

However, it is the appealing notion that Caxton could have used the Winchester MS as his actual copy text that has been the most hotly discussed point in the MS's history. An indulgence printed by Caxton in 1489 was used to repair fol. 243, and this has been interpreted as evidence that the MS was in Caxton's office. Oakeshott, however, shows how inconclusive this evidence is, since anyone could have sewn the small piece on to the torn leaf – and why should the MS have been in the printer's office four years *after* Caxton had printed the text from it? Hellinga's identification of an offset in the Winchester MS with one of Caxton's types is similarly inconclusive (Oakeshott 1977, but cf. Hellinga 1980 and 1982). What remains is the positive textual evidence that Caxton must have used a text that was closer to the French sources, and therefore to Malory's lost original, than W is – a view always held by Vinaver. Oakeshott quotes a few compelling readings and Barthos (1979) has more recently enlarged on the same subject.

The reproduction of the volume is excellent and deserves full praise; book and chapter references to Caxton's (and Vinaver's) edition are given at the foot of each facsimile page, thus greatly facilitating the simultaneous use of the two. The facsimile edition makes accessible one of the major 15th-century MS – which has, of course, itself become more accessible since being sold to the B.L. a short time after the facsimile was published.

2.9 *Facsimiles of ME drama manuscripts*

2.9.1 ME dramatic texts are different in many ways from ME lyric poetry or narrative prose: the flourishing of ME drama was mainly a 15th-century affair, but only a few contemporary drama MSS survive – and hardly any texts were printed by the early printers. The bulk of the drama cycles was written down very late (1580-1610), that is, after the staging of the plays had come to an end, and in a form that does not necessarily reflect the actual text as spoken on the stage.

Accordingly, 'critical' editions of ME plays have to use different methods from those of other forms of literature, and drama facsimiles fulfil a somewhat different function than do those of other ME manuscripts.

2.9.2 *The Chester Mystery Cycle, MS Bodley 175*

The Medieval Drama Facsimile (= MDF) series was started, appropriately enough, with a MS of the Chester Cycle, one of the four surviving cycles of medieval 'mystery' plays and one which is especially close to an assumed tradition of popular medieval drama. Of the eight MSS that have come down to us, only two short excerpts survive from the 15th century, the remaining six having been written down after the staging of the plays had come to an end around 1575. Copied between 1591 and 1607, they are likely to "represent reading texts made for antiquarian interest" (p. vii). The facsimile was prepared in connection with the same authors' EETS edition, of which the text volume appeared as SS 3 (Lumiansky & Mills 1974), the commentary volume being announced for 1986. This means that the facsimile volume was in expert hands; also, most of the "Introduction" (pp. vii-xiii) reappears, in the context of descriptions of other MSS and larger editorial questions, in (1974). An editor's choice of MS – whether for a 'critical' edition or for a facsimile – must obviously be made from among the six full versions, in particular between the divergent MS Harley 2124 (the base MS for Daimling/Matthew's old EETS edition of 1892/1916) and 'the group' of the other five (such as MS B.L. Additional 10305, as chosen by Wright (1843/47), or Bodley 175).

The Chester Cycle has been the object of one of the most thorough applications of editorial method: Greg postulated (as Daimling had done before him) that a 'best' MS could be established, and that the authorial versions, or at least hyparchetypes, are recoverable from the surviving copies, though these are as far removed as two hundred years from the original, by application of 'recension' (as explained in *The Calculus of Variants*, Greg 1927). However, such a procedure was inadequate for texts in which

> layers upon layers of accretions, alterations, and excisions by revisers, actors, or scribes from various regions and periods (hence sometimes speaking different dialects at several stages of linguistic change) have left even relatively homogeneous cycles like Chester and York looking like patchwork quilts. (Lancashire 1977:65)

Moreover, the original texts as heard on the stage were altered by being recorded in manuscript form:

> Chester and York are civic registers, administrative controls on a text's content, not promptbooks or even individual craft copies. How does a play exist unless as it is performed? (Lancashire 1977:65)

The conclusion to be drawn from these textual complexities is that *one* type of edition is not enough but that

> (1) Facsimile editions are necessary because they are the best arbiters of accuracy.
> (2) Critical editions of entire play-manuscripts must be available for their textual and philological introduction, their glossary, and their lineated reference text.
> (3) Because some play-manuscripts break down into play-groups or sub-cycles each of which invite analysis of authorship, sources, staging, [...] a medieval play series [...] is desirable
> (Lancashire 1977:66)

It is obvious that having the same pair of editors for the first two types of edition of Chester has great advantages. However, even here some doubts remain:

Lumiansky and Mills do not say why they started with a facsimile of Bodley 175. Their own evaluation of the six main MSS (1974: xxxiif.) shows Bodley to be much less attractive than Huntington MS 2, which they chose as the base text for their EETS edition. Their promise "to bring out in the future facsimiles of the other Cycle-manuscripts" (1974: vii) has been partly fulfilled by the publication of facsimile volumes of Huntington 2 (MDF VI, 1980) and Harley 2124 (MDF VIII, 1984). In consequence, we now have an old, unreliable edition and a recent facsimile of Harley 2124, a reliable, new edition (with additions from Harley 2013) and a facsimile of Huntington 2, and a facsimile of Bodley 175.

Lumiansky and Mills provide a specimen transcription of fols. 64^r-65^r on pp. xivf. "as an aid to readers beginning their study of earlier handwriting". Welcome as this feature is, it reminds one of how much more useful it would have been to have had a running transcription of the complete text such as Bevington provides in his facsimile of the *Macro Plays* (2.9.6 below). This is especially the case since the reproduction of the Bodley MS lacks half-tones: while this throws into relief the full strokes, many of the minor features are lost, not even the edge of the MS being visible in many places. The impaired legibility of some passages which resulted would have been much easier to bear if a transcription had been provided. Blank pages have apparently been photographed if they are rectos (14-16, 135), but not if they are versos (14-16, 25, 33, 40, 50, 71, 88, 103, 109, 116, 123, 143, 165) – the word *ffinis* and these physical breaks are the only indications in the volume that distinguish between the 24 individual plays, there being no list of contents in the introduction.

While the volume exhibits some weakness of photography and editorial method, it makes accessible one of the major drama manuscripts at an unbelievably low price (the work is now, alas, out of print, as is volume II).

2.9.3 *The Towneley Cycle, Huntington MS HM 1*

The second volume of the series shows a remarkable advance on volume I on many counts. The fine vellum MS, which now consists of 132 folios (formerly 160), measuring 305 x 200 mm (trimmed) may have been copied ca. 1450-60, but the two initial capitals on fols. 1 and 3, modelled on early printed books, and some features of the handwriting of the main scribe point to 1480-1500 as a more likely date. All this is discussed in great detail in the introduction (pp. vii-xix), which also provides information on early ownership, collation and lacunae, various other palaeographical features, errors, corrections, and stage directions, it concludes with the statement that:

> the variations in scribal practice in the Towneley manuscript are due not only to the peculiarities of the scribe's copy texts but to his efforts throughout a long manuscript to improve his methods of presenting the plays. (p. xiv)

The evidence of post-Reformation use is aptly summarized (and clearly reproduced in the facsimile); examples are the marginal comment "correctyd and not playd" which refers to the cancellation of eight lines referring to the Sacraments, and the anti-Marian corrections on various pages. Cawley, who had already made an exemplary edition of six of the 32 items (nos. II, III, XII, XIII, XVI and XXI) as *The Wakefield Pageant in the Towneley Cycle* (1958), has provided a clear account of many of the MS's problems, and this will serve until the projected new edition for the EETS (also by Cawley/Stevens) appears, replacing he unreliable account in the 1897 EETS volume "for which A.W. Pollard provided the first of several haphazard introductions he was to write for EETS play-editions" (Lancashire 1977:60). The greatest progress is visible in the reproductions: there is a beautiful colour frontispiece of fol. 111^v (Thomas Indie) and the 132 folios are reproduced on paper well suited for half-tone photography which guarantees legibility even of some of the badly worn pages. The low price is welcome - but the volume is unfortunately no longer in print.

2.9.4 The Digby Plays. Bodley MSS Digby 133 and e Museo 160

The two MSS combined in this volume have, for better or worse, formed a group ever since Furnivall, using a method not unlike that of late medieval assemblers of booklets, first combined the texts in his New Shakspere Society edition (1882) and again in his EETS edition in 1896: Baker and Murphy retain this traditional *mésalliance* in both the facsimile and their EETS edition which in 1982 at long last replaced Furnivall's.

MS Digby 133, a plain paper MS of 169 folios of 200-240 x 135-155 mm, contains, amongst Latin and Italian tracts, the four plays *The Conversion of St Paul* (fols. 37^r-50^v), *Mary Magdalene* (fols. 95^{ar}-145^r), *The Killing of the Children* (fols. 146^r-157^v) and (fragmentary at the end) *Wisdom* (fols. 158^r-169^v). The present combination of booklets in MS Digby appears to be a consequence of somewhat inconsistent 17th-century rebinding. But three plays carry Myles Blomefylde's signature, and therefore have connections with 16th-century Bury/Cambridge/Chelmsford, as confirmed by the other, full, copy of *Wisdom* preserved in the *Macro Plays* MS (see below) – relationships that are patiently unravelled on pp. viii-ix. The four booklets are described in detail on pp. x-xiv, the only early connection between them being that the scribe who copied *Wisdom* ca. 1490-1500 may also have copied *The Killing* in 1512, a date found in the MS.

In contrast to the Digby MS, e Museo 160 appears to be homogeneous, a paper MS of 172 folios measuring 210 x 145 mm, written by a Carthusian in Yorkshire around 1520 – which provides a context for the use (though not the composition) of the two plays of *Christ's Burial* and *Christ's Resurrection* copied at the end of the existing MS, on fols. 140ʳ-172ʳ.

As with the Chester Cycle above, the identical editorship of facsimile and text editions means that the arguments contained in the two introductions are virtually identical. The EETS introduction additionally has further detailed information on language, sources, and staging, and a few references to more recent findings, such as to the staging of the Digby plays at Chelmsford in the early 1560s (Baker/Murphy/Hall 1982:xv).

The relevant folios, eighty-nine from Digby and thirty-three from e Museo, are clearly reproduced in half-tone, the quarto size of the originals permitting the use of a smaller format while still allowing for ample margins around the reproductions: a book that combines perfectly with the EETS edition.

2.9.5 *The N-Town Plays, B.L. MS Cotton Vespasian D VIII*

The Cotton MS, a composite paper volume of 225 folios measuring 200 x 140 mm (trimmed) was – apart from interpretations – copied in 1468 (? if the date on fol. 100ʳ is relevant) by one scribe who "apparently had a pile of rough working play-texts before him" (p. viii). Meredith/Kahrl concentrate in their introduction (pp. vii-xxix) on "processes involved in the compilation" of the MS; they offer a few provisional findings of major significance for its structure (p. vii), namely:

1) the Marian (contemplacio) group (plays 8-11, 13) was a separate and self-contained composite Mary play;
2) the first Passion sequence (quires N.P.Q.R.) was undoubtedly a separate manuscript, though written by the main scribe, and incorporated into the present compilation in much the same way as the *Assumption of the Virgin* play (quire [W]);
3) the work of the reviser B was directed primarily at, once again, regrouping the plays, this time clearly for theatrical production.

Meredith/Kahrl have been able to build on Block's dependable edition (*Ludus Coventriae*, EETS, ES 120, 1922). Their improvements include a certain amount of renumbering and retitling of the plays (pp. viii-xii), and conclusions 1)-3) above, which are based on cumulative evidence drawn from collation, watermarks, the condition of leaves, handwriting, and rubrication, all described with care and caution on pp. xiv-xviii. Their findings are supported by a close interpretation of Reviser B's activities, whose "alterations are in the direction of prompt-copy, suggesting that [the Nativity and Resurrection sequences] were produced separately some time after the compilation was made" (p. xxiv). It will be interesting to see whether all these conclusions are reflected in the forthcoming EETS edition by Stephen Spector. (For another study of some of the textual problems of the MS see Meredith (1977)).

The MS is impeccably photographed and reproduced. It will be an invaluable complement to future critical editions, especially if later editors propose new hypotheses to account for the texts' history and their present combination in the Cotton MS.

With eight volumes published by 1984[10] the MDF series has made available in facsimile most of the important ME drama MSS, and has done so, with the exception of vol. I, in high quality. Only the light green paper covers, a trademark of all the Leeds books, are very badly suited to the precious contents: a clothbound edition should have been made available for libraries – and bibliophiles.

2.9.6 The Macro Plays

The *Macro Plays*, three originally independent paper booklets of 38 + 24 + 13 folios (*The Castle of Perseverance*, fols. 154-191, *Wisdom*, fols. 98-121, *Mankind*, fols. 122-134), measuring 210 x 143 and 220 x 160 mm, all written towards the end of the 15th century, were not included in the Leeds series for the obvious reason that Bevington's excellent edition came first. Though not itself under review here, it provides a useful comparison with the Leeds MDF volumes, showing certain potentials of drama facsimiles that they fail to realise.

In his introduction, Bevington pays great attention to the development of ME drama as a literary genre and to staging practices (pp. vii-xv) before turning to "The manuscript and this edition" (pp. xvii-xxiii). The great difference from the MDF volumes is the conservative transcription printed on the pages facing the facsimiles, and the provision on these pages of a critical apparatus listing emendations in Furnivall's and Eccles' editions and, in the case of *Wisdom*, variant readings from MS Digby, as well as scribal corrections, marginalia and other textual information. This makes Bevington's book an ideal complement to a critical edition (which it does not aim to replace, and which is already available in Eccles' EETS edition of 1969). While such a production will always be possible only for a few selected manuscripts, it illustrates what ideal help such combinations *can* extend to the reader.

---

[10] Bibliographical details of volumes 5 to 8 not included in the present review are:

Non-Cycle Plays and the Winchester Dialogues. Facsimiles of Plays and Fragments in Various Manuscripts and the Dialogues in Winchester College MS 33. With introductions and a transcript of the Dialogues by Norman Davis. MDF, V. Leeds: The University, School of English, 1979, iv pp. + 208 pp. in facsimile.

The Chester Mystery Cycle. A Reduced Facsimile of Huntington Library MS 2. With an introduction by R.M. Lumiansky and David Mills. MDF, VI. Leeds: The University, School of English, 1980, xvi pp. + 290 pp. in facsimile.

The York Play. A Facsimile of British Library MS Additional 35290. With an introduction by Richard Beadle and Peter Meredith and a note on the music by Richard Rastall. MDF, VII. Leeds: The University, School of English, 1983, lxi pp. + 551 pp. in facsimile and five colour plates.

The Chester Mystery Cycle. A Facsimile of British Library MS Harley 2124. With an introduction by David Mills MDF, VIII. Leeds: The University, School of English, 1984, xxii pp. + 284 pp. in facsimile.

3. Conclusion

3.1 Functions of facsimiles

After such a large survey of recent facsimiles some general remarks will be in order. They are here arranged in something like a systematic sequence, the intention being to show what a facsimile can and should do.

A facsimile is not a critical edition, nor should it be given this status in scholarly discussion.[11] Hudson, mentioning the meticulously diplomatic editions of the EETS *Ancrene Riwle* series, warns against raising change to the position of arbiter:

> The recent passion for the facsimile, even where no edition exists, is the modern counterpart to that enterprise. This method exalts palaeography as sole editor. The other method exalts textual and philological critics. (Hudson 1977:38)

On the other hand, Pearsall justly claims:

> The tyranny exerted by 'the critical edition' is now recognized, and scholars are learning the value of 'bad manuscripts': how in the work of interfering and meddling scribes [...] can be seen the activities of our first literary critics [...]. The manuscript context of particular works needs to be understood in detail; matters of layout and format give an insight into the ways in which medieval poems were understood to exist [...]. The excerpting, abridging and paraphrasing of certain major works give unrivalled access to the modes of thought within which such works were first read and used [...]. (1983:1)

There is little need to stress that facsimiles provide unique potential for studies like those outlined by Pearsall – but the point is not made in any of the introductions with such persuasive force as in the lines quoted above.

All the books here reviewed are *facsimiles*, not replicas of the bibliophilic kind in which an attempt is made to imitate specific kinds of vellum or paper, and frayed edges, and with covers imitating medieval book-bindings. Rather, the philological interest clearly predominates: while every hairstroke must be visible in the half-tone reproduction, questions of collation and binding can be left to the descriptions provided by specialists in the introductions (including, where relevant, a photograph of the binding, as in Hengwrt, p. xlf.). Illustrations are, however, important, and facsimiles should not be too sparing of colour plates, whether of complete leaves or of sections of particular interest.

If the textual aspect, then, is fundamental, the position of a facsimile vis-à-vis existing editions should be clearly defined. Is it possible to provide a conservative transcription, which guides the user but does not spoil the evidence, as has been successfully done with *Beowulf*, the Hengwrt *Canterbury Tales* and the *Macro Plays*?

---

[11] Note that the *Variorum Chaucer* text of the *Canterbury Tales* must not be mistaken for a new critical text, either; rather, it is "a modestly emended or corrected Hengwrt text", selected on the basis of the best-text method (*Hengwrt*, p. xii). There are similar warnings against overvaluing Shakespeare's First Folio (in form of Hinman's facsimile edition). This does not mean that a reproduction of an early print (or a unique manuscript text) cannot form the basis of a critical edition. R. Hands' excellent edition of portions of *The Boke of St. Albans* (Hands 1975) illustrates the possibilities of a type of edition that should be encouraged.

What is the status of the facsimile text and – possibly – its relationship to that printed from another MS? Can the chapter/line references to the printed text be provided to make the simultaneous use of the two possible? In the case of the Corpus Christi *Troilus* no such help is given in the facsimile – and no foliation is indicated in Windeatt's (1984) edition based on this MS.

3.2   *Which manuscripts should be facsimilized?*

Reflections such as those above lead to the basic question of which MSS should be made accessible in facsimile. Should they preferably be of MSS containing single works? How many variant versions of the same text do we need? What is the value of late texts, of miscellaneous collections, of fragments, of texts rewritten for different audiences or recast into different forms?

In Great Britain and the U.S. there has never been a single institution or publisher responsible for producing facsimiles. Decisions taken by the EETS Council, by D.S. Brewer Ltd. or by the management of Scolar Press are likely to be based on different principles. Is it possible (and would it be desirable) to draw up, by questioning a hundred leading specialists on ME, a list of twenty, fifty, or a hundred, MSS that ought to be given priority?

There has been a striking neglect of Chaucer until very recently, and neglect continues for Gower, Langland and Lydgate (unless portions of their work are found in 'Chaucer' MSS). Prose has also been treated badly: why is there nothing for the Lollards or the mystics, and why is there no ME Bible facsimile? If it is a question of accessibility, why not compile an even longer list of MSS worth facsimilizing and arrange for them to be made available in microfilm from one institution?[12]

3.3   *Information to be provided in facsimiles*

The amount of preparation (and money) a facsimile volume requires would lead one to expect that maximum information would be included in the introductions in order to help the reader make optimal use of the book. In fact, some of the introductions are quite short, concentrating on physical aspects of the MS (size, material, collation, ruling, handwriting, decoration etc.), and not even this information is always well organized: none of the descriptions of handwriting includes adjacent photographic samples of each scribe's work to illustrate the differences between them, or to show variation within one hand. In general, extensive descriptions of palaeographical details are of limited value unless they are made to bear on questions of date, provenance, and transmission of texts.

---

[12] Cf. the programme already offered by World Microfilms Publications (from which relevant MSS could be extracted); another microfilm project called "Britain's Literary Heritage: The Original Manuscript Record", which includes various medieval manuscript collections from London, Cambridge and Washington D.C. libraries, is now in progress (Harvester Microform). Full information is available from Harvester Press Microform Publications Ltd., 17 Ship Street, Brighton, Sussex BN1 1AD, England. For later centuries the monumental collection of microfilms of all English printed books from 1475 to 1700 contained in Pollard/Redgrave's and Wing's *Short Title Catalogues* can be compared.

Textual history, in so far as it can be reconstructed from handwriting, from the booklet structure of an existing MS or a similar structure in the presumed source(s), and – less so – from linguistic evidence, is receiving increasing attention. This is evident (and necessary) where 1) piecemeal accretion over several generations (Findern), 2) compilation by either one man or a group (Thornton, Auchinleck), or 3) changing textual combinations and relationships as a consequence of the absence of a canon (Chaucer's *Minor Poems*) have to be explained. Especially welcome is the attempt in many introductions to correlate former owners/compilers with the contents of their MSS (Findern, Ff. 2.38., Auchinleck[13]).

Other topics, however, are treated summarily or omitted altogether. The absence in some facsimiles of a chapter on the importance of the texts for medieval literature or the history of ideas is to be regretted; it is probably owing to a scholarly tradition which presupposes such knowledge on the user's part (not even referring him to relevant literature in the bibliography).

The general lack of linguistic discussion is much more awkward since dialect 'layers' in composite MSS have an obvious bearing on textual history and would seem to be indispensable (along with codicological and literary evidence) for a reconstruction of the pre-history of many collections. Convincing analyses of scribal language have been made for a great number of texts using a methodological frame of *Mischsprache* (cf. Benskin/Laing 1981), and the application of such methods to MSS of the Findern type would obviously be rewarding.

Samuels pointed out the linguistic importance of MS Auchinleck as early as 1963, regarding hands 1 and 3 as typical of Type II dialect, the pre-1360 dialect of the Greater London area, which has some Essex and generally East Anglian features as a consequence of mid-14th-century immigration (1969:409-11) – but there is nothing on 'language' in the Auchinleck facsimile. Similarly, A. McIntosh's findings (1962, cf. 2.3 above) were not taken further in the Thornton facsimile, Brewer's short statement (quoted in 2.3) not being as detailed or precise as one would wish.

Finally, lists of contents (a very useful section if supplied with relevant information) are not as helpful in many volumes as they could be. Such a list is completely lacking in the Chester facsimile; references to the *Index/Supplement* or *Manual*, customary titles and incipits are omitted in others. Only a few facsimiles provide information on whether the MS's version is available in print, or what relation the facsimile text has to the printed version, or whether a text is unique (33 items out of 62 are marked with an asterisk as being unique in Findern).

---

[13] Harris' (1983) article on the Findern MS shows how shaky our knowledge of owners, compilers and users is even for the close of the Middle Ages, and that some ascriptions such as to the country house at Findern may not be quite as certain as has been assumed. We must certainly beware of repeating an error of earlier generations of scholars who too readily ascribed anonymous poems to authors known by name, by now ascribing manuscripts to known collectors. Pearsall strikes a similar note in cautioning against naive socioliterary equations (cf. the quote in 2.1 above).

Many of these critical points reflect the obvious fact that the functions and readership of the books have not been clearly defined. It is to be hoped that subsequent volumes (or second editions of existing books) will be improved in such respects, which can be achieved with little additional cost.

3.4 *Research possibilities*

It is certain that the recent spate of facsimiles will stimulate new research in various fields. Scholars will still find it worthwhile to

a) establish from codicological, dialectal and literary evidence the 'pre-history' of existing collections[14] (continuing the work of Brewer, Doyle, Parkes, Pearsall and others), and investing in other texts the same kind of energy that has recently been devoted to the early transmission of Chaucer's works (cf. Doyle/Parkes 1978);

b) abstract the characteristic textual and linguistic features of particular manuscripts by comparing individual texts with versions preserved elsewhere, i.e. establishing the 'Vernon-ness', 'Thornton-ness' or 'X-ness' of such collections, and testing the alleged homogenisation thought to have been going on in the 'Auchinleck bookshop' etc.;

c) write a history of literary taste, summarizing all the evidence of principles of selection and textual adaptation found in existing collections (including collections of 'bad', 'late' and 'corrupt' texts, and correlating this with what can be reconstructed or is already known about individual compilers and their social backgrounds, carefully weighing individuality against the impact of fashion, etc. (For a sketch of such an approach cf. the chapter "Some 14th-century books and writers" in Pearsall 1977a:119-49). The discussions of such questions in the introductions to the facsimiles by Pearsall, Brewer, McSparran, etc. could well be a starting point[15];

d) write a history of ME textual editing, comparing 'critical' editions with the evidence the facsimiles provide: there have never before been such opportunities to compare authentic documents with 'cleaned-up' editions of the same texts;

e) reflect on the linguistic make-up of facsimilized MSS, concentrating on dialect translation as against retention of source language, and on modernization, misunderstanding, and the homogenizing tendencies evident in many scribes' treatment of copy-texts.

Much of this kind of research is well under way, and it is characteristic that so much is concerned with the very manuscripts that have become available in facsimile:

---

[14] Thompson (1983) illustrates how modern codicological research and a reconsideration of genres of ME texts can explain some of the mysteries of apparent haphazard arrangement, in this case of the 'inappropriate' items in Thornton's romance section which have baffled many generations of ME scholars.

[15] Such questions would be best treated in a monograph on the ME codex; they will, one hopes, be discussed in A.I. Doyle's projected book, based on his 1965 London lectures on "Later ME manuscripts" (cf. Doyle's reference in Pearsall 1982:143).

the collections of conference papers edited by Rigg (1977, cf. esp. Lancashire and Hudson) and by Pearsall (1983, cf. esp. Pearsall, Boffey, Thompson), important articles on Thornton and his two MSS by Stern (1976) and Keiser (1979), the new edition of *Troilus* (Windeatt 1984), the EETS editions of medieval drama, and finally the various projects within the *Variorum Chaucer* – all are related to existing or forthcoming facsimiles. There is, then, enough work to be done, and we can expect new insights related to, or made possible by, the existence of reproductions of major ME manuscripts. And, to recast the phrase "mirth in manuscripts" coined by R.H. Robbins, there is also fun in facsimiles.[16]

References

Alexander, J.J.G., M.T. Gibson, eds. 1976. *Medieval Learning and Literature. Essays Presented to Richard William Hunt.* Oxford.

Baker, Donald C., John L. Murphy, Louis B. Hall Jr., eds. 1982. *The Late Medieval Religious Plays of Bodleian MSS Digby 133 and e Museo 160*, EETS, OS 283. Oxford.

Barthos, G.A. 1979. "Caxton's edition of Malory based on a source other than the Winchester Manuscript", *N & Q*, 224:9-10.

Benskin, Michael & Margaret Laing. 1981. "Translations and *Mischsprachen* in Middle English manuscripts", in Benskin/Samuels (1981:55-106).

Benskin, Michael & M.L. Samuels, eds. 1981. *So many people, longages and tonges. Philological essays in Scots and medieval English presented to Angus McIntosh.* Edinburgh.

Boffey, Julia. 1983. "The manuscripts of early courtly love lyrics", in Pearsall (1983:3-14).

Brown, T.J. 1974. "Complete facsimiles of Mss in Middle English", in *New Cambridge Bibliography of English Literature*, pp. 219-20. Cambridge.

Brusendorff, A.A. 1925. *The Chaucer Tradition.* Oxford.

Cawley, A.C., ed. 1958. *The Wakefield Pageants in the Towneley Cycle.* Manchester.

Doyle, A.I., M.B. Parkes. 1978. "The production of copies of the *Canterbury Tales* and the *Confessio Amantis* in the early 15th century", in Parkes/Watson (1978:163-203).

---

[16] There are various discoveries to be made in the facsimiles relating to their less 'scholarly' contents, but illustrative of attitudes that led to old manuscripts being held in lower respect, or reverence, than they are today. What made 15th/16th-century users practice their ubiquitous pen-trials in sumptuous MSS? What made a reader copy a recipe for a clister into the vacant space on fol. 151^v of the magnificent *Troilus* MS Cp, or include an inventory of "the parcellys off clothys at ffyndyrn" on fol. 70^r of the less precious Findern MS? (The answer is surely not "because of the value of the MS and the hoped permanence its contents would give them", Robbins 1954:620 f.) Other marginalia are even more grossly 'irrelevant', such as many in the Macro MS on which Bevington comments: "Many [...] take on a playful turn, as though prankish scribes or young scholars were devising messages and even indecencies to one another under the cover of a secret code" (Macro, p. xix).

Furnivall, F.J., ed. 1871-80. *A One-Text Print of Chaucer's Minor Poems*, 2 vols. London.
Görlach, Manfred. 1981. "The Auchinleck Katerine", in: Benskin/Samuels (1981:211-29).
Gray, Douglas, E.G. Stanley, eds. 1983. *Middle English Studies Presented to Norman Davis in Honour of his 70th Birthday*. Oxford.
Greg, W.W. 1927. *The Calculus of Variants*. Oxford.
Guddat-Figge, Gisela. 1976. *Catalogue of Manuscripts Containing Middle English Romances*. München.
Hammond, E.P. 1908. *Chaucer: A Bibliographical Manual*. New York.
Hands, Rachel, ed. 1975. *English Hawking and Hunting in 'The Boke of St. Albans'*. A facsimile edition of a2-f8 of *The Boke of St. Albans* (1486). Oxford.
Harris, Kate. 1983. "The origins and make-up of Cambridge University Library MS Ff. 1.6", *Transactions of the Cambridge Bibliographical Society*, 8,3:299-333.
Hellinga, Lotte. 1980. "Review of The Winchester Malory", *The Library*, VI, 2:92-98.
---. 1982. *Caxton in Focus: The Beginning of Printing in England*. London.
Hudson, Anne. 1977. "Middle English", in Rigg (1977:34-57).
Kane, George, ed. 1960. *Piers Plowman. The A Version*. London.
---, E.T. Donaldson, eds. 1975. *Piers Plowman. The B Version*. London.
Keiser, George E. 1979. "Lincoln Cathedral MS 91: life and milieu of the scribe", *Studies in Bibliography*, 32:158-79.
Ker, N.R., ed. 1960. *Facsimile of Ms. Bodley 34*, EETS, OS 247. London.
Lancashire, Ian. 1977. "Medieval drama", in Rigg (1977:58-85).
Loomis, L.H. 1942. "The Auchinleck Manuscript and a possible London bookshop of 1330-1340", *PMLA*, 57: 595-627.
Lumiansky, R.M. & David Mills, eds. 1974. *The Chester Mystery Cycle*, I, EETS, SS 3. London. II (forthcoming?).
McIntosh, Angus. 1962. "The textual transmission of the alliterative *Morte Arthure*", in N. Davis & C.L. Wrenn, eds., *English and Medieval Studies Presented to J.R.R. Tolkien* (London, 1962), pp. 231-40.
Manly, J.M. & Edith Rickert. 1940. *The Text of the Canterbury Tales*. Chicago.
Meredith, Peter. 1977. "A reconsideration of some textual problems in the N-Town Manuscript (BL MS Vesp. D. VIII)", *Leeds Studies in English*, 9:35-50.
Müller, Ulrich. 1983. "Die mittelhochdeutsche Lyrik", in Heinz Berger, ed., *Lyrik des Mittelalters*, II (Stuttgart, 1983), pp. 7-227.
Oakeshott, Walter. 1977. "The matter of Malory", *TLS*, Feb. 18: 193.
Pace, George B. & Alfred Davis, eds. 1982. *Geoffrey Chaucer, The Minor Poems*, Part One, Variorum Chaucer. Norman, Oklahoma.
Parkes, M.B. & A.G. Watson, eds. 1978. *Medieval Scribes, Manuscripts & Libraries. Essays Presented to N.R. Ker*. London.
Pearsall, Derek. 1977a. *Old English and Middle English Poetry*. London.
---. 1977b. "The *Troilus* frontispiece and Chaucer's audience", *YBES*, 7:68-74.

---, ed. 1983. *Manuscripts and Readers in Fifteenth-Century England. The Literary Implications of Manuscript Study*. Cambridge.
Rigg, A.G., ed. 1977. *Editing Medieval Texts, English, French and Latin Written in England*. New York.
Robbins, R.H. 1954. "The Findern Anthology", *PMLA*, 69:610-42.
---, ed. 1955. *Secular Lyrics of the XIVth and XVth Centuries*, 2nd ed. Oxford (^{1}1952).
Robinson, P.M. 1972. *A Study of Some Aspects of the Transmission of English Verse in Late Medieval Manuscripts*. B. Litt. Thesis. Oxford.
---. 1980. "The *booklet*: self-contained unit in composite manuscripts", *Codicologica*, 3:46-69.
Root, R.K., ed. 1926. *The Book of Troilus and Criseyde*. Princeton.
Samuels, M.L. 1963. "Some applications of Middle English dialectology", *English Studies*, 44:81-94; repr. in R. Lass, ed., *Approaches to English Historical Linguistics* (New York, 1969), pp. 404-18.
Stern, Karen. 1976. "The London 'Thornton' Miscellany: a new description of British Museum Additional Manuscript 31042", *Scriptorium*, 30:25-37, 201-18.
Stevens, John. 1961. *Music and Poetry in the Early Tudor Court*. Cambridge.
Thompson, John J. 1983. "The compiler in action: Robert Thornton and the 'Thornton Romances' in Lincoln Cathedral MS 91", in Pearsall (1983:113-24).
Tyrwhitt, Thomas, ed. 1775-78. *The Canterbury Tales of Chaucer*. Oxford (^{2}1798).
Windeatt, B.A., ed. 1984. *Geoffrey Chaucer. Troilus & Criseyde*. London.

2 *The Vernon Manuscript. A Facsimile of Bodleian Library, Oxford, MS. Eng. poet. a. 1*, with an introduction by A. I. Doyle. Cambridge: D. S. Brewer, 1987, viii + 16 pp. + 12 pp. of (26) colour plates + 350 folios in facsimile + foldout contents page at end; from *Anglia* 107 (1989), 520-3.

The Vernon MS "in a unique way combines the criteria for (a facsimile) reproduction: the literary importance of its texts, beauty, and historical and linguistic interest", is how I ended my postscript to a survey of "Recent facsimile editions of ME literary manuscripts" (Görlach 1987). Although the Vernon facsimile (Vf) was not available at the time when I wrote the review article, it was not difficult to predict that this would be the crowning glory of such works for some time to come. Have these expectations been fulfilled?

The book is intended to be "a working facsimile" – no attempt has been made to reproduce the paper, colour, binding and other physical features of the original. Instead, greatest care has been given to photographing the huge pages (here reproduced at 92% of the original size) on black-and-white (orthochromatic) film with the explicit aim of bringing out the text as legibly as possible – and anyone who has ever worked with a microfilm of the Vernon MS (V) will quickly recognize how incomparably superior the facsimile (Vf) is as a means of research.

The book starts with an excellent introduction by Ian Doyle who has been working on the major ME manuscripts for the past forty years and is *the* authority on the palaeography, codicology and text of V. He concentrates on a close comparison of V and its sister MS Simeon (S) throughout, conveniently summing up his earlier research (Doyle 1974). After all, the two MSS not only share a very great number of similarities in content, but must have been produced together: textual and palaeographical riddles solved in one MS are always likely to throw some light on the other as well. Doyle points out the extremely high quality of the material used, and the care with which the gathering, pricking and ruling of the costly parchment was planned for both V and S. Such considerations are in contrast to the selection of the texts and their sequence which "were not necessarily determined long in advance of the copying" (p. 2) – apparently because not all of the texts were available at the same time, thus preventing careful planning: if such failures are obvious in smaller 'commercial' volumes such as the Auchinleck MS, they are much more likely in the huge schemes underlying V and S. (Such considerations are merely hinted at in Doyle's introduction who believes that this is not the place for such questions). It is obvious, however, that in both V and S scribes "must have transcribed a sequence of exemplars with rare instructions where to halt". Such complex questions of textual traditions combined with the actual make-up of V and S can now be followed up by a great number of scholars, who can build on Doyle's fascinating detective work on how the interrelated process of copying V and S could have proceeded, conjectures based on textual relations, codicological evidence and (fragments of) marginal inscriptions apparently reporting on the commissioning of sections of the copying of the work (p. 13). They may also, on the basis of new clues, come up with a new interpretation of who may have commissioned/compiled V and S, and for what purpose and audience, problems which still "elude" Doyle (p. 11). The very fact that MS Simeon and Vf can now be used side by side in the British Library suggests that Doyle's hopes may be fulfilled one of these years. Apart from a very detailed discussion of the characteristic features of the two V scribes, there is a meticulous description of signatures, punctuation, rubrication, decoration and border illumination, and what remains of V's illustrations: all this information not only helps the Vf user to visualize details which remain easier to recognize in the MS itself, but it is also related to comparable evidence in S throughout. Available evidence for dating and localization (through contents and dialect features) is conveniently summarized, as is the relevance of the mention in V of "Thomas Heneley" – clues which provide tantalizingly patchy information about V's and S's medieval history.

Difficulties in photographing the huge manuscript brought about some delay in Vf's publication, but now it is out it is clear that the photographers have done a very good job. (Note only some mismatch of rectos and versos, apparently a consequence of the difficulties of handling the bulky MS). All the text is remarkably easy to read, even parts close to the gutter or where letters have been partly rubbed off. Shine-through is much less conspicuous than in V itself, and although the staining of the vellum is slightly accentuated, this does not impede legibility. In fact, I found only one word that was easier to read in V, an instance of *in-*, where mutilation meant that identification of the word had to rely on the hairstroke not reproduced in Vf. By contrast, pencil marks do not show in Vf – not even the press mark on fol. 1! Colour reproduction is a different matter. Although it is claimed that red and blue initials are easy to distinguish by their greys throughout, I found that all colours – red, blue, green, gold and even black ink – merged in various hues of grey, an effect most obvious in the coloured frames and miniatures. So we must be grateful for the 16 pages of colour photographs – though even these come out somewhat darkish and certainly less brilliant than the originals.

All medievalists ought to be very grateful for this magnificent publication, and they certainly will be – though philologists more than art historians. However, it is also the reviewer's duty to list what could have been done better – and possibly will be in a second edition:

1) The contents of Vf are listed in tiny print on a fold-out at the end of the book. I would not only have wished for a more manageable size (on a detachable leaf?), but also some information on the status of the V texts, "the biggest surviving volume of ME writings ... for many of which it has the earliest and for some the sole known copy" (p. 1). Such information is given with exemplary clearness in the facsimile of C.U.L. Ff. 2.38 (McSparran & Robinson 1979).

2) There is no exhaustive discussion of what modern scholars have written about the textual, linguistic or codicological aspects of V. Some important articles *are* mentioned in 'side-notes', but a consolidated bibliography (including not just 'references') would have provided much useful information in little space.

3) It is good to have folio numbers repeated in the white margins beneath the facsimile pages, but there is nothing to warn the reader about gaps in the MS – why not have one blank page bound in with "fols. . . . missing", or at least give this information underneath the modern folio number?

The publication of facsimiles has slowed down greatly in recent years, certainly a consequence of rising production costs – in a time of decreasing university budgets – rather than a lack of worthwhile objects to reproduce. And as the facsimile of one of the two Thornton manuscripts whets the appetite for the other, the wish to have the Simeon MS out as a facsimile is a natural one with Vf in front of the reviewer. Let us hope that the (commercial) success of the volume under review will make such a project a viable one for the present publisher who has given us such a plethora of facsimiles of ME literary manuscripts already, and let us hope this will be as reliably introduced as Vf is.

References

Doyle, Ian. 1974. "The shaping of the Vernon and Simeon Manuscripts", in B. Rowland, ed., *Chaucer and Middle English Studies in Honour of Rossell Hope Robbins*. London, 328-41.

Görlach, Manfred. 1987. "Recent facsimile editions of Middle English literary manuscripts". *Anglia*, 105:121-51. (See preceding review).

McSparran, Frances & P.R. Robinson, eds. 1979. *Cambridge University Library MS.Ff.2.38*. London.

3   Julia Boffey and A.S.G. Edwards, eds., *The Works of Geoffrey Chaucer and The Kingis Quair*. A Facsimile of Bodleian Library, Oxford, MS Arch. Selden. B. 24, with an appendix by B.C. Barker-Benfield. Cambridge: D.S. Brewer, 1997. viii + 61 pp. + 478 unpaginated pages of the facsimile; from *Anglia* 119 (2001), 120-1.

The manuscript here reproduced is possibly the last major Chaucer codex to be facsimilized (compare earlier facsimiles of MSS Bodley 638, Tanner 346, Corpus Christi Cambridge 61, Cambridge University Library Gg. 4.27 and St. Johns Cambridge L. 1 published by Pilgrim Books, the reproduction of Hengwrt edited by P.G. Ruggiers, and two recent facsimiles of the Ellesmere MS edited by R. Hanna and by D. Woodward & M. Stevens). The present collection is also one of the latest, variously dated to the late 15th or early 16th century (possibly copied ca. 1488 by James Graye, protégé of Henry Sinclair, though this hypothesis was rejected by N. R. Ker in 1977). The manuscript contains 25 items, starting with *Troilus & Criseyde* (fols. 1-118v), of which it provides a late conflated text which is generally considered useful only as a specimen of how *TC* was read a hundred years after its composition. The most recent editor of the poem rightly states:

> S1 has tended to be discounted as a text of *TC* because its patterns of agreements reveal that it has been edited... and consequently offers a mixed text. But as such it offers significant evidence for some of the processes which may lie behind the features of composite *TC* MSS.
> (Windeatt 1984: 74)

Of the other texts only a minority are by Chaucer; they include *Truth*, no. 3; *Complaint of Mars*, no. 8; *Complaint of Venus*, no. 9; *Parliament of Fowls*, no. 13 and *Legend of Good Women*, no. 14. The late medieval collector also included poems by Walton (from his *Boethius*, no. 4), Lydgate (*Complaint of the Black Knight*, no. 6), Hoccleve (*Mother of God*, no. 7; *Letter of Cupid*, no. 16) and Clanvowe (*Book of Cupid*, no. 12). Of particular interest is the inclusion of the unique texts of the *Kingis Quair*, no. 15 and the *Quare of Ielousy*, no. 19.

The *Kingis Quair*, probably written by James I after his return from sixteen years of captivity in England (a text which is appropriately influenced by Boethius and by Chaucer's *Knight's Tale*), is the fountainhead of Chaucerian poetry in 15th-century Scotland, a debt acknowledged by James in the last of the 197 rhyme-royal stanzas of his poem:

> Vnto Impnis of my maisteris dere
> Gowere and Chaucer that on ye steppis satt
> Of rethorike quhill thai were lyvand here
> Superlatiue as poetis laureate
> In moralitee and eloquence ornate...

One of the most important texts of the early history of Scottish literature is thus inextricably mixed as far as its language is concerned, both because of the author's idiolect and (possibly) because the poem underwent further Scotification in the course of the sixty years or more that lie between its composition and the extant copy[17]. The facsimile now offers the welcome opportunity (not utilized in the book) to determine the scribal *Mischsprachen* and thereby come closer to a satisfactory interpretation of the poem's genesis. It also allows us to compare at leisure the make-up of similar compilations (such as those in CUL MS Gg. 4. 27 and the 'Oxford group', Bodley Fairfax 16, Bodley 638 and Tanner 346).

The introduction to the volume has an exemplary description of the physical features of the manuscript (with eight unpaginated pages of colour reproductions following p. 6) and insightful remarks on the contribution of the two scribes and later annotators, and the manuscript's provenance and later history. It ends with a bibliography. A uniquely detailed appendix, "Technical notes and collation chart" (29-60), documents the findings of meticulous codicological research undertaken when the manuscript was disbound (1992-94).

The decision to reproduce the manuscript not in full colour, but in black and white as a working facsimile, is to be welcomed: it makes it now accessible, at a reasonable price, in the major research libraries. It is a pity, though, that – for purist reasons also followed in other similar facsimiles – the user is not guided through the texts by having minimal information provided in the lower margins. The identification of the text copied on an individual page would have been greatly assisted by having, for instance, "TC V: 1828-62" printed at the bottom of fol. 118^r.

Reference
Windeatt, B.A. ed. 1984. *Geoffrey Chaucer. Troilus & Criseyde.* London: Longman.

4   *Studies in the Vernon Manuscript*, ed. Derek Pearsall. Cambridge: D.S. Brewer, 1990, xi + 238 pp.; from *Anglia* 110 (1992), 486-9.

The publication of the *Vernon Facsimile* (1987), together with earlier reproductions of ME manuscripts, opens up new research possibilities (see my review articles above), as is testified by the volume under review. It comprises 13 contributions, of which twelve were commissioned for this volume, with an older paper reprinted as an introductory essay: Doyle's "The shaping of the Vernon and Simeon Manuscript" (= V, S), first published in 1974, has become a classic, and is therefore rightly reprinted here with minor corrections (1-13). Doyle was one of the first to draw attention to the methodological interdependence of palaeography, codicology and literary history; unsurprisingly, his research is quoted by other contributors to the volume more frequently than that of any other modern scholar.

The presence of individual texts contained in such large collections as V and their form can be explained by close comparison of the textual traditions behind them and the

---

[17] Most of the 'Scottish' features could have been introduced later; for instance, *quhill thai were lyvand here* might well represent authorial (Chaucerian) *while thei were lyuynge here*, or any kind of mix.

adaptations made to fit them to the specific purposes and preferences of the compiler. Robinson's line of argument in "The Vernon Manuscript as a 'coucher book'" (pp. 15-28) is slightly awkward: the book was certainly not called that when copied and most coucher and ledger books were not of the Vernon type, but were large breviaries. Her article comprises rich documentation of such oversize books, but the relevance of all this for V appears to be somewhat marginal. Turville-Petre discusses "The relationship of the Vernon and Clopton manuscripts" (pp. 29-44); since the textual overlap between the two is confined to the *Euangelie,* the similarity of the two *collections* is not conspicuous. The major part of the paper is, in consequence, on the Clopton family and the other poems contained in the MS.

Blake's "Vernon Manuscript: contents and organisation" (45-60) neatly complements Doyle's account: Blake concentrates on contents, pointing out that V was never planned to contain more texts than the surviving index lists, that the collection is notably English in character, that all its texts are religious, many were quite modern in 1380, and many are of western/northern provenance. He warns us, referring to Lewis' findings relating to the *Prick of Conscience*, that the scriptorium is likely to have had available more than one copy of some texts, from which scribes could choose, and did. This hypothesis is confirmed by the *South English Legendary* texts (48, referring to Görlach 1974). Blake has very perceptive remarks about possible intentions that can be gathered from the particular selection and the arrangement of the individual pieces; however, there must have been much more improvisation than he admits. Further indications of this are Doyle's opinion, quoted approvingly by Marx (156), "that 'Part 3' was assembled almost at random" (compare the bookshop hypothesis formulated for MS Auchinleck which assumes that the compilers assembled the text in a much more systematic manner than is possibly true). Also, the 'legends' of the "luther briddes" Judas and Pilate were added later to V, and Micheal to S, which shows that collecting additional material went on even after a collection had been copied from one or more manuscripts – the texts in question were added later from a *third SEL* MS, although their marginal character does not permit us to categorize them as representing different strands of textual transmission. The compiler, even with his vast resources, was far from being in the position of a modern anthologizer. Moreover, questions like the addition of the short *Refrain Lyrics* ("added as an afterthought?", 56) remain unsolved (cf. Burrow, 187-99).

Blake's account is complemented by Hussey who provides more specific arguments in his "Implications of choice and arrangement of texts in part 4" (61-74), a section in which the compiler turned, in the main, to recent religious prose. Heffernan's treatment of V's *Northern Homily Cycle* first interprets the MS as evidence of the contemporary religious climate: he admits that V is exceptional; whether the contents, or parts of it, can be attributed to certain factions remains dubious – the author's discursive style probably reflects this uncertainty (cf. Henry, who also refers to "the difficulty of associating it with any specific group of religious or of the pious", 113). Henry, who interprets the doctrinal meaning of texts and make-up of V (89-113) sees "doctrine in V ... to be orthodox" (89), which she exemplifies with a close analysis of the 'carpet page' (f. 231v) which has a "Pater Noster in a table ypeynted" to precede the *Speculum Vitae* text, and then relates the illumination to the *textual* evidence in the Lord's Prayer and Creed.

Meale's discussion of "The Miracles of Our Lady" (115-36) places the texts of the (now fragmentary) section into V's devotional context; although the poems are certainly not by one author, their great importance to the compiler is confirmed by the high quality of the illustrations, which "are the work of a finer narrative artist than any other whose hand appears in the volume" (136). Marx, in his discussion of the "'Lamentation of Mary to Saint Bernard' and the 'Quis dabit'" (137-57), freely admits that "the reasons for carrying out the revisions in the ME text ... are not obvious" (156), but sees the poem placed in a network of texts that can be established by its being found together with other religious works: although no common descent can be assumed for them, compilers must have had a feeling of where the Lamentation belonged "in the tradition of instructional literature" (157), arguments that are similar to Thompson's with regard to the V lyrics (201-24).

Edwards in his "Contexts of the Vernon romances" (159-70) points to the fact that the three items in V so classified do not fulfil the *Manual's* definition; even Mehl's compromise term 'homiletic romances' is not quite satisfactory (cf. Reichl, 171 below). Whereas *Robert of Sicily* occurs in V and S and eight other MSS, *Tars* does so only in V., S and MS Auchinleck, and *Joseph of Arimathia* is unique – in more than one way. It also precedes the peculiar 'anti-legends' of *Judas* and *Pilate* from the *SEL*. Its content and 'half-alliterated' form make it a piece predestined as a 'filler'. Also, the poem may well be local: the connection with Bordesley Abbey, to which "Guy de Beauchamp bequeathed a French *Joseph* in 1306" (169) provides exciting circumstantial 'evidence' for the origin of V for all who have considered the abbey a likely place of origin on other, mainly dialectal, grounds.

Reichl's analysis of "*The King of Tars*: language and textual transmission" (171-86) is the only contribution that focuses on linguistic matters. His conclusion that the original poet must have used a mixed dialect has been suggested before, as has the hypothesis that both memorial and written transmission are behind the V text. Since this is far removed from the original in time and space, the details of this transmission are impossible to reconstruct, but the essentially written basis of *Tars* of course agrees with those of other V texts where the evidence is less ambiguous.

Burrow's treatment of "The shape of the Vernon refrain lyrics" (187-99) deals in very clear fashion with the most problematic set of texts in V: the 23 lyrics are here first recorded, they represent a new lyrical form, and one of the poems explicitly refers to the Peasants' Revolt of 1381 and the earthquake of 1382. They were clearly added at the end, and since only nine of them are found in other manuscripts (20 occurrences only, and only two MSS have the same set of three poems), there is little evidence available for reconstruction – even the differences between V and S are minimal.

Thompson discusses the same poems (plus four without refrains) in his "The textual background and reputation of the Vernon lyrics" (201-24). He agrees with Burrow on the V/S compiler's active editing of his text (205), keeping open the possibility that S (the second half of the section only?) was copied straight from V (206), possibly 'improving' the text in the process. It is not quite so easy to follow Thompson's claim that these lyrics were popular (212) – the fact that individual pieces are found in 14 MSS outside VS (mainly in commonplace books) is neither impressive nor does it throw any light on how conventional the combination of the lyrics was, or whether VS formed indeed the starting-point of a tradition that was never successful – even though some of its portions came to be included in the numerous anthologies intended for religious and moral instruction. Comparing the V collection with other "lyric clusters" in the 'London' Thornton MS or in MS Harley 1706 (219) or classifying them as "preaching fodder" (222) does not help, since this raises more problems than it solves.

There is a very full index of names and titles at the end of the book (225-38), but no list of references; since all the bibliographical information is contained in footnotes, it is often difficult to trace the *op. cit.*'s.

Discussion of V will and must continue, and there is indeed a great deal of spade work still to be done – Blake mentions how many texts have not been properly edited (or related to the edited text in critical analysis), and linguistic investigation, here represented only by Reichl, is certainly lagging behind. Also, none of the contributors mentions that he actually read S and the V facsimile side by side in the British Library – a unique opportunity to compare the two and impossible before 1977. However, the volume under review is a hopeful sign that the spate of facsimiles now available is coming to be used for philological work, thus justifying the great pains (and costs) involved in their production.

5 A Variorum Edition of the Works of Geoffrey Chaucer, Volume II: *The Canterbury Tales*, Norman: University of Oklahoma Press.
Part Three, *The Miller's Tale*, ed. Thomas W. Ross, 1983, xxix + 273 pp.;
Part Nine, *The Nun's Priest's Tale*, ed. Derek Pearsall, 1983, xxviii + 284 pp.;
Part Ten, *The Manciple's Tale*, ed. Donald C. Baker, 1984, xxvii + 146 pp.;
from *AAA* 11 (1986), 111-4.

No English author apart from Shakespeare can boast of a continuous history of scholarly comment such as Chaucer can, and it is timely that this wealth of criticism is now being assembled for the first time (for a history of the Chaucer reception cf. also Brewer 1978, and for allusions, Spurgeon 1925). The basis and point of reference for the three volumes under review (which are the first of 25 parts to be devoted to the *Canterbury Tales*, and are among the first five of the whole *Variorum Chaucer* = *VC*) is the excellent facsimile of MS Hengwrt (Ruggiers 1979) that started the series. This has made the text accessible in a form that has been established as the one closest to Chaucer's original (Ruggiers 1979, Blake 1980), providing a technically perfect photographic reproduction and transliteration together with a collation of the Ellesmere text – a combination that permits a close comparison with Hg's sister manuscript and age-old competitor for editorial favour. The facsimile was published with the explicit aim of permitting all the volume editors of individual *Canterbury Tales* to base their editions on it. (The facsimile series is to be continued with reproductions of MSS Tanner 346, Bodley 638, Pepys 2006, Cbr. Trinity R.3.19 and Cbr. St John's College L.1 for other portions of Chaucer's work).

There is no doubt about the textual excellence of Hg; its superior value is repeatedly stated by the three editors, thus Ross, p.75: "El displays its characteristic editorialization, however, and is thus not as authoritative as Hg." Pearsall confirms that "Hg is so remarkably free from scribal error and editorialization, so remarkably consistent in grammar, spelling, and meter, that it is clear that it must stand very close to the author's original" (3-4). The fact is most vividly expressed by Ross, 54: "The dazzling El is a showy (and demanding) mistress; the drab and 'rat-gnawn' Hg is a dependable wife". However, the editors do not take the rigorous stand favoured by Blake (1980), *viz.* rejecting as dubious everything not supported by Hg. Pearsall gets close to this position when commenting with regard to NPT 2981: "Emendation of Hg is here painful for the present editor" (p.132).

Careful planning has gone into the preparation of the huge project, shared among some forty scholars mostly from the United States and Britain. Baker's pilot edition of MaT was

> selected as the original model for the fascicles of the VC and has during the intervening thirteen or fourteen years been recast again and again as the editorial board has sifted and transformed the original concepts upon which this vast project was based". (Baker, p.xvii)

It has been a felicitous choice to select as models two undoubted masterpieces (MiT, NPT) and one (MaT) in which "the artistic value of the entire performance has been under debate" (Baker, p.3), at least before 1950, but whose "function within the closing argument of the Canterbury Tales ... makes clearer Chaucer's larger intentions" (Baker, p.3), and a piece whose appreciation has changed from Manly's verdict in 1926 ("a student's piece, full of rhetorical stuffing, ill-digested", quoted by Baker, p.11) to modern praises (Baker's summary ends in non-committed perplexity, 37ff.).

Coordination within the project has already been effective apart from the impact of Baker's pilot volume. Ross acknowledges the help that Pearsall's model provided:

> I consulted a draft of Derek Pearsall's exemplary introduction ... I follow Pearsall's model because it is remarkably lucid and comprehensive and also because conformity in our methods will produce a measure of uniformity in the Variorum Edition. (Ross, p.49)

All the volumes are, then, of similar appearance (slightly smaller than the facsimile) and are arranged according to the same pattern. An Introduction provides exhaustive information on the history of the text and its critics, arranged under the headings "Critical commentary" (comprising subchapters on "Sources and analogues", "Date", "Survey of criticism" and "Conclusions") and "Textual commentary" (including

"Textual tradition", "Glosses", "Order of the C.T.", "Table of correspondences" and "Descriptions of the manuscripts and printed editions"), and is then followed by the Text (with textual variants, and comments arranged by line). Two indexes (bibliographical and general) are provided at the end. Peculiarities of the individual tales and differences among individual editors have meant (and will continue to mean) that the emphases and hence the amount of space devoted to sections vary slightly. In general, the distinction between the two types of commentary appears to have worried the editors. The best solution seems to be that adopted by Pearsall, who has arranged the critical commentary analytically around clear-cut issues that have been prevalent in the history of interpretation of the NPT (Pearsall, p.13). The carefully documented introductions are mines of information, even in sections for which definitive results seemed to have been reached. For instance, in "sources" (a topic of less attraction for recent scholars than it used to be) Pearsall shows (22-27) how much remained to be done for the NPT even after Bryan-Dempster's summary collection, and what has been done in the 1970s, in particular by Blake and Pratt.

Since every volume is intended to be self-contained to a certain degree, there is some necessary overlap and repetition. However, I found the extensive descriptions of manuscripts tedious: Each of the three editors has based his description on the same sources, in particular Manly/Rickert, and since the individual manuscripts have few features relating exclusively to the text portion in question, reading these subchapters develops into a comparative study of summary writing.

There is excellent value in the description of the principles underlying the printed editions, a topic of eminent importance for a Variorum edition since earlier judgements were necessarily based on the quality of the text in front of the critic's eye. But again, much of the information derives from the same sources allowing the reader interesting comparisons: for Tyrwhitt 1775 (= TR) Pearsall (p.118) provides the full account of the Alderman Library copy of SP^2 (Speght 1602) that served as the printer's copy for TR, whereas Baker (p.70) draws attention to the fact that Tyrwhitt collated 26 MSS, but did not yet use Hg and El. (Pearsall merely states that TR "is the first of the printed editions to make systematic use of good manuscripts, but it was not set up from a manuscript"). For the full story of TR, the reader would do best to combine the relevant sections in the two volumes. It might have been a better solution to reserve an extra volume in the series to the description of manuscripts and printed editions. A similar method is apparently envisaged for the treatment of metre about which Pearsall says: "A special section of a volume of the *VC* will be devoted to this subject, which cannot be considered in reference to each work in the series." However, no further information is provided on this point.

As regards the Text, the general editors have sensibly refrained from demanding the establishment of a critical text of each tale by recension. They argue that Manly/Rickert's genealogical conclusions arrived at remain curiously detached from the text they created; the extraordinarily complicated system of constant groups still awaits refinement by careful computer program.

(p.xv in the "General editor's preface", printed in identical form in all the three volumes)

However, the individual editors stress that they place their aim very high; Pearsall states that

the ambitions of the present edition are more extensive than those of MR, who aim only to establish the readings of the archetype of extant copies . . The present edition assumes that the unique authority of Hg enables us to recover with some degree of assurance the text of the author's original. (cf. the very similar statement by Ross, p.61)

In practice, therefore, they follow Hg wherever possible, putting right only the very few errors that are unambiguously scribal. Baker accepts only six of these, retaining 22 Hg readings that modern editors usually reject in favour of El variants (Baker, 53-59). Pearsall accepts twelve emendations, Ross only six, as against 63 readings that he retains because he believes Hg's sense to be superior, or equally acceptable, or more difficult or arguable, or where the metre can be said to be more authentic. (The last point is directed against El readings, whose metrical regularity appealed to Augustan and Victorian poets and editors alike). An "editor must be absolutely sure of his grounds before he repudiates [Hg's] readings" (Pearsall, p.xviii). He will retain such variants as

the reading of line 4266, [...] as representing what Chaucer might have intended to revise but did not. (Pearsall, p.4)

On the other hand, the editors do not feel called upon to take sides in those notorious enigmas of the textual tradition where Hg is ambiguous, such as the break in MiT:

one may guess that a remote common ancestor of [...] made a shift in its copy text at about line 3480. There may have been available two versions of *The Miller's Tale*; the hypothetical source moved from one to the other at the midpoint. Perhaps the two versions were Chaucer's own first draft and revision. (Ross, p.75)

– with none of the (possible or plausible) "guesses" corroborated by evidence. The text follows Hg's spelling; however, whereas the facsimile is accompanied by a transliteration which retains some otiose dashes, italicizes expansions, and has the virgula as the MS punctuation (Ruggiers 1979), normalizations in the *VC* editions include modern punctuation and capitalization, expansions are not indicated, *th* is used throughout, and *u/v* are used according to their ModE value. The practice can be illustrated by some word pairs from the beginning of the NPT (the edited spelling given first): *grove/groue, that/þat, hireself/hire self, never/neuer*.

The huge masses of textual variants and interpretation in the two apparatuses must be read and relished at leisure. The textual apparatus includes all substantial variants from the ten major manuscripts and the major printed editions (the latter included not as an aid towards establishing a critical text, but because their readings formed the basis of contemporary readers' comments). The editors are of course aware of the problem that what constitutes a 'variant' (and not, say, an alternative spelling) is often a nice one; Baker frequently argues against MR's use of the term (cf. notes to MaT, lines 5,30,80,123,222,245 etc.). Individual preferences appear in the notes: whereas Baker often supplies translations of individual words, Pearsall hardly ever does so, sticking to the *VC* editor's proper job of collecting earlier editors' and commentators' interpretations of individual phrases and passages, which are often contradictory, occasionally far-fetched or over-ingenious, and sometimes silly ("certain details in Chaucer appear to have overstimulated some uncritical observers", Pearsall p.47). All this is documented in the notes with a kind of objective exhaustiveness. Editors take sides more explicitly in their introductions – at least Pearsall does so quite often, such as when he repeats his justified reservations about the interpretations of the Lumiansky school on pp.8, 34f. and 39f. Other views are characterized as "very perverse" (36) or "extremely dubious" (37).

The three books make an excellent start to the *VC;* my personal favorite is Pearsall's whose witty style is a perfect match for his subject matter (cf. his characterization of NPT as being "like a firework display that has got into the hands of a pyromaniac", p.10), but whose clear arrangement, lucid expositions and succinct evaluations make his volume a particularly successful achievement that other volume editors would do well to match. Printed in a beautiful typeface (and with very few errors) on high-quality paper, and lavishly bound, these volumes are even attractive (a rare feature in scholarly books) to those who "value books (as women men) for dress". The whole ambitious undertaking will further add to the concentration of scholarly interest on the *archipoeta* whose fame will continue to eclipse that of his contemporaries.

References:
Blake, N.F., ed., 1980, *The Canterbury Tales.* London: Edward Arnold.
Brewer, Derek, ed., 1978, *Chaucer. The Critical Heritage.* 2 vols. London: Routledge & Kegan Paul.
Manly, John M. & Edith Rickert, eds., 1941, *The Text of the Canterbury Tales.* Chicago (= MR).
Ruggiers, Paul G., ed., 1979, *The Canterbury Tales. Geoffrey Chaucer. A facsimile and transcription of the Hengwrt Manuscript* ... Norman: Univ. of Oklahoma Press.
Spurgeon, Caroline C.F., 1925, *Five Hundred Years of Chaucer Criticism and Allusion, 1357-1900.* 3 vols., Cambridge.

6   *Geoffrey Chaucer, Troilus & Criseyde. A new edition of 'The Book of Troilus'* by B.A. Windeatt. London: Longman, 1984, xii + 584 pp.; from *AAA* 10 (1985), 280-2.

It must come as a surprise to the non-specialist that there has been no modern scholarly edition of one of the greatest poems in Middle English literature, and what Chaucerians of many centuries thought the poet's masterpiece: Root's edition of *TC* of 1926 has been the only one available.

Dr Windeatt has now produced an edition that is remarkable in many ways. His text is firmly based – as indeed was that of most of the earlier editors – on what counts as the best (though not quite finished) MS, Corpus Christi Cambridge 61 (= Cp) for which the facsimile, published by Brewer in 1978, can be conveniently compared [2.7]. All the extant texts (there are sixteen major MSS) have been collated, not only with a view to getting as close as possible to the poet's final intentiont, but also to illustrate how Chaucer may have revised his own text and how scribes understood (and in consequence may have felt called upon to alter) their exemplars. A very detailed chapter in the Introduction (25-35) points out that

> the scribal responses to Chaucer's poetry ... are not to be despised as the equivalent of mere printing errors ... With varying levels of attainment, the scribes – as the near-contemporaries of Chaucer – can offer us the earliest line-by-line literary criticism of Chaucer's poetry (26).

Variant readings can of course also show the specific difficulties some scribes (and implicitly, other 15th-century readers) had with a proper understanding of the expressions and the syntax of the original (28ff.).

Windeatt's introduction covers all the important topics also treated in earlier editions, but he often provides new interpretations and insights, and his style is always clear and logical. There is, first, a well-balanced summary of how Chaucer treated his sources. His main source, Boccaccio's *Il Filostrato* (without use of the French translation, as Pratt had assumed, 19-24) was rendered "in the creatively adaptive medieval sense of translation" (3), which in this case means additions from various authors, above all the pervading influence of Boethius – a fact of far-reaching consequences for the genesis of the poem and, in consequence, for textual criticism. The very welcome parallel printing of *Il Filostrato* "enables us to look, as it were, over Chaucer's shoulder as he works." – The modern literary critic is here much better off than the medieval reader, but this advantage scarcely makes up for the losses in immediate contextualization, which shows that any modern evaluation must differ from contemporary judgments. Windeatt, however, brings out, with proper use of the huge scholarly literature on the topic, the decisive features of Chaucer's achievements.

Possibly the most complex problem of *TC* is competently tackled in "The text of the 'Troilus'" (36-54). Since Chaucer's combination of so many complementary sources "involved distinctly different kinds of poetic activity and suggests that Chaucer's composition of the poem was in practice a series of layers ... of writing" (36), Windeatt persuasively shows that such inherently plausible assumptions and claims put forward by Root and other scholars cannot be verified by manuscript evidence in any coherent way: the absence of 'Boethian' passages in some MSS is more likely to reflect scribal problems with disorderly copy texts rather than a 'first edition' of the poem. An analysis of minor textual variants yields, according to Windeatt, the same result (in contrast to Root's tenets): "The evidence for a sustainedly distinct version or state of Chaucer's text, earlier and closer line by line to the Italian source, does not exist" (43). The disconcerting fact is that MSS Ph etc. (Root's α, thought to represent a first version) do contain a number of readings closer to Boccaccio (listed in note 9, p. 52, and again mentioned in the respective places in the notes) – but there are as many instances in which Ph etc. readings are in fact further away (note 10, p. 52). There are, then, readings "which apparently go back to Chaucer's first translation of the Italian ... survivals, possibly corrupted, of a 'rough' early draft" (44). Windeatt concludes: "To all intents and purposes the Ph etc. family has no identity which is anything other than scribal, except in certain parts of Books I, III and IV. Here it sporadically produces some fascinating readings. But these should be seen with the implications of their isolation and scribal context ..." (45). Evidence for a distinction between two authorial stages among the remaining MSS (Root's β and γ) is even weaker. The necessary conclusion is summarized on p. 50 and in note 23:

> none of [the various MS groups] has a consistent integrity throughout as being equivalent to a distinct state of the author's text (50).
> More than one authorial archetype possibly existed, at a time when copies were rapidly proliferating, and the extant MSS themselves show scribes furthering "horizontal" influence between texts ...   (note 23, p. 53)

Although Windeatt's arguments impress as much by their logicality as by their readability they are likely to spark off a lively scholarly debate since they touch so much that has been taken more or less for granted since Root's edition. However, as Windeatt rightly points out, we should not be misled by the assumption that Gower's and Langland's revisions (and Chaucer's in *LGW*) were in any way typical and must therefore apply to the genesis and textual transmission of *TC*, too. After all this, it will be no surprise that Windeatt nowhere ventures to provide a stemma illustrating hypothetical textual relations (nor does he even use cover sigils such as α,γ, β – as Root and Robinson do – in the apparatus). He does provide some account of varying affiliations in "This edition" (65-67) and in "List of Manuscripts" (68-76), in which the 16 extant MSS are briefly described (and the 16 fragments and three early prints listed). It is unfortunate that Windeatt considered a full description of his base MS Cp to be unnecessary, M. Parkes having supplied a full codicological account in the facsimile edition (1978:1-13): it is important to be informed about the very careful execution of Cp on the one hand (which explains Root's statement that Cp "presents the γ text with a high degree of purity, and is spelled with exceptional consistency", 1926:liii), and its unfinished nature on the other. It is especially strange not to find any summary of which lines or longer passages are lacking in Cp (and whether this is owing to losses, such as of f.12^r, or scribal omission, with the correction not carried out, cf. Parkes 1978:1).

The Text section of the book (81-565) is laid out in four columns (two on each facing page), or which *TC* itself takes up the second, and is thus framed between *Il Filostrato* and the explanatory notes ("commentary") and the critical apparatus ("Readings"). Boccaccio's poem is printed in its entirety, with corresponding sections arranged opposite *TC*: where Chaucer did not use Boccaccio, col. II is vacant; where he followed other sources, col. 1 is. This ideal arrangement makes it possible not only to enjoy each work independently, but also to skip from one to the other (and further to the notes for explanation) – the enjoyment of the Italian text being somewhat restricted by the excessively small print. Windeatt's text of *TC* follows Cp quite closely, as any look at the facsimile will show. It appears that he has recourse to emendation only very rarely; for reasons given in the Introduction, 'better' readings (i.e. those closer to Boccaccio) have not been accepted into the text if attested in the Ph and R groups only, but where Cp's reading makes sense. Capitalization and punctuation are modern; the latter (, ; : . –) is less heavy than in Robinson's text. Contrary to normal editorial practice, deviations from the base MS are not indicated (with the exception of complete stanzas taken from other MSS to supply gaps in Cp); such cases are mentioned exclusively in the "Readings" – where they are very difficult to detect. Finally, I would have liked to have had the Cp folio numbers indicated in the text (as in the facsimile edition). Since the facsimile, in turn, does not give line numbers, cross referencing the two books becomes something of a party game.

The "Commentary" is much fuller than in Root: it is detailed, but not so cumbersome as to cause one to lose sight of the text. There are plentiful references to sources and textual parallels (but Windeatt does not jump to conclusions as regards, e.g., Thomas Usk's knowledge and use of *TC*), as well as linguistic and textual commentary.

Variant readings are listed much more exhaustively than in Root's edition; there they primarily had the function of justifying the constitution of the text, here (as emphasised by Windeatt) they allow us to deduce at least something about how the scribes read the text.

TC is generally assumed to have been finished by 1385. Dr Windeatt's edition gives us a fresh impetus to reread the text, and to discover new beauties and problems – a worthy celebration of the work's sescentenary.

7 Helen Cooper, *The Canterbury Tales*. (Oxford Guides to Chaucer). Oxford: UP, 1989, xiii + 437 pp.;
Barry Windeatt, *Troilus and Criseyde*. (Oxford Guides to Chaucer). Oxford: Clarendon Press, 1992, xiv + 414 pp., from *AAA* 19 (1994), 142-5.

Chaucer's work has been the centre of unabated scholarly interest, and it is becoming increasingly difficult, even for a specialist, to keep track of all the findings published in form of dissertations and articles. In consequence, there is a need for bibliographies and handbooks to guide readers through the maze of modern scholarship. The board of Oxford University Press a few years ago decided to bring out a set of three books devoted to Chaucer's works; the first two have appeared and will here be reviewed together. Publication of vol. 3, devoted to his Minor Poems, is announced for the near future.

Cooper's is the first comprehensive guide to the *Canterbury Tales* for many years; new approaches to a wide range of topics from manuscript research to women's studies, and from interpretations of individual lines to the sources, rhetoric and philosophical background make such a new survey timely – as does the availability of the 'new' Robinson Chaucer and many volumes of the Chaucer Variorum edition.

Cooper performs the complex task with admirable comprehensiveness and clarity: she covers the recent research literature exhaustively and produces a balanced synopsis of the present state of knowledge. A succinct survey of general problems relating to the work as a whole is provided on pp. 5-26, before the individual tales are treated one by one. The "General Prologue" rightly makes up the first and most extensive chapter (27-60). Placing the individual portraits in a literary and social perspective, Cooper achieves a good compromise between detailed comment and general information, and between data useful for the neophyte and more specialized interpretations of interest to medievalists who may have missed some of the many recent publications. Treatments follow the accepted sequence of the ten fragments (27-412); each of the tales is surveyed according to a set pattern, in which attribution, date, text, genre, sources and analogues, structure, themes, the tale in context, and style are successively discussed; exhaustive cross-references are included and relevant research is listed at the end of each passage. Since annotated editions are easily available, Cooper has generally refrained from providing information on individual lines; however a substantial number of new and stimulating arguments are embedded in the surveys and amply justify the new book. An attractive feature of Cooper's text is that it is eminently readable and at the same time precise and informative.

The author is a literary scholar: there is slightly less on language than one might have expected, and although the individual chapters contain insightful summaries of stylistic analyses, books dealing with Chaucer's language in more narrow terms (like those by Kerkhof, Fries etc.) are notably absent, as are discussions about Chaucer's "own language" (Samuels) and how this relates to the emerging standard language, or how his poetic diction survived in 15th-century English and Scottish authors.

The book ends with a chapter on "Imitations of the *Canterbury Tales* 1400-1615", which traces the 'afterlife' of the collection from the first attempts to fill in the gaps with texts like *Gamelyn* and ends with John Lane's *Squire's Tale* (413-27); this is followed by a "General bibliography" (428-30, listing the seventy works most frequently quoted) and an "Index" (431-71 – note that these do not help to trace the publications by individual authors embedded in the individual chapters). Dr Cooper has given us a very competent and reliable guide which should (and most certainly will) be used alongside Benson's revision of the Robinson text.

Windeatt rightly claims that *Troilus*, Chaucer's longest work and most ambitious achievement, which was enthusiastically praised by critics of the 15th century, but has since been overshadowed by the *Canterbury Tales*, is now receiving the scholarly and popular attention that it deserves. The book under review is likely to support this trend in a significant way. As the first modern editor of the text (1984) and as the author of eight papers on *Troilus* (cf. 405-6), Windeatt is in a particularly privileged position to write this guide – in it he summarizes the research which he did for a different purpose in his introduction and in the notes to his text edition, and complements it with the findings of more recent publications (the "bibliography", 383-406, lists some 500 titles up to 100 of which postdate the first printing of his edition).

Windeatt provides chapters on the date of composition (3-11, reviewing the accepted date 1382-85/6), text (12-36, summarizing the problems and solutions arising from variation among the surviving manuscripts), sources (37-137, an impressive conspectus of the complex situation in a book "that both draws on so many 'old bookes' and yet is profoundly original and new"), genre (138-79, discussing the variety of genres that have contributed to Chaucer's masterpiece), structure (180-211), themes (212-313, ranging from 'love' to 'the freedom of the human will'), style (314-59, pointing out the stylistic variation and linguistic resourcefulness that contribute so much to the poem's novelty in a depleted ME), and the afterlife: imitation and allusion, c1385-1700 (360-82). A bibliography and index follow at the end.

Readers may well be tempted to skip the more bony parts and go straight to genre, structure and themes, but those who do so would be wrong: Windeatt's important work on the text and its sources constitutes one of his major achievements (most of which is of course also used to justify his text edition). His interpretation of the more 'literary' chapters could not have proceeded, certainly not as persuasively, unless he had laid safe foundations; he makes at least an attempt to clear up "the perennially puzzling interrelation of authorial intent and scribal medium" (34), and to disentangle the sources Chaucer used, and then draw conclusions from the methods of their adaptation and combination about the aims of the author who created "a new unity which remakes everything it contains" (37). Windeatt's objective here is to re-create "the intertextuality of an already related group of narratives which successively reinterprets a common corpus of stories, characters and settings" (44) – an interpretative competence which Chaucer could expect in an educated contemporary audience, where modern readers have no such background available. This also applies where "the 'source' is the poet's use of his educated memory of accumulated reading rather than any particular book open in front of him" (46-7). Windeatt's very clear conspectus of how Chaucer's text relates to his main source, Boccaccio's *Filostrato* (54-69), into which the subsidiary sources (70-137) are then incorporated, is eminently useful.

The fact that Windeatt, in contrast to Cooper, has a single poem to comment, in a book of 400+ pages, means that he has space for discussion of details, and can do so in more leisurely style. This 'leisure' is put to great advantage when Windeatt discusses the fusion of 'epic', 'romance', 'history', 'tragedy', 'drama', 'lyric', 'fabliau', 'allegory' (140-79) – categories, of course, which are not as distinct as the author's separate discussion of them seems to imply. The "remarkable symmetry of structure (...) designed to reflect (...) the rise and fall of Troilus' fortunes" (184) has been noted by most critics, but Windeatt adds interesting details, also relating the plan to the structure of time and that present in the stars (198-211). Structure of a different but complementary kind is made explicit in the discussion of 'love', 'service', 'religion', 'death', 'pitee', 'secrecy', 'honour', 'trouthe' and 'freedom' (212-67), key concepts elsewhere in Chaucer's work, but arguably more important for the thematic structure of *Troilus*. (The second half of the "themes" chapter, 275-98, deals with the main personae and the ending of the poem – possibly better treated in a separate chapter).

Troilus contains the greatest number of explicit comments on language in Chaucer's works, and Windeatt rightly points out how the reader is alerted "to the accuracy and appropriateness of language used in the poem, and also to its range and variety" (317). Windeatt's chapter on "Style" therefore stresses the interplay of rhetoric, style and formal requirements of metre and rhyme (314-59). Finally, the reception of the work from Chaucer's contemporaries Gower and Usk to Dryden is summarized (360-82); the chapter does not contain much new information, but is useful to have for the light it throws on potential interpretations of the Chaucer text.

The two Oxford guides will prove very useful in academic teaching, the paperback price making the first accessible also to students. Both books are very carefully edited and printed and a pleasure to handle.

8 William Langland, *Piers Plowman. A Parallel-Text Edition of the A, B, C and Z Versions*, edited by A. V. C. Schmidt. I: Text. Harlow: Longman, 1995, xiv+762pp. (=S4);
William Langland, *The Vision of Piers Plowman*, A Critical Edition of the B-Text Based on Trinity College Cambridge MS B 15. 17. Second Edition, ed. A. V. C. Schmidt. London: Dent (= Everyman), 1995, lxxxvi+551 pp. (=SB);
from *Anglia* 115 (1997), 391-4.

The modern history of Langland research starts with Skeat's monumental editions of the three versions for the EETS (four volumes 1867-85), and his print of three parallel texts in two volumes of 1886, but it started anew with Kane's edition of the A Text (1960, ^{2}1988) and Kane & Donaldson's of the B-Text (1975, ^{2}1988) – the critical edition of the C-Text, expected for years (by Russell and Kane) is now announced for late 1996. Kane & Donaldson summarized their work on the text in editions which were new (some might say revolutionary) because they were based on the most rigid rejection of stemmatic principles in the reconstruction of the archetypes of the three versions they accepted as genuine and their interpretation of interrelationships and the growth of the text based on these insights. The 172 plus 225 pages of introduction in which their editorial methods are justified remain a monument of *PP* research and of the methodology of textual criticism in general.

What, then, is left for modern editors to do? They can, as Pearsall (1978=PC) did, print one version from the best manuscript, with corrections from the text closest to it, to provide a text accessible to the general reader, who can enjoy the poem assisted by a very readable introduction, plentiful notes, and a glossary. Such an edition of a single version can be more scholarly too and still remain clear to and readable for a wider audience, as is nicely illustrated by Schmidt's B-Text. A different purpose lies behind Rigg & Brewer's edition of the Z-Text (1983=RZ) in which the authors establish the existence of a fourth, early draft version of the poem. The alternative method is obviously to print the four (or three) versions side by side, as Skeat had done *after* editing the texts individually, and thus to permit readers to follow the process of rewriting on which Langland must have been active for more than twenty years (A: from 1360 on, B 1370s, C complete by 1387, cf. Pearsall 1978:9), much as readers may wish to see how the text of Wordsworth's *Prelude* developed over the years.

It is interesting to see that modern editors unanimously agree in their estimates of:

a) The distinctness of A, B, C as clearly distinguishable works, revised by the same author (rather than three states of countless intermediate versions, as might seem likely for an author continuously working on the same text for more than twenty years). This agreement does not include an acceptance of Rigg's claims for 'Z' (accepted by Schmidt, if critically, but rejected by Kane).

b) The choice of the best manuscript: all have spoken out, with verdicts based on irrefutable evidence, for Cambridge Trinity College MS R.3.14 (A), Cambridge Trinity College MS B.15.17 (B) and San Marino, Huntington Library MS 143 (C) – which makes it possible to compare easily editors' decisions about contested passages. (Since 'Z' is uniquely extant in Oxford, Bodleian Libary MS Bodley 851 the only difference between editions can be how many emendations are admitted).

The four-text edition (S4) consists of an editorial preface, a list of MSS, the symbols and abbreviations used and a note on the text and apparatus, which together take up seven pages and tell us little more than the practice used for the transcription of the texts; readers are referred to the "second volume which will contain a full discussion of the textual aims and procedures of this edition as well as detailed textual notes, an extensive interpretative commentary, and a comprehensive glossary" (p.viii). There are also four appendixes at the end, giving two additional passages, a list of rejected readings of the base MS insufficiently supported by other copies and one hundred instances of emendations on metrical reasons (far fewer than in Kane & Donaldson). The list of some eight hundred instances of rejected readings of R for the B text (pp. 745-53) and some six hundred rejected for C (pp. 754-60) are especially important since they contain all deviations from the best text not recorded in the main-sequence apparatus. Otherwise, for the time being (publication of the second volume not being in sight) we will have to gather information about the editor's principles from SB (reviewed below) and check this against the texts here printed. The B text in SB is evidently identical (apart from SB's modernized spelling), but a comparison with the other editions shows Schmidt's divergence in a number of features:

RZ/S4Z: Both editors hesitate to emend, but S does so three times as often as R (sometimes for linguistic reasons, or for sense, or in line 1,101 to make sense of R's crux). R indicates expansions; the punctuation differs slightly.

KA/S4A: K, on the basis of his reconstruction, is more willing to emend, even on the grounds of metre; not all deviations from T are marked: S4A emends less frequently. I find it disconcerting to have quite a few, even major emendations not indicated in the text: *Prologue* 22 Wonne] Whom T, 34 synneles] giltles T, 42 Fayteden] Flite þan T,

73 ȝe gyuen ȝoure] þei ȝouen here T – all these (and other) emendations being justified, or justifiable. Schmidt's decision avoids a highly cluttered text, but makes it much more difficult to take into account the textual evidence.

KDB/S4B: The contrast between the two is repeated: there are more emendations in KDB, many for metre and alliteration, but Schmidt's deviations from the base MS are not always indicated, e.g. Pr 29 cairen] carien W; 37 sholde] wolde W.

PC/S4C: The two editions are very similar, though PC is more conservative; S4C's emendations are not always indicated: Pr 18 ryche] pore, 28 ful] swythe.

The great advantage of S4 is of course having all four versions displayed on a single opening. The rest, however, is left to the reader – identifying the corresponding lines and finding the differences. Rigg, who prints lines and words exclusive to Z in bold, provides much more guidance here – as even SB does, which indicates the support of individual variants by **Z**, **A**, **C**, in the apparatus. So one wonders how many of the "Langland specialists and advanced students" (p.viii) will have the patience for a word-by-word comparison and thus make full use of the evidence provided.

As the publisher, the price and the make-up at once make clear, SB is intended for a different public. It will remain invaluable, until the second volume of S4 is out, for the meticulous account of the editorial procedure it gives – for **B**. In contrast to Kane Schmidt feels he is "unable to agree with Kane (here following Greg) that "striking (...) variants are *more* likely to be generated coincidentally by scribes than 'commonplace' ('minor') readings of little lexical, stylistic or metrical significance" (p. lvii). Having worked on a similarly complex corpus, the *South English Legendary*, I found that 'major' variants were essential for a classification of texts (Görlach 1974).

Schmidt's introduction (xvii-lxxxvi), totally revised from the text of the 1978 edition, is a solid piece of scholarship and will prove essential for Langland studies. He treats the versions, authorship and dates, the literary tradition, structure and themes of *PP*, and Langland's poetic art – all in a succinct but very readable style. Only where he delves into the textual and editorial problems (liv-lxxxii) does it become likely that most Everyman readers will not patiently follow him – but these highly informative sections are (as has been indicated) very valuable for specialists working with S4. The two books are excellently edited and printed; minor mistakes can of course not be avoided – I noted *this* in SB Pr 62 (which should be *thise*) and in S4A Pr 18 *perinne* the initial *p* should probably be a *þ*.

The two books under review, together with the author's *The Clerkly Maker: Langland's Poetic Art* (1987) and his *New Translation of the B-Text* (1992), constitute a rich harvest of a dedicated scholar's work over the past twenty years – to be crowned by the second volume of S4 which will make his text edition fully usable and, being complete in manuscript form, will hopefully be published quite soon.

References
Görlach, Manfred. 1974. *The Textual Tradition of the South English Legendary*. (Leeds
    Texts and Monographs New Series 6). Leeds: University.

Kane, George, ed. 1960. *Piers Plowman. The A Version*. London: Athlone Press [²1988].

Kane, George & E. Talbot Donaldson, eds. 1975. *Piers Plowman. The B Version*. London: Athlone Press [²1988].

Pearsall, Derek. 1978. *Piers Plowman by William Langland. An Edition of the C-text*. (York Medieval Texts 2). London: Edward Arnold.

Rigg, A. G. & Charlotte Brewer, eds. 1983. *William Langland, Piers Plowman, The Z Version*. Toronto: Pontifical Institute of Medieval Studies.

Russell, George & George Kane. fc. *Piers Plowman - The C Version*. London: Athlone Press (fc.?).

9 Angus McIntosh, M.L. Samuels & Margaret Laing, *Middle English Dialectology: Essays on Some Principles and Problems*, ed. and introduced by Margaret Laing. Aberdeen: UP, 1989, xiv + 295pp.,
The English of Chaucer and his contemporaries. Essays by M.L. Samuels and J.J. Smith, ed. by J.J. Smith. Aberdeen: UP, 1988, vi + 126pp.; from *Anglia* 109 (1991), 112-6.

The two volumes under review (= MED, ECC) bring together the most important articles on ME philology by members of the Edinburgh and Glasgow schools, who from the 1950s onwards have so largely contributed to our understanding of the language of ME manuscripts: there are twelve papers by A. McIntosh (all in MED), nine by M.L. Samuels (4 + 5), and two each by M. Laing (MED) and by J.J. Smith (ECC) plus two written by more than one author. Although the titles of the two books indicate that the focus is slightly different, there is also a great deal of thematic overlap which argues for a joint review. With the exception of two papers, all have been published (between 1956 and 1988) and are here reprinted with minor alterations only: apart from their methodological interest, they thus also serve as indispensable background reading for the development of the particular approach to ME dialects which culminated in the publication of the *Linguistic Atlas of Late Mediaeval English (LALME)* in 1986.

MED very appropriately starts with McIntosh's "The analysis of written Middle English" (1956, here 1-21) and his "A new approach to Middle English dialectology" (1963, here 22-31), stressing the need to base investigations firmly on the analysis of written evidence, and make deductions about pronunciation only at a later stage. The comprehensive documentation of ME graphematics, which necessitated the use of computers from the beginning, permitted the definition of the '*fit*-technique' on the basis of which much more precise datings and localizations of late ME manuscripts were attempted than had ever been done by scholars working with far fewer variables. This leads to the identification of "Scribal profiles from Middle English texts" (1975, here 32-45) – ideolectal fingerprints which make ascriptions of even mixed texts possible. (There are more than 1,000 of these profiles represented in *LALME*.) Such accumulative evidence made it possible for McIntosh in 1974 to sketch "Towards an inventory of Middle English scribes" (here 46-63) in which taxonomic procedures combining evidence from palaeography and graphemics are employed very convincingly. Samuels' "Some applications of Middle English dialectology" (1963, here 64-80) has proved one of the most influential papers of historical dialectology. His contrastive description of 'Wycliffite' ME, with two successive layers of London ME ('Auchinleck', and 'Chaucer's language'), supplanted after 1430 by 'Chancery standard', has greatly improved our understanding of the dynamics of ME dialects, 1330-1430. Samuels' paper now has *LALME* maps for SUCH, MUCH, ANY, SELF, STEAD, GIVEN, and SAW replacing earlier 'isographic' ones. A comparison makes clear that the evidence is not quite as tidy as suggested in 1963, but still the explanatory limits of the new maps, for all their objective correctness, become quite obvious. Concentration on the graphemics of ME has meant that the projects sketched in the next three papers remain unfinished: In "The dialectology of mediaeval Scots: some possible approaches to its study" (1978, here 81-85) McIntosh argues, as a first step, for "a preliminary survey of all ... potentially valuable local material together with one of all literary and other non-documentary texts" surviving from Scotland before 1450 (or including non-standard texts up to 1550?). Only then can dialectological work proper start. Word study is largely excluded from *LALME*, so McIntosh's "Word geography in the lexicography of mediaeval English" (1973, here 86-97) and his "Middle English word-geography: its potential role in the study of the long-term impact of the Scandinavian settlements upon English" (1977, here 98-105) as well as Samuels' "The great Scandinavian belt" (1985, here 106-115) are valuable illustrations of how much promise there is in a new investigation of ME lexis now that the *MED* is almost complete, and *LALME* provides the frame for dates and localizations: such work is still needed even for the much-ploughed fields of the Danelaw. (Cf. p. 187, n. 31, where McIntosh regrets that there has been so little follow-up work to Kaiser's *Word Geography* of 1937). A localized analogical development in verb morphology is treated in McIntosh's "Present indicative plural forms in the later Middle English of the North Midlands" (1983, here 116-122), which serves to show that the complex traditional view of verb inflexion in ME is still too simplistic to account for all the data.

Chapters 11-19 in MED have in common with ECC that they deal with individual manuscripts and authors, showing with impressive rigour how modern dialectology can be grafted on to traditional philology, as in McIntosh's "Two unnoticed interpretations in four manuscripts of the *Prick of Conscience*" (1976, here 123-35) and Samuels' "The dialects of MS Bodley 959" (1969, here 136-49 – showing traces of Wycliffe's ideolect?). Laing's "Dialectal analysis and linguistically composite texts in Middle English" (1988, here 150-69) continues her investigation of *Mischsprachen* on the basis of two complex manuscripts which show that forms used in them are not random, and that "they are no less valid for dialectal studies than the most methodologically written holograph" (165). McIntosh and the late Martyn Wakelin (who had made Mirk a special object of his research) combined to discuss the five scribes who wrote the *Festial* text in Bodleian MS Hatton 96 (1982, here 170-78); these scribes produced some 16 varieties of Middle English between them, partly as a consequence of different examplars – a complex set-up that is yet possible to disentangle with some plausibility. Robert Thornton receives detailed attention in McIntosh's "The textual transmission of the alliterative *Morte Arthure*" (1967, here 179-87) concentrating on two groups of texts for which he used sources written in more southerly language than his own, a piece of linguistic detective work supported by masses of data. Laing returns to the concept of linguistic profiles which she applies to R. Misyn's translations of Rolle's works to establish textual interrelationships, the old method of correlating linguistic parallels with textual affinities in a convincing new garb and supported by a great amount of evidence (unpublished, here 188-223). McIntosh, in his "The language of the extant versions of *Havelock the Dane*" (1976, here 224-236) makes a convincing case for an assignment to Norfolk (rather than Lincolnshire); the argument is complex because most manuscripts that can be listed in support are themselves complex (230-31). The textual transmission of the *Scottish Troy Book* (1979, here 237-55) is even more difficult since the question of how 'Scots' the original was is uncertain; however, a close comparison of the language of the four surviving fragments leads to a plausible reconstruction of the character of the poet's own text. Finally in this collection, there is Samuels' discussion of "The dialect of the scribe of the Harley Lyrics" (1984, here 256-63). The collection has long been ascribed to Hereford, and Samuels, comparing the language of the Harley MS with that of MS BL Royal 12C., copied by the same scribe, isolates a few diagnostic variant forms which fit with Leominster, the scribe's putative home.

Whereas the scribal dialects treated in MED range from Scotland to Norfolk and Leominster, ECC is mainly on the triad Chaucer, Gower and Langland; in particular, the interrelationship of textual criticism, palaeography, book production, dialectology and graphemics is here presented in exemplary studies of the language of the great Ricardian poets. It comes as a surprise to find that despite so many investigations into these texts, a number of important matters, such as the reconstruction of the authors' original dialects, had not been gone into efficiently. Scribal behaviour may be largely unpredictable, but it is not random, and in detecting these meaningful patterns in copies of Chaucer manuscripts Samuels succeeds in shedding new light on the age-old problem of "Chaucerian final '-*e*'" (1972, here 7-12): a great number of scribes of other manuscripts used -*e* in a 'grammatically correct' way, and since such use guarantees metrical regularity in most of Chaucer's lines, deviations are likely to be due to scribal corruption. Progress in palaeography and textual criticism combined with dialectology have even permitted Samuels to reconstruct "Chaucer's spelling" (1981, here 23-37); one of the findings is that the *Equatorie* is indeed likely to be "an authentic and autograph work of Chaucer" (p. 34). Spelling practice is again the decisive argument for *one* scribe for the Hengwrt and Ellesmere MSS, the slightly different preferences being explained by the difference in time and in the different character of the manuscripts (1983, here 38-50). The fact that individual scribes copied texts from various authors is used to detect 'layers' of dialect throughout this collection. Smith makes good use of such information in his "The Trinity Gower D-scribe and this work on two early Canterbury Tales manuscripts" (unpublished paper 1988, here 51-69); this neatly complements the best modern account of "The language of Gower" by Samuels and Smith (1981, here 13-22) in which the three stages of revision, their underlying dialects and a correlation with Gower's biography are lucidly set out and the very high quality of the Fairfax and Stafford MSS is safely established – indispensable background reading for every student of Gower's works. Smith returns to Gower when analysing with great diligence the spelling practices of 15th-century copyists of the *Confessio Amantis* (here 96-113), which includes a very useful classification of 49 major manuscripts, 108-10. Samuels' task in establishing "Langland's dialect" (1985, here 70-85) was much more difficult than in the case of Chaucer or Gower. He bases his new analysis on his alliterative practice (*heo* 'she'; *are(n)*: *beþ* 'are'; *f/v*-alliteration; 'h'-dropping) which excludes everything but SW Worcestershire – the Malvern area which tallies with autobiographical evidence. More intricate are the arguments from the spelling practice in the manuscripts: Samuels is able to confirm Skeat's hypothesis (77) that Langland may well have returned to the Malvern area when he wrote the C version – most of the C MSS come from that area. Although he chooses his words carefully, Samuels thinks it very likely that the 'Z' version *is* the very earliest draft of *Piers Plowman*, which would tally with the strongly SW Worcestershire dialect of the text (p. 85, n. 80). Finally, there is a look at conditions post-1450, a period in which the fast spread of written London features makes it increasingly difficult to localize manuscripts. Samuels' "Spelling and dialect in the late and post-Middle English periods" (1981, here 86-95) sketches the type of evidence and how it can be interpreted dialectologically and sociolinguistically, and provides clear guidelines for further research into a much-neglected area.

Both books have consolidated bibliographies, and indexes of persons and manuscripts (and of places and words, MED). As indicated above, the papers have methodologically so much in common that they could have been combined in one volume. They represent not only the gist of the new historical dialectology as formulated and practised by two leading historical linguists over almost forty years, but they also illustrate a very promising fusion of findings of dialectology, graphemic analysis, palaeography, literary history and the history of the late medieval book which have begun to make many earlier philologists' statements look somewhat dated. The two collections are excellently edited and printed with great care; they provide a very useful complement to *LALME* and are essential reading for anyone interested in Late Middle English.

2 Historical Linguistics and the History of English

The topics have been central to my teaching from the later 1960s, and prominent in my publications from my (German) *Introduction to English Historical Linguistics* (1974) onwards. My selection here concentrates on major books in the field 1980-2000, which have also determined much of my thinking. The long review article is here included since so little is known on the 19th-century grammatical tradition that a reprint seems to be particularly worthwhile.

10 Lyle Campbell, *Historical Linguistics. An Introduction*. Edinburgh: UP, 1998, xx + 396 pp.; from *Anglia* 118 (2000), 267-9.

Is historical linguistics in the classical sense a dying discipline? Competence in older stages of languages has certainly declined a great deal since the days of comparative linguists of the 19th century, but Campbell is certainly right in partly blaming insufficient reflexion on the aims and methods to bring a traditional discipline up-to-date, and a scarcity of adequate textbooks to make it teachable, for the neglect in academic teaching. A leisurely introduction (1-15) makes students aware of change in the history of English, and provides exercises to make it possible for them to test their comprehension. "Sound change" (16-56) introduces the reader to kinds of changes, allophonic/conditioned and phonemic ones, and their articulatory bases, with examples taken from English and Indo-European (and a few 'exotic') languages; all this is done in clear and precise definitions, with, again, exercises testing the students' comprehension on examples from languages they cannot be expected to know. Borrowing (57-88) and analogy (89-107) are of course the major factors disturbing the regularity of change presupposed for the comparison, and so an intensive discussion of the forms and consequences of the two phenomena comes next; in this context Campbell skilfully introduces cultural history and language structure as conditioning factors for the 'deviation' from the expected developments. With these preliminaries settled, the way is open for "The comparative method and linguistic reconstruction" (108-62) in which a succinct introduction is provided into *the* method of the 19th century, with intelligent summaries of the basic assumptions – and the restrictions of the method (e.g. with regard to the 'realism' of reconstructed proto-languages); to broaden the scope, extensive samples from American Indian and Finno-Ugric languages are included for exercises. A rightly short chapter on "Linguistic classification" follows (163-85): since the concept is here defined genetically (and not typologically), and much of the discussion is taken up by the misconceived method of glottochronology, Campbell's treatment is appropriately succinct and partly negative. The argument here presupposes the family-tree model, which is contrasted with alternative models (wave theory, and methods derived from dialectology, sociolinguistics and lexical diffusion) in the next section (186-200). "Internal reconstruction" (201-25) is again illustrated from a great number of languages and plenty of exercises. After phonological change was discussed above, syntactic change and semantic and lexical change follow next. Syntactic change (226-53) is lucidly explained by reanalysis, extension and borrowing – with due consideration of the problem that categories and structures cannot be expected to be identical cross-linguistically. (The chapter will, however, need cautious explanations by the teacher, rather than trusting the students' capacities to recognize the limitations of the method themselves). A very useful portion introduces 'grammaticalization', exemplified by various near-universal trends (238-42) and followed by necessary warnings as to reanalysis and borrowing as obstacles to syntactic reconstruction. Traditional categories of semantic change (254-67) are exemplified by appropriate (mostly well-known) examples from Germanic and Romance languages, with a few tentative explanations of the reasons added (267-73); various forms of coinages are adduced to illustrate the growth of English/French vocabulary, a section which (perhaps necessarily) lacks a coherent structure.

The final five chapters summarize the insights gained above and apply these to new concepts and questions: theories of explaining linguistic change (274-98 on internal and external causes, including compensation and the retention of communicative effectiveness, are complemented by a few remarks on areal linguistics, including sprachbund phenomena, 299-310). "Distant genetic relationship" (311-26) is more speculative, especially since 'genetic' is here largely a matter of faith rather than established fact – but Campbell's arguments are duly cautious. A short chapter on "Philology: the role of written records" (327-38) intervenes, before "Linguistic prehistory" links up with the speculative chapter above (339-73). A bibliography (374-85) and three indexes (386-96) follow at the end.

Campbell's book is in a well-tested tradition exemplified by authors like Bynon (1977). He introduces readers leisurely, but with great didactic skill to understand linguistic synchronic structures in a great selection of languages and to apply these insights to diachronic comparisons and historical interpretations. Whether we need more than 400 languages to do this, is of course controversial – I have always believed that English alone is largely sufficient (Görlach 1997): students can not only be taught more easily to see what makes the forms of *guest* and *garden* indicative of borrowing, but also to understand the cultural relevance more clearly than from Aztec or Bantu examples. Such remarks aside, I do not hesitate to say that Campbell has achieved a very difficult task, *viz.* to bring a seemingly untractable topic into easy reach of students and make a convincing case for the need of such approaches for all students in linguistics departments, at a time when so many believe that synchronic (statistical) analysis of variation can serve the same purpose.

References
Bynon, Theodora. 1977. *Historical Linguistics*. Cambridge: UP.
Görlach, Manfred. 1997. *A Linguistic History of English*. London: Macmillan [German original 1974.]

11 Recent introductory text books in (English) historical linguistics; from *AAA* 23 (1998), 118-9.

Historical linguistics experienced a notable low in the 1970s and 1980s, but interest has recently picked up to a considerable extent, a fact duly reflected in a great number of textbooks intented for undergraduate teaching in departments of linguistics and English. The new introductions do not normally continue where the old books stopped – there is now a marked interest in theoretical and methodological questions, in explaining the causes of present-day variation and the change in progress and in the possibilities of using the present to explain the past. Occasionally, too, there is more competence in theoretical models than in philological training – a problem that has riddled historical linguistics at all times but is becoming more visible under present conditions. In what follows, I will review three recent books of a very different character which will together illustrate trends of teaching in the 1990s (for a fourth type cf. Görlach 1997).

N.F. Blake, *A History of the English Language*. Houndmills: Macmillan, 1996.

Written "for undergraduates and the general public" (vi) Blake's book is the most general and traditional of the three: it is also largely concerned with the external history of English, which makes it less theoretical. Blake's central aim is to describe the development of Standard English (= St E). Accordingly, he divides his material along a chronological line into chapters devoted to following topics: before Alfred, the first English standard, its aftermath, ME leading to the new standard, changes 1400-1660, establishing the standard within social norms, emancipation, education and empire, and finally, world domination and growing variation.

For a book thus devoted to historical sociolinguistics, Blake's descriptions are notably non-technical; he tries to avoid linguistic jargon, frequently repeats arguments in modified phrasing (6, 30), but fails to bring out the details of the correlation between linguistic variation and choice and the social structures determining these as clearly as might have been possible, even with the intended general readership in mind. Nor is it clear in what way changes in literary diction and linguistic description (14) relate to the topic under discussion. The fact that complex discussions are printed as a running text, without tables, lists and other means to help the reader to structure the argumentation, adds to the lack of clarity – see, for instance, how the remarks on reconstructed pronunciation and on changes in the ME writing system are set out on p.20. As a consequence, the mixture of statements, qualifications, hypotheses and exceptions in long sentences is sometimes difficult to take in – a distinct disadvantage for a student's handbook. A chapter intended to outline the great structural changes in the history of English ("Background Survey", 24-46) thus becomes a medley full of generalizations, insufficiently structured, and leading away from what the author wishes to achieve.

In the next few chapters, chronology helps to define the argument so that it becomes more intelligible. However, avoiding detail leads to questionable statements. It is uncertain whether readers of the book ought to know about Verner's Law; but formulating this as "f → v, th → d, k → g" (50) is even more doubtful. Whenever technical distinctions are necessary, the description becomes difficult to understand, as with the phonological system and conditioned changes of OE vowels (59-63) and occasionally one encounters spurious generalizations (why claim on p.112 that Latin /k/ remained /k/ in Anglo-Norman, but developed into /č/ in French when the distinction applies to /ka/ only?)

The period between 1400 and 1530, possibly the most important for the emergence of the new standard language, shows Blake, unsurprisingly, excellently informed; this chapter contains very valuable information on the function of the Signet Office, the Chancery and the early printers, most notably Caxton (see esp. 175-88). As the author of an introduction to Shakespeare's language, Blake has very relevant remarks to make on the Elizabethan period, too, but I found his exposition again difficult to follow as a consequence of the great amount of data, not always arranged in optimal fashion, and because of generalizing statements and unexplained terms; also, Blake summarizes various books without including qualifying arguments or providing sources so that the readers can see for themselves. (This shortcoming is partly a consequence of a drastic reduction of notes – which does not, however, make the book more 'reader-friendly').

The widespread neglect of language history in the 18th and 19th centuries makes Blake's chapters on the period particularly welcome – even though he only presents the facts known from other publications. Since correctness and stylistic differences in proper usage are largely indicated by frequencies, the absence of such data makes Blake's statements often too general or vague to be really helpful for those who want to see the social mechanisms behind the developments. Still, his summaries of developments in the 19th century correlating social structure with linguistic expectations are useful and very readable.

In the final chapter, the historical account includes curricular reforms of 1988, the effects of the Gulf War, and the impact of feminism, political correctness and Americanization. There are short sections of notes (333-8), suggestions for further reading (339-40), a glossary of technical terms (341-52) and an index (353-82) at the end.

Jeremy Smith, *An Historical Study of English Function, Form and Change*. London & New York: Routledge, 1996.

In contrast to Blake, Smith focuses on the internal history of English; his methods are determined by those of his teacher Michael Samuels to whom the book is dedicated and whose *Linguistic Evolution* (1972) remains one of the major works in English historical linguistics of the more recent past (cf. Smith's ch. 3 which is significantly named "Linguistic evolution"). Smith is critically aware of the restrictions set by the surviving data and sees the limits of the explanatory power of functional analysis, pointing to the philological and historical competence necessary for the historical linguist. Insightful remarks draw our attention to variation, contact, tree and wave models and "language and chaos". Part II starts with an analysis of writing systems, in particular between 1100 and 1500, and processes of standardization (55-78). This is followed by a description of regularities of sound changes, including various instances of 'shift' and complex problems of 15th- and 16th-century developments (79-111). "Change in the lexicon" comes next (112-40); this includes a discussion of semantic change, borrowing, and the development of pronouns. Finally, there is a section on "Grammatical change" (141-62) which concentrates on the fascinating developments from OE to ME, including "innovative failures" and "successes"; Smith here provides some clear instances proving that innovations are non-teleological (151). Part II focuses on two modern varieties in context, *viz.* language in use in Scotland and in the London black community (165-96) – sketches which cannot do justice to the complex problems and linguistic histories involved, but which nicely illustrate the interrelation of diachrony and synchronic variation. Notes, further reading, references and an index conclude the book.

This is not an easy book since it presupposes a great deal of philological knowledge and a readiness to be involved in theoretical abstraction, with specimens taken from various sections of historical phases of English, rather than presenting a comprehensive and coherent description.

R.L. Trask, *Historical Linguistics*. London: Arnold, 1996.

Trask's book, as the title suggests, is not restricted to English (although a great proportion of the data and arguments relate to it). The book is rather in the tradition of Bynon (1977) selecting the evidence from a great number of languages – Basque, French, German, Greek and Turkish being quoted particularly often. Starting from the awareness of change and attitudes towards it, Trask first discusses "Lexical and semantic change" (17-51) giving particular attention to the integration of loanwords "Phonological change" is divided into articulatory changes in pronunciation (52-75) and the consequences for the *langue* level (76-101), with convincing illustrations taken from a large range of languages. "Morphological change" (102-32) stresses the universal principles of analogy and morphological typology, leading on to "Syntactic change" (133-64), which takes up recent ideas of reanalysis, grammaticalization, ergativity and the restructuring of grammars – unsurprisingly, English has little to contribute to this chapter, and the phenomena in the structurally divergent languages from which the evidence is taken are difficult to compare. The next two chapters look at the consequences of change, *viz.* the divergence of dialects (and the relatedness between languages, 165-201) and review the comparative method, developed to explain systematic correspondences by way of reconstruction (202-47); the discussion includes relevant remarks on the 'reality' of reconstructed items and, of great didactic interest, specimens of pitfalls and limitations – an exemplary chapter illustrating methods and findings in admirable succinctness. "Internal reconstruction" (248-66) is a natural complement; the reader is taken far back to a treatment of the laryngal hypothesis in IE. "The origin and propagation of change" (267-307) is exemplified, rightly, by a discussion of modern studies of variation and change in progress as documented in sociolinguistic investigations. Finally, there is a chapter on "contact and the birth and death of languages" (308-44). "Language and prehistory" (345-75) and "Very remote relations" (376-409) form a kind of appendix, containing a great variety of topics including some speculation.

All chapters have carefully selected exercises appended which permit readers to apply the knowledge recently acquired to new data – a necessary complement meant to avoid learning by rote or mechanical memorization.

The three books under review illustrate the great range of textbooks offered for university teaching. It will have become obvious that only Smith and Trask fulfil the readers' expectations of a modern, theory-oriented account, whereas Blake's description is not only more conservative, but also less well arranged to be useful in academic courses. By contrast, an objection that could be raised against Smith and Trask is that data and arguments based on them come from very different sources which makes it impossible for the learner to check many of the claims made, or even see the relevance of the discussion, at least in an undergraduate context.

References
Baugh, A.C. & Thomas Cable, [4]1993. *A History of the English Language*. London: Routledge.
Bynon, Theodora. 1977. *Historical Linguistics*. Cambridge: UP.
Görlach, Manfred. 1997. *A Linguistic History of English*. London: Macmillan.
Samuels, M.L. 1972. *Linguistic Evolution, with Special Reference to English*. Cambridge: UP.

12 *The Cambridge History of the English Language*. General Editor Richard M. Hogg. Vol. 1, *The Beginnings to 1066*, ed. Richard M. Hogg. Cambridge: UP, 1992, xxiii + 609 pp.; Vol. 2, *1066-1476*, ed. Norman Blake, 1992, xxi + 703 pp.; from *Anglia* 112 (1994), 130-5.

A comprehensive survey of the complex history of a language like English can no longer be achieved by a single scholar, as was the tradition in the age of Baugh or Brunner. As the handbook *Sprachgeschichte* (Besch *et al.* 1954) has shown for the history of the German language, everything depends on having a convincing framework, a dedicated editor or team of editors and a selection of authors who have the experience and stamina to survey particular sections comprehensively and with linguistic insight and didactic skill. The board of Cambridge University Press decided some eight to ten years ago that the time was ripe for a six-volume *History* to summarize the state of play in the 1990s and provide *the* work of reference for another generation of scholars and students. In contrast to the 180 chapters of the *Sprachgeschichte* written by some 160 scholars, the plans for the *CHEL* envisaged a general chapter written by the volume editor and another 49 chapters written by a similar number of scholars (there are a few chapters jointly written by two authors, and a few authors contribute more than one chapter).

In chapter 1, Hogg sketches Anglo-Saxon history and how it relates to the OE language and literature (1-25) succinctly and in non-specialist style which sets the tone for a treatment that is intended to reach both the interested layperson and the specialist. The editors, paying tribute to 19th-century traditions of comparative philology, decided that a chapter on the ancestry of OE was needed, and Bammesberger solves the problem competently. However, his style is somewhat technical and dry, and he devotes too little space to the limits, or usefulness, of reconstruction and, moreover, fails to focus sufficiently on the promise contained in the chapter heading "The *place of English* in Germanic and Indo-European" (26-66). The usefulness (or even need) of a sound exposition of the foundations of OE might have been set out more persuasively for scholars who believe that the internal history of English (or a discussion of its Germanic background) is sufficient. Hogg's "Phonology and morphology" (67-167) is a fine piece of scholarship; the author was, of course, able to build on the more detailed treatment in his *Grammar of Old English*, of which the first part (*Phonology*) appeared almost simultaneously in 1992. However, his chapter illustrates the problems of the project possibly better than many others: Hogg attempts to create an informal lecture-like style and to reduce the use of technical argumentation – but then involves the unprepared reader in quite abstract reasoning. This is followed by advice to read Hoenigswald's and Anttila's highly theoretical books on reconstruction, an indication that the tension between the different levels of description remains unresolved. Morphology (here understood as nominal and verbal inflection) is a 'messier' field; Hogg's clear exposition of the main categories and OE developments charts the domain perspicuously. (His restriction of the field to 'orderly' West Saxon of course helps to achieve transparency). As volume editor he has also been able to take opportunity to link his arguments with those in other chapters.

Traugott's "Syntax" (168-289) rightly focusses on "differences between OE and later stages of the language" (169); she bases her description on Mitchell, though her interpretations "are sometimes different from Mitchell's" (286) – leaning towards less conservative models. Where Mitchell's text, in its excessive detail of rules and exceptions, is difficult to take in over longer passages, Traugott's "focus ... on constructions that are of particular interest in the history of English" (169) and her skilful handling of style make her chapter, as far as this is possible with a technical field like syntax, a pleasure to read. For readers of German, there is, of course, Fries' (1976) chapter on syntax, which was done with similar skill, but for English Traugott's chapter must be the best combination of informativeness and readability in the field of OE syntax to date.

Kastovsky's job, describing "Semantics and vocabulary" (290-408), was even more difficult than that of other contributors – with the publication of the great Toronto Dictionary of OE just started, the London thesaurus unpublished, and comprehensive studies of OE word-formation and lexical semantics never attempted so far, this was virgin soil for large stretches, even for a scholar as experienced in the discipline, synchronic and diachronic, as Kastovsky is. He offers a convincing solution to the problem, stressing the Germanic and 'associative' character of OE (294) to explain the prevalence of word-formation, contact influences (few loanwords against an overwhelming number of loan translations and semantic calques, 299-338; he adds a detailed subchapter on Scandinavian, 322-36) and regional and stylistic stratification (338-55). A chapter-length treatment of word-formation follows (355-400): this is home-ground for the author, who provides the clearest and most comprehensive account of the field so far – which makes the need for an exhaustive book on word-formation all the more keenly felt. By contrast, his remarks on semantics are disappointingly short, especially since this might have been an opportunity to summarize the most important word-field studies, many of them written in German and difficult of access (cf. Strite's very useful survey (1989), which should have been mentioned in this context).

The comparative shortness of Toon's "Old English dialects" (409-51) reflects the meagreness of the material (which has led many scholars to claim that OE dialectology is impossible) and the consequent state of research. However, at least the discussion about the late West Saxon standard language and what is distinctively Anglian has recently been revived, and all this is reliably summarized. There is no need to stress that the main thrust of the chapter is a reformulation of the author's major thesis about the importance of Mercian in OE areal linguistics.

To what extent is "Onomastics" part of linguistics? The late Cecily Clark's two chapters (I:452-89 for OE, II:542-606 for ME) are admirably clear, listing the principles and problems of names of people and of place- and river-names and paying particular attention to their morphology and etymology. The relationship between onomastics and linguistics proper is, however, not explicitly described. The fact that the field is so peripheral means, of course, that most readers will find here a treasure-trove of information new to them which is of great relevance to settlement history and to cultural history more generally.

The particular importance, and distinctive character, of OE poetic diction made a separate chapter for it imperative; Godden's "Literary language" (490-535) of poetry rightly stresses the archaic and formulaic character and the formal determinants of alliteration and metrics that combined with the individual poet's creativity to produce a unique vocabulary, most of which, unsurprisingly, disappeared with the texts it had ornamented. The second part (513-35) is devoted to prose, with text types ranging from 'Alfredian' translations to Wulfstan's homilies. Much of this is formal, and derived from, or modelled on, Latin concepts of style, but there is an astonishing range, even though Godden excludes text types like laws (the distinction between 'literary' and other texts is not made sufficiently explicit). It is interesting to learn that in spite of literary ornament "contemporary writers generally refer to prose as an entirely functional medium" (520) in obvious contrast to the practice of many authors who modelled their prose on concepts of Latin *Kunstprosa*. For all the insights it provides, Godden's interpretation makes it clear that much remains to be done to describe the forms and functions of OE style.

In the second volume devoted to ME, Blake's Introduction (1-22) focuses on general topics like the tradition of scholarly description, languages functioning in a bilingual society, lack of standardization and social developments related to literary forms. Lass's Phonology and morphology (23-155) would have brought with it endless descriptions of systems coexisting in geographical space had all the major dialects been adequately covered and combined with descriptions of varieties following each other in time. His decision to concentrate on London speech, on developments of more universal interest and on features illustrating trends that led to the later standard is therefore an acceptable (and frequently attempted) method of cutting down the data. The author's strong bent towards systematicity has further helped to structure the unwieldy evidence. All the arguments are securely based (as they should be) on OE conditions – and often extend beyond this. Lass is at his best where he discusses theoretical questions of quantity and stress. In morphology, too, the messy data are organized by Lass's firm belief that evolution involves more than just simplification; there is a certain 'directedness', favouring particular categories at the expense of others (123). Many of the developments (to avoid Lass's term 'evolution') are of particular interest in exemplifying the impact of 'the north' on the London-based 'standard' language, an impact that would have been worth summarizing in a special paragraph.

J. Milroy's Dialectology (156-206) starts with a comprehensive discussion of 'traditional' ME dialect studies (156-91), although he sees (and implicitly criticizes the fact) that this interest arose from the needs of editors of literary texts, so that knowledge of regional variation has been seen largely as a contribution to studying textual transmission of particular documents (168). Milroy acknowledges the great value of the *LALME* project (McIntosh 1986), but is somewhat reticent about its limitations: he uses his description of its principles as a means of proceeding to a discussion of structured variation, which he somewhat disappointingly exemplifies only with [h]-dropping (which, according to Milroy, could make a contribution to a multidimensional history of the structure of the English language, 201). His move from this point to his central concern with speaker motivation (202) appears to be somewhat loosely argued; this is regrettable because one would have liked to see more clearly demonstrated the extent to which the principle can be applied to the kind of diffuse network of systems that ME was.

Fischer's Syntax (207-408) is a fine example of a thorough description on traditional lines which from time to time branches out into more abstract explanations, especially when she can refer to her own research of the 1980s (cf. p. 236 on 'impersonal verbs'), thus combining a competent resumé of existing research on the major syntactic features of ME with constructive criticism. Fischer's description, staunchly data-based, is eminently clear and well-argued; its length and comprehensiveness would make it a candidate for separate publication as a small monograph or (in completion of what Mustanoja (1960) never carried through) for expansion into a full *ME Syntax*.

Burnley's Lexis and semantics (409-99) concentrates on loanwords (414-39), word-formation (439-50, somewhat too briefly, but major investigations are lacking for the period), stylistic, social and regional variation (450-61) and semantics (461-96, a convincing subchapter in which he was able to build on his book on Chaucer). Blake in his chapter on The literary language (500-41) rightly selected a few texts in which the author's artistic intentions are obvious and the modern analyser's interpretations plausible: Layamon's *Brut*, *Ancrene Wisse*, *Sir Orfeo*, poems of the Alliterative Revival and of course Chaucer, but he does not skip drudges like Caxton.

Clark's chapter on Onomastics (542-606) is a rare case where an author has continued the description from one period to another; her ME chapter is particularly detailed – clearly a reflection of the increase in material available for the study of names in this period.

It is difficult to summarize one's impressions of the two volumes under review, the subject matter, methods and styles of description being so various. First a remark on what the collection does not contain: there are no chapters devoted to language in society (or external language history) such as play so conspicuous a part in books like Baugh's (^{4}1993), which could have helped to explain the changes that the functions and prestige of languages have undergone and which in turn could have done something to account for degrees of *ausbau* and standardization and provide points of reference for data in chapters like Clark's (cf. the subject matter treated in books like Kibbee's (1991)). There are no chapters comparing English with other European languages, and no chapters containing a comprehensive discussion of the criteria for fixing the beginning and end of the two periods (1066 and 1476 being the dates of historical events with mnemonic appeal).

One of the attractive features – and, at the same time, drawbacks – of the first two volumes (and, no doubt, of future volumes, in which the diversity of the contents is likely to increase rather than diminish) is the multiplicity of methods. This makes it impossible to read the chapters 'slice by slice', e.g. to follow up the development of English lexis through the two periods. It also means that authors have to provide their own definitions of terms and methods where a single author might have explained what 'inflectional morphology' is once and for all at the beginning (cf. Lass in II:91). As the general editor explains, it was obvious at an early date that it would be impossible to lay down a 'party line' on linguistic theory (II:xv); he expresses the hope that resulting contrasts, and even contradictions, are stimulating and fruitful. Not all will be willing to accept this, but most readers will close the two books feeling stimulated and enriched in various ways. There may be an opportunity, in a second edition, not only to correct the typos that remain in spite of careful proofreading (note those in titles in German), but also to introduce more cross-references linking the individual chapters in which identical ground is covered. Some authors may even find that their text should be modified, by rephrasing or omitting arguments, in the light of interpretations in other chapters.

The outstanding achievement of the first two volumes and, by projection of the remaining four, cannot be doubted. However, it is also clear that the project falls between the two stools of, on the one hand, a one-volume history, accessible, intellectually and financially, to a student of English (for whose use there might also have been more graphs, tables, facsimiles and maps than are here provided), and, on the other, a fully scholarly handbook series that would make no compromises as regards wealth of detail, abstractness of argument and production costs. The fate of the series, favourable it is to be hoped, will be decided in the academic market-place. It is obvious that no alternative project will be attempted in the near future – so the set is, in fact, doomed to success.

References

Baugh, A.C. & Thomas Cable. ⁴1993. *A History of the English Language*. London: Routledge.

Fries, Udo. 1976. "Grundzüge der altenglischen Syntax". In Hans Pinsker, ed., *Altenglisches Studienbuch*. Düsseldorf: Bagel/Francke, 125-74.

Hogg, Richard. 1992. *Grammar of Old English*. I, *Phonology*. Oxford: Clarendon.

Kibbee, Douglas A. 1991. *For to Speke Frenche Trewely*. (SHLS 60). Amsterdam: Benjamins.

McIntosh, Angus, *et al*. 1986. *A Linguistic Atlas of Late Medieval English (LALME)*. Oxford.

Mustanoja, Tauno F. 1960. *A Middle English Syntax*. Part I. Parts of Speech. Helsinki: Société Néophilologique.

Strite, Victor L. 1989. *Old English Semantic-Field Studies*. (American University Studies, IV:100). New York/Frankfurt: Peter Lang.

13 Suzanne Romaine, ed., *1779-1997*. (The Cambridge History of the English Language 4). Cambridge: UP, 1998, xix+783pp.; from *Anglia* 117 (1999), 273-5.

The volume under review has been expected for a long time, but although it has taken inordinately many years to produce, it has still overtaken vol. 3 (*1476-1776*) on which it was intended to build in many ways. The fact that it is the first survey of a much-neglected period is part of the explanation why vol. 4 has taken so long, but certainly not the only one. As we will see, uncertainties about aims and methods and an obvious neglect by the editor (whose interests are clearly in other fields) must have played a part.

In her "Introduction" (1-56) Romaine reflects on a great many things, but strangely misses out on aspects that readers have expected to find in an editorial outline intended to introduce us to the subject matter, methods of description and limitations; an exploratory survey is all the more urgent since the question of how we can do historical linguistics for quite recent periods is largely unexplored (cf. Görlach 1999). Such unasked questions relate to the interplay of social history (educational/literary, regional and social mobility, mass communication and the media) with the establishment of linguistic norms, overt and covert prestige, the functions of ordered heterogeneity, and the dynamic development of variation within English in the past two hundred years. It is significant that Romaine here misses the two recent books which at least partially deal with the relevant topics of 19th-century English, Bailey (1996) and Mugglestone (1995). Also, there is no information on how authors were guided on matters of synchronic vs. diachronic description in a period which includes the present time, or whether variation of the world language should be treated – readers might have assumed that since Scotland, Ireland, America etc. are covered in other volumes of the CHEL series, there would be cross-references at best, and they will be surprised to find US data included in many chapters, often without the necessary distinction from BrE evidence.

The subsequent chapter, Algeo's "Vocabulary" (57-91), is a case in point. Although surprisingly short, the author combines data from both America and Britain. His particular concern is with the expansion of English lexis after 1776 which he classifies according to the processes of creating, shifting, shortening, composing, blending and borrowing, a system he has used in earlier publications. The most problematic category here is 'shifting' which is meant to include "grammatical shifts" (otherwise known as zero-derivation, including transfers of product names), "semantic shifts" (covering various types of meaning extension) and pragmatic shifts (largely shifts of stylistic values and geographical range of application). The system appears to be more or less Algeo's, and many readers will prefer more traditional classifications, and they will also miss more sociohistorical aspects of the topic treated.

Denison's chapter on "Syntax" (92-329) is, with its book-length coverage, in stark contrast as far as detail is concerned. The painstakingly thorough description and rigorous methodological principles applied leave nothing to correct or add – but the sheer wealth of data makes it difficult to pick up the salient features, in particular to distinguish between properly 19th-century characteristics and the developments in, or surviving into, present-day English. Again, a proper consideration of sociolinguistic factors (correctness, prescriptive norms etc., cf. Görlach 1998) and stylistic characteristics (distributions according to medium, formality etc.) would have deserved to be extracted and represented in short subchapters that might have served to guide the reader through the maze.

Readers may well ask what the function of names is in a description of language and linguistics. CHEL IV has Coates' chapter devoted to the topic (330-72), as earlier volumes had, but again there is no explicit justification for its inclusion. The author stresses that there is less to discuss for the period than for earlier volumes (in which questions of etymology, settlement history, and language contact phenomena were more relevant). All the same, he provides a very extensive discussion of first and second personal names and place names in both Britain and the United States – one wonders why the U.S. part is not reserved for vol. VI or, if the survey is not restricted to Britain, countries like Canada, Australia and New Zealand are not included. There is hardly anything on statistics, although changing fashions in name-giving might have been easily presented in a succinct form: compare the survey of given girls' and boys' names of the past two hundred years in Britain and the US in Crystal (1994: 151) which permit interesting conclusions. In first names, again, period-specific choices might have been brought out more clearly, as indeed in place names in the US: why is there no treatment of the *Fredonia* type or German names replaced by more patriotic ones after 1914? Do present-day family names still reflect 19th-century settlement patterns, for instance in areas predominantly settled by Scotsmen and Irishmen? Also, the fascinating topic of reinterpretations of names by folk etymology is missed, although there are many cases falling into Coates' period, at least in America.

After the syntax chapter, MacMahon's on "Phonology" comes next in the amount of data it provides (373-535). The chapter was first announced as by Wells, whose system of referring to lexical classes by small caps is in fact taken over from him. MacMahon had enormous masses of historical sources to digest: the first peak of critical statements in the age of Walker, Sheridan and Elphinston in the late 18th century, then the age of the new phonetic science represented by Ellis and Sweet, and modern methods of description (including dialectology and sociolinguistics) all fall into his field – no wonder that, again, many readers might have preferred either more summary chapters bringing together the evidence under certain general headings (orthoepy, diatopic differences, prescriptive norms including the impact of modern media, etc.).

Finegan's chapter on "Grammar and usage" (536-88) is on a topic not singled out for separate treatment in earlier CHEL volumes. It includes a study of attitudes (popular to philosophical), norms and handbooks and a large number of topics under the heading "language and..." (...correctness, speech, dialect, register, variation, morality, etc.) While such a chapter is certainly to be welcomed, its relation to the preceding ones and to that on literary language might have been defined more clearly, also in order to exclude overlaps and repetitions.

One of the most necessary and best chapters is Adamson's on "literary language" (589-692), and it is very good to see it here even though the belated submittal delayed the production and has held up the entire volume (as has the respective chapter in vol. 3). Adamson provides very insightful sketches of how language was treated over a period extending from 18h-century poetic diction and the Romantic responses to the styles and linguistic experiments in highly diversified, and often idiosyncratic linguistic choices in 19th-century writers, which in turn formed the basis for even greater diversity, and in a way subjectivity, in the 20th. She is largely successful in bringing out the linguistic categories and evaluation in a field in which many authors tend to slide back into literary interpretations.

A glossary of linguistic terms, a bibliography and an index follow at the end of the book (693-783).

It is not quite easy to come to terms with this collection, the first of its kind. The individual chapters very much reflect the preferences of their authors and there seems to have been little guidance or interference from the editor. This fact is brought out most clearly from a comparison of the length of chapters (in percentages relating to the text portion, 1-692): Algeo's "Vocabulary", a topic often treated with great attention to detail, comes to a meagre 5%, wheras syntax (34%) and phonology (23%) are somewhat excessive. Also, there does not seem to be sufficient cross-referencing between the chapters; it is not possible to judge whether the chapters and authors' methods link up with the descriptions of the previous period, the publication of CHEL 3 (which has been ready in manuscript for more than seven years but for a single chapter) having been overtaken by the collection here reviewed.

The book is excellently printed. It is a pleasure to note that the bibliography and index were compiled and proofread with apparent care. It is to be hoped that the pattern set by this book will increase interest in, and multiply research on, this much neglected period – in which we can talk about 'historical' linguistics with greater justification than when dealing with earlier stages of the language. In particular, slimmer manuals might make the fascinating topic of English after 1776 available for teaching to provide topics of linguistic analysis for students concentrating on modern developments (cf. Görlach 1999).

References
Bailey, Richard W. 1996. *Nineteenth-century English*. Ann Arbor: The University of Michigan Press.
Crystal, David. 1994. *The Cambridge Encyclopedia of the English Language*. Cambridge: UP.
Görlach, Manfred. 1998. *An Annotated Bibliography of 19th-Century Grammars of English*. Amsterdam: Benjamins.
---. 1999. *English in 19th-Century England*. Cambridge: UP.
Mugglestone, Lynda. 1995. *'Talking Proper.' The Rise of Accent as Social Symbol*. Oxford: Clarendon.

14 David Denison, *English Historical Syntax*. (Longman Linguistics Library). London: Longman, 1993, xiv + 530 pp.; from *Linguistics* 32 (1994), 573-7.

A comprehensive survey of the historical development of the syntactical structures of English has been an urgent desideratum for a long time. Existing introductions are all too narrow in scope. Some cover only one period (Mitchell, Mustanoja, and the relevant chapters in the *Cambridge History of the English Language* to which Denison himself will contribute the chapter on Late Modern English syntax[in IV:92-329]). Others cover only one field (the verb, Visser) or concentrate on one method of analysis not necessarily the most adequate for description (Lightfoot). Denison's comprehensive survey attempts to avoid all these limitations. He does not hesitate to say:

> My approach is eclectic, often with a straightforward use of traditional terminology, in order to make the book accessible to people working within any of the formal or informal frameworks current today. (p. ix)

In fact, he frequently uses different methods and compares the results of such investigations.

His first part, "Groundwork", provides a clear exposition of the basic facts and methods of historical linguistics, the development of English, and the data used for his analysis, as well as a sketch of existing research. He adds a short account of the development of nominal morphology (i.e. inflexion) since this has obvious consequences for the emergence of certain syntactical patterns.

Part II, "Word order" (25-58), is placed first because, arguably, it is "of major overall importance in verbal syntax". As Denison freely admits, there is "some difficulty in reconciling different theoretical approaches" (25). Denison adopts the distinction between "synchronic versus diachronic, and non-generative versus generative" methods (30), which are discussed, on the basis of the most relevant research papers, in 18 subchapters (31-55) – the most comprehensive survey of the topic to date. The style of presentation is typical of the entire book: rather than offering his own model Denison is content with critical reviews of accounts proposed by other colleagues, which he summarizes with great acumen and comprehensiveness. His own points are often found in necessary warnings such as:

> for any period, just what constitutes relevant data, let alone how to assess it, depends very heavily on the theoretical assumptions of the analyst. (p. 30)

However, readers should not expect general verdicts, such as whether 'traditional' or 'transformational' explanations are more adequate. Even in the evaluation of individual interpretations, the commentator's "I" intrudes with some caution:

> "I see little prospect of confirming or disconfirming such a detailed specification". (p. 40)
>
> "But how, why, and indeed whether, remain unanswered questions." (p. 41)

In part 3, "Subject and verb phrase" (59-162), the first chapter is devoted to 'impersonals' (61-102), an extensive treatment justified (and possibly required) by the degree of attention the topic has had in studies of the historical syntax of English. Are there 'subjectless' sentences in OE (as in *him ofhreow þæs mannes*, 63)? Is the development of '*hunger, behove, rue, happen, seem, dream, avail* and *please*' verbs due to a reanalysis (and thus connected with a ME conflation of case distinctions) or not (as claimed by Fischer & van der Leek, 80ff.)? The development of a second ('indirect') passive is treated in ch. 6 (103-23), again in exemplary detail, on the basis of an (inherently) case grammar model: an excellent illustration of how the data and arguments of Visser (§§ 1967-75) can be improved by new analysis. Obviously, the topic is related to the 'prepositional passive' treated next (124-62).

Part IV is on "Complex complementization" (163-217); the chapter deals with the pattern verb+object/subject+infinitive (*aci* and *nci* in Latin terminology); various types exist in PDE, but all appear to have become more frequent in the course of the ME period. Since the surface similarities reflect quite different underlying (semantic) relations, the data have provoked divergent explanations, all here duly rehearsed. A shorter chapter on the history of "subject raising" follows on 218-51.

Part V, on "Auxiliaries", is probably the most exciting (and controversial?) section of the book. Ch. 10 provides a very useful summary of the almost endless discussion of the "origins of periphrastic *do*" (255-91), a topic which has fascinated Denison for a long time and on which he is particularly expert to judge. However, even he has no easy solution to offer. (Although Denison covers the literature quite exhaustively, he keeps us in the dark about what he thinks of Stein's book-length study of the problem). "Modals and related auxiliaries" (ch. 11, 292-339) receive full treatment, with the evidence presented first (292-325) – and a remarkably short section on "explanations" appended (325-37). This is obviously so because Lightfoot has dominated the discussion to such an extent that, apart from a few opponents of his views (most notably Warner) he has left Denison little to summarize or to argue about.

Still arranged under 'auxiliaries', ch. 12 is on the "perfect" (340-70); Denison's discussion centres on grammaticization, in particular on loss of inflection in the participle, the word-order distinction emerging between "I had my finger cut" and "I had cut my finger," and the replacement of *be* by *have*. Explanations (364-8) mainly illustrate "conventional wisdom". Ch. 13 (371-412) is devoted to what Denison hesitantly labels the "Progressive". He concentrates on the origins of the OE forms, and on whether any continuity can be postulated which leads on to the modern forms (these do not become frequent before the 17th century). Denison's exposition of the problem and interpretation of the data are of exemplary lucidity and especially helpful where he neatly summarizes the extensive studies by Mossé (in French) and Nickel and Nehls (in German) for an English (-only) readership. The "passive" (ch. 14, 413-45) receives the detailed treatment it deserves (the prepositional passive has of course already been discussed in ch. 7). Denison looks in detail at the following problem areas of change: function and meaning of the passive, form and function of the participle, choice of auxiliary verb (*be*, *weorth*, *get*), paradigm of the auxiliary, range of active verb-object syntagms available for passivization, and expression of agent (414).

Finally, there is a short chapter on the co-occurrence of auxiliaries and the regulation of *do* (446-71), the latter complementing ch. 10 above, and ending in valuable suggestions for further research (467). A "Glossary of technical terms" follows on 475-81.

With virtually thousands of examples discussed in the book it would be strange if were to agree with Denison in all cases. Let me mention one general and one more specific point of possible disagreement:

One of the problems of historical categories is illustrated by the equation of *sprecan ... ymbe* and *speak about* (p. 130) where 'preposition stranding' is difficult to postulate for a stage when *ymbe* was *not yet* the preposition we know in ModE but a much more flexible element, a fact which is likely also to affect other scholars' arguments in this chapter.

When discussing emphasis expressed by *do*, Denison quotes the early example [57] "but rewarde hym he dyd" of c1475 – a clear case of verb topicalization which should be kept distinct from emphasis in PDE (the pattern is used as a counterargument relating to Dutch *doen* by Denison himself, p. 284).

With all this comprehensiveness, are there also gaps – either because research is still lagging behind, or because topics did not fall into Denison's grid? The first is possibly true for case grammar, which promised to be very well qualified for the explanation of syntactic structures in highly inflected languages like OE or early ME, but is here mentioned only in passing (pp. 18-20, 53, 84, 140) and not indexed. (However, *Benefactive, Experiencer* etc. *are* indexed). Case grammar still provides obvious opportunities for further research, including contrastive studies with other Germanic languages. On the other hand, loan syntax, or syntactic influence exerted especially by Latin, clearly had no separate slot in Denison's system of description – which leaves not only a rich tradition of scholarship somewhat neglected, but also misses historical explanations for the emergence of certain syntactic patterns (especially in OE and EModE): note the mere allusion to such topics on pp. 192, 194, 203, 207; "always in dependence on a Latin original", pp. 222; 257, 279, 286, 287, 382, 398, 399, etc. Moreover, there is no coherent discussion of the importance of medium (written: spoken: written to be spoken), of text type (e.g. diary, letter, biblical prose, cooking recipe, etc.) and sociolinguistic determinants which are relevant not only in synchronic analysis but even more so in the establishment of correlations between styles and grammatical structures in the history of English. (There is one solitary reference to Biber & Finegan on p. 4). Finally note that Denison often deliberately excludes the *function* of the forms he discusses. Thus, the contrast between past and present perfect, and of simple and progressive forms is largely neglected. (On p. 406 he explicitly states that most of Nehls' "discussion is concerned with the *functions* of the progressive at the various stages and will not concern us further", but when discussing the passive he promises to look at "function and meaning of passive", 414). Finally, his discussion stops at the sentence level; the fact that developments in the patterns of English text syntax are at least as conspicuous as the ones here treated is not even mentioned.

For all the possible quibbles, it should be restated that Denison's book is an outstanding achievement for many reasons: it is the most comprehensive treatment of the topic, and written in a style that combines methodological rigour with comprehensibility. The author's diligence is exemplary: this is not only impressively documented by the ca. 400 references listed on pp. 482-501 but particularly in the considerate use he makes of these secondary sources in the summaries in his book. (Some readers will feel that this cornucopia is likely to intimidate their students). Finally, and importantly, Denison *knows* OE and ME and is not guided by modern preconceptions about what features these early stages ought to exhibit because they are found in present-day English. Again, some 300 to 400 primary sources quoted on pp. 502-18, and the judicious use he makes of these, testify to his firm philological basis ranging from OE to the 19th century.

Denison's book is likely to become a standard work in the field. Reading it is stimulating and challenging – but you should bring a sufficient amount of time (best found for an academic teacher when preparing a class or lecture course devoted to the topic). The book is also excellently edited and printed, and the paperback edition ought to bring it into the financial reach of all interested in the field.

15 A: *British Linguistics in the 19th Century*. With a new introduction by Roy Harris. 7 vols. London: Routledge/Thoemmes Press, 1993, 3088 pp.; from *Anglia* 117 (1999), 525-41.

The tradition of 19th-century English linguistics has been largely neglected by modern research. Whereas discussions of 18th-century linguists and their works are plentiful and considerable attention has been paid to dictionaries and (school) grammars and language teaching problems before 1800, there is a remarkable absence of such investigations for the time after 1800. There are three possible reasons for this relative neglect:

1) The 18th century had produced writers of school grammars like Lowth, Priestley and Murray in addition to highly original thinkers like Harris, Beattie, Monboddo, and Horne Tooke, linguists outstanding for laying the foundations for the later tradition and/or noted for the philosophical depth of their systems. Writers of the 19th century were, by contrast, largely copying from, or at best reacting to, the ideas handed down from the earlier grammarians.

2) What was new in the 19th century was thought to come mainly from abroad, in particular from Germany, whether it concerned comparative philology (Schlegel, Bopp, Schleicher, etc.), or school grammar (Becker, Mätzner, etc.), so that Britain again offered only a history of a somewhat belated acceptance of the new ideas developed elsewhere.

3) Largely as a consequence of these two points, there has never been a comprehensive reprint series of 19th-century works (with the partial exception of a few American titles brought out by Scholar, Delmar), so that scholars have not even been able to check whether the judgments summarized above are based on proper analysis or on prejudice. In fact there has not even been a comprehensive bibliographical account of 19th-century grammars (cf. Görlach 1998 for a first attempt) or of writings on linguistics. Both a bibliography and a reprint series have long been available for the time before 1800 (cf. Alston 1964-87 and 1968-70), and they have generated important research.

The gap that existed for reprints has now been partly filled by Routledge who have brought out a few sets in facsimile and in reprinted form. Two of these sets devoted to the 19th century are the subject of the present review article:

A1 Alexander Murray, *History of the European Languages*. 2 vols., Edinburgh, 1823, xi + cxxvii + 468 pp.; v + 508 pp.
A2 Richard Chenevix Trench, *On the Study of Words*. London, 1851, xi + vii + 216 pp.

A3 Max Müller, *Lectures on the Science of Language*. 2 vols., London, 1861, x + 399 pp.; 1864, 600 pp.
A4 William Dwight Whitney, *The Life and Growth of Language*. London, 1875. xi + vii + 326 pp.
A5 *Comparativist Controversies*. Dugald Stewart, Nicholas Wiseman, Robert Chambers, Charles Darwin, and Henry Sweet. xiii + 42 + 142 + 47 + 10 + 159 pp.

> **B**: *Language and Linguistics. Key 19th Century Journal Sources in Linguistics*. With a new introduction by Roy Harris. Wellesley Series. 4 vols. London: Routledge/Thoemmes Press, 1995, 1600 pp.; from *Anglia* 117 (1999), 525-41.

B1 *English Language and Language Teaching 1800-1865*, x + 415 pp.
B2 *English Language and Language-Teaching 1865-1900*, vi + 382 pp.
B3 *Language and Linguistic Theory 1800-1865*, vi + 436 pp.
B4 *Language and Linguistic Theory 1865-1900*, vii + 472 pp.

A1. Alexander Murray (1775-1813), the son of a Scottish shepherd and largely self-taught, died the year after his appointment as professor of Oriental Languages at Edinburgh. An unfinished manuscript of his was first thought unpublishable, but was then carefully edited and printed with a long biography of the author, in 1823. The text is of exceptional interest because it was written before Bopp had established the principles of comparative philology in 1816. As Harris says, "What (Murray's book) reveals is a linguistics in search of a method that it has not yet found." (I:v). What is, then, the value of this extensive essay in speculative pre-scientific linguistics, strongly influenced by Horne Tooke and apparently having little impact on the later history of language research in Britain? The abstruse ideas put forward here include a reconstruction of a proto-language on the basis of various languages ranging from Sanskrit to Celtic, which is claimed to have consisted of nine words rhyming on -*ag*, to form – to quote the author himself – "(a hypothesis) on which an edifice has been erected of a more useful and wonderful kind, than any which have exercised human ingenuity" (I:32). The editor found two related manuscripts left behind by the author, of which the second is an incomplete revision of the first, in more narrative exposition, and he must have taken great pains to produce what is a curiosity. It might have been sufficient documenting a specimen of 20-30 pages rather than producing almost 1,000 pages here offered in facsimile reproduction.

A2. Richard Chenevix Trench (1807-86), Dean of Westminster and Bishop of Oxford, was certainly one of the most important linguists of the mid-19th century. A late follower of Horne Tooke and an admirer of Richardson's *Dictionary* of 1834, he was convinced of the divine origin of speech and also that language was fossilized in early poetry, lexical meanings and ethics. By reading this book one gains insight in cultural history and is introduced to Victorian views on the moral decline from an earlier golden age. The speculative heritage is evident in many of Trench's etymologies, which show little influence from comparative philology. *On the Study of Words* (together with

English Past and Present, 1855) "did far more than any previous publication to make language study popular" (Aarsleff 1967:234-5): the author had obviously struck the right note, in combining contemporary interest in historicism with morality. His influence had its culmination when he became one of the godfathers of the *New English Dictionary*.

Of the volumes reprinted here, Trench's makes the most stimulating reading – and this is so in spite of his impressionistic and anecdotal presentation of the facts. If we seem to recognize many of his arguments and examples, it may well be because we have met them elsewhere – in the books by Bradley, Sweet and Jespersen. (A sketch of the impact Trench's book(s) had on later writers would have been a good complement to the volume). The six lectures originally "addressed to the pupils at the Diocesan Training School, Winchester" proceed from a general introduction, pointing out the information contained in words as documents of cultural history, to a chapter characteristically named "On the morality in words" (which looks upon some sorts of degeneration as tokens of sin and even reveals something about national character). His look at the history of English words shows exciting semantic developments, followed by reflections on how new designations come into being, changes which include the acceptance of archaisms and slang terms. A discussion of the competition of native and loanwords, of the distinction between doublets and of confusibles leads on to a very religious conclusion.

A3. Friedrich Max Müller (1823-1900), born in Germany, came to Britain to see his edition of the *Rigveda* published. He became first a teacher of modern languages in Oxford, then professor (1854) and in 1868 was appointed to a chair of comparative philology specially created for him. He was in an ideal position to combine Locke's *Essay* and the work of Horne Tooke and Trench with comparative philology – not surprisingly for a professor who held a chair for Sanskrit studies. As far as English work is concerned, he quotes, in his monumental *Lectures* of 1861/63, Horne Tooke, Trench, Marsh, Barnes, – but more frequently Adelung, Bopp, Grimm, Pott, Rask, Schlegel, Schleicher or authors of classical antiquity. *Science* is one of the terms mentioned most often: a scholarly discipline is said to evolve through an empirical stage to classification (comparative) and finally to the theoretical, or metaphysical stage (I:18). Although he questions whether "the science of language can be brought back to the standard of the inductive sciences" (I:21) he does little to this end. This is not just because of the lecture form used (which in the printed version has of course been edited in the direction of greater precision) – it seems to be more owing to the unsystematic methods which, though eminently displaying his learning and knowledge of languages from all continents, never goes much beyond butterfly collecting. Certainly his argumentation has little of the rigidity we would expect of the natural sciences (even allowing for the fact that chemistry in Müller's time was not yet far advanced in scholarly method). The axioms laid down (I:71) are that grammar is the basis for a classification and that there are no mixed languages. Otherwise there is not much of a system, beyond what had been formulated by the continental comparativists. His 'empirical' stage, described in

I:77-105, is mainly concerned with language-learning and teaching in ancient Rome and a discussion of the Greek influence, but he offers no methodological guidelines. In "the classificatory stage" (I:106-57) the aim is again frequently lost sight of; the coverage is here extended to almost all the languages included in *Mithridates*, but any general criteria of how a linguist proceeds in the classification are lacking. In the lecture "Genealogical classification of languages" (I:158-200) Müller has a great deal of new information to share with an insular audience, although his rambling presentation must have made it difficult for the audience to follow his arguments. "Comparative grammar" (I:201-61) was more concerned with roots and linguistic speculation à la Horne Tooke than served his purpose. "Morphological classification" (I:262-328) extends the scope to Semitic, Turkic and Finnic, presenting a principally sound typological categorization, though it is encumbered by endless detail and excursions. "The theoretical state, and the origin of language" (329-78) makes very stimulating reading, but the methodological foundations are not precise enough to justify the comprehensive conclusions he attempts.

Müller gave a second course of lectures two years later, here reprinted in a second volume. His intention was to make more specific or expand on points insufficiently treated in 1861; no coherence is, then, to be expected – least of all from the author. However, his individual thoughts are interesting and the great range of topics he was involved with are shown by the titles of the lectures: "New materials... and new theories" (1-43), "Language and reason" (44-94), "The physiological alphabet" (95-159), "Phonetic change" (160-97), "Grimm's law" (198-237), "On the principles of etymology" (238-95), "On the powers of roots" (296-333), "Metaphor" (334-83), "The mythology of the Greeks" (384-412), "Jupiter, the supreme Aryan God" (413-61), "Myths of the dawn" (462-524) and "Modern mythology" (525-80). There was little in the wide field of philology that he had not touched on by 1863 – and he was to continue his remarkably wide scope of activity in Oxford for another 37 years. Judgments about Müller were divided in his lifetime: his co-Sanskritist Whitney and many of his Oxford colleagues had great reservations about him. Harris rightly sums up: "Max Müller still ranks among the most ambivalent figures in the long history of linguistics: He has been described as 'one of the most talented and versatile scholars' of his day and also, by (...) W.D. Whitney, as 'one of the greatest humbugs of the century.' Neither judgment is without foundation."

A4. What a distance there is between Müller's lectures of 1861/63 and Whitney's *The Life and Growth of Language* of 1875! Since the two authors were both Sanskritists and German-influenced comparative philologists by training and each wrote a comprehensive book on the science of language (both in lecture form), the two studies should be comparable. That this is not the case can certainly not be explained by the mere twelve years between the dates of publication, but must have to do with elementary differences in the personalities and scholarly methods. Each can be regarded as the leading linguist of his country, but their methods were largely irreconcilable, and it is no surprise that their personal relationship was a hostile one. "Max Müller accused him of plagiarism" and Whitney, "following a prolonged clash with Max Müller, went to the unusual length of publishing in 1892 a brochure entitled *Max Müller and the Science of Language: a Criticism*," as Harris points out in his introduction. Many of the characteristics of Whitney strike us as modern, looking ahead to de Saussure and Bloomfield (who both knew and liked his work); this contrasts with Müller who carried on a heritage of linguistic speculation derived from Horne Tooke and Trench, a tradition which he never completely outgrew.

One striking feature of Whitney is his systematicity. In the first eight lectures his book treats general aspects of language (1-6), language acquisition (7-31), growth and change (32-44), formal changes (45-75), semantic changes (76-97), lexical loss (98-107), new words (108-33) and name-making (134-52). After laying the terminological foundations in clear and unassuming diction and argumentation, he proceeds to variation as a universal principle of language (153-78). Only then does he start to discuss the major distinctive features of the "Indo-European languages (179-212), using them as material for generalizations about linguistic structure (213-28). Other language families, and methods of classification, are treated next (228-77), before he returns to more general topics ("Nature and origin of language," 278-309) and his programmatic summary on "The science of language" (310-9).

Whitney unambiguously groups the science of language with the *Humanwissenschaften*, thinking that the alternative classification as a physical science is impossible to defend; he consistently adopts the French term 'linguistics' and explains language and its units as arbitrary and conventional (as de Saussure did): every language is "an institution, one of these which, in each community, make up its culture."

It is a prominent feature of Whitney's argumentation that he does not burden his readers with endless detail and carefully avoids speculation: his incisive comment about the worthless tradition of root comparisons (268, 313) is apparently levelled against a school of thought reaching from Horne Tooke to Müller. It is interesting to see that he feels he has also outgrown his German masters: "There is among (German scholars) such discordance on points of fundamental importance, such uncertainty of view, such carelessness of consistency, that a German science of language cannot be said yet to have an existence" (318-9).

The reprint of Whitney's book is one of the highlights of the series; it is a pity that not more of his writings were included: his diatribe against Müller, and his *Language and the Study of Language* (1867), or even Whitney's *Essentials of English Grammar* (1877) would have been useful complements – and many readers might have preferred them to Murray's two volumes (**A1**).

A5. The volume *Comparativist Controversies* includes contributions by five authors, mostly excerpts. Dugald Stewart (1753-1828) was one of the first to contest Horne Tooke's etymologies; the fifth essay from his *Philosophical Essays* of 1810 was appropriately called "On the tendency of some late philological speculations" (147-189). As a philosopher committed to induction, he strongly objected to appealing to etymology in a philosophical argument (a pursuit which is "nugatory", 166), contrasting "the conclusions of inductive science (with) the presumptuous fictions of human folly" (186).

Nicholas Wiseman's *Twelve Lectures on the Connexion between Science and Revealed Religion* of 1836 takes up some ideas of the new comparative philology, surprisingly finding its contributions compatible with the Tower of Babel – an argumentation as impressive for its ingenuity as it is devoid of sense (1-142 reproduced). The anonymously published work by Robert Chambers on *Vestiges of the Natural History of Creation* (1844, here: 277-323) discusses the five major classes of languages, which are seen to be correlated with the major races; the developmental interpretation of races and languages foreshadows some of Darwin's ideas, whose short chapter on "Language" (from *The Descent of Man*, 1871:53-62) appropriately follows. The major part of the present collection is taken up by a complete reprint of Henry Sweet's *The History of Language* (1900; xi+148 pp.) – a book worth re-reading (or discovering), as so much by Sweet is. Written as an introduction to the principles of Comparative Philology, the book combines methodological clarity with didactic skill, leading the reader with unpretentious language through the initial definitions to a descriptive account of sounds, followed by a discussion of their changes (with functional explanations). The chapter on morphological development includes syntax and the classic typology of languages based on their morphological properties. "Changes in language" includes various topics like dialects, styles, rapidity of change etc., and neatly points out the interconnections between factors. A description of the characteristic features of 'Aryan languages' is followed by that of neighbouring families (98-135). The arguments are elegantly concluded with a discussion of general features and the individuality of languages (135-45).

B1-4. The four volumes assemble 83 essays and articles written by literati, grammarians and famous word-watchers for 19th-century journals. Today it is difficult to imagine the immense influence these publications had in the 18th and 19th centuries, especially when it came to questions of good style, linguistic etiquette and grammatical correctness. Although the language of journalism was often seen as contributing to the decline, even decay, of the English language, there were also people who thought otherwise, but they possibly were not making judgments about daily papers.

Harris selected the essays from the following 25 journals:

Westminster Review (10 items)
Contemporary Review (7)
Edinburgh Review, Frazers Magazine (6)
Cornhill Magazine, Macmillan's Magazine (5)
Dublin University Magazine, Fortnightly Review, London Quarterly Review, London Review (4)
Blackwood's Magazine, British Quarterly Review, National Review, North British Review, Quarterly Review (3)
Longman's Magazine, New Monthly Magazine, Prospective Review (2)

Bentley's Quarterly Review, Home and Foreign Review, New Review, Nineteenth Century, Scottish Review, St. Paul's Magazine, University Magazine (1)

B1. It might be argued that the most important contribution to language research in 19th-century Britain was in applied linguistics. There was certainly no field in which publication of books burgeoned as it did in the area of grammar books (cf. Görlach 1998). There has been no comprehensive reprinting of these books which could be compared with Alston's *English Linguistics* series, which ends with 1800. Therefore, to include at least two volumes with reprints of 41 papers culled from journals (which are otherwise largely inaccessible) deserves particular praise. Harris has selected a smaller number (16) from the early period before 1865. Hazlitt was one of the most careful observers of the scene; his "Old English writers and speakers" (1825, 1.1-10) is, however, on EModE and mainly devoted to literary texts. The two contributions by Garnett survey the methods and deficiencies of "English lexicography" on the basis of Todd's Johnson of 1818, Webster's big dictionary of 1828 and the new two-volume work of Richardson (1835, 1:11-44). This selection captures the most important dictionaries before the *NED/OED*, and Garnett's contribution would be even more valuable had he not been almost exclusively concerned with etymology. Garnett's review article "English dialects" (1836, 1:45-77) deals with Grose's *Provincial Glossary*, 1811 ed., Wilbraham's minor Cheshire study of 1826, and Jennings' *West of England Dialects* of 1825, followed by Hunter's *Hallamshire Glossary* of 1829, the anonymous study of *The Dialect of Craven* of 1828, Forby's *Vocabulary of East Anglia* of 1830, Brockett's *Glossary of North Country Words* of 1829 and then turns to Scotland, dealing with Jamieson's grand *Etymological Dictionary* of 1808 and its *Supplement* of 1825. Finally, there is Boucher's compilation of *Archaic and Provincial Words* from 1832-3. These were the materials that were the basis of the late 19th-century dialectology of Ellis and Wright, and Garnett's comparison is valuable since it comes from a participant observer. It is a pity that his bias is very historical; he stresses the value of dialect evidence for reconstruction (if the data are properly handled) and he has little to say about the social aspects. De Quincey's "The English language" (1839, 1:78-89) offers a critical survey of English teaching materials among which his criticism of Murray's *Grammar* of 1795, though not new, is worth quoting:

> This book, full of atrocious blunders (some of which, but with little systematic learning, were exposed in a work of the late Mr. Hazlitt's), reigns despotically through the young ladies' schools. (1.82)

He stresses the need for proper English-language teaching, linguistic purism (but not advocating Saxonisms) and the relationship between language and nation and poetry. Morgan's proposal for a dictionary of humbug (1843, 1.90-100) is an ironic aside. Two papers on spelling reform (anonymous, 1849, 1.101-28; 1849, 1.129-37) review Ellis' books and pamphlets of 1848 and reflect contemporary attitudes on the need and desirability of a reform, one major argument being to qualify English as a world language (1.105-6). Rogers' extensive "History of the English language" (1850, 1:138-

77) claims to review two books by Latham (*The English Language*; *Elementary English Grammar*) and Harrison's *Rise, Progress, and Present Structure of the English Language*, but appears to be largely something else, considering the small number of references to them: it is a largely narrative account based on literary history and lexical change. Craik's "Curiosities of the English language" (1857-8, 1.178-222) is mainly on lexis, dealing with statistics about the foreign element in English and requirements of a new dictionary and ending with etymological concerns. A.F. & M.E. Foster's "Points in English grammar" (1858, 1.223-44) reviews Latham's *English Language*, the article on "Grammar" in the *Encyclopedia Britannica* (^{8}1856) and Head's *Shall and Will*; its title is a misnomer, since it is almost exclusively the latter that is discussed – a nice illustration of early Victorian priorities. Fitch (1858, 1.245-80) responds to Trench's *On Some Deficiencies in Our English Dictionaries* of 1857 in providing a background history of English lexicography and a thorough discussion of the weak spots in Todd's Johnson, in Richardson and in Webster; covering the same range as Trench, Fitch is best regarded as a critical complement to him. Freeman's "Modern English" (1860, 1:281-302) claims to be a review or commentary on three books by Trench and Bartlett's *Dictionary of Americanisms*; the author takes these as starting-points to write what is at best a spirited diatribe against the abuses of newspaper style and cheap novels, and idiosyncrasies marked by pedantry, affectation and vulgarity, especially the genteel diction of social climbers illustrated by misuses of such words as *celebrity*, *individual*, *party* 'woman' and *locality* which are variously called "vile pieces of slang, intolerable barbarisms, or mere vulgarisms." Coleridge's review of Wedgwood's *Dictionary of English Etymology* (1860, 1.303-11) is a series of corrected etymologies, some appropriate and some not. A.F. & M.E. Foster's "English literary and vernacular" (1860, 1:312-38) is a somewhat rambling account of the interplay of standard and dialect forms and functions, with particularly valuable remarks on the uses of dialect in England and Scotland, also with reference to religious education, where even dialect translations of parables are envisaged (337). An anonymous reviewer (1864, 1.339-68) tried the impossible when he discussed eight works together – and most blatantly failed; this is a pity because his collection included some of the best known works of the time: the Alford: Moon controversy, Müller's *Lectures*, Bain's *Grammar* and Latham's *Dictionary*, none of which receives the scrutiny it deserves. Similarly weak is Dasent's review of Latham's *Dictionary* (1864, 1.369-415): from a work written in a pseudo-facetious style, sprawling, not properly focused or intelligently arranged, we learn less about deficiencies, and remedies, than we might wish for. Dasent was disappointed with Latham, just as we are with Dasent.

B2. The last third of the 19th century is represented by slightly more (25), but shorter, articles. Hayles' sketch of the history of English (1867, 2.1-11) contains nothing new or exciting. Since it is both amusing and educational to see mistakes in eminent stylists corrected (a tradition incorporated under 'false syntax' in school grammars between 1750 and 1830) readers will enjoy an anonymous review (1867, 2.12-32) of Breen's *Blemishes,* where he had taken great pains to ferret out inadequacies in the expressions of great writers and is here corrected himself – an excellent exercise in Victorian stylistics. Seeley's "English in schools" (1867, 2.33-48), a plea for mother-tongue education, is directed against classicists – a hot debate at the time – but his arguments are not new and they are phrased too vaguely. His follower Abbott (1868, 2.49-58) complements this by "the results of experience" (49), illustrating the use of parsing for a better understanding of native texts (Shakespeare in particular). Baynes' reviews of various new dictionaries (1868, 2.59-88) concentrates on Latham's which is treated very systematically and with a great deal of insight, quite in contrast to other reviewers, who tend to discuss individual words. Bain's article "On teaching English" (1869, 2.89-102) is an excellent specimen of careful reasoning based on experience: grammar teaching must be justified by the aim of composition, and is best done in the mother tongue; to teach scientific method other disciplines, such as mathematics, are far more adequate. Nicol's account of "English philology" (1872, 2.103-21) neatly sums up the editorial and linguistic foundations that lay behind the great enterprises of the EETS and Ellis' historical dialectology, and the establishment of a phonetic transcription for linguistic reconstruction. Tyler's account (which he himself calls a 'lengthy dissertation') on the lexicography of 19th-century English (1873, 2.122-53) is, despite its prolixity, a valuable description of the dictionary scene before the *NED/OED*. A similar service is rendered by an anonymous writer (1874, 2.154-81) who made a very careful comparison of six school grammars (by E. Adams, Morell, Bain, Angus, Mason and W. Smith – the leading authorities in the early 1870s). He points out very clearly how the new principles of linguistic description are relevant to the teaching of the mother-tongue. All items, categories and relations are compared in the six authors, with critical judgments about ideal solutions, and the characteristics of a good English grammar are repeated in summary form at the end. Baynes' review of Hall's *Modern English* (1874, 2.182-204) is an insightful anti-polemic, complaining about Hall's "Mordent appetite and acrimonious proclivities" in caustic phrasing, though acknowledging the author's critical intelligence and the factual justness of many of his remarks. Müller had been interested in spelling reform since the early 1850s; his "On spelling" (1876, 2.205-29) reviews the proposals made by Pitman and many others, taking due account of difficulties and objections. The topic is taken up in two articles (1877, 2.238-49; 1878, 2.250-71) by Newman; he mainly objected to eccentric spellings and stressed the difficulties of teaching, including those which are bound to arise world-wide. Bradley reviews the principles of etymology that should be considered in the study of local names (1877, 2.230-7). An anonymous account of the beginnings of the *NED/OED* (1879, 2.272-86) provides some insight into the difficulties of the first stages of the enterprise. Lovett's review (1884, 2.303-19), apart from reviewing reprints of three historical dictionaries, is an evaluation of the *NED*'s first fascicle, *A to ANT*, generously quoting from entries for illustration. Allen's "Superfine English" (1885, 2.320-7) discusses, in a light vein, hypercorrections and meaningless platitudes, pedantic niceties and specimens of the etymological fallacy. Two papers by Freeman also cover general topics. His look at AmE (1882, 2.287-302) is discursive and very selective, concentrating on a few words and pronunciations and offering little that is precise or new with regard to social history. His reflections "on some modern abuses of language" (1885, 2.328-44) quote a handful of 'objectionable' terms used with vague or misleading meanings. Waugh draws attention to an ongoing stylistic change in "The tyranny of the paragraph" (1893, 2.345-49); his arguments are answered by Fry's "In defence of the paragraph" (1893, 2.350-5). Courthorpe's spirited plea for English as a part of a liberal education (1893:356-68) came at a time when (the history of) the English language had established itself as a subject even in Oxford and Cambridge, but Eng.Lit. was still outside the curriculum. "Can the English tongue be preserved?" asked Lloyd (1897, 2.369-75) who pointed to the influence of big cities (like London) on changes in pronunciation, and the counter-balance of a national standard in Britain. The book concludes with Leftwich's "English as the international language" (1897, 2.376-82), which points the way to the 20th century.

B3. The first two thirds of the 19th century are represented by twenty papers – those from 1851 onwards dominated by contributions by or about Max Müller. (It might have been preferable to have a Müller volume combined from 3+4, to contrast the views independent of him). James Browne's "Origin and affinities of languages" (1830; 3.1-31) is a remarkable fusion of Murray's abstruse theses with modern insights from comparative philology; it is still brimful of speculation, and in spite of bringing in Jones and Adelung it remains devoted to Noah and the ark. The correct interpretation of Oriental writing systems, after Champollion had deciphered the Rosetta Stone, is the topic of two not very clear papers by Wills (1836, 3.32-61; 1840, 62-78), which are followed by two philosophical papers. Bain discusses "Abuse of language" (1847, 3.79-98) with regard to 'flimsy conceptions' and connects these with the fact that "Language is apt to be an obstacle to our observation and study of realities" (84); he devotes much space to the problem of vagueness and ambiguity, including the metaphorical use of language, basing his arguments on Locke, Hume, Campbell, Coleridge and Leibniz. Mansel's paper (1850, 3.99-124) discusses "two methods by which grammar may be treated as a science ... sensationalism and idealism" and accuses Tooke of a "premature attempt to reconcile the two methods by the application of a hasty and partial philology to a crude and one-sided theory of mind" (105). By contrast, Stoddart is praised for his "valuable contribution to the science of grammar ("the science of the relations which the constituent parts of speech bear to each other in significant combination," 109) from the psychological point of view" (106).

With 1851, we enter the age of Friedrich Max Müller. With two contributions in **B3** and five in **B4**, his dominant position is appropriately acknowledged; in fact, he is represented much more fully, since most other linguists included review his work or discuss ideas proposed by him. Even his great rival in America, Whitney, was ready to admit, though with a strong ironic touch, Müller's "great fertility as a writer, and his position as accepted guide and philosopher, beyond any other living man of the English-speaking people" (4.244). His "Comparative philology" (1851, 3.125-62) uses the recent translation of Bopp's *Comparative Grammar* to describe the principles of the not-so-new continental discipline – this of course remained his major function as a mediator of the German tradition. Strettell's review of Humboldt's *Kauri Language* (1851, 3.163-92) makes a nice contrast, introducing English readers to a different strand of continental thinking. Kenrick's review of a book on glossolalia (1852, 3.193-204) and Kingley's on the linguistic and pedagogical problems of stammering (1859, 3.205-23) remind us of how broad the concept of linguistics was at the time. Two reviews of Müller's *Lectures* follow. An anonymous one (1862, 3.224-46) was the first to object to Müller's grouping of linguistics as an inductive science among the physical disciplines; the remainder forms an intelligent summary of Müller's tenets, and of progress in linguistics in general. Cox's review is also supportive ("The deep learning of Müller has left but scanty room for criticism", 3.278). It was again Cox's turn to review the *Second Series* (1865, 4.14-41), where Cox is less interested in linguistics, concentrating instead on Greek and Sanskrit mythology. Taking over Müller's arguments and examples, Cox is imbued with the feeling of progress, as when he discusses the onomatopoeic (*bow-wow*) and interjectional (*pooh-pooh*) origin of languages:

> Such views deserve, indeed, little tolerance now; but, hard as it may be to understand how such theories could ever have found any acceptance, the conjectures of a past generation, groping without clue through the vast labyrinth of language, deserve the gentle handling which they receive from Professor Müller. (3.273)

Irwin also reviewed both parts of Müller's *Lectures*. In (1862, 3.299-308) he provides a very selective, generally approving account; his descriptive summary in (1865, 4.1-13) is again without a hint of criticism. Two reviews bring together Müller and F.W. Farrar, a scholar who is now largely forgotten: Paley (1862, 3.309-27) critically reviews theories that had been proposed – that language was innate and God-given, that it was originally imitative and monosyllabic, that it arose from interjections and that a common origin of all languages was a likelihood (3.313). The other (anonymous) reviewer to combine the two (1866, 4.71-102) draws on Plato, Bopp, Tooke to describe "that ultimate intellectual region where the laws of nature and the laws of thought are seen in their closest combination" (3.71). The very learned author gets involved in the mimetic origins of language, reflections which must needs remain highly speculative.

Two more reviews of the *Lectures* testify to the attention that the publication of the first volume received: Swayne's "Characteristics of language" (1862, 3.280-98) reporting on a continental conference of philologists, belongs to the chatty tradition, abounding in misleading generalizations like when the "entire absence of vulgarity in the ancients" is said to be "because wealth-worship was comparatively unknown to them" (3.290). An anonymous reviewer (1862, 3.329-358) unreservedly accepts the notion that "Language is not the manufacture of man; it is the work of nature; it is the work of God" (3.331), but admits that "Language is continually undergoing change; and in this it seems to resemble a historical science like that of government, rather than a physical science like that of astronomy" (3.331) – but these are "changes of phenomena and not of laws" (3.332). The somewhat rambling account is notable for cutting the treatment of Müller's "Theoretical stage" down to five lines (3.358). Wedgwood (1862, 3.359-68) praises the graceful style of the lectures, but then takes up the controversial issue of the imitative origin of language. Müller gave the second series of lectures in 1863; the introductory one appeared independently (1863, 3.369-85) and is here included for comparison with the full text. An anonymus starts the row of reviewers of the second volume (1864, 3.393-413), praising Müller's achievement: "the enthusiasm with which the new philosophy of human speech has been cultivated is greatly due to the genius, learning, and eloquence of the distinguished foreigner" (3.393), a paragraph which culminates in an unreserved (and undeserved) encomium. Smith (1864, 3.414-35) is more skeptical but not really more critical because he does not provide alternatives to Müller's claims.

B4. The last third of the century is represented by 27 contributions, again overshadowed by the figure of Müller. Irwin's and Cox's reviews have been mentioned above; Tylor's "On the origin of language" (1866, 4.42-57) takes up one of the most debated topics; he is close to Tooke in his faith in onomatopoeia and interjection as the basis of the origin of language and defends the bow-wow theory against Müller's caustic criticism (4.43). Smart (1866, 4.58-64, 65-70) on "Thought and language" sees grammar as subservient to logic, a position the author claims is innovative.

Turning to Müller, the author, we have his nationalistic speech to students of the university at Strasbourg, then Strassburg, in 1872, in which he neatly summarizes his main objectives in studying language under "On the results of the science of language" (1872; 115-29). This is followed by his stimulating two "lectures on Mr. Darwin's philosophy of language" (1873:152-221), which fits language into the system of Evolutionary Materialism of Darwin and Haeckel and brings in Spencer, Kant, Berkeley and Hume to produce a sophisticated, comprehensive sketch of the Mülleresque science of language. "The simplicity of language" (1887; 310-23) is a return, after 23 years, to the Royal Institution, a relaxed, but necessarily speculative lecture on the origins of speech. In "My predecessors" (1888; 324-43) he reflects on the philosophers that he has based his *Science of Thought* of 1887/88 on, focussing particularly on the controversy between nominalism and realism, including D. Stewart and M. Taine, before he again turns to IE roots and their function in the origin of speech. Müller's final paper is surrounded by a larger number of articles on various related topics which must have been controversial in those years: Campbell's "The identity of thought and language" (1888; 344-62) very modestly but convincingly criticizes Müller for not admitting that "we can never have concepts (abstract ideas) without words" (349), where this is said to be possible for sensations and perceptions. Campbell refutes Müller's 'fallacies' one by one, showing how shaky many of his claims were, a criticism which found a sympathetic reaction from Müller's (1889; 363-74). Garner's "The Simian tongue" (1891-2; 375-90) and Barham's "The relation of language to thought" (1895; 409-15) both try to complement the discussion by looking at the "mental continuity between the brute and man."

Skipping a few articles mainly relating to speculative explanations of the origin of speech, we come to *the* great transatlantic rival of Müller, Whitney. He is praised by G.H. Darwin (1874; 222-32) for his "successful refutation of the somewhat dogmatic views of our Oxford linguist", a statement supported by extensive quotations from Whitney's criticism of Müller. Whitney finds that:

> While the present century has witnessed a truly wonderful advance in the study of languages, it has not yet yielded equal results for the science of language. Comparative philology has thus far borne off the palm over linguistics. (233)

In particular, he complains about Germany:

> Germany is the home of philological and linguistic study; but the Germans are rather exceptionally careless of what we may call the questions of linguistic philosophy. (234)

His major contribution is his well-reasoned 'Yes' to the question raised in the title of the article "Are languages institutions?" Otherwise the paper is a document of how impossible it was for Whitney and Müller to understand each other.

There are articles on various other topics, illustrating the scope of late 19th-century linguistics: Freeman's problematic views on "Race and language" (1877; 261-88) – Müller had, almost prophetically, spoken out against the reconstruction of an Aryan race in 1872 (122), discussions about the expressiveness of language, and another comment on the eternal subject of spelling reform (Leftwich's "Reading at sight for illiterates" 1898:443-8).

Conclusion

Is it possible to sum up one's impressions from 4,700 pages of 19th-century texts on linguistics, and the English language in particular, written by some forty authors? The unifying impression is, I believe, that we here have texts largely written by amateurs for amateurs – and this applies of course to the reviews and other contributions to the journals which provided educational reading matter on a great variety of (semi-) scholarly topics to a vast audience – not just the educated leisured classes, but through lending libraries, Mechanics Institutes and other educational institutions to the upwardly mobile in the middle classes. Our judgment of the material should not be based purely on modern expectations of how a scholarly expository text should be structured and phrased, but the datedness of the arguments and their expression is still apparent. Most important, it is unexplained why there are so few Whitneys or Sweets among the 19th-century authors, whose clear exposition and succinct and lucid style are strikingly modern and a pleasure to read even though they wrote at the end of the last century.

For those who wish to plough through the 4,700 pages, a fascinating panorama of a period more distant than many realize will unfold. The delight will be impaired, however, by a few problems which have to do with the selection of the texts and their presentation.

1) The selection of book-length treatments is restricted to four, and this selectivity demands very explicit justification. I fail to see that Murray is important enough

to justify his taking up some 35% of the space of the first set of reprints, especially since so many other authors, or other works of those included, or other types of books dealing with language, had to be excluded. I would have willingly exchanged Murray for more Whitney and Trench. Specimens of school grammars (of which there are some outstanding examples), of Alford's and Heald's treatments of the Queen's English, and of conduct books (such as the anonymous *Vulgarities* of 1826 and Savage's *Improprieties* of 1833) warning against linguistic misbehaviour, might also have been included at least in the form of excerpts.

2) The pieces reprinted from journals are of eminent value and interest. There must be many more potential candidates, but rather than sending readers to the *Wellesley Index*, which provides titles only, Harris might have listed 'rejected' papers by topic, with full bibliographical information. Such a survey might also have included more detailed arguments about why Müller is so prominent in this selection – his importance is undoubted, but his relative weight for the thinking of an entire century is difficult to estimate.

3) The articles are arranged in chronological order, which can serve to represent historical sequence. However, this principle separates authors, topics and methods – since texts by or about Müller, or treatments of lexicography before the *NED* are spread over several volumes. There are no guide-posts, footnotes or cross-references to help the reader.

4) There is no index to guide the reader to points where individual authors or topics are treated. Such an index need not have been comprehensive and could still have been very useful. Why not index at least authors frequently discussed or quoted from (or represented as writers of articles) – such as Alford, Angus, Bain, Bopp, Campbell, Darwin, Ellis, Freeman, Furnival, Grimm, Harris, Hobbes, Hume, Johnson, Jones, Kant, Latham, Leibniz, Locke, Müller, Murray (A. & L.), Newman, Pitman, Pott, Rask, Richardson, Schlegel, Stewart, Stoddart, Sweet, Tooke, Trench, Walker, Webster, Whately and Whitney? Why should very general topics not be indexed to serve as cross-references – such as AmE, bible, comparative, dialect, etymology, false syntax, French, German, Greek, history of English, Indo-European, language teaching, Latin, lexicography, literacy, literary style, loanwords, morphology, natural science, *NED*, philology, phonetics, poetic diction, prescriptivism, science of language, Scots, style, syntax, tense and world language?

The texts in **A** were reproduced in facsimile from the best copies available; the 83 papers in **B** were reset. These difficult texts were printed with great accuracy; there are very few typographical errors. But such major enterprises have their price; the limited number of libraries able (or willing) to buy these sets have apparently forced the publishers to put astronomic prices on their reprints, which makes it almost impossible for private scholars to acquire them – cheaper originals might be found amongst the treasures of the local secondhand bookshop.

References

Aarsleff, Hans. 1967. *The Study of Language in England, 1780-1860*. Princeton: UP.

Alston, R.C. ed. 1968-70. *English Linguistics*. Facsimile reprints. Menston: Scolar Press.

Alston, R.C. 1964-87. *A Bibliography of the English Language from the Invention of Printing to the Year 1800*, 12 vols. & supplement, corrected reprint. Ilkley: Scolar Press.

Görlach, Manfred. 1998. *An Annotated Bibliography of Nineteenth-Century Grammars of English*. Amsterdam: Benjamins.

3 Dialectology, Sociolinguistics and Contact Linguistics

The topics here treated are an obvious complement to my major research interests in historical linguistics, a discipline which must have a social component in it if it has a claim to the name. Exciting developments in all these disciplines are documented in many important works which I have tried to cover in reviews of the major books. A survey of the most important publications of the related field of world English, with a reprint of selected relevant reviews, is found in my *Still More Englishes* (Amsterdam, 2002): there was no room to accommodate these here, and they are somehow better placed in the other book.

16 William Labov, *Principles of Linguistic Change. Internal Factors* (Language in Society 20). Oxford: Blackwell, 1994, xix + 641 pp.; from *JEL* 25 (1997), 156-9.

This is the first of a set of three books, the next two planned to contain "social factors" and "cognitive factors": the three will make up some 2,000 pages summarizing the life work of a linguist who has dominated modern thought in the field as nobody else has, with the single exception of Noam Chomsky. The reviewer, then, approaches his task with some trepidation, increased by the insight that the three books should ideally be reviewed together, and that vol. 2 may in fact be the centre of the whole work, usefully read before vol. 1 – in principle. However, it does make sense for writer and readers to have the internal mechanisms clarified before social conditions, causes and consequences are dealt with.

Labov has continued to describe the mechanisms of linguistic change for more than thirty years; he has raised the descriptive rigor and sophistication to a level without precedence before the 1960s – for all the massive evidence sifted by 19th-century scholars. In fact, Labov has consistently pursued the approach laid down in the seminal article of 1968 (Weinreich, Labov & Herzog 1968), having to fulfil the expectations raised in one of the most important papers of this century. A historical linguist is up against a series of obstacles, many not strictly surmountable: long-term changes are more or less well documented, but they do not provide detailed evidence on the initiation and spread of a change; many individual facts are 'messy', and we do not know whether they represent idiosyncrasies, mistakes, or undiscovered rules, and so on. All this leads up to the "fundamental paradox of historical linguistics":

> The task of historical linguistics is to explain the differences between the past and the present; but to the extent that the past was different from the present, there is no way of knowing how different it was. (21)

However, a cautious "use of the present to explain the past", guided by the uniformitarian principle (21) is, with all its inherent dangers, the only approach possible – according to Labov. As the Neogrammarians well knew "this principle is a necessary precondition for historical reconstruction" (24); Labov reminds us that the principle is not a solution to the paradox but a working assumption. (Scholars more skeptical of the uniformitarian principle will agree, but come to a different conclusion).

Since historical data are as restricted as they are, Labov concludes that the synchronic study of linguistic change in progress must be used to explain historical problems – this has of course been his message from the beginning of his career. He rightly mentions the "natural alliance of dialect geography, sociolinguistics, phonetics, and historical linguistics – fields that share a common interest in objective data" (25). Very much as with 19th-century 'predecessors', *phonetics* is given a special role in Labov's approach, being both open to technical measurement at a high degree of detail and largely unaffected by deliberate kinds of change. However, historical material being sparse and ambiguous even for more recent periods, and not available at all for others, we are thrown back to accepting the regularity of sound change, so Labov claims, as the Neogrammarians had postulated.

However, the modern linguist has at his disposal both sophisticated technical instruments (tape-recorders) and various computational methods for the multivariate analysis of huge amounts of complex data, all of which can be used to confirm, or falsify, his hypotheses.

Ch. 2 (28-42) repeats in greater detail the methods outlined above, before Labov turns to the vital question of "What we can learn about change in real time from distributions in apparent time", i.e. the analysis of linguistic variables across age levels. Labov duly lists the dangers of accepting such evidence naïvely or estimating shifts on an impressionistic basis. He admits that the noteworthy refinement in measuring data can have adverse effects: "As accuracy has increased, the difficulties in using these data to track sound change across the community have become more serious" (56). In this predicament multivariate analysis measuring the effect of many factors simultaneously is a great help in interpreting complex correlations. Labov shows this when he compares thirteen linguistic variables from Philadelphia with twelve social variables (56-58) and arrives at patterns ranging from incipient to completed change (65, using the model of the famous S-shaped curve). A better check is to contrast real-time changes – where such data are available, and of sufficient quality (ch. 4, 73-112); again, earlier studies of Philadelphia dialect serve for comparison (79), as well as replications of previous investigations (including Labov's own department store one, 86-94).

The next two parts apply these principles to the phenomena of chain shifting (113-291) and mergers and splits (295-418) – the central data-based sections of the book. Three principles are formulated for vowel movements in chain shifts. Based on developments in some twenty languages, shifts can be accepted as regular, with the few exceptions serving to formulate constraints. The findings are then applied to the English Great Vowel Shift (145-54) where "the issues are clear-cut, but the controversy is unresolved" (147). Labov here formulates a set of paradoxes since no fully convincing explanation seems to be possible. The modern linguist is of course in an infinitely better position when describing chain shifts in progress, as Labov does in the summary of his research on the "Northern Cities Shift", which here serves to modify one of the principles above (200; various other English dialects are adduced for support). A solution is offered for the paradoxes of ch. 5 on pages 222 to 244: varieties of phonological space apparently permit sounds "to pass each other in front or in back" (226) – a principle necessary also for Labov's explanation of 'near-mergers'. Misunderstandings are used to define subsystems in ch. 9 (271-91), which in turn serve to explain how chain shifts work across subsystems – if a shift spreads it must obviously do so beyond the group where it originated.

If shifts (or rotations) preserve distinctions, then the complementary processes of mergers and splits eliminate and create them (295) – this insight is of course common lore. Labov discusses with great acumen the problem cases of EModE *ea* (*great*) and the *loin*/*line* confusion to lead on to mergers and splits in general, rightly pointing out that "mergers are irreversible by linguistic means" (311). A great number of mergers and splits is then discussed in various English dialects (including speakers' efforts to learn words exemplifying the split), and it is in this chapter that Labov's decision to restrict himself to functional/internal arguments and leave out social factors proves impossible to keep up. "Near-mergers" (349-70) includes a highly relevant discussion of 'discreteness' as a consequence of systemic reasoning, with insightful arguments on speakers' production and perception, and the reality of minimal distinctions in phonetics. The existence of near-mergers in various speech communities is persuasively discussed in great detail with *line* : *loin* words in Essex, and *meat*: *mate* words in Belfast (371-90). Detailed tests exploring the (lack of) discrimination between near-mergers of *merry*: *Murray* words among Philadelphians point to "the suspension of phonemic contrast" (391-418).

The interpretation of these findings is summarized under "The regularity controversy", starting with "evidence for lexical diffusion" supplied for Chinese consonants and Philadelphia short [a] – clear indications that the Neogrammarian tenet of regular sound change "affecting all words at the same time" seems impossible to defend. However, Labov feels that "expanding the Neogrammarian viewpoint" (440-71) to include "tools of statistical analysis" (470) is a legitimate procedure; also, we realize that "there appear to be far more substantially documented cases of Neogrammarian sound changes than of lexical diffusion." Whether this really finishes off the opposite view that every word has its own history is doubtful – both statements are true but one does not necessarily disqualify the other. Dialectology is therefore the real test case (472-501); Labov, in a convincing line of argument, shows that data from BrE dialect can be interpreted to confirm Neogrammarian tenets rather than the favoured explanation by lexical diffusion. Since both lexical diffusion and regular sound change are involved in the transition, Labov chooses to look at Philadelphia [a] again; after applying very sophisticated tests he states: "The splitting of short [a] is clearly a classic case of lexical diffusion. By contrast, the vowel shifts of Philadelphia are classic cases of Neogrammarian sound change" (526) – which finally leads to defining the two processes as complementary. Lexical diffusion involves abrupt substitution and illustrates change from above, and regular sound change illustrates a gradual change from below (542). Is there room in all this for functional explanations? Labov points out that his experience has made him skeptical "of arguments for the controlling effect of meaning on language and language change" (549). If chain shifts are adduced as evidence for retaining contrasts, why then are mergers more frequent? (551) And if speakers cannot hear all contrasts properly, how can they use them to distinguish meaning? (552) Drawing on a great variety of cases from various languages, Labov concludes that variants are "chosen without regard to the maximization of information" (568). How then is systemic readjustment achieved? After all, languages preserve meaning distinctions in change. Labov plausibly connects this with the learning device of "probability matching" (596), a process which "proceeds without conscious attention" (597).

One of the striking limitations of Labov's study (admitted by himself, 600) is his concentration on sound change, neglecting morphological and syntactical change. How far the principles reformulated in remarkable clarity (600-5) can be seen as near-universal for phonological change and applied to other levels, remains open – and will not be addressed in the two volumes still to come. The most exciting features of the book are the very detailed and convincing arguments for the restricted importance of functional aspects in change, which will be a must-read for all who are too ready to jump to plausible explanations, and for the confirmation, in principle, of the Neogrammarians' tenets of the regularity of sound change, a model which had been all but given up by most linguists under the impact of the alleged universal validity of lexical diffusion. It is likely that the relative weights are different on the levels of morphology, syntax and lexis: however, anyone willing to take up research into these fields will now have an excellent basis for comparison in Labov's tightly argued book.

The great attraction of the book is certainly that Labov has with great persuasion drawn together the findings of thirty years of research to illustrate a theory of linguistic change. It is consistent and coherent, all arguments being within a Labovian paradigm: whatever criticism some scholars may have (and there certainly will be some) will have to come from without, from different positions.

Reference
Weinreich, Uriel, William Labov, and Marvin Herzog, 1968. "Empirical foundations for a theory of language change". In W. Lehmann and Y. Malkiel, eds. *Directions for Historical Linguistics*. Austin: University of Texas Press, 95-188.

William Labov, *Principles of Linguistic Change. Social Factors*. Oxford: Blackwell, 2001, xviii+572 pp.; *EWW* 22 (2001), 326-30.

The second volume of Labov's *magnum opus* summarizing his life's work now follows at a greater remove from the first than most readers had expected: whereas vol. I (above) was devoted to *Internal Factors*, the impressive volume under review is now on what is rightly considered the core of Labov's interest and the field in which he has become a landmark of modern linguistics – to explain the social motivation of linguistic change which has been his driving force ever since his early study undertaken on Martha's Vineyard, that is, for almost forty years.

The present book is divided into four parts. "The speech community" (1-145) introduces us to "The Darwinian paradox" (1-34), "The study of linguistic change and variation in Philadelphia" (35-73) and "Stable sociolinguistic variables" (74-145). This introductory section makes evident a few features continued in the later discussion. It is not really introductory in a way that terms and methods are explained for beginners, and it is idiosyncratic in concentrating on parallels between biological development models à la Darwin and language change – if these similarities exist they cannot be taken as constitutive, however stimulating such comparisons are (and to whatever extent they were felt as establishing linguistics as a scientific discipline by scholars in the 19th century). Labov, then, is very well informed on the history of linguistics, more than many would have expected, such as when discussing earlier proposals to account for linguistic change, like "the principle of least effort" (16-8), the functional approach of Martinet (20-3), or the social causes of change, referring to Meillet and Sturtevant (29-31). Labov's discussion here is, and continues to be, (almost) entirely on sounds, disregarding morphology, syntax or lexis. It concentrates (with a few references to his earlier work in New York) on his research in Philadelphia (1973-77) and Eastern Pennsylvania (1977-79). It summarizes almost exclusively Labov's own research (including collaborative investigations), but refers to only few other scholars (such as Chambers, Rickford and Trudgill) by way of very brief remarks, mostly in support of his own claims. The approach is centred on the past few decades, the aim being to describe ongoing change.

The study is, then, a uniquely detailed conscientious description of how Labovian sociolinguistics has developed over the past forty years. Chapter 2, "The study of linguistic change and variation in Philadelphia" (35-73) provides a meticulous description of the speech community and the reasons for the choice of the neighbourhoods to be investigated. Readers will, however, have to take the distinction between the town and its hinterland and the embedding into a larger US context for granted – some indications of what makes Philadelphia singular will, we assume, become clearer when the *Atlas of North American English* (*ANAE*, hinted at in several places) is published. In Philadelphia, Labov retained the system of sampling (in both the direct interviews and the complementary telephone survey), using networks for the interpretation later on. "Stable sociolinguistic variables" are first treated in order to properly investigate change, *viz.* (dh), (Neg)=negative concord, and (ing). 'Stable' does not mean of course that these variables have no social history to them: (Neg) and (ing) became socially relevant in the 18th century. One of the exciting findings is that change from above, exerted through educational systems, has apparently not quite levelled out syntactic differences predating the merger of *-inde* and *-yng(e)*: Labov's research shows that the more verbal the form, the greater the proportion of [-n], whereas nouns have more [-ŋ]. (This contrast has not been tested on BrE varieties, where it is likely to yield even more conspicuous results). Ch. 4, "The Philadelphia vowel system" (121-45) sketches the developments of ten sound changes in apparent time as evident from the Neighborhood Study.

The correlation with "Social class, gender, neighborhood, and ethnicity," the topic of Part B (149-322), is the central part of the book in more than one sense. The "location of the leaders in the socioeconomic hierarchy" (149-92) establishes members of the upwardly mobile sections of the local community, mostly women, as the sources of innovation; arguments are supported by highly complex statistical methods in order to provide a safe basis for the locus of the initiation of changes. A short complementary chapter discusses the explanatory value of tests using self-reports and subjective reactions (193-224). "Neighborhood and ethnicity" are treated next (224-60): however descriptively adequate purely quantificational correlations of linguistic and social variables are, they need complementation through networks to explain the why's and how's of changes. Obviously, the Belfast study, which used similar methods, had to employ different parameters because of the radically different social-class structure of the community, and different linguistic variables. Whereas 'neighborhood' and social class are established as highly relevant, 'ethnicity' surprisingly is not (247) – with the exception of African American Vernacular English (AAVE). 'Jewish' and 'Italian' features are controversial, and certainly not related to the substratum.

"The gender paradox" (261-93) is a particularly important contribution to the ongoing discussion. How can females be conservative and close to standard on the one hand and leaders of linguistic change on the other? They obviously accommodate more readily to changes from above, that is, follow overt norms, but they take the lead in phenomena where the norms are not codified – as in the Northern Cities Shift of vowels (which affects all parts of the region as will be demonstrated in detail in the forthcoming *ANAE*). Sociolinguistic analysis has to consider "The intersection of gender, age and social class" (294-322) which confirms the importance of female leadership in ongoing change and its diffusion.

"Social networks" have been stressed as important factors by sociolinguists such as the Milroys and Chambers. Labov underlines the importance of the model for his Philadelphia study (325-65) in establishing the leaders and resolving the gender paradox (366-84). Portraits of these leaders are given in great social detail (385-412) to make plausible that these persons can be believed to have had the influence ascribed to them.

Having established the principles of actuation, Labov can now, true to the stages established in 1968 (Weinreich *et al.* 1968), look at "transmission" (415-45), "incrementation" (446-65) and "continuation" (446-97), stages in the spread of linguistic change which are documented with a barrage of statistical interpretations. The interrelation of structural factors (à la Martinet and Moulton) with social parameters is explained as "socially motivated projection" (498) – whereas some changes are transparent from functional causation, social motives are needed to explain structurally opaque changes (500). Changes are explained by the "Nonconformity Principle" by which they "are generated in the social milieu that most consistently defies these norms" (516), but they are "generalized to the wider community by those who display the symbols of nonconformity in a larger pattern of upward social mobility" (516), which "links it to the Curvilinear Principle" (516) – a formulation of Einsteinian elegance.

It is obviously impossible to summarize the densely filled 572 pages of largely abstract high-powered argumentation in a short review like this. As was to be expected, Labov's book will provide a cornerstone of sociohistorical linguistics. A few questions remain, though, which I'd like to summarize under five points:

1) The account of Philadelphia is totally convincing. However, we lack similar descriptions of other speech communities outside the U.S. Where such exist, the differences are sometimes as conspicuous as the similarities (Belfast; even less similar: Norwich, Bradford, Glasgow, Sydney). The question therefore remains how far comparisons are misleading or worse – among the few sociolinguistic investigations referred to for various individual points there are studies of palatalization in Cairo Arabic, of intonation in Sydney and of shift to German in an Austrian village. How far can Labov's Philadelphian conditions, and the methods developed for their description, be generalized or adapted? The question is not answered – and is possibly not answerable.

2) Similar questions as to the applicability of the findings also relate to language history of a more distant past. Labov does refer, in a few isolated cases, to 18th-century conditions, but only to support his claims, and there is no indication of how far it is legitimate "to use the present to explain the past."

3) There is hardly a recent sociolinguistic study without mention of Labov's work. By contrast, the number of sociolinguists mentioned in the book is very small and their methods are not really discussed. Labov's study gives the impression of self-containedness, not to say isolation, in which stimuli are proceeding increasingly in one direction. Readers might wish to learn how far the voices echoing Labov have in turn influenced his work – *not* just investigations conducted by his pupils.

4) The discussion is almost exclusively on pronunciation – understandably, considering the salience and easy elicitation of relevant data. However, a sketch on how the other levels of linguistic structure are correlated (or contrasted) with the phonic evidence might have been supplied. There is a solitary reference to "the most important studies of the elaboration of syntactic structures in developing pidgins and creoles..., which will play a prominent role in this volume and the following one" – but only *bai* (423-5) is here discussed from the rich data and interpretations in the field, and the relevance and comparability of pidgin data for Labov's arguments do not become clear.

5) A number of statements are strange. The parallel with Darwinian categories (6-10) is too far-fetched to justify the space, and for the central position it has in Labov's argumentation; Swadesh (13) might be better passed over in silence – and he is in the index; finally, to say that "learning German, French, Spanish, or Russian, languages that were once mutually intelligible dialects of proto-Indo-European" (5) is putting it in a very awkward way, indeed.

This central portion of a gigantic triptych makes stimulating reading throughout. Many lines indicated in vol. 1 are here followed up in painstaking detail and treated with scholarly rigidity. We look forward to having solutions to a few open ends supplied in vol. 3, which will hopefully not take another seven years to be published.

17 Werner Besch, Ulrich Knoop, Wolfgang Putschke & Herbert Ernst Wiegand, eds., *Dialektologie. Ein Handbuch zur deutschen und allgemeinen Dialektforschung.* (Handbücher zur Sprach- und Kommunikationswissenschaft 1.1 + 1.2) Berlin/New York: de Gruyter, 1982/83, xxxiv + xix + 1714 pp.; from *EWW* 6 (1985), 308-11.

The foundation of an ambitious new series in linguistics, with the present huge work as an appropriate starter, comes at a time when linguistic variation and its relevance for language change have again become a focus of interest within the discipline; on the other hand, hypotheses put forward and methods applied in dialectological research have been greatly affected by various 'modern' schools of linguistics in the course of the last twenty years. The time to publish a state-of-the-art account of relevant research into one of Europe's best documented and most diversified languages is, then, well-chosen. And although this is a work written on German by German-speaking scholars and in German, the international relevance of the undertaking will be obvious to everyone who cares to browse through this work of breath-taking proportions. In fact, dialectological findings and methods have always been taken over from one language and applied to another, and the impact of German schools was particularly strong in the early stages of the discipline – when British dialectologists studied at Göttingen and Heidelberg. With Hans Kurath in the U.S., Eugen Dieth and Eduard Kolb for England, and Hans Speitel in Scotland (to name only the most conspicuous scholars) the personal link with the German tradition has remained considerable: their roots can now be assessed much more easily than has hitherto been possible. For in spite of these strong links, publications on English dialects tend to neglect the Continental origins and parallels – Kurath's *Studies in Area Linguistics* (1972) and Francis' recent handbook (1983) are among the rare exceptions. (Influences the other way are not in evidence until the more social and urban-oriented research of the Labov and Bernstein schools: the German tradition had always looked to France).

The two volumes comprise 104 articles (ranging from three to ninety-three pages) written by ninety scholars predominantly from West Germany, Switzerland and Austria (the absence of contributions from East Germany is especially to be regretted). They describe the history of the discipline, procedures, findings and needs for future research, without aiming at encyclopedia-like exhaustiveness: the field is the (historical and present) ordered heterogeneity of the German language and its native speakers mainly in Central Europe (with sketches of dialects outside the major cohesive area, but with no treatment of German dialects spoken in the New World, such as Pennsylvania Dutch or Hutterite in the U.S., or Hunsbucklerisch or Pommeranian in Brazil; Mennonite Low German is discussed with regard to the Ukrainian settlements, but the migration to

Canada is mentioned in one sentence only on p. 928). There is also some treatment of Low German (as far as it can be considered as functioning as a dialect of German; for more exhaustive information, the reader can now be referred to Cordes & Möhn's Handbook of 1983) and there is, more unexpectedly, a chapter on the dialectal structure of Yiddish, which is certainly a different language (but again no treatment of the Yiddish influence on German dialects, which has been considerable). The selection of material in the volumes under review was also determined by the contents planned for two other handbooks in the same series, *viz. Historical Linguistics* (1985) and *Sociolinguistics* (forthcoming): it is striking that the social/communicative aspects of dialect are not treated as exhaustively as might have been expected, though there is no explicit formulation of this policy in the foreword.

The contents of the two volumes are, then, in greater detail and arranged according to the fifteen sections in which they are grouped by the editors:

I (1.-11.)	Main approaches in the tradition of German dialectology;
II (12.-15.)	Theories of 'classical', structural, generative and communicative dialectology;
III (16.-19.)	Case histories;
IV (20.-26.)	General problems relating to aims and methods;
V+VI (27.-41.)	Data collecting, processing and interpretation;
VII (42.-46.)	Computational applications;

and in the second volume:

VIII (47.-49.)	Surveys of the regional structure of German dialects inside and outside the cohesive Central European area, and of historical reconstruction;
IX (50.-53.)	How did dialects influence the emergence of the standard language?
X (54.-67.)	Phonetic/phonological features;
XI (68.-78.)	Morphological and syntactic features;
XII (79.-83.)	Lexical/semantic features;
XIII (84.-93.)	The dialect speaker in society;
XIV (94.-99.)	Interdisciplinary aspects;
XV (100.-102.)	Dialect in literature.

There are recurring patterns in regional speech throughout Western Europe, and many discussions of individual topics are likely to stimulate research on related questions elsewhere; one thinks of treatments of possible historical reconstruction of dialect boundaries or areas (16., 49.), generative rules for the derivation of ablaut forms (18.), register switching (19.), interpretations of dialect maps (24.), tense and mood in dialects (73., 74.) or dialect words in standard dictionaries (83.) or indeed of recurring topics such as standard vs. dialect, written vs. spoken language, dialect erosion and death, dialect and education, diglossia and contact phenomena.

Although the huge masses of material to be dealt with in dialectology (and the type of gentleman amateur characteristic of early stages of the discipline) favoured empirical, positivistic approaches in the 19th century, the sometimes highly theoretical discussions of the present collection make nonsense of the often repeated charge that dialectology lacks theoretical abstraction: true though it is that dialect research depends on a firm data base, the elicitation and collection of this, its processing and interpretation is only possible with methodological clarity within a theoretical framework. The majority of essays, especially in section IV (see those by Heger, Löffler, Mattheier, and the ones on dialectometry), testify to this.

The work ends with an impressive index of names and terms (pp. 1667-1714), which comprises more than 2,000 entries. The books are excellently produced, with a lavish use of multicoloured maps (many folding), and printer's errors are laudably few. It is to be hoped that the impact that the work ought to have will not be partly thwarted by the use of German as a medium: it should be a stimulus to dialectologists to brush up their German sufficiently to read these 1,700 pages packed with scholarly information. It would also be rewarding to contrast the situation described here with that in similarly diversified language areas (such as that of Italian) and with the distribution of dialects in centralised states such as France and Great Britain.

18   W.N. Francis, *Dialectology. An Introduction.* (Longman Linguistic Library 39). London: Longman, 1983, xii + 240 pp.; from *EWW* 6 (1985), 329-30.

Every 'language series' is bound to include a dialectology volume – after introductory textbooks by Chambers & Trudgill, Davis, Petyt and Wakelin, however, Francis comes rather late in the Longman series. Was there still room for another introduction? In spite of the above-mentioned books, it will soon become clear that there still was. Francis' book is especially strong on methodology: how to select informants, how to compile questionnaires, how to print the answers or to edit them in the form of various lists or types of maps, and to analyse the responses in a traditional, structural, generative or sociolinguistic framework is here dealt with in exceptional breadth and with considerable conspicuity. Francis takes his readers – in a scholarly, but always readable style – through the questions of "What is dialectology?" and "Why and how to practise it?" in ch. 1 (1-14) to variation as a universal linguistic phenomenon (ch.2, 15-47) and four chapters devoted to a careful and detailed description of methods (ch.3, "Sampling the language", 48-65; ch.4, "Sampling the speakers", 66-77; ch.5, "Collecting the data", 78-103; ch.6, "Publishing the findings", 104-44). Two very important chapters at the end are meant to prove the value of insights from dialectology for linguistics at large, and to establish the discipline firmly as a branch of linguistics: chs.7-8, "Dialectology and linguistic theory: traditional, structural, generative" (145-92) and "Sociolinguistic" (193-214). For the advanced student (and for academic teachers not primarily interested in dialectology) these two well-structured and carefully reasoned chapters may well constitute the heart of the book – but they should not forget (and will not after ploughing through the preceding chapters) the "body of thought and speculation which has accompanied the hard work of the field collector" (viii): dialectology is likely to be the subdiscipline of linguistics in which it would be most dangerous to lose sight of the data.

A special asset of the book is that it makes available to the English-speaking student the gist of European (Continental) dialectology, as far as this is possible within such limited space. Francis rightly says:

> Much of this writing – primarily in French, German and Italian – has been neglected by British and American dialectologists; one aim of this book is to show the truly international nature of the discipline. (viii)

A look at the index makes it clear that Gardette, Gilliéron, Jaberg, Jud, Moulton, Séguy and Wenker – all working with non-English data – are among the most quoted authors. The advantage of such a wide catchment area is especially evident in chs. 8 and 9, where the possibilities of mapping are illustrated with raw data maps, map and list combinations, edited; and interpretative (isogloss and structural) maps – a feature that would have been difficult or impossible to achieve on the basis of the published English material available. The volume is excellently produced and lavishly illustrated with tables, facsimiles of worksheets and various maps: it is a pity, though, that maps have often suffered so greatly from reduction in size as to make them hardly legible to the naked eye – a price that one must pay, it seems, if the price of the book itself is to remain moderate.

19 Peter Trudgill, ed., *Language in the British Isles*. Cambridge: UP, 1984, xii + 587 pp.,
Glanville Price, *The Languages of Britain*. London: Arnold, 1984, 245 pp.;
from *EWW* 5 (1984), 283-90.

Britain ranks among the most monolingual countries in the world – as a consequence of the spread (or imposition) of English which has been going on for more than a millenium. In 1588 Harrison (in his Introduction to Holinshed's *Chronicle,* when dealing with "The languages spoken in this island") could still list Cornish and Norn as living languages as well as English, Welsh, Gaelic – and Standard Scots. Nevertheless, the fact that indigenous languages are still spoken on the islands, that new ones have been imported by immigrants in the present century, and that regional variation of English worth preserving still exists – all this has received greater attention from the seventies onwards. Lockwood's (1975) book was the most recent summary of multilingual Britain, and by some curious coincidence (if it is indeed a coincidence) two substantial books have now appeared in the same year to testify to the continuing interest. Trudgill's collection is by far the weightier one, as is evident from the number of chapters, of languages and dialects treated, and from the number of contributors, whereas Price's is an admirable one-man effort, and greatly differs in its accentuation.

Trudgill puts English first, because of its undoubted hegemony. Milroy's introductory chapter on "The history of English in the British Isles" (5-31) is the only historical treatment in this section, and the restricted number of pages allocated to this topic means that the contents cannot be quite satisfactory in all respects. But since the function of the chapter for the whole book is not made explicit, it is difficult to criticise the weight given to and the arrangement of certain topics, such as the preponderance of matter on phonological change, and the limited space given to the social history of English (Leith 1983 is a useful complement here). Next to follow is Trudgill's brief description of "Standard English in England" (32-44), which is mainly about some characteristic features of St E, and its delimitation as against other national standards, but which also has a short section on ongoing changes (41-43). This is complemented by two chapters on pronunciation, Gimson's "The RP accent" (45-54), in which changes within our time receive some attention, and Wells' "English accents in England" (55-69), a technical description, sound by sound, of pronunciation habits outside the small group of RP speakers. Such regional characteristics of accent must not be confused with 'dialect', as Wakelin's "Rural dialects in England" (70-93) makes clear. This concise sketch is admirable for its selection and arrangement of heterogeneous material; however, more information on present-day functions of broad dialect, and on the social history of this restriction, would have been welcome. (Such treatments are found for the other regions in Part IV, but there is none on rural England provided there). Scotland receives a chapter to itself; Aitken deals competently with 'Scottish accents and dialects" (94-114): rather than separating ScE from Scots (whose status as an independent language as represented by rural and urban dialects and by the Lallans literary tradition might have been argued for), Aitken here sees the situation as a sociolinguistic continuum – which it certainly is for the great majority of its speakers, whatever the linguistic history of Scots. His exposition of the Vowel Length Rule and of coexisting phonological systems is wonderfully clear; in the second half of his paper, when he comes to discuss covert and overt Scotticisms, vulgarisms, Morningside English, 'dying' Scots (*Thise been the cokkes wordes and nat myne*), the Highland Line and the Border, there is some overlap with Chapter 30 ("Scots and English in Scotland", 517-32, also by Aitken) which is reserved to bidialectalism and its social consequences. (Here, as in the case of Celtic-English bilingualism in Wales, Scotland and Ireland, the editorial decision to split off the sociolinguistic situation has resulted in some incoherence which makes it difficult for the reader to correlate linguistic features and social functions).

Reflecting the historical divergence, two chapters are devoted to Ireland: Harris treats "English in the North of Ireland" (115-34); again, a discussion of pronunciation features predominates, these being most distinctive and best researched. Matters are different in the Republic, where the Celtic substratum influence is much stronger, and where divergent lexical and syntactical features are more conspicuous, a state of affairs adequately treated in Bliss' "English in the South of Ireland" (135-51). Again, more on the uses of the varieties would have been welcome – the two corresponding chapters in Part IV, Douglas-Cowie's "The sociolinguistic situation in Northern Ireland" (533-45) and Edwards' "Irish and English in Ireland" (480-98) being not closely correlated or correlatable to the earlier 'linguistic' chapters. Historical considerations are apparently behind the decision to group the Englishes of four former Celtic-speaking areas together and place them after "Ireland". Shuken's "Highland and Island English" (152-66) and Thomas' "Welsh English" (178-95) are on speech forms largely used by bilingual speakers (or at least those in whose families the shift to English is not too far away so that interferences are still noticeable) – the tendency being, however, towards Englishes without obvious Celtic traces apart from some articulatory and intonational features. Both accounts are sketches, as a consequence of the neglect of these L2 varieties by traditional dialectologists and modern sociolinguists. The situation is different with Barry's "Manx English" (167-77) and Wakelin's "Cornish English" (195-8); these could have been included under "Rural dialects" and were of course covered by Ellis' and Wright's investigations and by the Leeds SED collections (which also make the body of available material much larger for the two areas).

Two more recent developments are treated at the end of the English section: Milroy's "Urban dialects in the British Isles" (199-218) justly covers the complete area since methodological problems of urban surveys and of quantitative linguistics in general are similar for Norwich, Bradford, Glasgow and Belfast, however much the linguistic data and their social correlates may differ. The greater part of her account is an annotated summary of existing research, especially of the last twenty years after the completion of the SED opened the way for Labovian and post-Labovian sociolinguistics. It is a pity that Milroy – who would have been in an excellent position to do so – did not expand on "the typology of urban dialects" which forms the conclusion of her chapter (214f., and cf. Romaine's critical account, 1980). Sutcliffe's "British Black English and West Indian creoles" (219-37) deals with one important variety of immigrants' English, investigating how far a post-creole continuum of the Jamaican type persists in Britain; he first supplies a description of significant features of JamC and then adds a contrastive sketch of its British descendant. (Other ethnic Englishes, such as Gujerati English, and the state of research on them are treated later in the book, by Reid in his "The newer minorities: spoken languages and varieties", 408-24, and by Martin-Jones, "The newer minorities: literacy and educational issues", 425-48 – whereas the 'applied' equivalent of Sutcliffe's paper is placed right at the end of the book, where V.K. Edwards, the expert on the subject, deals with "British Black English and education", 559-72). Such an arrangement, however, makes it difficult to contrast BrBE as a second dialect with English as a second language for Asian speakers.

Section II is reserved to Celtic languages; Thomson's useful introductory survey on "The history of the Celtic languages in the British Isles" (241-58) is followed by Awberry's "Welsh" (259-77), Thomas' "Cornish" (278-88), Ó Doghartaigh's "Irish" (289-305), Thomson's "Manx" (306-17) and Clement's "Gaelic" (318-42). All of these are technical, with a few remarks at best of the history of the language, the weight being given to spelling, pronunciation, morphology, syntax and varieties; moreover their arrangements differ greatly, without apparent reason. This makes the chapters less accessible to the non-initiated than they might have been, and if a reader feels tempted to skip a few pages in this huge book, this section is a likely choice.

"Other languages" are treated in Part III: they have never had more than a peripheral position in Britain, and are fast receding today if they survive at all. But their marginal status also means that information about them is not easy to come by and for many readers of Trudgill's collection the topics may be completely new. Spence writes on "Channel Island French" (345-51), which is still spoken by a few (bilingual) speakers. Right at the other geographical extreme, "Orkney and Shetland Norn" (352-66) is now a matter of linguistic archaeology; Barnes summarizes the history and structure of this Scandinavian dialect which was supplanted by Scots, and later by English, in the course of the 16th to 18th centuries. Hancock writes on four languages without a geographical base, and which are probably even less known: "Romani and Angloromani" (367-83) are Travellers' languages or rather two ends of a continuum of the traditional languages of North Indian provenance still current, with morphological adjustments, all over Europe, and a variety which is English in everything but a section of the vocabulary (and which, therefore, it is very problematic to classify as either 'Romani' or 'English'). Even less known (and less investigated) are "Shelta and Polari" (384-402), the former a secret language of Irish tinkers with Irish roots but excessive deliberate modifications, and Polari, probably not a full language, but rather a cantlike relexification of English, with a very reduced lexicon, and now moribund or dead.

Part IV, "The sociolinguistic situation" has already been referred to, *passim*. Two chapters on immigrants' speech are followed by three on societal and individual bilingualism in Celtic areas: Bellin's "Welsh and English in Wales", 449-79: J. Edwards' "Irish and English in Ireland", 480-98, and MacKinnon's "Scottish Gaelic and English in the Highlands" (499-516). These are competent and realistic accounts of Celtic speech communities crumbling along the fringes, essays which permit interesting comparisons with the treatments of the same topics in Haugen (1981). Finally, there are four essays on various forms of bidialectalism and its educational consequences: on Scots vs. English, on N. Ireland, on nonstandard English and education, and on Black English and education. In many ways this part IV could have been the heart of the book, but it is now pushed to the end where the reader's attention may have flagged – but since knowledge of the contents of the preceding portions is assumed it is no use starting the book at p.405.

References to further reading are at the end of the 33 individual chapters. This was probably the most convenient solution with so many and so divergent topics, but this arrangement also means some overlap – and some diligent searching for those who wish to check bibliographical details. An exhaustive glossary of linguistic terms and a very useful index conclude the book.

This is an admirable collection, and some individual chapters are among the best summaries written on the topics in question. Despite the great number of contributors the editor has achieved comparatively similar treatments (abbreviations and phonetic transcriptions should probably be standardized further). There is only one major snag – as will have become clear from my remarks above: a strictly geographical arrangement, which would have kept the distinctive structural features of each variety together with the socio-historical factors that condition them, the historical development of the variety, its expansion vis-à-vis competing languages, and continuing influences exerted by StE receding or continuing bidialectalism and their causes – all these are parts of an ecological whole, and an understanding of the system is necessary for a correlation and explanation of its parts. *Disiecta*, in the present volume, are not only the *membra*, but since these were written by different people, some of the pieces of the puzzle are missing.

Coming from Trudgill's collection, one soon becomes aware how much the contents of Price's book differ from it; in fact, Price's text shows only minimal overlap with it (e.g. in the chapters on Channel Island French and Romani where the material is very limited). Historical (or even prehistoric) stages of languages clearly predominate in Price: a comparison of the number of pages devoted to individual language families with those in Trudgill (in parentheses) will illustrate the difference in focus: Prehistoric 15 (-), Celtic 130 (104, not counting the chapters on "X + English"), Latin 12 (-), Germanic, including English 37 (252, not counting the 'applied' chapters), French 25 (7) and Romani 9 (17). Moreover, of the 17 languages treated in Price, eleven are extinct (Pictish, Irish in Britain, Irish in N. Ireland, Manx, British, Cornish, Cumbric, Celtic Pictish, Norse, Anglo-Norman, Anglo-Latin – if all of these are really separate languages).

Price's aims are, then, to cover all "the languages that have been spoken for some considerable length of time ... in the United Kingdom, the Isle of Man and the Channel Islands" (p.9; Eire, which is included by Trudgill, is here omitted). Scots is accorded a chapter "even though I consider it a dialect of English rather than a distinct language" (10). The languages are described in "roughly chronological order" (10), which groups them into those of the "Early Arrivals"; the Celtic languages; Latin; the Germanic languages; French; Romani. Price (who refers the reader to Lockwood (1975) for detailed information on the grammatical structure of the languages treated) explicitly states that he "is concerned with the languages as social phenomena ... with their role as standard or literary languages, with their decline and ... disappearance" (11) – this modern approach is partly thwarted, however, by the fact that relevant data are not available for at least half of his languages, or even more, considering how little we know about, say, the sociolinguistics of Anglo-Norman.

It is a precarious enterprise to write on the language(s) of "Prehistoric Britain" (13-19) since even placename evidence is ambiguous, and it is not much easier to give a sober account of "Pictish" (20-27), but Price carries out the tasks with a healthy degree of caution. "Irish in early Britain" (28-38) can at least be based on some Ogam inscriptions in South Wales, but the material is admittedly scanty, so that the main account of Irish (Eire being excluded) is in the chapter "Irish in N. Ireland" (39-47), which traces the expansion of English from 1169, but especially after 1600, and the decline of Irish as a combined result of English settlement, English schooling, the Famine and consequent emigration. The account of "Scottish Gaelic" (48-70) is much fuller: Price outlines its social history through the Middle Ages (which saw an increasing anglicization of the Lowlands) on to the Statutes of Iona (1609), the consequences of the 1745 Rising, and the Clearances after 1782, the Education Act of 1872, and 20th-century losses through the schools, the media and increased mobility. "Manx" (71-84) is another language that has succumbed to English, if only so recently that it was possible to make tape recordings with the last native speakers. Price is back to placename evidence in "British" (84-93), the all-England predecessor of Welsh/Cornish, which had, however, receded to almost modern linguistic boundaries in late Anglo-Saxon times – except for the southwest (Cornish) and the northwest (treated in chapter 10 under "Cumbric", 146-54). Although British, Cumbric, Welsh (and possibly also "Celtic Pictish", 155-7) can and should be treated as independent languages, their combination in one chapter would have given a better balance – after all, Price has no qualms about putting Danelaw Scandinavian and Norn together in one chapter. The story of Welsh (94-133) has been retold repeatedly in the past few years; Price's account, though the longest chapter in the book, adds little except that the early history of the language is given more room than is usual. Its decline is documented with care, from the Act of Union (1536) to its modern shrinkage in spite of recent improvements in its official and legal status. One interesting aspect of "Cornish" (134-45), extinct for some 200 years, is the recent attempt of revivalists to raise it from the dead, and Price has some critical remarks on the quality of such neo-Cornish. "Latin" (158-69) is here treated only as the natively spoken language of pre-449, which is in accordance with Price's principles, but curiously inadequate considering the real impact of Latin all through English history, and the history of English. The small space reserved for English (170-85), Scots (186-93) and Norse (194-206) speaks for itself. In particular, the history of English is a mere sketch concentrating on the emergence of successive standards, the resulting devaluation of dialect, and some account of traditional dialectology. The impression one gets is that the reader is expected to know about the history of his own language from other sources, and that its present-day varieties and functions are not Price's central concern. Scots is reluctantly given a chapter although Price does not commit himself and treats it as an independent language. He provides a competent summary of its development, which is, however, too sketchy to leave room for detail. The two sections on "Norse" (194-206) are again useful for quick information: the story of the Scandinavian dialects of 10th- and 11th-century England is summarized from many sources, and there is an outline of Norn based on Marwick and Jakobsen. Two chapters on French follow: his "French in the Channel Islands" (207-16) is based on both his own fieldwork and on every bit of printed evidence available to describe the history and present-day decline of the three island dialects. His chapter on medieval Anglo-Norman (217-31) has the qualities of the other accounts: a diligent summary with cautious conclusions (Berndt's research in the field might have been mentioned). Finally, there is a chapter on "Romani" (232-40), an objective estimate of the obsolescence of the inflected variety, and a description of varying degrees of retention of Romani words, and the vitality of Anglo-Romani as a secret language acquired in adolescence.

Price has produced a carefully and cautiously written account of Britain's languages; his concentration on the earlier stages of the languages treated makes his work a good complement to the essays collected by Trudgill.

References
Haugen, Einar, ed. 1981. *Minority Languages Today.* Edinburgh: UP.
Leith, Dick. 1983. *A Social History of English.* London: Routledge.
Lockwood, W.B. 1975. *Languages of the British Isles Past and Present.* London: Deutsch.
Romaine, Suzanne. 1980 "A critical overview of the methodology of urban British sociolinguistics", *EWW* 1: 163-98.

20 Peter Trudgill, *Dialects in Contact.* (Language in Society). Oxford: Blackwell, 1986, viii + 174pp.; from *EWW* 8 (1987), 128-31.

This necessary and eminently stimulating book has been in the making for a long time. Announced as *Sociolinguistics and Linguistic Change* in 1983, it is still "concerned with the subject of linguistic change", though admittedly with "a very restricted set of all the possible types of change that can occur in the language" (1).

The question of dialects in contact obviously has to do with speakers of one variety accommodating their speech to that of another, newcomers adjusting to old settlers, salesmen to customers (or vice versa), campaigning politicians to audiences of voters, or scholars changing places in a small world to their new linguistic habitats (Trudgill's own experience in the U.S. as reflected in ch.1). Trudgill shows that the phenomenon is sadly underresearched, but that his own Norwich interviews of many years ago, now relistened to, exhibit such accommodation even in his own questioning. He starts by explaining in detail how linguistic accommodation works in its short-time form (4-5) and leads on to types of partial accommodation in the style of British pop singers imitating AmE (13-14). Such behaviour can be explained by the salience of individual features (markers), which leads speakers to acquire these in a certain order (20). The process will be speeded up where comprehensibility is at risk (23), but features can also be too salient to be affected. Accommodation in inflected languages also affects the morphology, as Trudgill shows in the speech of Swedes living in Norway (24-28). However, accommodation is always partial, even with young children, as is illustrated by case histories from Australia, Canada and Norwich (31-37). Chapter 2, on "dialect contact" (39-82) sets out, then, to explore how linguistic forms are transmitted from one geographical area to another at the level of the individual speaker (diffusion, 39-40). On the basis of recent developments in his native East Anglia, Trudgill lucidly demonstrates how transfer of London items and various forms of adaptation arise. He carefully weighs the complications resulting from incomplete and variable accommodation based on individual lexical items, classifying the 'new' dialects as 'mixed', 'fudged' or 'interdialect' (60-64). Whether these three types are clearly distinguishable in reality must remain an open question: the case of Reading auxiliary shows that "dialect contact via accommodation, with or without diffusion, is a complex process. We must be alert to interaction among dialects, rather than straightforward influence, as being instrumental in the development of interdialect" (65). The picture is further complicated by hyperdialectalisms, where dialect features are applied in the wrong lexical sets or in wrong functions, thus neutralizing earlier contrasts (67-70); compare the detailed discussion of 'wrong' [r] (71-78) and 'Bristol' [l] (78-81).

There is no doubt that such processes lie behind the growth of new dialects, the topic of chapter 3 (83-126). Mixture is first exemplified by the fascinating case of Fronteiriço on the Uruguay/Brazil border, and by the St Kitts post-creole continuum (86-91). In divergent (bi-dialectal) speech communities a new regional norm can develop through a fudged dialect; Trudgill here adduces examples from Sweden and Norway (88-99) and from Fiji Bojpuri (99-102): Scottish and German instances might here have provided even more compelling illustrations. Simplification, too, is a normal result of contact where inflections are in conflict, as is illutrated by Norwegian (102-6) and Trinidadian Hindi (106f.) examples – processes that are in fact likely to have occurred in the early history of English in the Danelaw. Finally, Norwich and Belfast pronunciations demonstrate that forms originally from different dialects can (but need not) be retained as social alternatives rather than be levelled out (118): re-allocation and accommodation combine in the formation of the new compromise system. (The process if referred to as koinéization, a descriptively adequate, but somewhat unwieldy term in English). Much of the above discussion is something of an overture to chapter 4 (127-61), in which several colonial Englishes (mainly of Canada, Australia and South Africa) are – rightly – interpreted as cases of such koinéization: the new, focussed dialects cannot be regarded as survivals of earlier speech forms, and a naive hunt for predecessor forms in British dialects must therefore be fruitless. It is, however, possible to establish the regions the early emigrants must have come from. There is, for instance, no British (English or Scottish) dialect with the distribution of diphthong qualities found in 'Canadian Raising' (156) – but similar features are found in other colonial varieties (160), which proves that all must be the results of new levelling processes in mixed colonial dialects in which diverging diphthong pronunciations in settler dialects were redistributed as allophonic variants. Trudgill's interpretation of AusE, as originating from koinéization on Australian soil (129-46) is the most plausible explanation of the phenomenon to date, and the interpretations of 'Canadian Raising' offered by J.K. Chambers gain further plausibility when viewed within the larger colonial framework.

Trudgill's arguments are convincing throughout. They might have had even greater weight if the existing literature on dialects in contact had been taken into account. This applies in particular to the vast literature dealing with comparable situations in German-speaking areas: dialect 'islands' resulting from internal migration, levelling (Ausgleichssprache) in emigrant communities of the 12th to 19th centuries in Central and Eastern Europe and in Pennsylvania and Brazil – and re-migration, with subsequent (still on-going) accommodation after 1945. These remarks should be taken as suggestions for further study; they are not meant to detract from the value of the book. Such inclusion of all available evidence might finally bring us closer to a decision about whether we are entitled to make any prognostication on language development. Although Trudgill is somewhat pessimistic about the prospects himself, there is to my mind too much positivist assurance in his claims when he says:

> The ultimate goal of work of this type will be to predict exactly what will occur when one dialect, with a given set of linguistic and demographic characteristics, comes into contact in a particular way with another dialect with different characteristics. (2)

A theory that adequately explains what has already happened would surely be much more than we have at present, and would seem an aim worthy of our energy.

21 Charles Jones, ed., *The Edinburgh History of the Scots Language*. Edinburgh: UP, 1997, xi+690pp; from *Linguistics* 37 (1999), 358-64.

The monumental collection under review is, strange as it may seem, the first entirely devoted to Scots, dealing with the variety as a historical entity in a comprehensive way; earlier surveys of the type were sketches of less than book length or concentrated on individual topics. The most satisfactory account to date is therefore McClure's (1994, a title strangely overlooked in Jones' book), but McClure's chapter is misnamed "English in Scotland" and it misleadingly appeared in a volume devoted to *Englishes*. The uncertainty on whether Scots should be regarded as a language or as a dialect of English in fact partly explains the absence of comprehensive scholarly treatments of it: where would we expect to find a university course devoted to the analysis, let alone the teaching, of Scots outwith Scotland?

Jones' book comprises 15 chapters organized in three parts. The first covers "the beginnings to 1700", that is, the time corresponding to EModE and roughly to the period of at least partial Scottish political independence (which ended with the Union of the Parliaments in 1707).

By way of introduction, Meurman-Solin gives a succinct survey of the "Differentiation and standardization in Early Scots" (3-23), discussing the criteria that make it possible for historical linguists to call Scots a 'language' (cf. Görlach 1991:18-23). Basing her statements on the historical (Helsinki) corpus of early Scottish texts of various genres, she provides much new information on how the distinctive features that make up the Scottishness of a text are spread through individual genres, thus neatly complementing earlier research by Devitt (1989). That her analysis is now based on a computerized corpus (so far untagged) should of course not blind us to the provisional nature of many statements; this preliminary character is caused by the comparatively small size and consequent selectiveness of the corpus used (as Moessner rightly points out on p. 115, giving seven unambiguous instances of auxiliary *do* from *The Complaynt of Scotland* where Meurman-Solin's excerpt of the text produces none). The spread of *do* into Scots, 1560-1700, is in fact far from adequately documented; Meurman-Solin's conclusions (1993) are misleading being largely based on a highly anglicized text, James VI/I's *Counterblaste* of 1603, which was written after his move to London.

Kniezsa's "The origins of Scots orthography" (24-46) is on a topic which has proved most fruitful for the history of standardization in any of the vernaculars rising to, or being raised to, the status of a national language in the Renaissance. Kniezsa treats her topic in great historical depth, starting from OE conditions. The obvious impression (especially when developments are compared with those in contemporary EModE) is that in the Renaissance when Scots came close to being a standard language, there was no institution, nor at least an élite, in Scotland that took seriously the question of distancing their *leid* from English on the level most easily affected by language planning – spelling. The sociolinguistic reason for this is only too apparent: the so-called the anglicization of Scottish culture left no room for language-planning measures vis-à-vis the predominance and higher prestige of Latin and English. It is well to remember that full confidence in the resources of English to provide an alternative to Latin dates only from 1575-80, when the decline of Scots was already in full progress.

Johnston, in his "Older Scots phonology and regional variation" (47-111), was able to build on the insightful research of the late A. J. Aitken – a name which is sadly missed among the contributors; his seminal article of 1977 has provided the basis of most recent descriptions, including discussions of 'Aitken's' Law. As the length of the chapter indicates, Johnston's reliable description is painstakingly detailed, taking the reader through developments from OE segments to present-day dialect representations resulting from unconditioned and conditioned sound changes. However, his (and Kniezsa's) chapter lacks a succinct survey correlating graphemes and phonology – after all, in the absence of orthoepists dealing with Scots of the calibre Hart or (the Scotsman) Gil, spellings are the best evidence for a reconstruction of pronunciation and, with expected delays in recording them, for phonetic change.

Moessner's "The syntax of Older Scots" (112-55) is a solid and well-ordered account of the indigenous structures in a largely structuralist-descriptive framework. There is only little contrastive consideration of EModE which would have been helpful to explain the why's and how's of the impact of *Sudron* and the gradual erosion of specifically Scots syntax – but, then, these developments, such as the takeover of *do*, aspectual distinctions and word-order regularities modelled on English have been insufficiently investigated, scholars having concentrated on other syntactical features, e.g., the modals and relative pronouns. King's chapter on "The inflectional morphology of Older Scots" (156-81) is justifiably short, the loss or merger of endings having by 1500 done away with many distinctions (as in EModE, which is strikingly similar by way of parallel development). It is, however, strange to find only half a page (178) devoted to tense marking in strong verbs, since the situation in this field is complex and lends itself to detailed analyses, whether synchronic or diachronic, Scots-internal or contrastive with EModE (cf. Görlach 1996).

Macafee's "Older Scots lexis" (182-212) summarizes the evidence in a handy manner, and includes a discussion of the lexicography of Scots. Her position is a bit precarious since many statements, especially quantificational ones, are provisional as long as the *Dictionary of the Older Scottish Tongue* is incomplete and not available for computer-based research. In spite of these restrictions, she is able to provide very informative statistics on the sources of Scots lexis (the predominant aspect here treated). Jack's "The language of literary materials: origins to 1700" (213-63) supplies a great deal of valuable information on forms and functions of literary texts in the period; however, it is disappointing in that obvious answers to linguistic topics are not provided (and the relevant questions were probably never asked): Jack's chapter is one written by a literary scholar who was insufficiently aware of what exciting contribution his field had to make to the history of the language, a neglect which is particularly sad and consequential, since the later history of Scots was based so much on the literary language/poetic diction from the 'Scottish Revival' of the 18th century onwards. Even where Jack promises to concentrate on "linguistic issues" in ch. 7.5 on John Knox and James IV (253-6), he fails to provide a clear analysis.

The second part on "1700 to the present day" duly opens with the editor's chapter "Phonology" (267-334); as in Johnston's account, the amount of detail is stunning – of course there is much more comprehensive information on pronunciation from the 18th century onwards (and Jones was here able to fall back on his relevant research and lifelong interest in the subject matter, cf. Jones 1991, 1996); however, much of Jones' discussion is on Scottish English rather than on Scots, and it is difficult to say how much of this bias is caused by the character of the sources available – educated Scotsmen writing on language would tend to be concerned, as 'North Britons', with the correct pronunciation and grammar of the new standard language rather than with their provincial vernacular.

Beal's "Syntax and morphology" (335-77) combines the two linguistic levels, since the subchapter on inflection is short (again, less is said on strong past-tense formation than might have been expected). In 'syntax', Beal has very relevant remarks on relatives, the definite article, modal verbs, negation, progressives and discourse features. The account is descriptive, and implicitly contrastive with the English system – but it does not link up properly with Moessner's chapter (and it cannot in cases like 'negation', a topic which is not treated by Moessner). Here, as elsewhere in the book, the division into two periods results in the failure to achieve a coherent linguistic history.

Tulloch's "Lexis" (378-432) rightly concentrates on that part of the vocabulary which is exclusive to Scots. He skilfully sets the problem of lexical expansion against the background of the 18th-century 'Revival' and continues with what Gaelic, Irish, Welsh, Latin, French and Germanic languages have contributed. Word-formation, extension of meaning and revivals are all illustrated with well-chosen examples, as is his treatment of losses and geographical distributions. In all this, Tulloch is able to build on the excellent lexicographical tradition from Jamieson to MacLeod from which he expertly drew his specimens and much of his argumentation.

Johnston's "Regional variation" (433-513) is impressively detailed – a necessary consequence of the fact that dialects and regional norms are the soul of present-day Scots, and of the atomization of varieties as a result of the 'non-roofed' situation and the communicational break up into many small speech-communities. This left no choice for the author but to deal with the forms and functions of regiolects one by one – and he has done so with a great deal of success. Since his interest is concentrated on phonetics, the careful analysis of vowel systems takes up an enormous space (449-99); however, this apparent bias is partly justified by the salience of vowels in the distinction (and recognition) of dialects.

Research in progress is summarized in Macafee's "Ongoing change in Modern Scots. The social dimension" (514-48). There has been a great deal of research on Glasgow (including her own), but other rewarding areas have been sadly neglected (including Aberdeen where the author is now based). Her remarks, provisional as they still are, make stimulating reading, in particular as regards the question of how many Scotsmen can be considered (or consider themselves) speakers of Scots, and her clear summaries of the results of sociolinguistic studies undertaken in speech communities in Glasgow, Edinburgh, Ayrshire and the Borders are excellent.

Part III has three papers on Scots outside the Scottish Lowlands. Ó Baoill looks at "The Scots-Gaelic interface" (551-68), starting with the decline of, and attitudes towards, Celtic, and leading on to the history of language contact in the Highlands and its consequences. Montgomery and Gregg deal with "The Scots language in Ulster" (569-622) – a most felicitous choice of authors, who have contributed so substantially to our understanding of the emigrant Scottish community and their changing speech in Northern Ireland: the political history, demography, religion and changes of norms and linguistic prestige are here presented in a convincing account which combines clarity and reliability with great readability. Tulloch's "The Scots language in Australia" is much shorter, but no less stimulating, covering much-neglected aspects of the survival of Scots in the Empire. Tulloch here provides a fascinating sketch of how the speakers initially retained their identity but were ultimately merged in one of the great melting-pots by way of colonial levelling. (For the demographic history, Jupp [1988: 759-90] might have been mentioned). It is a pity that no attempt is made here to contrast the ethnic and linguistic history of the Australian Scots with their fate in other colonies, such as the United States., Canada and, particularly, New Zealand (cf. Bauer 1997).

The structure of the book shows some peculiarities which are partly a result of the nature of the data and the specific character of Scots, but which also depend on the organization of the project. Phonology prevails (with 65+71 pages) over syntax (including inflexion: 44+26+43 pages), and lexis is less prominent than might have been expected. The chapter on spelling in the first part has no modern equivalent, nor has that on literary language, whereas the early part lacks equivalents of the modern regional and sociolinguistic treatments. Finally, 'standardization' is only dealt with in a special chapter in part I. "Is Scots a language?" might have been a good corresponding title for a chapter in part II.

However, the most striking absence in part II is that there is no equivalent to Jack's chapter on the language of Scots literature in I. This is particularly grievous since much of the tradition of Scots is literary, and there would be no norm for the modern language at all if it were not for the forms standardized for literary genres. Due to this neglect, one of the most important figures for a discussion of 18th-century Scots, Robert Fergusson, is, as the index shows, mentioned only three times, with references worth quoting: "the poems of Fergusson and Burns" (50); "Scots usage in the poetry of such as Allan Ramsay, Fergusson and, of course, Burns" (338); "initiated by Ramsay himself, Burns, Fergusson and others" (501) – as if the name came up only as a conditioned reflex of a mention of Burns. It is therefore not surprising that most of the writers who have given Scots a great deal of distinction in this century are not even mentioned (Annand, Garioch, Gibbon, Leonard, McLellan, Scott, Soutar and many others). Since excellent authors for such a chapter on literary Scots (such as Aitken or McClure) would have been available, it is difficult to see why it was not provided.

Although it is precarious to summarize one's impressions and criticism of a complex book of this size in a few lines, I will point out a few features which might warrant reconsideration and possibly revision in a second edition:

1) The links between individual chapters should be closer and more explicit. This is most obvious along the historical dimension since this is the objective of the collection: chapters on phonology, syntax and lexis should be so geared to each other that whatever historical continuity there is should be brought out clearly.

2) Obvious gaps, as in the case of the modern Scots literary language, should be filled. It might be useful to reflect on whether the wider concept of 'text types' (which has literary sections as a subdivision) might not do better justice to the phenomenon of a language which has experienced a continuous shrinking in its functions for the last four hundred years (cf. Görlach 1997). Also, it would have been very useful (many would say, necessary) to have had another introductory chapter on the sociolinguistic changes, including the degree of 'languageness', right at the beginning of the collection. This would enable the reader to put the detailed and insufficiently connected treatments in individual chapters in context.

3) Cross-references might be increased to refer to relevant arguments in other chapters, as on p. 435 where the situation in Ulster is documented by older literature, but no reference is made to the excellent chapter in the same book (569-622).

4) Since the history of Scots cannot be seen in isolation but is closely linked with that of English, methods should be devised to indicate parallel developments and contact phenomena in a clear way. Ideally, the book could be geared to a history of English. (I suggested many years ago that the Cambridge History of the English Language might be supplemented by a seventh volume on Scots, but the idea was not taken up).

5) In many contexts, socio-stylistic interpretation of the evidence could be provided or at least extended. To give a single example: lexical innovation was largely

stopped with the dialectalization of Scots. Most of what new words we get in modern Scots are the result of literary, often purist, attempts. However, words like *yearhunner* (for 'century') are widely considered artificial and therefore lack acceptability.

In conclusion it seems fair to say that the collection, for all its limitations, is a major event for the Scots language. Following a long and sophisticated tradition of lexicographical description and promising, but never completed, dialectological research, we here have a long overdue historical description of a *halbsprache* that never made it to independence, a unique variety in the compass of the English world language. As a first attempt of its kind it is open to various kinds of critique which will hopefully be duly considered to produce an improved second edition quite soon. Only then will the book have a chance of becoming a standard textbook which (for all *its* limitations) the *History of the English Language* by A.C. Baugh has become.

References

Aitken, A.J. 1977. "How to pronounce Older Scots". In A.J. Aitken, M.P. McDiarmid & D.S. Thomsen, eds. *Bards and Makars: Scots Language and Literature, Medieval and Renaissance.* Glasgow: UP, 1-21.

Bauer, Laurie. 1997. "Attempting to trace Scottish influence in New Zealand English." In Schneider, Edgar W., ed. *Englishes around the World. Studies in Honour of Manfred Görlach.* (VEAW G 19) Amsterdam: Benjamins, II: 257-72.

Baugh, Albert C. and Thomas Cable. [4]1993. *A History of the English Language.* London: Routledge (first ed. 1935).

Devitt, Amy J. 1989. *Standardizing Written English: Diffusion in the Case of Scotland 1520-1659.* Cambridge: UP.

Görlach, Manfred. 1991. *Introduction to Early Modern English.* Cambridge: UP (2nd ed. of the German original, Heidelberg: Winter 1994)

---. 1996. "Morphological standardization: the strong verb in Scots." In Derek Britton, ed. *English Historical Linguistics.* Amsterdam: Benjamins, 161-81.

---. 1997. "Text types and the history of Scots." *JEL* 25: 209-30.

Jones, Charles, ed. 1991. *A Treatise on the Provincial Dialect of Scotland, by Sylvester Douglas.* Edinburgh: UP.

---. 1996. *A Language Suppressed: The Pronunciation of the Scots Language in the Eighteenth Century.* Edinburgh: John Donald.

Jupp, James, ed. 1988. *The Australian People.* Sydney: Angus & Robertson. ("Scots", pp. 759-90)

McClure, J.D. 1994. "English in Scotland." In Robert Burchfield, ed. *English in Britain and Overseas: Origins and Development.* (CHEL 5). Cambridge: UP, 23-93.

Meurman-Solin, Anneli. 1993. "Periphrastic and auxiliary do in early Scottish prose genres." In M. Rissanen, M. Kytö & M. Palander-Collin, eds. *Early English in the Computer Age: Explorations through the Helsinki Corpus.* Berlin & New York: Mouton de Gruyter, 235-51.

22 John Corbett, *Written in the Language of the Scottish Nation. A History of Literary Translation into Scots*. Clevedon: Multilingual Matters, 1999, vii+199 pp; from *European English Messenger* 8:2 (1999), 155-6.

Translations have played an important role for literature in Scots and in the quest for a standard form and the enrichment of the national language (if it is ever to be one). Therefore it comes as a surprise that we have lacked so far a comprehensive account of what translations have meant for Scots in the course of the past six hundred years. Corbett provides such a survey which combines a great deal of information with succinctness and legibility. He starts from general principles of the interfaces of translation and literature, language planning and nationhood, and a reasonably short précis of forerunners to 1500 and then proceeds to give a well-reasoned account of the major translations (and their authors) of the 16th century – Douglas's *Eneados* of ca. 1513, Bellenden's *Chroniklis* of 1531 and the activities of the court poets of James VI. He points out what function as models for imitation the two early works might have had, if a fully fledged standard language had come into being in Renaissance Scotland, and stresses Douglas's enormous achievement in creating the first epic on British soil. The failure to print a Scottish translation of the Bible is convincingly explained by the hypothesis that English versions fulfilled Lyndsay's (1554) demand of having the text available "in the vulgar (vernacular) tongue." Drummond and Urquhart are interpreted as illustrating the major change in the 17th century, when the translator's choice was reduced to English (neutral or high style) or Scots (for low style) – a development that was to be dominant well into the 20th century.

In 18th- and 19th-century Scots literature translations are not prominent; Corbett places the works by Ramsay, Fergusson, Jamieson, Buchanan and a few others (many of the texts resembling paraphrases rather than translations) into proper context. The revived interest in translation in the 20th century was largely prompted by MacDiarmid's appeal to make Scots a truly European language, by the desire to fill the gaps left in former centuries and by language-planning considerations of enriching an impoverished vernacular; all these topics are treated with a great deal of insight. The history of biblical translation is justly included in the survey – Lorimer's outstanding *New Testament* is as much a literary achievement as it is a neglected text for public and private worship. Corbett also includes fascinating specimens of translations from OE elegies and of course of the two recent Scots renderings of Shakespeare's *Macbeth*; he does not mention a marginal category which Scotophiles hope will never flourish – translations of Scots texts into English.

Corbett has here drawn together a surprising amount of detail, reliably summarizing a large number of scholarly publications, carefully reducing the evidence to the most relevant arguments and propping these up with excellent quotations and excerpts from the translations discussed.

There are, then, only a few topics a reader might have wished to see treated more extensively. I will summarize these in five points:

The great range of texts here treated raises the question what should come under the label of 'translation'. An introductory chapter devoted to the problem might have put the reader in a better position to evaluate some of the statements. Does translating into a *Halbsprache* add specific problems, and which?

The concentration on Scots has meant that the English tradition is not sufficiently taken into account. However, if it was an argument as early as 1560 that a Bible in Scots was not necessary because various English versions were available, must we not assume that e.g. Golding's *Ovid*, North's *Plutarch* or Pope's *Homer* made Scots translations equally unnecessary, especially since Scots had not created proper styles as demanded by the classical requirement of genre-specific decorum? A conspectus of the major English translations of the works of individual authors available to contrast with Scots attempts might have been helpful here.

This omnipresence of English as a written standard is also somewhat neglected in the discussions of the linguistic background. The fact becomes quite obvious from the bibliography, which does not list any of the major handbooks of the history of English, in particular those dealing with EModE which cover a great deal of common ground (e.g. Görlach 1991). Also not mentioned are more technical discussions of the linguistic evidence like that analysed in Devitt's book (1989) – which would have been useful for the discussion of anglicization between 1560 and 1660.

Corbett was clearly forced to select, but there might have been a compromise in at least listing other translations not discussed in detail. Thus, many readers will be likely to miss some of their favourites – as I do the excellent renderings of *Max und Moritz*, which also permit a comparison of four translations into different dialects of Scots (Görlach 1986).

Finally, the admirably full bibliography has only few omissions. Apart from the ones mentioned above, the fact that Jones (1997) is missed is probably the greatest surprise. Was the book too recent to be included?

The book fills a desideratum, and does so in exemplary form. It should be on all Scotophiles' bookshelves, complementing Lorimer's *New Testament* and the *Concise Scots Dictionary*.

References

Devitt, Amy. 1989. *Standardizing Written English. Diffusion in the Case of Scotland, 1520-1659*. Cambridge: UP.

Görlach, Manfred, ed. 1986. *Max and Moritz in English Dialects and Creoles*. Hamburg: Buske.

---. 1991. *Introduction to Early Modern English*. Cambridge: UP.

Jones, Charles, ed. 1997. *The Edinburgh History of the Scots Language*. Edinburgh: UP.

23 Graham Tulloch, *A History of the Scots Bible*, with selected texts. Aberdeen: UP, 1989, x + 184 pp.; from *EWW* 11 (1990), 158-61.

For those brought up on the creed that there has never been a Bible in Scots, nor even substantial portions of it, before Lorimer's *New Testament* (published in 1983), it must come as a surprise to find a title like that of the book under review. According to the author himself, who knew about Nisbet's (ca. 1520), Smith's (1901) and Lorimer's (1983) versions of large parts of the Bible when he began his research, he was astonished when he found how much else there was besides. Even though, the dictum still holds that the Scots language would be in a different sociolinguistic position and shape if there had been an *accepted* version of the Bible in the Renaissance or, failing that, in the 18th/19th centuries – so long as there was a homiletic reason for it, i.e. so long as preaching and reading the sacred texts in the mither tongue served pastoral aims, and not just literary, nationalistic or nostalgic purposes, for the majority of Scotsmen.

If we accept the view that the Scots language became separated from English in the 14th century, then Nisbet's scoticising of Purvey's version of ca. 1390 is indeed the first 'translation' of the Bible into Scots. However, like Bugenhagen, who transposed Luther's translation and thus created the most influential Low German Bible, Nisbet was content with adapting the orthography/phonology and inflexions, changing the lexis only where diachronic rather than diatopic differences in a version some 130 years old made such changes necessary. Tulloch analyses Nisbet's text in great detail and more favourably than others have done before, defending Nisbet's habit of retaining words shared by English and Scots (8). This practice conspicuously contrasts with that of modern translators who wished to indicate the Scots identity of their texts through the choice of unmistakably Scots words wherever available (and even coining new words where they were not). If Nisbet's text had been printed in his time, it might have helped to establish a formal standard language: "What was needed to maintain a standard of written Scots distinct from that of English was a separate spelling and grammar" – features that the 18th-century 'revivalists' like Ramsay and Burns would possibly not have neglected as they did, had there been such norms available. There was no attempt at biblical translation into Scots in the 17th and 18th centuries, the English Bible becoming the unquestioned authority, and biblical English, together with other formal registers, left the Scots no alternative. New attempts in the 19th century characteristically were motivated by dialectological aims – the versions of portions commissioned by Prince Louis Lucien Bonaparte (19-37), and Murray's *Ruth* (47-54): their significance lies in the fact that they exhibit increasingly realistic, informal features, not being hampered by expectations of a formal style. However, the greatest achievement of the age was Waddell's *Psalms* of 1871 (re-ed. by Tulloch, cf. *EWW* 9, 1988:141f.) and his *Isaiah* of 1879: these texts are rightly seen as the acme of Scots religious language in the 19th century, although it is doubtful whether Waddell struck the right sort of compromise between conflicting demands of retaining as much of the biblical tradition as possible and enriching it with as many Scots features as appeared stylistically justifiable. In his desire to distance Scots from English, Waddell rejected the formal Latinate terms shared by both languages and coined new compounds and derivations instead. He was convinced that Scots had remained truer to its Germanic roots than English had, and consequently felt justified in calquing on the German of Luther (a practice continued by other purists in our *yeirhunner*), which gives his style forcefulness, but also artificiality.

The most exhaustive of more recent attempts came from a Scottish emigrant to Canada: W.W. Smith translated *Matthew* first, and then produced the whole of the *New Testament in Braid Scots* (1901). His aim, as formulated in his Preface, was to render the text into colloquial Scots; in practice, he did not come very close to this, partly because he retained too much from his source text, *The Revised Version*, especially in syntax and style. However, his example is visible in the next two translations, again from English sources, *viz.* Paterson's *Proverbs* of 1917 and Cameron's *Genesis* of 1921, the latter translated by another emigrant, to Australia this time, where among foreign animals he "haes hard athin his saul and abune them a' the 'saft, couthie' müsick of the Doric" (65). Cameron is a good example of how the various strands of the tradition, especially Waddell, Smith and Paterson, come together.

Among recent translators Tulloch unreservedly approves of Borrowman's *Ruth* (printed posthumously in 1979) and finds J. Stuart's modernized and consistently scoticized selections, intended for public performance, worthy of note. However, the highest praise is reserved for Lorimer's *New Testament in Scots* on which the translator worked for many years, working straight from the Greek and comparing a great number of translations into European languages (cf. *EWW* 4, 1983:325-7). Lorimer, born near Dundee but not himself a native speaker of Scots, produced a text that combines extreme faithfulness to the original with high literary quality and a rare feeling for the potential of Scots, including convincing specimens of its colloquial vigour, as Tulloch brings out in his detailed and insightful analysis, an exemplary piece of linguistic stylistics. Lorimer went further than all his predecessors in creating biblical Scots prose, as an antistandard to the all-pervading British variety. He felt justified in this by the character of the Hellenistic koiné used in the New Testament: Tulloch convincingly interprets Lorimer's note "Jesus spakna Standard Aramaic – for ordnar oniegate – but guid ('braid') Galilee" as implying that Scots is an ideal language to translate the N.T. into since "Scots can itself be seen as a standard language, an alternative standard to Standard English but one which follows in many cases the usages of everyday speech (...). What this means for Lorimer is that he can translate the New Testament into informal Scots and thus draw on one of the areas in which Scots has been most vital, the area of colloquial language" (76). Lorimer does accept, on the other hand, those "lang-nebbit dictionar words" that are shared by English and Scots, only indicating in their spelling that they belong to Scots and are not English loans. Tulloch summarizes Lorimer's achievement as follows: "what really makes his work so important and successful is his creative ingenuity as a translator, his ability to find new and exciting ways of translating familiar passages, in short his ability to revitalize the text" (83). In all this he refrains from judgment on the linguistic impact the book is likely to have.

Although it was an immediate (and quite unexpected) commercial success, the texts have hardly ever been used in church, and it is to be doubted whether many of the buyers are also devoted readers. In Lorimer's text it is only the devil who speaks English (in a discarded draft), but for the majority of Scotsmen English remains the unquestioned sacred language of church services – Lorimer's version comes centuries too late to change this fact.

Apart from the 19th-century versions, Tulloch includes no translations into regional Scots. As readers of [*EWW*] are aware, there are Northeastern and Shetland renderings of short passages, of "The Prodigal Son" in *EWW* 4, 1983:85-91, and of the "Christmas story" in Görlach, ed., *Focus on: Scotland* (1985:211-6), both texts accompanied by Smith's and Lorimer's renderings – and further standard Scots translations by Annand and Low. Although this additional corpus does not amount to much, it would certainly have been worth mentioning.

The second half of the book (95-179) comprises a rich selection of passages from the various translations: this is a very welcome idea, since many of the sources are out of print, and the excerpts are long enough to retrace Tulloch's evaluations. (A reprint of Paterson's and Cameron's translations will seem desirable to all whose appetites have been whetted by the selected passages).

Tulloch has brought his near-native competence in Scots, his erudition and his linguistic-stylistic expertise to bear on the interpretation of this important facet of the Scots tradition to produce a book that equals, and in some ways surpasses, his classic study of *The Language of Sir Walter Scott*.

24 John Holm, *Pidgins and Creoles*. Vol. 1, Theory and Structure. Vol. II, Reference Survey (Cambridge Language Surveys), Cambridge:UP, 1988/1989, xix+257 p. and xxv+447 pp.; from *IF* 97 (1992), 312-4.

To illustrate the recent increase in pidgin and creole languages (PCs) and the explosive growth of information about them, there is, perhaps, nothing better than the fact that one volume was not enough to encompass all the arguments and data of the work under review. Holm, whose interest in the field started in the mainland Caribbean some fifteen years ago, is a specialist in 'Atlantic' English-related PCs, especially the varieties ranging from Black English to Guyanese Creole, and with special expertise in the creoles of the Miskito Coast and the Bahamas. However, not only has his research long since expanded to include other English-related PCs, but he has also complemented his scope by adding the standard and various creole forms of French, Spanish, Portuguese, Dutch and German. His polyglot interests and dedicated and meticulous work made him an excellent choice for the project, the most comprehensive description of the discipline to date. (The list of 159 scholars that he thanks for their help in I:xiii must certainly be unprecedented: it is about the most complete directory of creolists I know of.)

Vol. I is, then, devoted to systematic, historical and structural features of PCs as special types of language. He starts with a necessary definition of terms (including his suggestion that *pidgin* derives from Portugese *baixo* (*português*), the trade language that preceded pidgin English in the Far East). Holm sees his goal as bringing "together the most important information relating to [PCs] as objectively as possible, avoiding tendentiousness in matters of theory" (11), opting for a "moderate substratist position" (§ 2.13). "Theory: a historical overview" (13-70) provides a very readable guided tour of how PCs have been described from antiquity onwards, with prominence given first to Schuchardt, Coelho and Hesseling (27-36) and then to Reinecke, Hall and Taylor (36-44), whose views, much in advance of their time, have recently been 'rediscovered'. The remainder is 'recent history' – with B. Bailey, Whinnom, Stewart, Hancock, Cassidy and Le Page all building the foundations of the modern discipline, with early theoretical tensions becoming apparent between adherents of monogenetic vs. universalist, continua and substratum explanations. For the rest of the book, Holm discusses the three major levels of grammatical organization, "Lexicosemantics" (71-104), "Phonology" (105-43) and "Syntax" (144-215) – the sequence probably reflecting the author's predilections rather than internal cogency. He starts from the assumption that all the creoles he treats share the same semantic structure so that the English- (French- etc.) related *form* of a particular word is a historical 'accident'. Creole lexicons also share the same features (such as archaisms, regionalisms, and particular changes of meaning) and word-formational principles (such as reduplication and multifunctionality). Africanisms (i. e. words surviving complete, or the meanings of words whose form derives from a European language) have had an important position in theories about the early PC lexicon; Holm's summary is balanced and well argued (80-89). On the whole, it becomes clear that the lexicons, apart from the historical links they may prove, contribute little that is constitutive for PCs – the fact that these were originally spoken languages with a minimal lexicon makes certain semantic changes almost inevitable. Similar remarks are in order with regard to the sound systems. Holm justly criticizes the energy that has gone into Cassidy/Le Page's identification of 'reflexes' of English sounds in Jamaican (105): if we assume that pronunciation is the most stable level in language shift, including pidginization, then the quest for English forms, even if there is evidence for them in the early overseer's dialects, is methodologically ill-conceived. Apart from that, there are the expected mergers when lexifier languages of 40-50 phonemes have to be adapted to the phonological habits of speakers of languages that have only 30. In addition, there are modifications arising from differences in phonotactical rules – and this applies to PC words (Sranan *mofo* < *mouth*) as it does to loanwords (Hausa *sukurudireba* < *screwdriver*). Interesting as it is to see the effects of epenthesis or metathesis (110-1) or the nature of low central vowels (117) described in a cross-PC comparison, it does not really tell us much. Not even for the suprasegmentals (137ff.), which have often been thought of as characteristically different in PCs, is there an uncontroversial typological or historical interpretation – the 'survival' of tone in various Caribbean PCs has been a matter of debate for some time.

Syntax has often been claimed to be the most revealing diagnostic level for PCs. Holm's chapter on "Syntax" is, accordingly, the longest of the three, and in some ways the most difficult. Syntax has long been the favourite playground of the various schools of creolists, but evidence for the statements made often rests on what level is chosen for comparison (the basilect or mesolect), and in particular, syntactical units and features must be assumed to be identical in a cross-linguistic contrast, a fact that cannot be expected nor can it be proved through analyses of contrast in individual languages: thus whether 'aspect markers' in Yoruba, Sranan, and Haitian Creole really 'mean the same' and/or are historically related is strictly incapable of proof. ("Many of the creole syntactic features discussed below are viewed here as historically linked to similar features in substrate languages, rather than as constituting any kind of typology of creole languages in general," 147). Not that Holm is unaware of methodological pitfalls – his arguments are normally phrased with great caution. He has chosen twenty syntactical variables (assumed to be identical in function/meaning) for comparison in West African and various Atlantic PCs, starting with preverbal tense and aspect markers (cf. table 3, p. 149; the difference between 'tense' and 'aspect' is not explained here, and the distinction given on p. 154 is not entirely satisfactory). The universal character of the PC system is, however, challenged by Papiamentu (153), and the identity of categories at least doubtful in sentences such as: "A number of African languages use the same durative or non-punctual marker to indicate both progressive and habitual actions" (158), which leads to speculations such as: "There is a plausible substrate explanation for the link between habitual, progressive, and future markers", and the consequences developed from this (159). He continues with the striking similarities in complementizer constructions (168-71), negation (171-4) and the much-debated forms of 'be' (174-82). With 'serial verbs' (183-90) we are on somewhat safer ground again, such structures being more diagnostic of PCs (and African languages). Finally there is the noun phrase (determiners, possessives etc.), where the section on pronouns makes most exciting reading (201-5), whereas conjunctions and prepositions, and even word order, appear to be less conclusive.

Whereas volume I permits interesting comparisons with, e.g., Mühlhäusler's recent manual (1986), volume II is unique and much needed. It provides succinct information on 121 varieties thought or claimed to be PCs/to have PC characteristics, as follows: Portuguese-based (16 varieties), Spanish- (7), Dutch- (8), French- (22), English- (37), African-based (6) and others (25). Each of these is given one to four pages (rarely more) on: numbers of speakers, sociolinguistic status, history of speakers and of research, linguistic features (including specimens of texts) and a discussion, where relevant, of how far we can be certain about a variety's PC character. This applies, e.g. among the English-related varieties, to the speech of the Cayman Islands (479), the Bay Islands (480-2), American Indian English (506-10) and Pitcairn-Norfolk (546-51), Moreover, no claim is made as to whether all the varieties treated are really distinct, or whether some actually consist of more than one, which means that the figure given should not be interpreted to mean that there are exactly 121 PCs on this globe.

The amount of information collected for these varieties is enormous. Although individual readers may find data on their favourite PC incomplete or even misleading, there is no doubt that Holm, although relying on second-hand information most of the time, has given us a remarkably reliable, well-documented survey, and it would be nitpicking to search for oversights, misprints or doubtful judgements. The set of two books under review is certain to be accepted as one of the basic works on PCs, and it deserves to be read closely, and used as a basic reference book.

25 Jean D'Costa and Barbara Lalla, eds., *Voices in Exile. Jamaican Texts of the 18th and 19th Centuries.* Tuscaloosa, Al. and London: University of Alabama Press, 1989, xvi + 157pp. [*ViE*],
Barbara Lalla and Jean D'Costa, *Language in Exile. Three Hundred Years of Jamaican Creole.* Tuscaloosa, Al. and London: University of Alabama Press, 1990, xvii + 276 pp. [*LiE*]; from *AS* 69 (1994), 187-91.

The publication of these two books in close succession, by the same authors and by the same publisher, marks an important step in research into Jamaican Creole (JC). Before discussing the two books in detail, I think it will be helpful to look at their history as I know it. There is nothing in the two volumes to throw light on their interrelation apart from a single sentence in *LiE*, p. xiv: "In the companion volume (*ViE*), the reader may gain an even wider view of the language and culture of this vanished Jamaica in the collection of songs, tales, sermons, and other material selected for that volume". No word about the fact that *both* selections come from one original collection which would have come, with introduction and annotations, to some 400 pages, a size obviously considered too bulky to be publishable. So the available texts were evenly split, and *ViE* published as a bibliophile book with a mere eight pages of introduction – omitting all the linguistic interpretation that appeared to have been the motivation for the collection. When I submitted my first review, I expressed my concern at this departure and bafflement about such a change of policy from the original intentions. I would have been more at ease if there had at least been a single reference to a second volume which was to contain what I had expected to find in *ViE*. However, even now, with both books in front of me, I cannot help complaining about the negative consequences of tearing apart closely related material:

a) Many of the excerpts in both books come from identical sources: from Moreton (*ViE* p. 12/*LiE* Text 4), from Hugh Crow (24/T5), Walter Jekyll (28/T6), M.G. Lewis (30/T8), C.R. Williams (37/T10), Marly (41/T11), M. Scott (48/T12), [B. Martin] (56/T13), J.M. Philippo (62/T14), R.R. Madden (67/T15), J. Williams (75/T16), H.G. Murray (88/T17) and W.G. Hamley (111/T19). There is only one overlap, T17 forming part of a longer passage excerpted for *ViE* (107-9), but there is no information in the books as to the complementary nature of the excerpts, or as to *why* the texts were split up the way they are. On the other hand, there is necessarily quite a lot of duplicated information on authors and functions of texts, since the two books are intended to be self-contained.

b) The linguistic history and the description of individual levels of JC in *LiE* is based on, and refers to, the material printed in the volume; the identical amount of data in *ViE* is not explicitly used in the analysis at all.

All this means that the two volumes would have been much easier to use as text books had their complementary character been made more evident. (Line numbering in the texts would also have been useful).

This introduction may sound unduly critical, but it is not intended to disguise the high quality of research, editing and printing that is behind ten years of diligent work by two conscientious linguists, both highly qualified as Jamaicans and with great experience in Caribbean creolistics.

The texts they have chosen are excellent – not only because they contain the best data available by way of coherent texts from all possible genres, but also because they are exciting documents of social (colonial) history, reminding one of the geographically more widely spread excerpts in Abrahams & Szwed (1983). Such more general, anthropological interest is highlighted by historical illustrations scattered throughout *ViE*. Each individual text is introduced by carefully selected information about the author, the situation, and the linguistic reliability (in *LiE*) of the excerpt. The method is very similar to that used in Rickford (1987) and the *Varieties of English Around the World* series which are likely to have served as models. In a few cases, the two authors had to work as linguistic archaeologists, meticulously piecing together the shards of a forgotten culture – a metaphor that is in fact particularly appropriate as a characterization of the reconstruction of one of the most exciting specimens, the "Quaco Sam Song" reconstructed with great care by Lalla, which is also preserved on pottery, 144). Both books have adequate notes sections and glossaries; entries in the bibliographies contain few entries for 1985-86, only two for 1987, and nothing more recent – probably indicating the books' long gestation period.

For a linguist, the detailed first part on "Early Jamaican Creole" (*LiE*, 1-123) is the weightiest section of the set. The authors carefully document what is known about settlement, slavery, social and economic history and education, linking all this with cautious guesses about the history of languages used in Jamaica, in particular the emergence of JC. Largely accepting the hypothesis formulated by Niles (1980) for Barbados, namely that the formative early years of English in both islands saw large proportions of white speakers of various nonstandard British Englishes, Lalla & D'Costa rightly claim that undue concentration on African roots must distort JC's linguistic history. (It is remarkable that no reference is made in this context to the question of the prior creolization of Black English in the U.S., for instance to Schneider (1989/81)). However, the discussion of the plausible dialect input suffers from a great many uncertainties, many caused by the patchy documentation of varieties in both Britain/Ireland *and* in the colonies; but there is also too much reliance on Niles' claims, and a neglect of recent research by Harris (1986), Rickford (1986), Williams (1987) and others who have advanced our knowledge of dialect input in early Caribbean communities quite considerably. Moreover, the authors have not made any effort to expand on varieties in Britain beyond what is textbook knowledge, and since most of this is based on the speech of educated Londoners as described by Dobson and others, the data do not represent the regional non-standard forms imported into 17th- to 19th-century Jamaica. It is also not quite clear how the authors see the pidgin/early creole phase of JC. Was it, for the first years, a *dialect* of English, with a pidgin emerging in the plantation context – or did it remain a 'broken' form of nonstandard English which developed straight into a creole/creoloid? And how homogeneous can this speech be assumed to have been? The authors tend to interpret the recorded texts as mixtures of basilect and acrolect, the latter being due to influences from the written medium. However, variable use of, say, verbal inflections can also be interpreted as evidence of unstable *broken* English, with a stable creole possibly developing later than has generally been assumed. (The authors make an attempt at breaking up 'basilectal' features among Jamaican speakers of different social classes (84-96) but are of course severely hampered by the scarcity and doubtful nature of this evidence).

The problem with the few, and in many ways not quite authentic, texts is that either interpretation makes sense (again, a comparison with BEV would have been helpful). However, it could also be argued that sociolinguistic reality at any stage of early Jamaican does not permit us to define developmental stages, as Crowley also finds impossible in the more recent and better documented history of Bislama (Vanuatu):

> It is probably not possible to characterize Bislama at any stage of its development as a jargon, a stable pidgin, an expanded pidgin, a creole or a post-creole (or post-pidgin) continuum. It has probably been all of these at once, with different speakers having learnt the language under different conditions. (Crowley 1990:385)

In the reconstruction of individual levels of JC, the above cautions have to be kept in mind. The sound system (47-67) shows the expected merger of African and BrE nonstandard usage, but with so little known about the input, it is difficult to interpret the data in detail: why do more clearly African features (in consonants, syllable structure, tone etc.) not survive? Does their absence support the assumption of a *dialect* origin for JC? "Morphosyntax and lexicon" (68-78) is surprisingly short – possibly because the 'pure' creole system (no inflection, no tenses, no passives) cannot be convincingly illustrated from the texts. As regards the lexicon, many more sources were of course systematically tapped in Cassidy & Le Page, so that the authors cannot add much that is new; it is interesting that they calculated that among the words in need of glossing (a total of 250 in their corpus) "180 derive from dialects of English, 36 are of West African origin; 14 are Hispanic; and 25 are either unknown or of multiple origin" (77).

The two books in combination constitute a major breakthrough in the historical documentation of Jamaican texts, an achievement that is to be compared, on a more modest level, with the definitive collection and interpretation of Jamaican lexis in Cassidy & Le Page (^{2}1980), and this statement holds in spite of the drawbacks mentioned in my first paragraph. The books are excellently produced; typos and other mistakes are amazingly rare for projects of such complexity – the high quality is especially conspicuous when the finished products are compared with the book manuscript of six years ago. It is to be hoped that other collections of this type will appear in due course so that the linguistic patchwork of the 17th- to 19th-century Caribbean will become much clearer, and that such additions will combine social history and linguistic variation in the exemplary way that D'Costa and Lalla have done, adding important chapters to the sociohistorical linguistics of English.

References
Abrahams, Roger D. & John F. Szwed, eds., 1983. *After Africa*. Extracts from British travel accounts and journals ... in the British West Indies. New Haven: Yale UP.
Cassidy, F.G. & R.B. Le Page, 1980. *Dictionary of Jamaican English*. Second ed. Cambridge: UP.
Crowley, Terry. 1990. *Beach-la-Mar to Bislama. The Emergence of a National Language in Vanuatu*. Oxford: Clarendon.
Harris, John, 1986. "Expanding the superstrate: habitual aspect markers in Atlantic Englishes." *English World-Wide* 7:171-99.
Niles, Norma. 1980. "Provincial English dialects and Barbadian English." Ph.D. diss. University of Michigan.
Rickford, John R., 1986, "Social contact and linguistic diffusion: Hiberno-English and New World Black English." *Language* 62:245-89.
---. 1987. *Dimensions of a Creole Continuum*. History, Texts, & Linguistic Analysis of Guyanese Creole. Stanford: UP.
Schneider, Edgar W., 1989. *American Earlier Black English*. Morphological and Syntactic Variables. Tuscaloosa: University of Alabama Press (German original, 1981).
Williams, Jeffrey P., 1987, "Anglo-Caribbean English: a study of its sociolinguistic history and the development of its aspectual markers." Ph.D. diss. University of Texas.
Winer, Lise. "Early Trinidadian Creole: The *Spectator* texts". *English World-Wide* 5, 181-210.

26 Magnus Huber, *Ghanaian Pidgin English: A sociohistorical and structural analysis* (VEAW G24). Amsterdam: Benjamins, 1999, xii + 321 pp.; from *JPCL* (2001).

The English-related pidgins of West Africa have become a focus of linguistic interest from the 1970s onwards, and there has been decisive progress concerning central questions such as: "Are they imported or indigenous?", "Is there a distinction between 'broken' and 'pidgin English'?" "How did pidgins spread in the 19th century?" Nevertheless, the empirical data basis of hypotheses and conclusions has often been slight, and this is particularly true for Ghana, for which the very existence of an indigenous pidgin has often been denied (Hancock 1977). Huber's welcome book, slightly revised from his 1999 Essen doctoral thesis, sets out to remedy the situation. Basing his description on four years of fieldwork, collection and analysis, Huber scrutinizes all available evidence from the 18th century to the present, starting with a very detailed account of the social history of the Gold Coast. He provides an excellent survey of the period when simplified Portuguese and Lingua Franca were dominant in regional communication, and the successive period when various European powers fought for hegemony in the area. There are indications of a restructured English from 1680 onwards. Huber's reconstruction of the sociolinguistic setup, with particular reference to the mulattos of Elmina, is excellent, and the addition of a chapter on Sierra Leone more than justified, considering the intimate linguistic connections along the coast.

Linguistic analysis proper starts in chapter 4. Individual features are presented in very legible form and then analysed with exemplary precision. Huber's account conclusively shows that there is a much more reliable basis for a description of the sociolinguistics of coastal West Africa than was thought some thirty years ago, and that we need to reconsider previous hypotheses on the emergence of an 'Atlantic Creole' (as proposed by Hancock, 1986, and many other linguists). In this context, Huber's discussion of how individual features spread, and of how these facts are related to demographic mobility, is of particular relevance; his approach includes another look at possible connections between Krio and WAfE pidgin. Again, historical documents on repatriation permit the author to add relevant details. Foreigner talk, as the most likely form of the English input, is reconstructed from evidence in other PC languages.

The analysis of present-day GhPE is built on a well-informed account of the polyglossic distribution of English and African languages, which includes a very detailed description of modern forms of pidgin, as observed in situ by Huber himself. A central portion deals with a close-up study of the complex speech community of Tema Harbour, a locality that is ideal for studying sociolinguistic factors that have contributed to the stabilization and expansion of GhPE in its function as an interethnic lingua franca. This is complemented by an account of the more recent spread of pidgin in middle schools and the army, where it coexists with various kinds of unstable jargon ('broken'). The stigmatization of pidgin as the language of less educated Ghanaians is compared with the situation in Nigeria.

All this forms the basis for a structural description of the GhPE basilect. Included is a short phonemic analysis (which is problematic because of the existence of so many native languages) and a very detailed analysis of the grammar of pidgin. Huber's account is highly informative and clearly among the best descriptions of its kind. Explanations are all supported by samples from the corpus (accompanied by English translations). Wherever necessary, the structures are contrasted with those from the mesolect or acrolect.

The book under review is an exemplary study which combines a comprehensive awareness of the state of research, innovative analyses of newly discovered material, scholarly precision and eminent readability. The addition of a CD-ROM version has delayed the publication for a few months, but most readers will find it was worth the wait, as the electronic version opens up new technical facilities for further analysis. (The contents are detailed in the book, p. x). In particular, a few colour photographs of coastal factories and maps, and more importantly, the phonetic recordings of texts in ch. 6 which provide an easily manageable comparison of spoken evidence and printed representations, which in earlier *VEAW* volumes would have been supplied by more unwieldy cassettes.

The book is excellently edited and printed – a welcome addition to the historical and present-day languages used along the west coast of Africa, and a must for all creolists and sociolinguists.

References
Hancock, I.F. 1977. "Appendix: Repertory of pidgin and creole languages". In A. Valdman, ed., *Pidgin and Creole Linguistics*. Bloomington: Indiana UP, 362-91.
---. 1986. " The domestic hypothesis, diffusion and componentiality: an account of Atlantic Anglophone origins". In P. Muysken & N. Smith, eds. *Substrata versus Universals in Creole Genesis*. Amsterdam: Benjamins, 71-102.

27 Stephen A. Wurm & Peter Mühlhäusler, eds., *Handbook of Tok Pisin (New Guinea Pidgin)* (Pacific Linguistics, C70). Canberra: Pacific Linguistics, 1985, iv + 725 pp.; from *EWW* 7 (1986), 147-50.

This impressive book, which has been announced for many years, is the most exhaustive scholarly description to date of one of the most important and best known English-related pidgin languages. In 25 chapters eight authors have attempted to cover the history and present-day functions and features of Tok Pisin (= TP), or, to put it more correctly, Mühlhäusler has contributed three quarters, the other authors sharing in the fourth quarter. A short introduction, written by the two editors, is followed by 6 chapters on "Historical Aspects", *viz.* Mühlhäusler's "History of the study of TP" (15-33) and "External history of TP" (35-64); Wurm's "Status of TP" (65-74), Mühlhäusler's "Internal development of TP" (75-166); Wurm's "Writing systems and the orthography of TP" (167-76); and Mühlhäusler's "Etymologising and TP" (177-219). A debatable cover term "The Nature of TP" joins the next three chapters: Laycock's "TP and the census" (223-31), Mühlhäusler's "Variation in TP" (233-73) and his "Good and bad pidgin" (275-91). Treatments of individual levels of TP grammar follow: Laycock's discussion of segmental phonology (295-307), Wurm's of intonation (309-34), and Mühlhäusler's of inflectional morphology (335-40), syntax (341-421) and of the lexical system (423-40) - the importance of the individual levels neatly reflected by the number of pages devoted to each. Mühlhäusler's "TP and its relevance to theoretical issues in creolistics and general linguistics" (443-83) is followed by a final mixed section entitled "Issues and problems". It comprises Piau's and Holzknecht's two sketches of "Current attitudes to TP" (487-93), Laycock's treatment of TP as a literary language" (495-5 15), Siegel's "'TP in the mass media" (517-33), Dutton's "Teaching and TP" (535-7), Ross's "Effects on TP of some vernacular languages" (539-56), three chapters by Mühlhäusler on "The scientific study of TP", *viz.* on "Descriptive TP grammars" (557-75), "TP dictionary making" (577-93), and "Language planning and the TP lexicon" (595-664), and, forward-looking, Laycock's "The future of TP" (665-8). A joint list of references

(669-704) and an index (705-25, indispensable in such a huge and heterogeneous book) conclude the volume.

The book is innovative in many ways. It contains the fullest description of the grammar of TP published to date, which includes Laycock's succinct account of TP segmental phonology and Wurm's reliable description of TP intonation, as well as Mühlhäusler's eminently clear exposition of TP syntax. This is "based on a very large corpus of materials produced by indigenous speakers...", "maximally descriptive and minimally prescriptive or normative" (341). Mühlhäusler rightly gives priority to "observational adequacy" over "descriptive consistency" (342). He elegantly and persuasively solves the difficult problem of the fusion in TP of European and indigenous categories of parts of speech and constituents, openly admitting where further research is necessary, as in his discussion of transitive (and causative) and intransitive (and equative and locative) verbs, and predicative adjectives on p.358, and of aspect and tense markers as part of the predicate (rather than the verb), 377ff.

Theory-oriented readers should not miss Mühlhäusler's discussion of the relevance of TP to theoretical issues in creolistics and general linguistics. It is well known that TP presents a difficult case for adherents of the relexification hypothesis, or of universalist approaches. Mühlhäusler takes the interested reader on a tour involving terms and methods; universals, related speech forms such as foreigner and baby talk, substratum and language mixing, discontinuity, and the bioprogram hypothesis, lucidly concluding that no approach presupposing a homogeneous or stable language system can do justice to the realities of TP. Equally fascinating is Mühlhäusler's "Internal development of TP", in which he provides an exhaustive functional history of the language, never attempted with such consistency before.

On the other hand, much of the information in the *Handbook* is not new, at least to readers acquainted with the main authors' recent publications. This fact is not surprising in a handbook summarizing the state of the art. (It is less easy to justify why some passages within the present book should be identical, as is the case with pp.275-9 = 597-600, and shorter sections on p.196 = 636, where Mühlhäusler uses identical formulations in two different articles). In particular, Wurm's collection *New Guinea Area Language and Language Study* of 1977 (cf. my review in *EWW* 5:1984, 104-6) exhibits some overlap. However, the fact that only 142 pages (497-638) were then devoted to TP makes it clear how different the *Handbook* is in depth and width. A comparison of two corresponding sections will serve to illustrate more general problems: Laycock's (1985) account of creative writing adds very little material from the time after 1973 to his previous account in (1977: 609-38) – because the high hopes that TP would develop into a viable literary medium have not been fulfilled so far; the impression is, rather, that the peak of TP use in literature was over before it ever began (see in particular Laycock's sober remarks to this intent, 509-10). Dutton's very short 1985 account of TP teaching is explained by the absence of reliable recent information: " The present stage of knowledge is poor and unreliable and the situation unknown" (537). The reader is therefore referred to the extensive section of ten chapters in the earlier book (1977: 639-757) if he wishes to be informed about teaching by the churches, in the army, in the Highland, to medical and agricultural staff and to Europeans.

The present collection has been in the making for at least ten years. Apart from organizational problems which are likely to have held up progress the book was delayed by three facts ((a) and (b) being mentioned in various forms in a great number of places):

a) The authors are aware of how many aspects of TP have been insufficiently investigated so far. Many statements or hypotheses have been based on anecdotal evidence or idiosyncratic impressions. Central questions, such as Bickerton's assumption that a continuum is likely to develop between TP and English (1975; cf. p.28), that attitudes towards TP have been changing dramatically (cf. p.285), or whether speakers of TP accept linguistic change, especially that arising from creolization (cf. p.288) have been asked but not answered in any satisfactory way. Also, most treatments of TP available are by expatriates (as are, with the exception of the few pages written by J. Piau, all the contributions to the volume under review; cf. Mühlhäusler, p.291).

b) The authors agree that the forms and functions of TP are in a state of flux. Therefore, any description of individual linguistic aspect will be 'historical', i.e. it will be in need of updating and correction by the time he description has reached the printed page, cf. Mühlhäusler p.387 on tense markers becoming obligatory, p.390 on verbal chaining as a recent phenomenon, etc.). The greater is Don Laycock's courage in writing a few words on "The future of TP" – such statements will at least provide interesting historical documents in a few years' time. Independence in 1975 has not brought stronger centralisation and greater mobility of speakers, and with it, an increased need for Tok Pisin. Rather, growing regionalisation after 1975 means that more and more speakers can get along with regional languages – or with English. Whereas the knowledge of TP is still expanding in, e.g., the Highland areas, it is said to be receding in others - geographically and by domains (newspapers, creative literature).

c) The contributors may have also felt a sense of unease since scholarly descriptions of TP's grammar and lexicon are based on European concepts of orderliness, but may not do justice to a language whose speakers do not generally care for the 'correctness' of their utterances as long as successful communication is achieved. One cannot help feeling that most of the language planning arguments (and there are many of these in the *Handbook*) will have little impact, if any – Papua New Guineans apparently see little use in such activities. This applies especially to purist attitudes – why avoid anglicisms in morphology, lexis and syntax, if the English term or phrase is at hand, and a TP equivalent non-existent, clumsy or denotatively unprecise? Mühlhäusler's very considerate suggestions, especially in his "Language planning and the TP lexicon" (595-664) could therefore provide future generations of scholars with a nice illustration of "what might have been".

Despite certain gaps in the coverage and presentation (why, again, only one map in the whole volume?), there is no doubt about the *Handbook* establishing itself as the scholarly work of reference on Tok Pisin (hopefully to be complemented by a more adequate dictionary to replace Mihalic 1971; cf. Mühlhäusler's critical remarks, 577-93) in linguistic departments. It is quite a different matter, and will be worth while documenting in detail whether the book will contribute to developing a consciousness of a grammatical norm among PNG speakers, even though the authors were *not* aiming at a "Proposal for correcting, improving and ascertaining the pidgin tongue".

28 Peter Mühlhäusler, *Growth and Structure of the Lexicon of New Guinea Pidgin.* (PacL. C52) Canberra: Pacific Linguistics, 1979, xx + 498 pp., (= *Growth*); from *EWW* 5 (1984), 111-3.

The amount of information included in this book, its perspicuous arrangement and, above all, its rigorous linguistic methodology and observational adequacy make the book P. Mühlhäusler's *magnum opus*, the results of which he has himself summarized in various articles, and which have found their way into a great number of publications on pidgins, language change and sociolinguistics. As a thesis, the book is technical in nature: a more popular account of the findings is promised for the *Handbook* which "will serve the purpose of providing a reference book which can be consulted more readily by the layman") (iii). *Growth* is much more than its title promises, and its author explains in his introduction why he diverged from the narrow aim of an account of the growth of the NGP lexicon, and the share that word-formation had in it. he felt obliged to take into account various changes in the social context, "the development of non-referential dimension, as manifested in the development of new registers and sociolects" (iv), its applicability to the sociopolitical situation in PNG, and language planning needs.

The data for the book were collected mainly in the Sepik and Madang Provinces (Rural NGP) and in Malabang village on Manus Island (Creolized NGP), these two being "the most stable and sophisticated varieties, with Lowlands Pidgin becoming increasingly accepted as the basis for standardization of both written and spoken NGP" (4). There is an exemplary documentation of the external history of NGP, which Mühlhäusler divides into the jargon stage of 1800-60 (56-59), the development of stable pidgins 1860-80 (59-65), the years 1880-1914, when NGP acquired a new identity (65-83 – a subchapter in which the author provides stimulating new information), the years between the wars, which saw a geographical and functional expansion of NGP (83-97), and the years after 1945, when NGP expanded into the Highlands and acquired new media (97-103). Mühlhäusler then gives a survey of the history of attitudes towards NGP (103-40, with ample documentation from German administrational and missionary sources). This external history provides the explanation for the social and regional varieties of present-day NGP and their setting (140-61). The author's exposition includes his now widely accepted categorization into Tok Masta, Bush Pidgin, Rural Pidgin and urban Pidgin (146-53); this is followed by "special registers and their functions" (161-8) and a discussion of creolized varieties (168-78). Much of the descriptive framework has been devised by Mühlhäusler, who skilfully structures the complex situation which to many must have looked like the chaos preceding genesis. Only after his structuring is it meaningful to describe in purely linguistic terms the diachronic development of the NGP lexicon and word-formation (179-288) which led from paraphrasis to stable patterns via many conflicting developments, most of which were surprisingly detached from English patterns. When NGP came into renewed frequent contact with English after 1920 in some towns, the foundations were laid for Urban Pidgin with a grammatical basis far removed from that of the (re-)lexifier language (288-315). This new influx of English has already begun to restructure NGP on all linguistic levels – the inventory and distribution of phonemes, occasional morphological marking of number and tense, the addition of word-formation patterns, some syntactical and semantic changes, and above all, lexical expansion which makes most English words in reach of a speaker potential tokens of his NGP utterance. Such new loans are not only in conflict with existing structures, they also break up word families (as in *bung* 'gathering place': *bungim* 'gather' > *bung: kolektim*, 307). This process reminds one of ME developments which led to pairs such as *town: urban* – some of which are now being borrowed into Urban Pidgin (*taun: eben*, 437). Creolized Pidgin is remarkable for its relaxation of some of the traditional constraints such as multiple derivation (314), and since Urban and Creolized NGP are likely to indicate the path of future development it will be interesting to see how far these tendencies, observed in nuclear form, have expanded – changes may well be apparent even today, ten years after Mühlhäusler collected his data. Three productive patterns of lexical derivation (multifunctionality, compounding and reduplication) are then extensively documented from Rural Pidgin in chapter 5 (345-418). The detailed semantic-syntactic descriptions of underlying forms of the first two categories, also present in English, facilitate rewarding comparisons: where NGP structures diverge from English, as they often do, changes are likely to occur towards English patterns. Mühlhäusler's findings could well be applied to language planning (if there is a desire for it), as he shows in chapter 6 "Vocabulary planning for NGP" (419-48); it is a pity that Mühlhäusler's suggestions do not appear to have been taken up – he does not stop at negative criticism but makes very convincing proposals on how modern concepts could be adequately expressed in NGP. The precarious problem of how parts of speech are defined is solved in an elegant way: the author distinguishes between "lexical bases which ... contain information about their lexical categorical status (noun, verb, adjective) and lexical items containing categorical information relevant to syntactic operations (nominals, verbals, adjectivals)" (38), and justifies this distinction with the different word-forming potentials of lexemes as a consequence of their derivational history, and with the possibility of morphologically marked items to function in other syntactic frames, such as *harim* 'dialect'. Mühlhäusler has aptly demonstrated the uniqueness of NGP, which has a "more powerful derivational lexicon" (vi) than most other pidgins and most creoles, a potential which is in danger of being slowly lost through anglicization unless utilized in judicious language planning – soon. As with other pidgins of the region, the speakers of NGP do not seem, however, to be prepared for such measures, nor are there institutions to implement them.

29   Sarah Grey Thomason & Terence Kaufman, *Language Contact, Creolization, and Genetic Linguistics*. Berkeley: University of California Press, 1988, xi+411 pp.; from *IF* 97 (1992), 315-6.

'Mixed languages' (Mischsprachen) have long been a topic in historical linguistics; discussion arose in the late 19th century when scholars had difficulties in fitting languages whose history was characterized by a great amount of contact-induced change into neatly arranged stemmata of genetic relations. Schmidt's wave theory and the research of Schuchardt were prompted by related reflections – Schuchardt's dictum "Es gibt keine völlig ungemischte Sprache" is therefore rightly placed as a motto on p.1 of TK; a reply to the earlier tradition represented by Max Müller who claimed that there were no mixed languages (1). However, TK reject the claim that mixture makes most languages unclassifiable genetically (3), extreme cases being restricted to a small minority of languages which include, but are not coextensive with, pidgins and creoles (PCs): "languages arising outside of normal transmission are not related (in any genetic sense) to *any* antecedent systems" (10). All this is not completely new (as TK admit) but is here cogently argued and well illustrated by compelling case histories. TK show that none of the linguistic levels – not even morphology and core vocabulary – is exempt from contact-induced change (6) as had been claimed by Weinreich, Greenberg and others. In such languages "it will not be possible to show that both grammar and lexicon derive from the same source" (11). However, this definition can be applied only to cases of relexification as evident in, e.g., Anglo-Romani and Ma'a.

In chapter 2 TK provide an impressive array of evidence to the effect that "the purely linguistic constraint on contact-induced change will not work" (16). In particular, there is no evidence for the widely held opinion that "Internal language change typically involves simplification, i.e. loss of marked features, while creolization, language change through external contact, involves complication, the development of marked features" (27). Rather than the structure of the individual language, "it is the sociolinguistic history of the speakers (...) that is the primary determinant of the linguistics of language contact" (35). This is the keynote of chapter 3, and indeed a hypothesis that few would (nowadays) wish to quibble with. How far can linguists, then, predict "extent and kinds of interference" (46 ff.) from the factors determining contact situations? Table 3 (50) tries to provide such answers for change in language maintenance and in language shift, but (rightly) leaves pidgins out of such reflections.

TK detail their hypotheses in chapters 4-7, each devoted to interference phonemena in one type of language: ch.4 on those retained by their speech communities ("Language maintenance," 65-109), ch. 5 on "Language shift with normal transmission" (110-46), ch. 6 on "Abrupt creolization" (147-66) and ch. 7 on "Pidgins" (167-99). If we grant that we can find out, in not too distant historical times, which languages were maintained, and that these can be expected to share certain types of loans, then all depends on whether we agree on what "normal transmission" is and whether it can be established in the case of the history of an individual language. TK have gone a long way establishing criteria and methods, but cannot of course be held responsible where the evidence from diachronic linguistics or from the social history of the speech community is insufficient to decide the case.

Eight case studies are appended in ch.9 (214-342); the authors included these "to avoid (...) the use of isolated examples from a given case to support theoretical claims" (214). They discuss, then, Asia Minor Greek (215-22), Ma'a (233-8), Michif (228-33), Mednyj Aleut (233-8), Uralic substratum interference in Slavic and Baltic (238-51), Afrikaans (251-6), Chinook Jargon (256-63) and, finally and in great detail, "English and other coastal Germanic languages, or why English is not a mixed language" (263-342). Whereas the first set of seven cases exemplifies all important types of language mix imaginable, the application of the framework to the history of English is a sustained and convincing combat of the "creolist faddism" (357) as evidenced in some linguists' recent writings (cf. my own rebuttal of such claims, Görlach 1986). In particular, simplification of the morphology may have been speeded up by contact influence, but cannot have been the (only) cause (277), but then simplification does not make a language a creole, nor does extreme lexical mixture, as from French. In general, then, a welcome and necessary chapter, even though some of ME dialectology has been neglected in the survey of features documenting 'Norsification'. (The preface is dated "December, 1985", so the authors could obviously not include the results of *LALME* (= McIntosh *et al.* 1986) which one would wish to see taken into account in a second edition of their book). Also, some condensation and some amount of greater orderliness could be then introduced into this chapter to bring out the authors' conclusions even more poignantly.

TK provide an impressive amount of data from a very large range of languages, among which Bantu, Cushitic, Dravidian, Indic, and Uralic languages feature widely, but English, French, Norse and Portuguese receive even more detailed treatment – all this is a successful attempt at detecting universal or at least wide-spread contact-induced developments and avoiding the dangers that lie in basing too general hypotheses and explanations on too limited an array of types of languages and situations. The authors have not only helped to re-open the discussion about language contact and 'mixed languages' but also written a weighty contribution to the question which it would be unwise to neglect for any scholar interested in the topic.

References

Görlach, Manfred, 1986, "Middle English – a creole?" In D. Kastovsky & A. Szwedek, eds., *Linguistics across Historical and Geographical Boundaries*, Berlin: Mouton de Gruyter, 329-44.

McIntosh, Angus, *et al.*, 1986, *A Linguistic Atlas of Late Medieval English*, Aberdeen: UP.

30 Hans Goebl, Peter H. Nelde & Zdeněk Starý, Wolfgang Wölck, eds., *Kontaktlinguistik, Contact Linguistics, Linguistique de contact*. (HSK 12,1 & 2) Berlin & New York: de Gruyter, 1996, volume 1, xxxix + 936 pp.; 1997,volume 2, xxv+(939)-2171 pp.; from *Journal of Sociolinguistics* 1 (1998), 134-9.

The monumental collection of papers commissioned for the work under review represents the most wide-ranging survey of the new discipline of contact linguistics (= CL) ever compiled; the first volume comprises 115 chapters written by scholars from all continents. The book is divided into eight sections, all devoted to more general aspects of the discipline, *viz.* the history of CL (2), interdisciplinary framework (9), individual linguistic levels (8), external factors (6), basic concepts of CL (17), central issues (45), empirical methods (13) and applied CL (13).

The editors rightly stress that the "new sub-discipline of CL ... has not yet developed a coherent, conceptual, methodological and substantive framework of its own. The programmatic scope of the pragmatic realities of speech and language is too wide to easily fit a compact system." (xxx) One of the major aims of the project was, then, to provide a state-of-the-art account reducing the complex field to charterable order – and one of the points of criticism whether they have succeeded.

Oksaar's and Clyne's historical surveys provide a very useful introduction to the history of the discipline and its methods, esp. in the course of the past thirty years – however, the useful surveys suffer from the fact that too many things had to be forced in, as is illustrated by the 145 titles assembled in the "Bibliography (selected)" appended to ch. 1.

Connections of CL with neighbouring disciplines are explored by Hartig (sociology, 23-31), Hamers (psychology, 31-40), Liebkind (social psychology, 41-48) Véronique (anthropology, 49-57), Paradis (neurology, 57-62), Williams (geography, 63-75), Sonntag (political science, 75-81), Van de Craen (pedagogics, 81-89) and Eichinger (comparative literature and philology, 89-97). Whereas the interrelations with sociology and social psychology, geography and pedagogics are obvious, and the short chapters are a must for all interested in the fields, the findings and research possibilities in literature and CL are less obvious but excellently elucidated by Eichinger.

The section devoted to more narrowly linguistic aspects will provide a special attraction to many readers. Campbell discusses "Phonetics and phonology", 98-103) mainly using 'exotic' languages for illustration. The complementary chapter on "Spelling and graphemics" by Coulmas (104-9) is even more comprehensive ranging from Sumeric to problems of the integration of modern loanwords. Wilkins' treatment of "Morphology" (109-17) compares seven classificational schemes proposed to explore constraints on transfer as a consequence of CL. Muysken's chapter on "Syntax" (117-24) deals with a great number of topics, failing to do justice to the topic proper on the two pages he reserves to the problem of syntactical borrowing. It should have been easier for Mathiot & Rissel to explain the CL connections in "Lexicon and word-formation" (124-30), but their exposition is poorly structured and too general to be convincing. Ameka & Wilkins in their "Semantics" (130-8) wrongly decided to restrict themselves to summaries of views found in the literature, and since there is no consent about methods, they (and the readers) get lost in aspects divided between "the psychology of bilingualism, lexical borrowing, morphological transfer, social factors in second language learning, pidgins and creoles, and so on" (136).

If these hard-core subdisciplines were difficult to reduce to order, "Discourse analysis and pragmatics" (by Schiffrin, 138-44) and "Stylistics" (by Spillner, 144-53) were even more so. All these chapters are much stronger in formulating research needs than in discussing preconditions and conclusions. How far, in particular, can units like phonemes, suffixes, senses be compared cross-linguistically and what kind of contact is necessary for what particular consequence? The obvious statement, for instance, that styles (and text types) were imitated in Renaissance vernaculars because Latin provided prestigious models is not even mentioned, nor is the effect that colonial languages have had on the pragmatics of 20th-century vernaculars in Africa and Asia.

In "External factors" we return to conditions of contact: "Nation and state" (by Heraud, 154-60), "Language legislation" (by Turi, 160-8), "Speech community" (by Madera, 169-75), "Language boundaries" (by Melis, 175-80) provide background information more or less relevant for individual contact situations – chapters which are no doubt necessary in a comprehensive handbook, although their immediate importance is not always evident. The two chapters on "Migration" (by Ehlich, 180-93) and on "Colonialisation" (by Laroussi & Marcellesi, 193-9) are obviously more relevant, and Ehlich's summary is particularly well-done, too. It is not easy to see why three more chapters on "Migration" are separated from Ehlich, coming on 311-32.

The boundary to "Basic concepts" is not well defined. Oliversi's "Nationalisms" (200-3), Devetak's "Ethnicity" (203-9) and Labrie's "Territoriality" (210-8) very much belong to the preceding section. Their importance for CL is marginal as is Haarmann's (stimulating) "Identity" (218-33). By contrast, Lüdi's "Multilingualism" (233-45) and Kremnitz's "Diglossia" (245-58) are both excellent summaries and very closely related to the topic, as are Weisgerber's expansion to include "Dialect, vernacular, standard" (258-71), Mackey's "First and second language" (271-84) and Wode's "Language acquisition and teaching" (284-96) – the social and individual loci of CL well summarized. "Power" is thematized by Allardt and by Argemí & Ramon (342-51, 351-7) and "Accommodation" (by Niedzielski & Giles, 352-42) and "Self-determination" (by Wynants, 357-63).

What the editors subsume under "Central issues" is more or less a domain-oriented classification: introduced by four chapters on two age groups, and the family and the couple, we proceed to "Multilingualism in ..." – "Religion", "Politics", "Administration", "Economy", "Science and technology", "The mass media", "Telecommunication", "Advertising", "Toponymics", "Urban areas", "Literature" and "Education" (with various subchapters on immersion, tests, ESP, and language acquisition). A heterogeneous group on "Language change", "Borrowing" and "Onomastics" is followed by a highly relevant and stimulating group of papers on language in society: "Lingua franca" (by Metzeltin, 554-8), "Transference and interference" (by Gass, 558-67), "Language maintenance" (by Hyltenstam & Stroud, 567-78), "Language loss" (by de Bot, 579-85), "Language shift" (by Gal, 586-93), "Code-switching" (by Heller & Pfaff, 594-609), "Standardization" (by Bossong, 609-24), "Literacy programs" (by Verhoeven, 624-34), "Abstand and ausbau" (by Muljačič & Haarmann, 634-42), "Pidginization" (by Mühlhäusler, 642-9), "Creolization" (by Valdman, 649-58), "Endangered languages" (by Bereznak & Campbell, 659-66), "Linguicide and linguicism" (by Skutnabb-Kangas & Phillipson, 667-75) – all these are central topics of sociolinguistics, here dealt with by eminent scholars and specialists in their fields. Their presence is further justified by the focus on CL – which is, however, not convincingly achieved (or even attempted?) by all authors.

A final group comprises topics related to social psychology: "Linguistic awareness" (by Fenoglio, 675-84), "Language conflict" (by Dirven & Pütz, 684-91), "Language attitude" (by Vandermeeren, 692-702), "Prestige and stigma" (by Edwards, 703-8), "Discrimination" (by Baugh, 709-14), "Loyalty" (by Niculescu, 715-20), and "Sex and Language" (by Holmes, 720-25). The next group is even more a field for core sociolinguistics, the accommodation to CL research methods being slight in chapters on "Surveys", "Representativeness of sampling", "Survey design", "Interviewing", "Participant observation", "Language demography", "Data analysis", "Ethnography", "Network analysis", "Linguistic islands" and "Research ethics" (726-825).

Much of the above is 'applied', but there is also a final section named "Applied SL", quite a heterogeneous group of essays ranging from "language policy" and "Language planning" to "Purism" and "Artificial languages", "National languages and language revitalization" and "International English" (chs. 101-115 = 826-936) – however great the problems of a proper arrangement were, there would have been more obvious positions for many chapters. It certainly does not speak for a well-ordered or orderable discipline to end a volume with medley like this.

The second volume has 124 chapters dealing with the multilingual composition and resulting contacts in 39 states, the number of contributions devoted to the individual country depending on its size and linguistic complexity: Norway (4), Sweden (3), Finland (3), Denmark (4), Iceland (1), Great Britain (3), Ireland (1), Belgium (4), the Netherlands (2), Luxemburg (1), France (9), Spain (4), Portugal (1), Italy (11), Malta (1), Yugoslavia (1), Slovenia (1), Croatia (1), Bosnia-Herzegovina (1), Macedonia (1), Albania (1), Rumania (3), Bulgaria (4), Greece (6), European Turkey (4), Cyprus (1), Poland (8), Czechia (4), Slovakia (6), Hungary (6), Germany (6), Austria (4), Switzerland (5), Western CIS States (1), Estonia (1), Latvia (1), Lithuania (1), Byelorussia (1), Ukraine (1) and Moldavia (1). Only Yiddish (1) and Romani (1) as the most important supraregional languages not represented by a nation state are given one extra chapter each. The chapters are accompanied by sixteen linguistic maps (A-P, pp. 1973-2068) with helpful annotations. The book concludes with an index of authors and a topical index (2069-2171).

The chapters in vol. II are of exemplary thoroughness; many provide information not easily accessible, and here made even more valuable by the contrastive aspects provided by the framework. (However, there might have been more cross-references). The arrangement chosen has several general consequences which it may be useful to point out:

1) The focus is on indigenous languages, i.e. those which had traditional speech communities at least in the 19th century or before; in consequence, there is a chapter on East Frisian/German, although the language is now spoken by fewer than 1,000 speakers – but there is no mention of the more than three million people of Turkish descent living in Germany. (But compare statistics including new immigrant languages for Finland, p. 1000, and discussions of such speaker groups in Britain (1070-1), the Netherlands (1145-6), and especially in France (1178-83)).

2) The scheme excludes languages of wider communication (most notably French, English, German and Russian) acquired as additional languages through the schools, and their impact on the speech community is treated very marginally at best. Thus, the fact which languages are or were taught in the schools in rarely mentioned (1002); only Switzerland (p. 1848) has a few lines on English.

3) Many contacts are discussed from the viewpoints of two groups. For instance, German is discussed as a partner of Slovene, Croatian and Hungarian in Austria, and again under Slovenia, Croatia and Hungary; Polish, Czech and Slovak are treated twice in all three possible combinations.

4) The descriptions are largely demographic, focusing on historical aspects and language in society and less so on sociolinguistics; borrowing and other contact-based influences are somewhat unevenly treated, but often neglected. A typical instance of this preference is the extensively detailed treatment of German as a minority language in Belgium (1130-42).

5) What is considered to be a 'language' and thus qualifies for a contrastive treatment is not quite obvious. Bokmål is contrasted with Nynorsk although "Linguistically, Bokmål and Nynorsk are not different languages" (949). How far can we talk about contacts between Bulgarian and Macedonian, if the contact is between dialects in a continuum? If Occitan is paired with French, then why not Franco-Provençal (which is treated in contact with Italian only). Why are, in this context, Scots (vs. English) and Low German (vs. Dutch and German) not included, or the problem at least discussed?

6) The data on the speakers and functions of second languages are very scarce; normally statistics detail the number of native speakers (dominant languages); only for minority languages, statements about the multilingual composition of the speech communities are common.

It is difficult to select any contribution for particular praise since readers' reactions will be greatly determined by their previous knowledge and particular interests; however, the sections dealing with France (1172-1269), Spain (1270-1309) and Italy (1318-98) – not surprisingly nations with many indigenous minorities – deserve to be singled out for the compact and well-presented information they provide, including a great number of tables and maps (which are very helpful on top of the linguistic maps of the appendix). On the other hand, many readers will be especially grateful for the extensive coverage of Eastern countries which makes the collection one of the first truly European ventures after 1989-90.

The editors left it to the authors to use German, English or French for their articles, the 239 chapters of the two volumes now being divided among German (96), French (58) and English (85) – this was a democratic decision even if the number of linguists reading all three languages is (possibly) diminishing.

It is to the credit of the editors that they have tackled the problem of a handbook on an ill-defined field. The quality of most chapters certainly justifies their enterprise. To focus arguments on European languages was a wise decision – and doubts about comparability or transferability increase wherever authors have diverged from this principle (cf. an unconvincing justification p. 116). The statement made by Wilkins on his rather well-defined topic of morphology is *a fortiori* true for the complete project:

> Given the vastness of the topic of contact morphology and the limited space available, this article is of necessity somewhat piecemeal and selective in its structure and presentation of topics. (116)

However, it has been worth the effort. The book is excellently edited (an enormous task) and printed. The huge size of the enterprise has resulted in an enormous price; however justified this may be economically, it will restrict access for those who in a way need the information most urgently – sociolinguists in Eastern Europe.

4 Lexicography

Lexicography has, among all the systematic linguistic disciplines, probably held the greatest attraction for me, especially where it was related to historical periods or varieties of English. Although dictionaries can be claimed to be the most difficult books to review, the different types here discussed will, I hope, provide a survey of what dictionaries can achieve and where they do not quite live up to our expectations.

31   Jane Roberts and Christian Kay, with Lynne Grundy, *A Thesaurus of Old English*. 2 vols. London: King's College, 1995, xxxxv + 1555 pp.; from *Anglia* 116 (1998), 398-401.

The work under review is the first thesaurus of a historical period of the English language ever undertaken; it forms, so to speak, the foundation of the *Historical Thesaurus* (= *HT*) expected out at Glasgow in a few years' time. The complementary nature of the two projects reflects the age-old lexicographic tradition of having OE lexis collected by itself, and let English vocabulary proper start in 1150 – the principle established by the *OED*. But in this case the *TOE* is a pilot study for the *HT*, and its materials will be incorporated within the main thesaurus.

It is almost impossible to do full justice to Roberts' and Kay's achievement; Roberts' patient work over more than twenty years involved her in reviewing all the sources available and a meticulous checking of dictionaries, linguistic monographs and original texts, establishing a notional pattern according to which the huge material could be organized – and solving endless problems relating to computer technology in a period when this was pioneering work. The result is an impressive set of two volumes (at a moderate price) which can claim to be *the* most important contribution to OE studies for years. For experts the set makes fascinating browsing, as I hope to illustrate – even though for others less specialized readers it will have, as reading matter, the interest of a telephone directory.

In vol. I, acknowledgements are followed by a brief "Introduction" (xv-xxxv) in which the source dictionaries and the history of the project are discussed; readers are also introduced to the important frequency/stylistic labels attached to a minority of the lexical items in the thesaurus, *viz.*:
o= infrequent (possibly a *hapax legomenon*);
q=questionable/dubious word;
p=poetical/attested only in poetry (cf. the practice in Clark Hall's dictionary);
g=restricted to glossed texts or glossaries –
categories that are discussed in greater detail, with illustrative examples, further on in the introduction. It is also helpful to have semantic fields pointed out in which poetical words or meanings are found particularly frequently, and to have the problem of semantic vagueness or ambiguity of words found in poetry admitted so clearly.

By contrast, the reasons given for the classification used in the thesaurus are disappointingly brief. To be told that the materials were at first sorted according to the divisions of an edition of Roget of 1962, later modified for the Glasgow Thesaurus, with further changes introduced when the 48,000 senses of the OE lexis here treated required them is not precise enough information for readers to formulate their criticism.

The thesaurus itself has a classification of up to six digits with modern headings assembled under modern lemmata. In a simple case this means (3) to list under **Ground** twelve generic terms which can be assumed to be more or less equivalent, synonymous or coreferential, followed by four hyponyms differentiated by distinctive qualities, then the generic adjective followed by adjectives designating qualities of possible 'grounds'.

For readers well acquainted with OE such collections can make fascinating reading, especially where the lists provide an unprecedented wealth of equivalents, as is the case with thirty items for 'marsh, swamp' (7), or many words reflecting nice distinctions between moving and stagnant forms of water (10-13). When reading through sections like 'emotions' or 'warfare' it is difficult not to jump to Whorfian conclusions about the Anglo-Saxons' *weltbild* – were it not that we are warned that the character of the surviving texts may have something to do with the selection.

All of volume II (717-1515) is taken up by an index in which the OE lemma is followed by its classifications and meanings – 30,000 words or so, with 48,000 senses. This index is of course a necessary feature of the project – however, one wonders whether there should not also have been room for 20-30 pages on which the ModE words used to indicate the classifications could have been listed alphabetically. (I doubt whether the notional system is clear enough to guide the reader to the section wanted by using the contents pages).

What we get in this impressive compilation is, then, a comprehensive analysis of the fullest vocabulary that survives from any Old Germanic culture arranged in sets of minimally different items, inviting us to investigate what distinctions Anglo-Saxons felt important enough to make in the lexicon, for everyday uses or in poetical texts as the case may be. The system offered is static, or ahistoric, the style labels not covering diachronic, diatopic or diastratic distinctions; whether we can link the evidence here set out with developments of later English language history will become clear only when the Glasgow *Historical Thesaurus* is out.

This said, it will be in order to reflect critically on a few limitations and point to decisions which might have been taken differently:
1. The notional structure. There are two ways of organizing the lexis of a period language in thesaurus form: the compiler can use an 'accepted' pattern, say of an established edition of Roget, or von Wartburg, to permit diachronic or cross-cultural comparisons – but forcing the lexis in question into the bed of Procrustes. Alternatively, the thesaurist can base the notional arrangement on the lexical and cultural structure of the world and world view of the respective speech community. Roberts and Kay decided to employ the second alternative which much better reflects OE conditions than a universalist framework could have done.

There could (and possibly will) be endless discussions about whether Roberts' and Kay's structure is adequate for the OE data and is organized on the basis of a logical and intelligible internal structure. It is a pity that the authors do not discuss the problems involved in their decisions and the arguments in favour of present solutions in greater detail in their introduction. Thus, the 18 categories here chosen are of very different status, their sequence is not easily explained and the length of the chapters varies a great deal:

1 The physical world (22 pages), 2 Life and death (111), 3 Matter and measurement (51), 4 Material needs (63) 5 Existence (108), 6 Mental faculties (47), 7 Opinion (24), 8 Emotion (31), 9 Language and communication (28), 10 Possession (12), 11 Action and utility (39), 12 Social interaction (57), 13 Peace and war (18), 14 Law and order (23), 18 Leisure (6). It is difficult to see why e.g. 'property' is not part of 'possession', why 'peace and war' should not be grouped with 'law and order' etc. Problems multiply when we wish to account for a specific concept being classified as it is, e.g. 'township' under 'social interaction'. There may be good reasons for all these decisions – but Roberts and Kay leave it to the readers' intellectual capacities or their creative guesswork to find explanations.

2. Locating a concept (and check whether there is a word for it in OE) can be very time-consuming. Thesauruses are of course made for native speakers, and there are none of OE. No help is provided in this book to establish whether

    1) there is a word for a concept (assuming we know the OE culture had a need for this), or

    2) there is none (a lexical gap), or

    3) no word survives (but later history or comparative philology suggest that there may have been).

Thus, in order to find out whether there is an OE name for 'horse-shoe', we are thwarted by the facts that there is

    a)   no index for ModE *horseshoe*;

    b)   no compound mentioned on *horse-*;

    c)   no entry under 'shoe' or under 'harness'.

Can we now assume that there is no record of an OE name for the object? Is there any possibility of establishing notional or lexical gaps using the *Thesaurus* collections?

3. Most entries are organized under nouns. This appears to make sense for derived adjectives and verbs, and may also be supported by the nominal structure of OE. But is it really reflective of a notional structure to list adjectives according to their possible combinations, i.e. together with the nouns they qualify?

4. The editors do not even discuss whether their system is based on semantic or encyclopedic/notional categories, or whether such a distinction makes sense in a historical corpus (I firmly believe it does). They thereby make it impossible to use their material to distinguish between notional and semantic developments in English. However, any such study should try to keep apart the history of objects (say, forms of houses, ships etc.), of notions (say, the conceptual classification of animals, with bees and dragons counted as 'birds', and otters and crayfish as 'fishes') and of meaning (say,

the semantic changes affecting *bird, fowl, meat* etc. in the course of their development from OE).

It will be interesting to see what stimulus the OE *Thesaurus* provides to further research, and to more practical matters such as revised dictionaries or manuals of OE. It will certainly keep Anglo-Saxonists busy for some time to come.

32 Werner Hüllen, *English Dictionaries 800-1700. The Topical Tradition*. Oxford: Clarendon, 1999, xvi + 525 pp.; from *IJL* 14 (2001), 63-6.

The arrangement of the lexis of a language on the basis of conceptual structure, or onomasiological principles, is of great antiquity; in fact, the pattern dominated the lexical analysis of individual languages in the early stages here reviewed, alphabetical arrangement being largely, before the 16th century, restricted to bilingual dictionaries. For a discussion of different world views or noematic structures reflected in a specific language, and for semantic analysis, the thesaurus type of reference work is of course of greater information value than a bilingual word-list of translation equivalents can ever be.

The author here summarizes the results of at least ten years of dedicated research devoted to the topical tradition in (Western) antiquity and the branches and ramifications in the individual languages (cf. Hüllen 1989, 1994). He traces the development from Aristotle and Plinius through the major medieval representatives such as Isidore of Seville, Bede, and Hrabanus Maurus to Bartholomaeus Anglicus, but focuses on the English contribution to 1700 – which gave us, in the more recent period here excluded, the prototypical *Roget* (of 1852), which looks back on a respectable array of precedessors. However, Hüllen covers a much greater range of book types, adding to word-lists/dictionaries of various subtypes also tracts on terminology, dialogues written for language teaching and of course encyclopedias proper, in which the established factual knowledge was summarized and arranged according to logical/conceptual distinctions.

Hüllen first provides a very clear survey of lexicographic practice and theory with regard to alphabetical and topical order of entries, the relationship between encyclopedic and semantic factors, and the complementary approaches of onomasiology and semasiology (3-27); all this is seen from a European (largely Continental) viewpoint of semantics, employing distinctions which prove to be very necessary in the application to the individual works discussed in the main part of the book. These considerations are first applied to early cases of word-lists surviving from ancient Egypt, China, India and compilations for Graeco-Coptic and Arabic-Syriac, all of which serve to show the old age and autonomy of the onomasiological tradition (28-39) – even if the individual works are, of course, not in any historical interrelationship.

The English branch (43-77) starts with glossaries like the Leyden one of around 800, based on the *Hermeneumata*, complemented by text types like *capitula* and glosses/glossaries which often exhibit topical arrangement (such as lists enumerating names of plants). The most comprehensive of these is Aelfric's *Glossary*, appended to his *Grammar* (993-5?). The semantic macrostructure of this work is enlightening: its eight sections (comprising 18 parts) start with "God, heaven, earth, mankind" (64) and progress through a heterogeneous section 2 with eight parts, then covers animals and plants, to end in another composite section of four parts. Clearly, the contents are not yet fully comprehensive covering only selections from Isidore's *Etymologiae*, and the sequence is far from logical. (Why is 2.5 "negative features of human character" separated from 8.4 "human vices"? etc.) A pupil of Aelfric's also provided a colloquy, a text type which became central in foreign-language teaching. In these books, topics are arranged in encyclopedic/situational sections (much as in many modern school books). The encyclopedic coverage is of course even more limited here, being restricted to topics useful for the learner of Latin (79-81). Finally, the medieval tradition is complemented by *nominales*, word-lists which (as the name implies) concentrate on nouns, which have always been the focus for encyclopedic information. The *Mayer Nominale* is analysed in great detail (66-77). As in other text types, the OE tradition impresses us with its wealth of material, which is especially remarkable when we compare other European vernacular literatures of the time.

Starting from Aelfric's pioneering colloquy, Hüllen provides a very comprehensive survey of such books, leading up to Miège (1658) in his next chapter (78-139). With all their limitations, largely explained by their teaching function, the rich medieval English tradition supplies us with comprehensive data not found in other text types. "Treatises on terminology" (140-67) can range from husbandry to rhetoric, and from medicine to sailing. Obviously, the information supplied in these is topic-specific, but it covers special languages not normally found in common text types, thus adding interesting lexis otherwise unrecorded. Of these books some 40% were arranged alphabetically, and another 40% topically, between 1480 and 1640 (141); among these, the numerous treatises on rhetoric (149-54) are (and were) possibly most widely known. However, the lexicographic importance of such collections rests rather in the data they provided for dictionaries, which increasingly expanded their coverage by the inclusion of special diction.

Withal's bilingual *Short Dictionary for Yonge Begynners* of 1553, planned as an aid to learning Latin (168-201), has a 1574 edition with topical order which (173) arranges the lexis under "universe, elements (air, water, earth), man (crafts, housing, city), society (law, church, family) and life and death (human body, war, senses). Hüllen's detailed analysis concentrates on selected encyclopedic fields, showing that the compiler was guided by a set of heuristic principles (esp. gender differences); the importance the work has for the tradition also lies in its concentration on the native core vocabulary (201). Almost a hundred years later, Howell's four-language Dictionary of the *Genteel* (*Lexicon Tetraglotton*) of 1660 (202-43) has an onomasiological part (nomenclature) of some 390 pages comprising some 20,000 headwords; the data are arranged in 52 sections, starting with the human body and ending with the universe – a system being based on de Noviliers' *Nomenclatura* of 1629 (218). It is not clear how many conclusions we can draw from the arrangement and individual items in this work since "Howell's technique of writing entries is very *ad hoc* and pragmatic" (214); the data are moreover selected to "mirror the human activities of a social group which is convincingly defined by its lifestyle, its amusements, and its scientific interests" (217). Hüllen's interpretation of the evidence in selected sections brings out this structure very clearly. The work comes nearer to both "the idea of an encyclopedic dictionary ... (and) a thesaurus" (241) than anything before it.

With Dalgarno (1661) and Wilkins (1668) we arrive at the period of the quest for universal languages and, politically, the Restoration. The fusion with the topical approach resulted in a peak of such endeavours in the context of the Royal Society, all dominated by Wilkins' *Essay* (250-301), which receives the detailed analysis it deserves. His description of the universal encyclopedic structure of language goes far beyond his predecessors' lists of items of selected fields; Wilkins' method depends, as far as possible, on binary oppositions (but the author was aware of the limitations of this approach, see Hüllen's quotation, p. 254, from 1668:22). The ranking of categories is signalled by an intricate system of typographical distinctions, illustrating a three-level structure in the tables, ultimately based on traditional logic (257). One of the innovations apparent from the collection is that the major parts of speech, *viz.* nouns, adjectives and verbs, are listed side by side (obviously because zero derivation restricts the value of such formal distinctions, and derivations serve to cross part-of-speech boundaries). This approach includes even a treatment of 'transcendental particles' for notions such as "radical PAST (*time past*)", p. 271. It is highly stimulating to contrast the classification of objects (such as 'herbs', 1668:95, p. 279) with abstract notions (such as 'events', 1668:42, p. 267, or 'virtues', 1668:210-1, p. 282-3), and Hüllen's analysis. He rightly compares 16th-century books on logic, rhetoric and botanical taxonomy, which may have at least partly suggested Wilkins' method (288-99).

The discussion of the English scene breaks off after this highlight; in fact, there are no major works of the type until it resurfaces with Roget's *Thesaurus* in 1852. Rather, Hüllen expands his discussion to cover "The European scene (1400-1700)" (306-430). This is a magnificent survey brimful of information, beginning with "Multilingual dictionaries and nomenclators", which permit a comparison with English (though the parallels and contrasts might have been made slightly more explicit). The survey culminates in the chapter devoted to the writings of Comenius (361-430), clearly the most important Continental writer on topical lexis, widely imitated in individual European speech communities, and translated into English. The English tradition peters out with Greenwood's *London Vocabulary* of 1713. Hüllen rightly sees a boundary around 1700 which, if it did not end the topical tradition, at least constitutes a watershed (442-4), to be replaced, in a way, by what he calls "mental lexicography", represented in particular by Locke's *Essay* of 1689 (445-7).

Appendixes (459-90) contain conspectuses of the contents of the works treated; this is followed by an impressive bibliography (491-514) and an index of names, titles and topics (515-25).

The book will permit expansions in various directions; there was clearly no space for Hüllen to write extensively on such future research (but he might well have charted out the territory on a few pages). The most exciting, and necessary, extension would be to investigate the following interrelated topics which have to do with the continuation of the topical tradition in modern times:

1) How far do the macro- and microstructures of pre-1700 works (in particular, Wilkins) survive in modern thesauruses – a study of the changing arrangements in various British and American works still published under the name of Roget will supply infinite material. What about other works of the kind using non-Roget methods and categories?

2) What happens in modern translations of Roget, such as Wehrle-Eggers' adaptation for German? How far can we expect conceptual structure to be translatable, and at what cost? How far do independent conceptualizations, such as Dornseiff for German and Hallig-von Wartburg for French, reflect differences in time and culture (rather than difference in methods of classification)?

3) How far can we be certain of diachronic stability of conceptual structures? Does the recent thesaurus of OE (Roberts & Kay 1995) reflect OE structures à la Aelfric, or modern ones à la Roget, or a third system, and for what reasons? What does the analysis of works treated here tell us about the feasibility of the *Historical Thesaurus* being compiled, on the basis of *OED* material, at Glasgow (Samuels & Kay forthc.)?

4) What is the relationship of concept (noematics) and meaning (semantics) in a diachronic and cross-cultural investigation?

We ought to be grateful to the author for writing this survey, which is brimful of information, careful analysis and reflexion, taking in the research of some 400 titles listed in the references, and still retaining readability, at least for readers who know enough of the ancient, medieval and Renaissance tradition of lexicography to be able to understand and correctly evaluate the immense amounts of data, comparisons and links between types of encyclopedic books, traditions and national adaptations. Although the text is forbiddingly complex, it was printed with a very high degree of correctness (only the peculiar form of the *thorn* disturbing the impression). The book can certainly stand beside the classic accounts of early English lexicography written by Schäfer (1989), Starnes & Noyes (1946, 1954), and Stein (1985).

References
Dornseiff, Franz. 1922. *Der deutsche Wortschatz nach Sachgruppen*. Berlin: de Gruyter.(^{7}1970)
Hallig, Rudolf & Walter von Wartburg, 1952. *Begriffssystem als Grundlage für die Lexikographie*. Berlin: Akademieverlag.
Hüllen, Werner. 1989. 'Their Manner of Discourse'. *Nachdenken über Sprache im Umkreis der Royal Society*. Tübingen: Narr.
---. ed. 1994. *The World in a List of Words*. Tübingen: Niemeyer.

Roberts, Jane & Christian Kay. 1995. *A Thesaurus of Old English*, 2 vols. London: King's College.
Roget, Peter Mark. 1852. *Thesaurus of English Words and Phrases*. London: Longman etc.; facs. ed. London: Bloomsbury, 1992.
Samuels, Michael & Christian Kay, forthc. *A Historical Thesaurus of English*.
Schäfer, Jürgen. 1989. *Early Modern English Lexicography*. 2 vols. Oxford: Clarendon.
Starnes, DeWitt T. 1954. *Renaissance Dictionaries. English-Latin and Latin-English*. Austin: University of Texas Press.
--- & G.E. Noyes, 1946. *The English Dictionary from Cawdrey to Johnson 1604-1755*. 2nd ed. Amsterdam: Benjamins, 1991.
Stein, Gabriele. 1985. *The English Dictionary before Cawdrey*. Tübingen: Niemeyer.
Wehrle, Hugo & Hans Eggers,[13] 1967. *Deutscher Wortschatz. Ein Wegweiser zum treffenden Ausdruck*. Stuttgart: Klett.

33 C.I. Macafee, ed., *A Concise Ulster Dictionary*. Oxford: UP, 1996, xli + 405 pp.; from *IJL* 10 (1997), 336-8.

The need for a comprehensive dictionary of Irish English (IrE) has been stated in various publications (most recently in Görlach 1995) – it is in fact strange that one of the most promising dictionary projects in the English-speaking world has never been started in earnest. As far as (the old) Ulster is concerned, there have been a great number of word-lists compiled by amateurs and linguists from the 19th century onwards (apart from the data included in general dictionaries of English, in the *English Dialect Dictionary* and the *Scottish National Dictionary*). Plans to compile from these word-lists an *Ulster Dictionary* were revived in the 1960s but the formal decision to go ahead with the project dates to 1989, when newly developed computer programs made the completion within a reasonable time possible and when the felicitous choice of an energetic editor-in-chief saw the publication within a comparatively short time.

The dictionary is, then, restricted in several ways – a wise decision to concentrate on what was feasible is the basis for a successfully completed book which fills an important gap. The board decided not to include the South and thus produce an all-Irish dictionary (because the material available was far too patchy), and they also decided not to systematically gather new data but to proceed on the available collections held in the Ulster Folk Museum (with additions sent in during the past few years when the compilation was in active progress.)

The vocabulary comprises some 15,000 items – it is difficult to give a precise figure since variant spellings made so many cross-references necessary, and derivations and compounds are normally nested in the main entries. The dictionary is explicitly meant for classroom use (and is therefore not 'over-academic'), a fact also indicated by the very moderate price. It is intended as an exclusive dictionary: items found in St E are accepted only if meanings are notably regional. Relying on the word-lists has meant that the editors had to accept many of the data *bona fide* – however much they corrected obvious errors; however, the evidence collected by non-specialists many years ago, and with very different aims and methods, has meant for Dr Macafee and her team many "instances of obscurity and confusion."[18]

Spelling presents a special problem for all non-standard vocabularies, like those collected in dialect dictionaries, and the *CUD* is no exception. It must have been quite difficult to summarize items under individual headwords; there are 20 variant forms for *potato* and 21 for *pismire* (some fanciful distortions), and among Celtic-derived items there are 15 for *jory* 'smallest of a litter', and *greesach* 'ashes' has three different entries devoted to it. Accordingly, it can be difficult for the user to find the respective entry, for all the cross-references provided (*praiseach* 'mess' is found under **pracas**; cf. the old problem of the citation form for *bonham/bonive* 'young pig', here two entries). Difference from St E in pronunciation and spelling does not normally qualify a word for inclusion – but there are hundreds of Scots words which are distinctive only with this regard (**ableeze, aboot, efternoon, alane,** ...) and there is even an entry "**attrection** *noun* attraction" for the local pronunciation (cf. **cat, caut, ket, kyet** *noun* a cat).

The sources used made it not possible to provide of stylistic or regional labels[19], a fact which is particularly regrettable with regard to the Scots vs. Ulster English items; nor was it feasible to indicate the currency of individual words – many, collected in the 19th century and conspicuous for their unusual form, must be dead today. The entries are, with all their limited detail, of great linguistic interest for

a) the large number of words retained in Ulster dialects (and often in dialects of BrE) that became obsolete in St E a long time ago – the allegedly 'Shakespearean' character of IrE: **afeard, affright, agone, ambry, cask, fenster,** .... Compare archaic meanings in **ban** 'swear', **brave** 'fine' etc.

b) The great number of Irish items, many apparently shared with SIrE dialects (although a comparison is not strictly possible, see below – but it would make sense to test the Irish words in *CUD* in the south to see how many are current there).

c) The many Ulster Scots words. Although the settlers are unlikely to have imported the full range of Scots lexis in the 17th century, and many words must have been lost quite recently, their representation is still very prominent[20] – in number and

---

[18] Whereas many of the limitations were impossible to overcome, it is surprising to see that a very simple but informative indication of the sources was missed: The word-lists mentioned on p. 405 could have been easily reduced to sigils – B(yers), G(regg) Li(ndsay) ... T(raynor) and appended to the entries to indicate date, region and reliability of the source, and frequency of attestation in the case of several sigils.

[19] The major exception is "Co Donegal" (see **carmeliagh, coheen, cornamailye, diswander, hoge, shalk**[1] etc.); I fail to understand the editor's note on p. xxv where she says:

> Hints on the geographical range of some items can also be obtained by noting the range of sources in which they appear...

This is only possible by identifying the source and then checking the words in the original word-lists – which are unlikely to be accessible to the *CUD* user.

[20] Since the data can be checked against the excellent dictionaries of Scots it might be worthwhile to find out how may Scots words survived in the relative isolation of Ulster which became obsolete in Scotland, thus forming a parallel to archaisms from BrE.

conspicuous form, as in the case of words derived, it is alleged, with an intensifying prefix: **carnaptious, cornatrakate, cumsloosh, curcuddockly, currymushy, curwhiggit** – which look like ghostwords (and some possibly are). It would be one of the most rewarding follow-up studies to find out how many originally Scots items have spread to other English dialects.

d) The great amount of cultural information on (obsolescent) folk life – no surprise for a dictionary based on the collections of the Ulster Folk Museum – mainly on farmer's implements and homestead, plants and animals, children's games and superstition. It proved a very wise decision to include a few hundred illustrations – a definition for **booltyin** the swipple of the flail' would easily be lost without an accompanying drawing.

e) The unusually rich data for colloquial speech – which tends to be less fully represented in printed sources. There is, e.g., a huge collection of terms signifying awkward, clumsy, silly persons (**habergallion, hallion, herrim-skerrim, hippel** and **hobbledehoy** in **H** alone).

Most of the few phrases and proverbial expressions included also fall into this category illustrating local humour, like **foot-harp** 'spinning wheel', **drive Irish tandem** 'go by foot', **Paddy's eye-water** 'poteen', **look seven ways for Sunday** 'squint' etc.

Etymologies were also added at a later stage of planning; they prove to be of exceptional interest in this "great feast of languages". I found those given for words of Irish provenance particularly helpful – especially since the ones provided in the *OED* are not always to be trusted.

How far can the *CUD* be used to read texts from Ireland? The aims of the *CUD* were different, and it is not fair to expect from it things the editors did not promise. However, I checked the list I used to test the coverage of Irish items in general dictionaries (Görlach 1995) and found that 49 of my 135 were not included in the *CUD*. The absence is not surprising in the case of historical terms, because these are unlikely to be dialect items (but *CUD* includes **Fenian, galloglass** and **hedge school**) or modern political words current south of the border (**Dáil, garda, taoiseach**) – but many of my dialect words were also missing. Here are just a few of those ending in *-een*: **alpeen, bawneen, cruskeen, drisheen, jackeen, mavourneen, shoneen, squireen** and **streeleen** are not in the *CUD*, although dozens of other *-een* words are. Does this point to regional differences, or just to incomplete coverage?

It would be good to be able to end in an optimistic note, seeing this as a first step towards a *Dictionary of Irish English on Historical Principles*; the preface does hint at this possibility but the chances do not appear too bright, for financial, political and staff reasons. But since *CUD* readers are asked to name their wishes on what should come next (p. xiii), here are a few steps that would be highly rewarding:

a) Which of the words listed are still current, and what are their stylistic restrictions?

b) What are the regional distributions of the items that survive, especially with regard to the major Scots vs. Ulster English divide?

c) Is an arrangement according to conceptual fields feasible, as has been attempted with great success for Scots?
d) What is the overlap with the vocabulary in the Republic?

The editor mentions that

> the project has also provided dialect scholars with a most important resource in the electronic database produced in tandem with the dictionary. It contains a vast amount of material that could not be included in the present publication, and it is hoped that at some future date it may be possible to use the database as the foundation for a fully fledged historical dictionary, based on a reading programme of dialect literature.

This does not sound wildly optimistic and is notably vague – but is likely to reflect the state of affairs. We ought to be all the more grateful to Dr Macafee that the more limited dictionary is out.

References
Görlach, Manfred. 1995. "Irish English and Irish culture in dictionaries of English." In M.G. *More Englishes*. Amsterdam: Benjamins, 164-91.

34 Frederic G. Cassidy, *Dictionary of American Regional English*. Cambridge, Mass., Belknap Press of Harvard UP. Vol. I: A-C, 1985, clvi + 903 pp., vol. II: D-H (associate editor Joan H. Hall), 1991, xv + 1175 pp., Frederic G. Cassidy (Chief Ed.) & Joan Houston Hall (Associate Ed.). *Dictionary of American Regional English*, vol. III: I-O. Cambridge, Mass., Belknap Press of Harvard UP, 1996, xv + 927 pp.; from *IF* 103 (1998), 322-3; from *IF* 103 (1998), 318-21.

With two volumes published of one of the major dictionary projects under way, vol.3 at galley stage and the next volumes not yet in sight, it is in order to review the achievements of Cassidy and his team – even though the books were published a few years ago.[21]

When Cassidy started planning the new dictionary in the early 1960s, he had just finished the *Dictionary of Jamaican English*, jointly compiled with R. B. Le Page (Cassidy & Le Page 1960, ²1969). The state of American dialect lexicography was in a sad state, although scientific study of American dialects had begun with the foundation, as early as 1889, of the American Dialect Society. It is generally assumed that one of the major aims of the ADS was to produce a dictionary. However, contrary to the English Dialect Society which was founded in 1873 and disbanded in 1896 when the publication of Wright (1898-1905) was in sight, the planning of an American dictionary was never competently undertaken nor was editing properly begun in the first fifty years of the Society. When it came, it came without the sanction of the ADS (Wentworth 1944). Publication was especially ill-timed because work on the *Dictionary of American English* and the *Dictionary of Americanisms* was still in progress, and the

---

[21] Part of this review is taken from my earlier account (Görlach 1990), written when only vol. I was available. For the history of the project see the Introduction to vol. 1, and Wolfram 1986.

Atlas material was not yet available: Wentworth did use the ADS publications *Dialect Notes* and, starting in 1925, *American Speech*, the unpublished archives of the ADS and private collections, but the 15,000 items do not nearly exhaust American regional vocabulary.

Wentworth included the following categories:

> dialect in the sense of localisms, regionalisms, and provincialisms; folk speech, urban as well as rustic; New England and Southern United States dialects viewed in their deviations from General Northern, or Western, American English: [...] conventional and traditional dialect; locutions and usages having a dialect flavor or association, those on the fringe of colloquiality; old-fashioned, archaic, and poetic turns of expression, particularly when known to be still current in certain localities and to some extent, the sometimes inseparable class and cultural dialects.

But he did not deal with the following:

> slang; occupational terms; technical and scientific (botanical, zoölogical, geological) terms, excepting certain popular names, nor with broken English, as used by [...] American Indians as represented in literature; impeded or mutilated speech or that of very young children: mere misspellings, downright malapropisms except occasionally as they may exhibit dialectal traits or illustrate linguistic processes bearing significantly upon dialect. (1944: vii)

Atwood ([1965] 1986: 65) voiced widespread disappointment when complaining about the absence of very common dialect words (such as *eaves troughs*, *firedogs*, *rainworm*, *snake feeder* or *toot*).

This desolate situation has been remedied since the 1960s. Cassidy, after outlining the inglorious past of the project, made a formal proposal in 1963 on how to make a new start with collections for the *Dictionary of American Regional English* (*DARE*). The fruit of more than thirty years of continuous work, which involved re-doing much that had been handled incompetently before, is now in the process of being published (Cassidy 1985-, and cf. the very informative analysis of the *DARE* data in Carver 1987).

A number of features make *DARE* an exemplary regional dictionary which will set standards for all future works of its kind:

a) Utmost care was taken to consider every possible source of written evidence:
> the entire published collections of ADS, the Linguistic Atlases, the Wisconsin English Language Survey, special private collections donated to *DARE* ..., original American diaries, newspapers from every state, all obtainable folklore journal articles, all the State Guides, special studies of American language, items taken from about 400 regional novels, plays, poems, and many contributions from individuals in every state. (*DARE* brochure, ca. 1984)

In addition, thorough dialectological methods were employed to complement these data by exhaustive spoken evidence. An enormous questionnaire comprising over 1,600 questions was worked through with 2,777 informants during fieldwork in 1,002 selected communities in 1965-1970; the informants were carefully sampled so as to include representative portions of the American population according to age, sex, educational and occupational groups, and ethnicity (there was, however, a bias towards untravelled older speakers of the local type of AmE). Such spoken data were supplemented by 1,843 tapes of free speech and readings of a set text.

b) The use of sophisticated electronic machinery, with programmes specifically developed for the project, made the editing of the huge masses of evidence possible and it will also facilitate the retrieval of all the information included in *DARE*. (The most conspicuous of these developments are the computer-made maps which accompany many entries, but the use of the computer has also permitted statistical comparisons and multivariate analysis correlations which resulted in very reliable usage labelling).

c) The presentation of the evidence in the individual entries is excellent. It includes the expected information on variation in spelling and pronunciation, etymology (tracing words back to regional use in Britain where applicable), meaning, regional, social, age-specific and ethnic currency, and well-selected quotations, as well as some features not found in comparable works:

– computer-drawn maps neatly illustrating the regional currency (and density) of individual items (occasionally combined with the distribution of heteronyms);
– extensive definitions and usage descriptions drawn from earlier dictionaries and dialect monographs;
– long quotes from *DARE* files in which informants have given valuable information in addition to the replies to the questionnaire proper.

The regional lexis of AmE is, for historical reasons, not as diversified as that of BrE – as a look at Wright's *EDD* or a dictionary of Scots will easily show. However, the netting of the *DARE* collections was enormous: some 21,700 headwords plus 8,800 additional senses in the first two volumes covering more than a third of the entire *DARE* corpus make the *ADD*'s 15,000 look quite small. The selection principles applied by the *DARE* editors were wide: every word or expression that had a claim to being 'local' was accepted. This includes (a) local dialectalisms (words and meanings) in the traditional sense; (b) localisms and occupational lexis; (c) some ethnic speech, in particular Black English (including Gullah) and words from various immigrant languages if attested in English contexts (e.g. Chicano, Pennsylvania Dutch, Polish or Hawaiian). Although *DARE* is intended to cover the regional variation of *contemporary* AmE, the time depth of the written data (and the datedness of some items recorded from spoken usage twenty years ago) also make it a historical dictionary; this fact is also shown by the quotes arranged in chronological sequence, and by markers such as *obs*.

The first volume includes a very detailed introduction (x-cl) which provides information, in chapters written by different authors, about the history of the project, the maps and regional labels, language change, and pronunciation, and contains the full text of the questionnaire and a list of all informants. The bibliography of sources will appear in the final volume, V or VI.

The two volumes published comprise, then, some 21,700 headwords (and some 8,800 additional senses, as well as many cross-references, mainly spelling variants) – an unprecedented and unexpected wealth of lexical variation in a post-colonial society that was thought to be largely free of the regional vocabulary so typical of European countries developing into nation states from multilingual or highly polydialectal medieval units. The detailed information on forms, meanings and distributions of individual items is very usefully complemented by some 1,100 computer drawn maps which show regional patterns at one glance, much better than anyone can piece together the data contained in verbalized form.

At 87, Cassidy is still the heart of the magnificent enterprise he started more than thirty years ago. Although he will not see the final volume out, the sections published are more than sufficient to judge how necessary and far-sighted his move was in the 1960s. The *DARE* data will in due course be further complemented, in a minor way, by the atlas projects in progress (compare the acknowledgement to Lee Pederson for LAGS data in II: x) – and the data files of *DARE* will be analysed in various ways other than arranging items in alphabetical order. Two of the recent aids extended to *DARE* users (Carver 1987, Metcalf 1993) have already greatly enhanced *DARE*'s usefulness. However, there is also the major need to make the questionnaires available: the most reader-friendly form would certainly be to condense the replies to the over 1,600 questions and thus produce a dictionary arranged on onomasiological principles – all who have looked at the *DARE* files know how much exciting information is certain to be forthcoming from such a book. (Responses will be included as the *Data Summary* in the last volume).

With *DARE* published very fast, there is hope to see the next volume out in 1996. We are looking forward to reading more about *jackeroo, jalopy, jambalaya, jayhawker* – and many other words.

It is a fitting tribute to F.G. Cassidy, who celebrates his ninetieth birthday in 1997 and is still the major driving force behind the dictionary he founded, to see the third volume of *DARE* out. It follows in all details the format of the first two volumes published in 1985 and 1991 (see my review above), adding another 10,000 entries to the 21,700 already available. With Carver (1987)[22] and Metcalf (1993) published we are now in an even better position to make full use of the most comprehensive collection of America's regional lexis.

The new volume contains the expected amount of exciting information, for instance in some 200 compounds with *Indian* as their first element – quite a few facetious, as also in forty compounds in *Irish* + . A special feature of *DARE* are the lists of heteronyms which can be looked up under their alphabetical entries, providing information on co-existing designations for the same referent: thus *killdeer* has 21 equivalents mentioned, *killfish* has 16; cf. *mallow* with a large number of names of various malvaceous plants (this type of evidence will be much more accessible when the replies to individual items of the questionnaire are published). There is only little 'ethnic' on dialect, but a number of specifically African American expressions and meanings include *member, mercy seat, mess over, misery, Miss Ann(ie), Mister Charlie*. Archaisms are likely to be found more frequently in regional folk speech than in the

---

[22] Note that there are slight differences in the regional classification of Carver (1987) and *DARE* III which probably reflect new decisions made in the course of the past ten years.

standard language (see *methinks* recorded from the Appalachians and Ozarks). It is interesting to find that derogatory ethnic designations can also be geographically restricted (see *kike, mick, mocky, moke*).

The special type of *DARE* maps now supply very useful evidence on regional concentrations (discussed in Carver 1987), such as NE: *jack* v., Jersey *mosquito;* Nth, N Midl. *jeez*; Nth, NMid, West: *kitty-corner, liverwurst*; Sth, S Midl.: *jackleg, jaybird*; Sth, S Atl.: *light wood; liver pudding*; S Midl.: *jake leg, jarfly*; West: *jerky (beef), King's ex, lariat, lug, maverick*. There are also much more restricted distributions (see *juneberry, Kaiser blade, kernel, lister 2, locker 2, low grounds, maniportia, mall*). Some of these are loanwords from European languages (the following are not all accompanied by a map): *kermis, kimmelweck, kip, knepp, kolacky, kram, kringle, Kriss Kringle, lagniappe, lingonberry, lutefisk, motte*; others are from Native Indian languages like *kiskitomas, kokanee* and *kyack*, and from Hawaiian like *kukae, kukui, kuleana, kulikuli* and *kuloto* on p. 261. Some words are said to be scattered, i.e. they are really non-regional but general non-standard (to *learn* = 'to teach'); it is surprising to find *is it?/isn't it?* as an invariable tag not mentioned under this category. Occasionally, there are suggestive pieces of evidence for the survival of BrE dialect words (*lerrupy* in swWI from Cornwall), but colonial levelling has reduced the number of this type to very few instances.

The third volume is, as its predecessors before it, a rich mine of information, impeccably edited and printed and a joy to read. We are looking forward to the volumes still to come, hoping they will be published soon.

References
Algeo, John. 1990. "American lexicography". In Hausmann, *et al.*, 1987-2009.
Atwood, E. Bagby. 1986. "The methods of American lexicography" (first 1963/64). In Harold B. Allen & Michael D. Linn, eds. *Dialect and Language Variation*. Orlando, Fl: Academic Press, 63-97.
Carver, Craig M. 1987. *American Regional Dialects. A Word Geography*. Ann Arbor: University of Michigan Press.
Görlach, Manfred. 1990. "The dictionary of transplanted varieties of language. English". In Hausmann, Franz Josef, *et al.*, eds. 1990. *Wörterbücher. Dictionaries. Dictionnaires*. II. Berlin: de Gruyter, 1475-99.
Metcalf, Allan. 1993. *An Index by Region, Usage and Etymology to the Dictionary of American Regional English, vol. I & II*. (PADS. 77) Tuscaloosa: University of Alabama Press.
Metcalf, Allan and Luanne von Schneidemesser. 1993. *An Index by Region Usage and Etymology to the Dictionary of American Regional English, vol. I & II* (PADS. 77), Tuscaloosa: University of Alabama Press.
Wentworth, Harold. 1944. *American Dialect Dictionary*. New York: Thomas Y. Crowell.
Wolfram, Walt. 1986. "A repentant sceptic looks at *DARE*" (review article). *American Speech* 61: 345-52.

35 *Dictionary of Jamaican English*. Edited by F. G. Cassidy and R. B. Le Page. Second edition. Cambridge UP, 1980, lxiv + 509 pp. (=*DJE*)
Dictionary of Bahamian English by John A. Holm with Alison W. Shilling. Cold Spring, New York: Lexik House Publishers, 1982, xxxix + 228 pp. (=*DBE*); from *Anglia* 103 (1985), 157-65.

The two dictionaries under review are on the same region, the languages treated in them are historically connected, and the *DBE* is explicitly modelled on the *DJE*: "later prunings required more precise guidelines, drawn from the *Dictionary of Jamaican English*, as Cassidy and Le Page drew on the principles of the *Dictionary of American English* before them, which in turn followed the historical principles of *The Oxford English Dictionary*" (*DBE*: xii). All this is enough to justify a joint review which also tries to bring out the advantages and drawbacks of each through a comparison, on the assumption that one of the objectives of each book – important as they are for their respective speech communities – is to contribute to a better understanding of the complex relations of varieties of English and English-based creoles in the region (including the U.S.), and ultimately towards a monumental *Historical Dictionary of English in the Caribbean*[23]. This wider use is also stated in the Foreword to *DBE* by Cassidy, co-editor of *DJE*, and editor of the *Dictionary of American Regional English*: "The *DBE*, unique for its own area, will also be of great value for the wider comparative studies to come in the future" (*DBE*: ii).

When the first edition of the *DJE* came out in 1967, it was greeted with much enthusiasm, and deserved it: after all, this was the first "Third World" dictionary using the methods and principles of the *OED*. Only information which adds to the *OED* and its *Supplements* is included (new entries, new meanings, and antedatings, or later dates for words marked as obsolete). As regards the scope of the dictionary, the editors decided to include the whole range of varieties from broad creole (locally known as 'patois' or 'dialect', and always labelled "dial." in the book) to West Indian Standard English, since the existing continuum permits a rough classification of the use of a word as typical of one of the two poles, while the overlap along the continuum would make two separate dictionaries questionable. (The book's title is, then, as misleading as it would have been if it had been named *Dictionary of Jamaican Creole*).

The Oxford pattern is also apparent in many other respects, which range from typographical presentation, designations for parts of speech, usage labels, to the detailed documentation: although oral sources were extensively used, as is appropriate for a

---

[23] Related projects have either not been published (Holm 1978), or are very provisional (Dayley 1979), or are in the planning stage, such as Winer's *Dictionary of Trinidadian English*, or Highfield's vocabulary of the US Virgin Islands dialect. Of great comparative value – whatever historical conclusions can be drawn from the evidence will be William Stewart's forthcoming *Dictionary of Gullah Usage*, and a new *Dictionary of Black English* (Hirshberg 1982) – [both projects cancelled, but cf. the review of Allsopp below].

dictionary that includes creole, the Oxford principle that printed evidence is somehow better or more reliable shines through. It is also in the Oxford tradition that historical evidence is given as much room as it is in *DJE*: this is not a dictionary only of present-day varieties (contrast the long-awaited and much needed *Dictionary of Caribbean English Usage*), but also of Jamaica's creole roots.

There are, among the ca. 10,000 entries, two groups distinguished by typography: words recorded from printed sources are in upper case letters, those from oral sources (almost all of them "dial.") in lower case. The more standard groups (1-3) comprise (xii):

1) Words or senses now (or once) general in English but of which the earliest or latest record is in a book about Jamaica ...
2) (a rather dubious category) Words not otherwise especially associated with Jamaica, but recorded earlier or later, in a book about Jamaica, than they are known to be recorded elsewhere.
3) Words, spellings, or senses used in Jamaica though not a part of the English language outside the Caribbean.

It is here that it becomes clear that the dictionary makers saw Jamaica as a representative of the larger English- (or creole-)speaking Caribbean community, and one of the new features of DJE^2 was to introduce sigils for other countries of the region for which the use was also recorded. However, this additional information, though a step in the right direction, is patchy and unreliable: the evidence is based on a single informant per region[24], and there is of course no information on how frequent the word is elsewhere, nor on what persons use it in what contexts, let alone on dates that could elucidate linguistic history.

The 'dialect' words are classified in groups (4-7) as:

4) Dialect words that have been given written forms more or less in the manner of traditional orthography.
5) Dialect words written down by their collectors in naive spellings, whose spoken form is unknown.
6) Dialect forms known only from oral sources.
7) Dialect forms which, though sometimes printed in dialect literature, have no established spelling and are known chiefly from oral sources.

---

[24] Informants as listed on p. xv: Walter Edwards for Guyana (G), Donald Winford for Trinidad (T), Richard Allsopp for Barbados (BA), Barbara Assadi and John Holm for Nicaragua (N) and Colville Young for Belize (BL). The frequency of occurrence of individual sigils in *DJE* entries does not appear to reflect present similarities or historical relations of a variety with Jamaican Creole: What is, for instance, the numerical significance of the fact that in letter L there are, for a hundred entries unmarked (= assumed to be restricted to Jamaica?), ca. 20 parallels for Guyana, 15 for Belize, 12 for Barbados, but only 3 for Trinidad and 2 for Nicaragua? Has the ratio anything to do with settlement history, decreolization, language contact in the various communities, recent influence of Jamaican abroad, or is it mainly owing to different standards of information or knowledge?

Words of groups (1-5) are often accompanied by a broad phonemic transcription, with tone indicated where necessary; this orthographic system, specifically developed by Cassidy for Jamaican Creole is always used for words of type (6-7), which makes an indication of their pronunciation only necessary where variants are to be recorded[25].

Finally, the editors' historical slant is expressed in the weight given to etymologies and the reconstruction of the sources and development of creole phonology. Cassidy was the first to draw attention to how widespread mixed etymologies are in Jamaican Creole, and how plausible it is that they are so frequent in all creoles: the slaves' rapid acquisition of rudimentary English would make the conflation of an African and an English expression very likely wherever the senses were identical or similar. There are hundreds of words with unknown etymologies, and wherever parallels from African languages are to be found that could have been related to present-day Jamaican words, these are duly noted (especially from Twi, Ewe, Akan, Bambara); the use of a wedge (<) in etymologies is, however, dangerous since it suggests that the derivation is certain.

The "Linguistic introduction" comprises a single chapter, "The historical phonology of Jamaican English" (xxxvi-lxiv), a painstaking analysis of the bases of individual Jamaican phonemes, which are related to Dobson's reconstructions of EModE sounds and to *EDD*'s statements about dialect pronunciations of the second half of the 19th century. The editors here encounter the same difficulty that Bliss (1979) met with when interpreting 17th-century literary IrE, *viz.* that Dobson almost exclusively treats London usage, an area that settlers in Ireland and Jamaica are least likely to have come from (a problem compounded by the differences in social background). However, together with the known or reconstructed geographical provenance of the early white settlers and overseers, the history of Jamaican phonemes makes it likely that BrE dialect pronunciations, especially North country, Scots and Irish, have had an important influence on the formation of the new language[26]. Syntactical information is not, as many might have wished, summarized in the introduction, but broken up into dozens of lexical entries. Reading the entries A^{5-7}, A-GO, DA^{3-5}, DE^{3-4}, DO vb^2 DONE adv, GWINE etc. is no substitute for a grammar of the Jamaican Creole verb phrase, and the form in which it is here given, without a coherent syntactical frame, will not make all linguists satisfied with the treatment.

---

[25] In the absence of any orthographic norm, the *DJE* has already exerted great influence on how creole words/texts are represented in scholarly writing in the Caribbean (cf. *DBE*). Cassidy & Le Page unfortunately did not consider a possible extension of their system to other Caribbean varieties; fitting new sounds into the system has resulted, e. g., in the infelicitous combination *ohy* for /oy/ in *DBE*. Problems of the choice of a lemma, and the need for frequent cross-references, are illustrated by such words as *asunu* (7 pronunciations: 5 spellings), *banjo* (3:9), *carry* (8:3) or *coratoe* (4:9).

[26] There appears to be a contradiction in the underlying assumptions, which is unresolved in *DJE*: if – as is widely admitted – the phonology is the most tenacious element carried over into a new language, then African features are most likely to be retained in the pronunciation (and illocutionary acts), a view that would seem to conflict with the editors' claim, *viz.* that etymologies are frequently mixed, but that the sounds are more likely to derive from dialects of BrE.

All this is not meant to detract from the great achievement that the first edition was; it was with high expectations based on DJE^1 that one turned to DJE^2, but the book is not the "completely revised edition" that the flap promises. The "greatly extended supplement" (491-509) has some 700 entries, and one cannot help feeling that there could have been more: Rastafarian uses, one important source of innovations in the seventies, appear to have been tapped only sporadically[27]; and the addition of sigils to indicate the distribution of "Jamaicanisms" elsewhere in the Caribbean, or to mark them as a common heritage of the Atlantic creoles, is – as has been stated above – far from complete. On the whole, one can only assume that the editors did not continue their editing and collecting of material with the same energy that they invested in preparing the first edition. It is cause of additional regret that the price of £30, though justified for a difficult book, will restrict DJE^2 largely to the European and U.S. market: few copies are likely to find their way to native speakers of Jamaican English – who would then find that the book is no help with their sociolinguistic problems of usage and 'correctness'. As a scholarly monument, DJE stands as a great achievement, and it is hoped that there will be similar dictionaries from the Caribbean, but also from other English-speaking countries especially from the Third World.

Whereas Jamaica has been the centre of linguistic interest for creolists around the world for a long time, research into Bahamian English dates back only to the seventies, and is still represented largely by the names of the two editors of the *DBE*. The present book is accordingly based on Shilling's early collections connected with her 1977 dissertation, and Holm's preliminary work with written sources, and intensive and quite exacting fieldwork by both authors and their students on eight major Bahamian islands in 1979, which made it possible to verify the first 4,000 lexical items as well as add some 1,500 new ones. These activities resulted in a first draft in 1980, and the publication of the finished book some 4-5 years after it was first conceived, which must have set a record at least in modern lexicography[28].

The introduction, substantial portions of which appeared in Holm & Shilling (1980), provides the best survey of the sociocultural history of the islands, including settlement and present-day varieties, available for the Bahamas so far. One of the major stimuli that the dictionary is meant to give (and which makes it of especial interest to US scholars, and to creolists in general) is the renewed discussion of the possible creole roots of American Black English. Holm takes it for proven (or granted?) that BahE forms a (if not *the*) missing link between Caribbean creoles and BlE since here "American plantation creole of the eighteenth century was preserved by the slaves of

---

[27] V. Pollard's research into Rasta talk is not mentioned, and insufficient use is also made of other important research of the seventies by Alleyne, Allsopp, Lawton, and evidence in various dissertations submitted to the UWI and US universities.

[28] Considering the speed with which the project was completed, typographical errors are few – except in the introduction, where even the slip-in errata list only mentions a fraction of the actual errors, and where the important double page illustrating lexicographical conventions is made up of entries at proof stage (xxvif., taken over from the Prepublication Special advertisement).

American loyalists brought there in the 1780s. The creole English has not only survived but flourished, developing along its own lines in this predominantly black country" (iii). A proper evaluation of this claim will rest on various factors: it will be necessary to learn more about early Bermudan E., since the Bahamas were settled from there from 1648 on. Holm admits that the infusion of American Blacks is likely to have "altered the identity of the creole speech" (v), but that "It is unclear what sociolinguistic forces prevailed in the eventual blending of what were almost certainly two distinct varieties of creolized English" (v). However, he sees a realistic chance of reliable reconstruction because "on the out islands that had been largely unsettled before the coming of the loyalist plantations, it is certain that the American creole predominated in that it had no real competition, especially after the white owners who presumably spoke uncreolized English abandoned these plantations" (v). If speech forms from such islands as San Salvador and Exuma were treated in isolation (as more likely to continue early BIE), these could be compared with what other evidence from US slaves is available, in the US, possibly in a few features in Krio and Liberia (where US BIE was added to local pidgin in the early 19th century) and especially from the Samaná peninsula (Dominican Republic), settled by Blacks from the Philadelphia region in the 1830s and almost completely isolated from other forms of English ever since (cf. Holm 1983, based on fieldwork by José Vigo).

Since the creolist lexicographers' eyes (whether in *DJE* or in *DBE*) are focussed on differences from international English, which again are more plentiful in early speech, it is not surprising to find that their aims become very similar to those of traditional dialectologists, who also wanted to document individual words of however rare occurrence, and likely to come from NORMs (non-mobile, old, rural males) – the linguistic present becoming more and more homogeneous, at least as far as lexis is concerned:

> With the coming of black leadership in government in 1968 and independence from Britain in 1973, many middle-class jobs have opened to blacks. In the rush to join the middle class (whose badge of identity is the ability to speak standard English), the creolized English of the Bahamian dialect is losing ground to the standard except in very poor or isolated communities.
>
> (*DBE*: vii)

The Introduction is also significant because it provides much more detail than has been usual about the techniques and the history of the data-collecting for *DBE*. One of the points that the user should bear in mind when judging the lexis represented in *DBE* is that the fieldworkers systematically searched for regional words in certain onomasiological fields which appeared most promising; this could indicate that some other areas are not represented as fully because these received less attention.

For an item to be included in *DBE*, it must add information not found in other dictionaries such as *OED*, *DAE*, *W3* etc. In fact, "with only a slight modification of *DJE* guidelines to retain certain items of particular cultural, sociolinguistic, or historical interest which would have to be excluded otherwise, (the editors) accepted as Bahamian regionalisms:

1) those words whose first occurrence in print was in a book written on the Bahamas (...),
2) words or idioms occurring in the Bahamas that have become obsolete elsewhere (...),
3) words whose Bahamian form differs from that used elsewhere,
4) words whose Bahamian meaning differs from that elsewhere,
5) words whose frequency of occurrence is notably higher in the Bahamas than elsewhere (...),
6) words or expressions apparently coined in the Bahamas (...)."

It is obvious that there must have been hundreds of doubtful cases of whether a word ought to be in or not (5 is an especially subjective category), and while it was good that the editors opted for inclusiveness, it might have been interesting to know the ratio of the six categories among the 5,500 entries (or to have a sigil in each entry giving the reason for its inclusion), or, by way of an appendix, to be supplied with lists of retentions (2) and innovations (6), for the intrinsically interesting information such lists would provide, and because new information about the lexis of other creoles is likely to change such lists, giving the remainder a better claim to being 'Bahamianisms' than the normal entry words.

Like other creole dictionaries, *DBE* includes grammatical function words which supplement the core grammar of the introduction (but which are of course no substitute for a much needed exhaustive grammatical description of BahE): a^{1-3}, be^{1-2}, da^{1-4}, de^{1-2}, *does, done, gwine* etc. There is also a category of entries that readers will be especially grateful for if they should happen to browse through *DBE*: a number of encyclopedic entries are constructed so as to provide a coherent text which includes as many cross-references to items from certain encyclopedic fields as possible; I found it of particular interest to read through *African words, Agriculture, Buildings, Bush medicine, Conch, Cooking, Courtship and marriage, Death, Fishing, Games, Obeah, Pregnancy* and *birth*.

Fauna and flora are, expectedly, among the most frequent entries, and one wonders how current the knowledge of various designations (a great number of them are heteronyms) can be. Whether such words should be included at all is always an open question; compare Jean Branford's decision against inclusion (1980: xx): "It is not, I think, justifiable to attempt a detailed treatment of flora and fauna in a dictionary, since it is not designed as a biological glossary". Another marginal type of entry is represented by a dozen or so Haitian creole words (*lapli* 'rain' etc.), few of them, probably, of general currency, and most of them used only if speaking to immigrant Haitians – a topic that would deserve an investigation to itself.

A typical *DBE* entry can contain information on 1. variant spellings (up to four, with cross-references if necessary), 2. pronunciation (revised *DJE* system), 3. etymologies and parallels from other creoles (drawing on the most important historical dictionaries), 4. part of speech, 5. obsolescence, 6. meanings and encyclopedic information, 7. syntactic restrictions, 8. citations from written and spoken sources preceded by the year, and with the island indicated if from fieldwork, 9. cross-references to semantically related items, 10. usage notes, and 11. social and regional distribution. Some of these reward closer attention: 3. covers the external, 11. the internal distribution of an item; and 3. also clearly shows the supplementary aim of *DBE*, as is shown by information such as "W3 idem; not in DAE, OED", "Scots idem CSD; US dial. North, Mid DARE". Other Caribbean dictionaries and wordlists, although not normally mentioned in the *DBE* entries themselves, are the source for the labels indicating regional distribution (cf. the key on p. xi), in descending order: 'Pan-creole' (equivalents found in French and Portuguese creoles etc.), 'Atlantic' (found in Caribbean and West African English-based creoles), 'Car' (found throughout the Caribbean), 'W Car' or 'E Car' (found only in the parts of the Caribbean indicated). It is obvious that the information available is much too fragmentary to be exhaustive; in our present state of knowledge some may even doubt whether a category such as 'Atlantic' is justified at all, because of its wide-ranging implications for the history of creole languages. The internal distribution, incomplete as it is as a consequence of the limitations of the fieldwork, is a valuable beginning. It is interesting to find that the label 'Black' is most frequent (with very few items marked 'white'), but that the items marked 'Gen' (general throughout the Bahamas) are much less frequent than those current on individual islands (mainly the ones investigated more thoroughly: San Salvador, Exuma, New Providence, Andros, Eleuthera, Inagua, Mayaguana) if taken together – no doubt a consequence of the great isolation of many island communities at least up to the 19th century.

    The two dictionaries are milestones on the road towards a proper description of the complex relations obtaining among varieties of Caribbean Englishes and English-based creoles. Apart from the great value that they have for the respective regions, they are likely to be of eminent value for other dictionaries of the Caribbean – and ultimately, one hopes, for a Dictionary of Caribbean English on Historical Principles which could complement the projected *Dictionary of Caribbean English Usage* [see **36**]. Hirshberg (1982) has shown what the incomparably larger resources of *DARE* permit one to retrieve for BlE, and although the aim of a future Dictionary of BlE – listing intra-American race-bound features – is different from both *DJE* and *DBE*, his conclusions can show what, ideally, remains to be done for the Caribbean: some sort of quantification of uses of lexical items, meanings and phrases according to region, class, race, age (of speakers), and obsolescence of words. Finally, Hirshberg points out that "the most salient characteristics of the glossary are rather the restricted or unique senses attached by blacks to words known or used by virtually every other speaker of the language; and the combinations of similarly common words to create new phrases and expressions largely unknown to the nonblack community" (1982:169). It is easy to see that such a detailed description is beyond the possibilities of the existing Caribbean dictionaries, whether finished or in the planning stage.

References

Bliss, Alan J. 1979. *Spoken English in Ireland 1600-1740*. Dublin.

Branford, Jean. 1980. *A Dictionary of South African English*, 2nd ed. Cape Town.

Dayley, Jon P., *et al*. 1979. *Belizean Creole*, 4 vols. Brattleboro, Vermont.

Fyle, C., and Eldred Jones. 1980. *A Krio-English Dictionary*. London and Freetown.

Hirshberg, Jeffrey, "Towards a Dictionary of Black American English on Historical Principles", *American Speech* 57 (1982), 163-82.

Holm, John. 1978. *The Creole English of Nicaragua's Miskito Coast: its sociolinguistic history and a comparative study of its lexicon and syntax*. PhD thesis, London.

--- "On the relationship of Gullah and Bahamian". *American Speech* 58 (1983), 303-18.

--- & Alison Shilling. "Accountability and verification in regional lexicography". *EWW* 1 (1980), 229-34.

Stewart, William. *A Dictionary of Gullah English Usage* [cancelled].

36 Richard Allsopp, *Dictionary of Caribbean English Usage*. With a French and Spanish Supplement by Jeannette Allsopp. Oxford: UP, 1996, lxxviii + 697 pp.; from *EWW* 17 (1996), 289-96.

The dictionary is the result of the dedicated work of the author over almost thirty years; the book under review was announced in various forms and often delayed (partly because of technological developments made it necessary to reorganize the material) – but the major aims have remained the same:

1) To document the varieties of English in the area,[29] concentrating on the acrolectal (standard) end, but allowing in large proportions of the local creoles where these are current and no standard alternative is available.

2) To make the book a reference work for teachers and other users who want to have a guideline on linguistic correctness.

3) To show both the distinctiveness of CarE (by including words and meanings not listed in the *OED*) and its internal diversity (by providing equivalents for individual areas corresponding to the meaning of the headword), as well as pointing out the links with other varieties of IntE.

The result is an original and enticing work. It may be useful to summarize the achievements under a few general points, concentrating on methodology and questions which are of potential interest to an international readership:

1) The data were collected in extensive fieldwork over many years, concentrating on the author's main scholarly interest, the coverage of equivalents; this field work was combined with a comprehensive reading programme (cf. the titles listed 627-66),

---

[29] Data are gathered from 22 territories in 18 states, but Allsopp never discusses how 'Caribbean' is to be defined. He includes Bermuda, but never mentions the Miskito Coast (also failing to mention Holm's dictionary (1978) for this variety) and all other Central American communities (for these varieties see Holm 1983).

resulting in some 20,000 words and phrases covered. Completeness is obviously impossible to achieve because even these efforts cannot be expected to provide a comprehensive haul, and because it is not quite clear in all cases what is distinctively Caribbean.

2) Allsopp was fascinated by different designations for the same referents, equivalents which prefers to call allonyms (and for which I prefer to use 'heteronyms', cf. Görlach 1991). The investigation of such items formed the beginnings of dialectology in England when the biologist John Ray was struck by the diversity of the terminology of flora and started to collect the evidence systematically (Ray ^{2}1691).

Allsopp has published extensively on the topic (cf. Allsopp 1984); looking at his full evidence in the dictionary we may be surprised there is not more of it. The evidence comes, unsurprisingly, mainly from flora – a field which swelled Morris' collections (1898) and which was deliberately excluded from Branford's South African data (^{4}1991). But even here, the striking cases for which some 10-20 heteronyms are recorded are few; see, for plants, the entries *birch-gumtree, bird-pepper, bluggo* (plantain), *cattle-tongue, cerasee, eggplant* and *Jamaica plum* – the need for a designation was originally solved on a local basis, and no standardization has ever taken place. It is more surprising to find widespread heteronymy in items of daily life (*bottle-flambeau* and *crepesoles*) and dishes (*dukuna*). Note that counting heteronyms presents a problem, because many items here differentiated are perhaps better classified as phonetic variants of one item (cf. the problem in *Jew plum, dew plum,* and *June plum*). But there are excitingly complex mixtures, as in the calqued noun for 'tale-bearer', *bring-and-carry, bring-come-and-carry-go, bring-go-and-bring-come, busy-lickum, carry-come-and-bring-come, carry-go-bring-come* and *lick-mouth*. Compare the various blends documented for *likerish,* adj. 'gluttonous' which is also called *cravicious, craven/raven/scraven, cravenous* and *licky-licky*. In cases like the latter identity of content is of course difficult and sometimes impossible to establish, and entries like *boucan* do illustrate a complex interplay of the same form designating different plants, and the same plant having different names. In general, items are more often distinctive of an individual area rather than shared; if they are shared this is often between regions closely related geographically (Trinidad & Tobago, Bahamas & Turks and Caicos) or through settlement history (Jamaica & Belize). There are a few indicating retentions of older lexical layers (say Barbados & Guyana & Jamaica) – these await closer analysis. However, for a full analysis Allsopp's data are not sufficient for two reasons: where a region is not listed, it is not clear whether a term was not elicited, or whether the standard word only is in use – or whether the object/concept does not exist.

3) The Caribbean area can be expected to provide extensive lexical evidence on a) African survivals; b) the retention of English dialects, including ScE and IrE; c) 'colonial lag' through isolation and fossilization of the early input; d) the interplay of various European colonial languages and those of more recent indentured labourers, e) the competition of BrE and AmE, f) the spread of pan-Caribbean items (as evidenced in reggae culture and Rastafarianism), and g) the impact of political unions established

in post-independence days (such as the new state of Trinidad & Tobago). All this could ideally be combined with the heteronymic data to reconstruct from linguistic reflexes the settlement and social history of the individual communities. How far does the dictionary help with this?

a) African survivals are generally recessive; many of these are connected with obsolete cultural items, and their retention cannot be used to reconstruct a pan-Caribbean early layer. Consider the attestations of five cultural items and one grammatical feature in six areas:

	Ant	Bdos	Gren	Guyn	Jmca	T&T
Cudjoe				x		
Kongkongsa					x	x
quackoo				x	x	
quashie	x			x	x	
shango			x	x		x
unu		x			x	

If we wish to take this as evidence of early settlement the data are conflicting to say the least.

b) As is well-known from Australia and the United States, BrE dialect evidence is difficult to establish, and clear cases of survival are much rarer than might be expected (Cassidy 1985, 1991). The Caribbean does not appear to be an exception, and it may come as a disappointment for those who had hoped for fuller documentation of words from, say, IrE in the area, but the evidence for this is almost completely lacking. (This may be partly due to the incomplete data here included. Note that *bonnyclabber* is attested for Jamaica (Cassidy & Le Page *baniclava*) and Barbados, but not found in Allsopp).

c) There is a great deal of 19th-century English surviving in the Caribbean, West Africa and India. Allsopp points out such cases with reference to last attestations in the *OED* in a number of places (see *beknown, biddy, tinnen* and compare *dickie* in a motorcar surviving in Grenada, St Vincent – and India). Much is more specifically biblical, as in *beforetime, bounden duty* (and literary: the impact of Milton, Bunyan and Victorian literature), but this feature not being specifically Caribbean, is only selectively covered – and not summarized in any place (there is no entry *teacheress* etc.).

d) French and Spanish played important roles in the area in general[30], and in the Windwards Islands (including Trinidad), with their surviving *Patwa* in particular. It is no surprise that French-derived items are concentrated on Dominica, St Lucia, St Vincent with Grenada and Trinidad often joining in (a statistical

---

[30] The supplement by Jeannette Allsopp (677-97) provides equivalents in French and Spanish (and Latin in the case of fauna and flora) but has otherwise little connection with the dictionary.

analysis of this impact would be valuable to have). The following eleven entries show different distributions but in general confirm our expectations as to the frequency of French-derived loans (only two attestations outside the six regions here shown):

	Dmca	St Lu	St Vi	Gren	Trin	Tob	
bèf	x	x					2
diablesse	x	x		x	x	x	5
djep	x	x			x		3
djab-djab	x	x		x	x	x	5
djanmet		x	x		x	x	4
mamman poule		x		x	x		5
palmiste	x	x	x	x	x		5
zabòka	x	x	x	x	x		5
zafè	x	x		x	x		4
zatwap	x	x					2
zèb-a-pik				x	x	x	3
	9	10	2	7	9	5	= 42

It is likewise not unexpected to find Indic words mainly in Guyana and Trinidad, since 19th-century indentured labour concentrated on these countries. (Recent Chinese influence is less focused and much less predictable).

e) There is no substantial evidence for the alleged Americanization of the area; the respective lexis was not Allsopp's interest, and so the impression the readers get from the dictionary is one of a staunchly British tradition and presence. How misleading this interpretation possibly is can only be found out by new research with a different focus.

f) Most Rasta terms like *i-anter*, *I-man*, *i-ration* are marked 'CarA' (whereas others remain Jamaican); this means that Allsopp accepts that the former are current throughout the Caribbean. There are a few other new terms of the same distribution, and it is noteworthy that many non-BrE derivatives are not restricted to the communities that coined them (see 4. below), an indication that there is a certain tendency to a more homogeneous CarE.

g) Political units are reflected in the distribution of formal terms (from administration etc.) but are confirmed also by the frequent attestations of words from Trinidad & Tobago; since their Englishes have quite different histories behind them at least some shared items are likely to be a reflex of a new national variety. (More evidence on this is expected from Winer fc.).

4) Word-formation was largely absent from the early pidgin and creole stages – with the exception of compounding. The great number of descriptive compounds is therefore no surprise, whether they are calqued on African languages (*day-clean*, *door-mouth*,

eye-water) or not. The many 'fanciful' derivations, most of them apparently dating to the 19th or early 20th century are more striking. Many of these were coined in defiance of English structure, are now felt to be incorrect (and thus marked x, or informal) and often obsolescent or used facetiously only, see *badmanism, begrudgeful, biasness, biggitive, cravacious/cravichous, don't-carish, facetiness, friendsing, jokify, studiation* and *stupidy*. (There *were* Victorian models like informal *botheration*, now a Caribbean survival). Note the official Bahamian term *belonger* (*-ness*).

5) Etymology is a nightmare under these conditions; Allsopp has succeeded, with a great deal of soberness and caution, to indicate or suggest the plausible provenience of most of the items included. One complicating factor is the prevalence of folk etymology. The fact is impossible to detect with many African items, but can be difficult enough for words of French ancestry (*bull-jowl* from *brule-gueule*, a sharp dish). Also note the great number of onomatopoeic items (conveniently collected under a collective entry *Echoic words*).

6) The explicit reference to correct usage and its deliberate intention to provide a norm for teachers and newspaper editors make the dictionary unashamedly prescriptive in places. This is indicated by [X] only, or by extensive advice on why a term should be avoided (*batty* 'behind'). Most of the items thus affected appear to be grammatical or other creole interferences (*becausen* "An illiterate form from Cr surviving in semi-literate speech" – a phrasing which encapsulates all the hesitation to accept the creole past as a legitimate part of language history). However, these indications are inconsistent. Why have *worse* x'ed for the superlative, and *worst* for the comparative, but not *worser*, and mark *worserer* and *worstest* as 'jocular'? Advising (or pontificating) on correctness is always difficult, but certainly more so under Caribbean conditions.

What does the dictionary give to the scholar? – a legitimate question since the price of £50, justified for European conditions, is likely to make the book as rare in the Caribbean as Cassidy & Le Page (^{2}1980) have been to date. The indication of the regional distribution of heteronyms, and their stylistic values, in the greater Caribbean area is one of the major contributions of the book. However, there is some evidence to collect to make the presentation more complete than it is (and there is some hope that readers will point out misleading statements and gaps.[31] A complete dictionary (or possibly the original dictionary files) will make it possible to reconstruct from the regional restrictions of some words important details of the history of English – a full dialectology of the area is in sight. The indications of regional currencies were of course half-heartedly begun in the second edition of Cassidy & Le Page (^{2}1980), but the method is here carried through much more consistently. Even if we must reckon with an extreme loss of linguistic evidence owing to the scarcity of early documentation, there are some data to make use of.

---

[31] To start with two random remarks: I find the word *rimlands* on the frontispiece map, and a *calabash* is said to be used as "a container or *dipper*" p. 130 – are these words Caribbean? Or Allsoppian? The impact of IrE is called *barbadoesing* "a unique place name verb in the English language" (xliii) – but there is no entry for it.

It is quite a different question whether, in due course, the dictionary should not be split into two complementary volumes – with all its high quality it appears at present to be sitting between two stools. For advice extended to teachers on whatever usage is to be considered as correct in cases where there is a choice, and thus to provide a reference book for active language planning, the number of entries and the scholarly documentation could be drastically reduced – which would permit the publisher to put on the market a book at a price that the intended users can afford. The scholarly audience, on the other hand, could be satisfied by a book concentrating on dialectologic and historical information.[32] The same community would have been pleased to have a more coherent exposition of the lexicographic principles (summarizing the author's earlier studies – which are not mentioned anywhere, as indeed other investigations of the field are almost totally neglected) and a statement of what differences he sees between his project, and the consequent methods, and Cassidy & Le Page (^{2}1980) and Holm (1982) to which his dictionary is in many ways complementary.[33] It may appear to be a churlish request now that we are happy to see this important book out, but it could provide a long-term perspective for making a good dictionary into two different books serving very different needs and expectations.

References:

Allsopp, Richard. 1984. "Cross-referencing many standards: some sample entries for the *Dictionary of Caribbean English Usage.*" *EWW* 4: 187-97.

Branford, Jean.^{4}1991. *A Dictionary of South African English*. Oxford: UP.

Cassidy, Frederic. *Dictionary of American Regional English*. Cambridge, Mass.: Belknap Press. *A-C* 1985, *D-H* 1991, *I-O* 1996.

--- & Le Page, R.B. ^{2}1980. *Dictionary of Jamaican English*. Cambridge: UP.

Görlach, Manfred. 1991. "Heteronymy in International English." (*EWW*) In: *More Englishes*. Amsterdam: Benjamins, 1995: 93-123.

Holm, John A. 1978. "The Creole English of Nicaragua's Miskito Coast." Ph.D. London.

---. ed. 1982. *Dictionary of Bahamian English*. Cold Spring, N.Y.: Lexik House.

---. ed. 1983. *Central American English*. (VEAW) Heidelberg: Groos.

Morris, Edward E. 1898. *Austral English. A Dictionary of Australasian Words, Phrases and Usages*. London; repr. Wakefield: S.R. 1971.

Ray, John. ^{2}1691. *A Collection of English Words not Generally Used*, London; facs. Menston (EL 145).

Winer, Lise fc. *A Dictionary of Trinidad & Tobago English*.

---

[32] The need is admitted by Allsopp himself but he does not indicate whether there are any concrete plans for such a book: "Although a dictionary on historical principles such as Cassidy & Le Page's *DJE* needs to be undertaken on a regionwide scale at some time, the present is not such a work." (xxxv)

[33] It is, however, easy to overlook titles of books and articles used since these are integrated into Allsopp's References and sources, 627-66, are arranged according to 'Codes' and quite difficult to handle.

37 Jean Branford, *A Dictionary of South African English.* Cape Town: Oxford UP, 1978, xxvii + 308 pp.,
D.R. Beeton and Helen Dorner, *A Dictionary of English Usage in Southern Africa.* Cape Town: Oxford UP, 1975, xix + 196 pp.; from *Anglia* 99 (1981), 196-201.

The last ten years have probably seen greater progress in the description of English as used in South Africa than all the years before. When D. Fanaroff published her *South African English Dialect: A Literature Survey* (Pretoria: HSRC, 1972) the picture was still rather bleak, although two projects had already been started whose (partial) results can be seen in the two books under review. However, a combination of various factors was necessary to make possible the recent flow of publications on South African English (SAfE): the concentration of linguistic interest on social problems of language and coexisting varieties, the special interest in bi- or multilingualism and language planning, and the political drifting apart of what at least until the Second World War had been a fairly homogeneous society of English speakers around the world, united in an Empire/Commonwealth. For South Africa, the vital dates are 1948 when the (Afrikaander) National Party gained power, and thereby visibly expanded the use and raised the prestige of Afrikaans and reduced that of English, now the minority native language of the white population. Many factors, often conflicting, have contributed to the research behind the two books: the desire to retain the close links with Britain versus a growing awareness of being different, and the desire to retain a conservative standard of speech versus the feeling that English must necessarily be different in different ways of life.

Preliminary work on *A Dictionary of South African English on Historical Principles* (*DSAEHP*) started at the Institute for the Study of English in Africa at Grahamstown in 1968, when a pilot study was begun that continued until 1970. The title shows that the dictionary team (among whom Professor W.R.G. Branford has been prominent) saw it as their goal to complement the *OED*, using basically the same methods, and thus forming part of a wider plan for regional dictionaries of English which includes the existing dictionaries of American English, of Canadian English, and of Jamaican English, with the Australian counterpart in preparation for 1988, and the dictionary of Indian English postponed indefinitely.

The dictionary work, which was able to make use of older compilations by Pettman (1913), Swart (1934-65), Jeffreys (1962-67) and van Blerk (1961), has already resulted in the publication of a pilot dictionary appropiately called *Voorloper* (Grahamstown, 1973: only some twenty copies printed). Since publication of the complete work will be a matter of many years, it was an excellent idea to publish the smaller dictionary first. Dr Branford is in the particularly lucky position not only of being highly qualified and keenly interested in the subject, but also of having at her disposal the institute's material.

Jean Branford has produced a reliable documentation of the lexis of SAfE where it differs from international English, especially from BrE and AmE, a purpose which came out even more clearly in the title originally proposed for the work, *viz. A Dictionary of South Africanisms in English* (the original subtitle was *Form features, adaptation and loanwords characteristic in South Africa*). Her book is halfway between a book for the interested amateur and a work of scholarly reference. Despite modest disclaimers, it leans towards the scholarly side, and will be a substitute for the larger *DSAEHP* as long as the latter remains unpublished, and indeed even afterwards it is likely to be of use, because it is handy and easily updated by way of new editions

In a multilingual society such as South Africa, the main question for a lexicographer is whose English is to be described, and what lexical items have a claim to being regarded as English, for transfers from other languages occur all the time and not only in the case of L2 or L3 speakers of English. This is a problem that is most obvious in societies like South Africa's, though it crops up elsewhere, too. Dr Branford makes it clear in a prefatory note on p. xi that SAfE is not "only that complex of forms spoken by what are sometimes called 'ESSAs' (English speaking South Africans) White or Black, but a *lingua franca* among those to whom English is, and many to whom English is not, their mother tongue." This inclusiveness is obviously reflected in the wealth of 'loans' from Afrikaans and Bantu languages, whose status as *English* will be questioned by many. But especially in domains/registers dominated by Afrikaans, such as in army slang, it seems sensible not to be too narrow if the dictionary is to fulfil its aim. Nor does Dr Branford evade the difficult question of recent political vocabulary (so sparsely represented in Beeton & Dorner) as she indicates herself on p. xii ("more recently the vocabulary of a different and yet deeper conflict – *apartheid, verkramp, amandhla, hippo, troopie* and *terr* – has begun to figure increasingly in the international press.") This is also borne out by her inclusion of new compounds or words with new meanings in *book of life, classify, classification, immorality (act), influx control, job reservation, separate development, to zone* and the recent (1977) *Chicken Run* 'the exodus of Rhodesian Whites', as well as common names such as *Azania, Robben Island, Turnhalle* and *Zimbabwe*.

The book is not a historical dictionary in the sense that the *OED* and the forthcoming *DSAEHP* are, but a fair number of obsolete and obsolescent words useful for reading older literature in SAfE is included. In some entries Dr Branford freely quotes from the older collections of Pettman (see *doodgooi, erf, gubu, mali*, etc.) and one can therefore only speculate on the reasons why quite a few 'Africanderisms' are left out. Apart from the conventional entries with a single lemma (including a few names, the more important placename elements, and a very few abbreviations), there are a few articles on 'correct' usage, such as *adjective with infinitive; articles; -ed, omission of; redundancies*, a feature much more prominent in Beeton & Dorner. There is also an article on *Indian terms*, which conveniently sums up the peculiarities of Indian English (but there is nothing comparable for Black or Coloured English). Dr Branford started her collections by arranging her material in "thirty-four categories chosen to cover the principal fields of South African English experience". This made it easy to give the whole the right sort of balance (e.g. by purposely omitting a large number of names for

South African fauna and flora) when, at a later stage, the entries were arranged in alphabetical order. However, it is with some regret that one does not find this earlier categorization retained in, for instance, a wordlist in an appendix: not only could this have illustrated why and how SAfE has developed differently in different lexical fields, but it could have provided a basis of comparison with other regional varieties of world English.

The material on which the work is based has been drawn from a wide range of sources, printed, written and spoken; it is here, and in the meticulous documentation at the end of the entries that the use made of the larger *DSAEHP* collections becomes most obvious.

As regards the organization of the entries, the orthography and parts of speech were unproblematic. Pronunciations are given for all words likely to present problems, i.e. all containing non-English elements. They are in IPA and include a few alternatives, such as more or less adapted pronunciations of Afrikaans words. This can still give the false impression of greater homogeneity than there is in SAfE, but in general the decision to give the form in which a word is likely to be heard in an English context is sound.

Definitions are linguistic as well as encyclopedic. For anyone willing to piece information together, this book provides a good deal of cultural information in the sense of M.M. Mathews who says in his *Dictionary of Americanisms*: "This dictionary is an index of the history and culture of the American people" (see, for instance, the subdivided entries for *boer, kaffir, kraal*, and *veld*).

Dr Branford was aware of the risk of including references "to items or usages from other variants of English comparable in form or idea with the South African terms e.g. '*randlord* cf. Anglo-Indian *nabob,* Hong Kong *tai-pan*'" (p. xvi). She goes on to say: "While this is not part of conventional lexicography, I think it is of great interest to match certain current themes in English vocabularies across the world. Thus *brak* is paralleled by Anglo-Indian *pye-dog* and Australian *mong; sugar baron* by Canadian *sawdust nobility, lumber king* and British *merchant prince; verkrampte* by Australian *wowser,* Canadian *mossback...*". Amusing as these 'parallels' can be for those who have access to the cultures involved, I think the dangers in comparing incomparables in this way are greater than the advantages.

Status labels are a problem in all dictionaries. Dr Branford makes (sparing) use of *substandard*, mainly for transfers from Afrikaans, *colloquial* and *slang* (the main distinction being that *slang* words are not normally found in print), *rare, regional* and *obs.*; other remarks on obscene and objectionable terms are verbalized in the definition of the word. There is full etymological information, which includes a discussion of doubtful cases, and there are generous quotations, with full documentation.

Beeton & Dorner's book, although covering much of the same ground, is in many ways quite different and hard to compare with Branford. It is firmly placed in an apparently old SAfE tradition of prescriptivism and as evidenced, for instance, by Pettman's verdict: "it gives an Englishman, who loves the sentence that is lucid and logical, a shock to hear his native tongue maltreated by those who are English in blood as himself" (1913: 16). The purpose of the book is most bluntly outlined on the back cover:

> This most unusual and exciting dictionary ... does not stop at merely giving the derivation and definition of words - it offers guidance as to the acceptability or otherwise of the vocabulary and usage listed. ...The aim of this compilation is prescriptive. It is, however, not intended to be a dogmatic and infallible guide ...

The compilers must be complimented on their derring-do: it is certainly most unusual in our age to reduce acceptability to a yes (+) and no (×) decision, even if '+' is sometimes qualified by 'rest' (indicating acceptability restricted to certain domains/registers), by 'reg' (regional) or by 'coll' (allowed in colloquial use). Quite unambiguous guidance on 'correctness' is, then, the main aim of the book; this includes advice on all kinds of 'confusibilia' which can be classified under

1) Orthography. "*chance/change.* sp frequently confused as a result of poor pronunc by Afk-speaking S Afr".
2) Pronunciation. *car* [kah] 'cor' ×, eg *'Where are you going to pork the cor?'* ×.
3) Grammar ("bad and *grammar* should not be combined as an expression; it is either grammatical or ungrammatical").
4) Latinate words ad usum Mrs Malaprop: *eminent/immanent/imminent, militate/mitigate.*
5) Near-synonyms: *close/shut, hire/lease/let/rent* and guidance on 'correct' meaning (*nostalgia*).
6) Registers such as officialese (*cognizant*), vogue words (*escalate, finalize, shock, viability*) or Americanisms (*paper packet*).
7) The main thrust is against influences from Afrikaans (and African languages), words from which have the greatest proportion of '×' markers, and are frequently labelled 'vulgar' in addition.

The principal inconsequence appears to be in the inclusion of up to one thousand items from South African fauna and flora, since these designations do not normally involve the question of acceptability. This highly specialized vocabulary is (as Dr Branford states) better served in encyclopedic reference books, especially since the main aspect of linguistic interest, namely the regional distribution of competing designations, is not adequately treated. Nevertheless, if one wishes to supplement the information in Branford, it is this field in which the effort would be most rewarding (see, for instance, the twelve alternatives offered for the shrub *African Wattle*).

As regards the structure of the entries, the lemma is followed by part of speech, source language, acceptability marker, then the pronunciation where thought necessary. Unfortunately the system was changed from IPA in the earlier EUSA version to a rather complicated notation. Lexical alternatives ('more correct' ones where necessary) are supplied, followed by lexical/encyclopedic information, which is not quite as comprehensive as in Branford. Detailed reasons why a term is objectionable or not, and indications of changing usage are found throughout.

After what has been said above it will be clear that no straight comparison of the two books is possible. The 3,700 entries in Beeton & Dorner (against 3,000 in Branford – with 10,000 on record in the *DSAEHP* collections) misleadingly suggest better coverage: inclusion of advice on orthography etc. and names of plants and animals in Beeton & Dorner swell the dictionary without making it the richer book. An extreme case of how little overlap there can be is found in the FA-FE section where there are 17 entries exclusive to Beeton & Dorner, 19 only in Branford – and a single entry found in both (*Fanagalo*). Beeton & Dorner's comparative reticence about recent political vocabulary, absence of historical SAfE, limited inclusion of loans and colloquial speech – all combine to make the book less useful for a foreign user: it is expressly a book meant for South Africa.

As regards the style of the entries and the amount of information, Dr Branford's more scholarly-neutral wording is often in contrast to Beeton & Dorner's more popular-emotional-evaluating style (see *Khalifa*).

Both books combine to bring us up to date from *aardvark* to *Zulu* – although it should be mentioned that *aandblom* +, *aandpypie* ×, *aapkop* × (see *vooihaakdoring*), *aapsekos* × , *aardbos* × and *aardroos* + reg precede *aardvark* in Beeton & Dorner, and *zut, zuur-, zwager,* and *zwart-* follow *Zulu* in Branford. The two books sufficiently illustrate the wealth of SAfE vocabulary not covered by the *OED* and whet our appetites for the even more comprehensive documentation in *DSAEHP*.

38 Penny Silva, managing editor, *A Dictionary of South African English on Historical Principles* (= *DHP*). Oxford: UP/Dictionary Unit for South African English, 1996, xxx+825 pp.; from *IJL* 10 (1997), 330-5.

Some twenty-five years of patient work of a dedicated team of lexicographers have now borne fruit: it is a consolation to find that the originators of the *DHP* project, William and Jean Branford, see their life work published, over a period of five years brought to completion in a comprehensive form and meticulously edited by Penny Silva and her team of four editors. For a few years it seemed as if the two dictionaries on historical principles prepared for Australia and South Africa might be published together – but then Australia's bicentenary in 1988 led to concentrated efforts to meet the jubilee, and Ramson's sister dictionary won the race by eight years (Ramson 1988). Eight years is little to most lexicographers, and, as it happened, the delay meant that the *DHP* could not only make full use of modern computer technology but also that it was possible to include in it the full linguistic evidence of the period before the peaceful change was initiated in 1991 – some sources and authors were 'banned' and not allowed to be quoted before the turnaround – and to reflect the new situation of the new South Africa at the same time.

The 5,000 entries of the *DHP* contain the most complete documentation of the special lexis of the national and local forms of English; since these items relate to South African culture and society they also form a fascinating history of the multilingual speech community, especially in the last two centuries.

According to the Oxford tradition here adopted, the headword, pronunciation (in IPA), etymology and definitions are followed by quotations (predominantly from printed or written sources – some 2,000 of these are listed in the "Select Bibliography," 811-25)[34].

As was to be expected, the special lexis is made up mainly of loanwords (Afrikaans predominating over Bantu/Khoi languages) and calques; the latter can be translations of the respective Afrikaans words, the similarity of the two languages making such interpretations easy, or new meanings suggested by the Afrikaans equivalents or independently developed.[35] *DHP* includes a full account of special vocabularies such as those of flora and fauna, law, army and church.[36] Among the most fascinating items are the historical relics of the apartheid era, the great number of ethnic designations (many no longer current as a consequence of political correctness)[37] and other offensive terms. Words not originating in South Africa are not normally included even if they have a special relevance for the cultural history of the country or present-day conditions[38]. Readers will therefore miss items like *TRC* = *Truth and Reconciliation Commission* or *affirmative action* (did these become current after the manuscript was sent to Oxford?).

Otherwise *DHP* leaves very little to be desired, as a comparison with the smaller dictionary shows:

DHP is of course closely related to Jean Branford's *Dictionary of South African English* (*DSAfE*) – after all, William Branford started the *DHP* project and Jean B. was an editor for some 18 years. If we compare the *DSAfE* (^{4}1991, with William B.) it

---

[34] Oral sources were used for items not likely to be documented from print, such as slang or grammatical peculiarities (cf. *yes-no*, whereas in *ja-nee*, *just now* and *now-now* printed sources predominate). Overall, the extensive use of quotations from speech is a notable modification of the 'Oxford' principles.

[35] No statistics are provided on the composition of the *DHP* lexis. It would be interesting to compare the figures given by W. Branford (1987: xiii). He estimates there are in the 1500 *SAPOD* entries some 570 compounds and diminutives, over 300 specialized SAfE senses, and about 70 acronyms; by way of etymology, some 52% of the words come from Afrikaans, 18% from English, 11% from Bantu languages and 1% from Khoisan (18% others).

[36] Terms of minority cultures are included as is testified by a substantial number of designations for African customs and institutions. Other cultures are covered more sparingly (cf. *abdas* referring to the Cape Muslim community), and many Indian terms were deliberately omitted as a comparison with Mesthrie (1990) shows (cf. *agharbathi, al, azan/adhan, back sari*, etc.).

[37] Cf. the over 70 compounds with *kaffir* as their first element documented on 343-9; many of these relate to fauna and flora and were not at all derogatory when coined, but had to be replaced when *kaffir* came to be a term of abuse.

[38] For a more liberal policy of greater inclusiveness cf. Craigie & Hulbert (1938: Preface); they state: "(*DAE*) includes, however, not only words and phrases which are clearly or apparently of American origin, or have greater currency here than elsewhere, but also *every word denoting something which has a real connection with the development of the country and the history of its people.*" [my emphasis] Their statement has often been quoted, and their principle been followed, by editors of dictionaries of -isms intended to supplement the *OED*.

becomes clear, however, that the smaller book is not just a short form of *DHP*, nor is *DHP* an expansion of the smaller. The relationship is much more complex; there are many words found only in *DHP*, about the same number is shared between the two, and a smaller number is found only in the *DSAfE*. Differences include in particular the more marginal lexis, such as:

1) The language of law and politics is more comprehensively covered in *DHP*: *absolution*, *absolve*, *accrual*, *achterborg*, *adiation* and *advice office*, *affected*, *Africanism*, *Africanize* are not included in the *DSAfE*.
2) The *DHP* includes more acronyms and abbreviations (*AAC*, *AB*, *ACF*).
3) In the case of Afrikaans words, the evidence is inconsistent. *DHP* has a great number of not integrated items (‖ *aanneming*, *aapsekos*, *aarbossie*) not found in the *DSAfE*, but the latter has *aanbod*, *aandag*, *aap*, *aardpyp*, *advokaat* and *afkak* missing from *DHP*,[39] whereas others are shared (‖ *aasvoel*, *afdak*).
4) The story repeats itself with words from Bantu (here: *Sintu* for p.c.) languages: the *DHP* includes *abakhulu* and *abalumbi*, the *DSAfE* includes *abadala* and *abaphansi*, whereas *abafazi*, *abakhana*, *abakwetha*, *abalungi* and *abathagati* are shared. (The fact that these words occur with a number of morphological variants necessitates many cross-references between $a \sim aba \sim um \sim m \sim \emptyset$, which makes checking not easy).
5) The *DSAfE* includes entries on usage and grammar (*a* 'article', *adjective with infinitive* etc.).
6) The more recent date of the *DHP* has of course meant that a few modern items were added for the period 1990-94; others are now marked 'obs.', marking the political changes of the past few years in particular – a practice of indicating usage which had to be more cautiously applied when the *DSAfE* came out in 1991. (It is a pity that the latter work is unlikely to see a new edition which could in turn serve to update usage in the *DHP*).

The new dictionary substantially adds to our knowledge of South Africa and the forms of English used in the country – its comprehensiveness, meticulous correctness and readability make it a monument to the new nation, and to all the lexicographers who devoted much of their lives to it. The fleet of Oxford dictionaries supplementing the *OED* is now almost complete – the New Zealand equivalent to be expected next. The *DHP* will remain the point of lexical reference for SAfE, but it will also provide an excellent basis for the smaller dictionaries planned for use in schools, in newspaper offices and for general readers.

References
Branford, Jean (with William Branford). 1991. *Dictionary of South African English*. Cape Town: OUP (4th ed.)

---

[39] The explanation probably is that the *DHP* needed attestations from three different sources, whereas inclusion in the *DSAfE* was often on a less strict basis.

Branford, William, ed. 1987. *The South African Pocket Oxford Dictionary* (= *SAPOD*). Cape Town: OUP.
Craigie, Sir William A. & James R. Hulbert, eds. 1938. A *Dictionary of American English on Historical Principles*. Chicago: UP.
Mesthrie, Rajend. 1990. *A Lexicon of South African Indian English*. Leeds: Peepal Tree Press.
Ramson, W.S., ed. 1988. *The Australian National Dictionary*. Melbourne: OUP.

39 W.S. Ramson ed., *The Australian National Dictionary*. A Dictionary of Australianisms on Historical Principles. Melbourne: OUP, 1988, xvi + 814 pp.; from *EWW* 10 (1988), 145-9.

When, in 1919, Sir William Craigie suggested complementing the *OED* with various period dictionaries and dictionaries of non-EngE varieties, he little thought how much time it would take to complete such a large-scale project. The book under review is part of this scheme, and the weightiest contribution to the lexicography of world English for many years; it is, however, to be joined by a similar dictionary of SAfE in the near future.

The subtitle of Ramson's book makes it clear that the compilation is quite deliberately modelled on the 'mother' dictionary, the *OED*, and the criteria used for inclusion of headwords clearly show the influence of Craigie/Hulbert's *Dictionary of American English* (1938), Mathews' *Dictionary of Americanisms* (1951), and Avis' *Dictionary of Canadianisms* (1967) – all explicitly designed to complement the OED, too. Ramson includes some 6,000 main entries (with the nested sub-entries, the total easily comes to double the number), which were elicited on the basis of *Instructions* handed out to readers, who were asked to be alert to:

- words and phrases they believed were Australian
- words and phrases in occupational vocabularies, especially those used 'on the job'
- words and phrases in other specialized vocabularies
- names for animals, birds, fish, plants, and geographical features
- words and phrases apparently borrowed from Aboriginal languages
- colloquial expressions
- proverbial expressions and catch-phrases
- familiar words and phrases used in unusual ways
- family or local expressions
- words and phrases not in common use, especially those which appear obsolete
- words and phrases which others have found unfamiliar. (Introduction, p. vi)

The 250,000 or so citations were edited to record in *AND*

> those words and meanings which originated in Australia, which have a greater currency here than elsewhere, or which have a special significance in Australia because of their connection with an aspect of the history of the country.

Apart from such models for non-Australian varieties as those mentioned above, Ramson gratefully acknowledges the benefit his team derived from existing dictionaries and word studies of AusE in particular works by E.E. Morris, S.J. Baker, G.A. Wilkes and the monographs published by the Australian Language Research Centre. Close cooperation with the editor of the *OED Supplement*, R.W. Burchfield (a New Zealander like W. Ramson), proved not only very profitable in the making of *AND*, but also guarantees that *AND* is fully compatible with the *OED*, and that its data can be used once all these 'word-hoards' come to be conflated in the *NEW OED*. The availability of all these earlier dictionaries has certainly helped speed up the *AND* project, but for its completion in the record time of only ten years full credit must go to the lexicographic expertise and organisational skill of Dr Ramson.

Work started in 1978, three years before the publication of the *Macquarie Dictionary*, which Ramson served as a member of the Editorial Committee. The *MacqD* is basically synchronic-descriptive, and it is inclusive: "not merely a dictionary of Australianisms; that is, of the words and phrases that are peculiar to Australia, that represent its institutions and express (even glorify) its folk ways. Instead, it takes the whole general vocabulary ... and describes the range of uses of each of the words of the vocabulary in the Australian context" (*MacqD*, 12). The complementary character of *AND*, in this respect being precisely what *MacqD* explicitly is not, is made clear in the previous quotation, i.e. it is an exclusive and historical dictionary. The two should, between them, include every item that is current in AusE or is recorded from earlier texts. In practice, this is often not so, and it is difficult to see exactly *how* the two dictionaries complement each other. Why is it that only eight *bush* compounds of the first 25 in *MacqD* (*-ballad, bash(ing), brother, carpenter, fire, house, lawyer, man*) are also in *AND*, which, however, contains another 42 in the same section (*bush ballad to Bushman*)? And which of these 67 can be considered AusE is a question that remains unanswered in both these dictionaries – because Australianisms are not marked as such in the *MacqD*, and because the criteria of admission to *AND* are liberal enough to allow in words that were recorded earlier in Australia than elsewhere, or which just have a particular historical relevance for the country. In fact, the problem of 19th-century 'colonial' English is incompletely taken account of in *AND*. Also, the interrelationship between AmE and AusE still calls for further investigation. (The discussion of the interrelationship between the two varieties in Ramson 1966:132 ff. certainly needs to be updated in the light of the new evidence – not even all the words mentioned in 1966 for the 19th century are in *AND* (cf. *dubersome, roust*, 1966:132. The origin of *bush*, derived from AmE in 1966:141 (against the SAf provenance assumed by the *OED*) is now left open: "Used earliest in S. Afr. and U.S.").

Another problem affecting completeness is presented by words of local currency. For one thing, those included in *AND* need to be tested as to whether they are or were restricted. Ramson warns (*AND*, vii) not to use "regional labels for many items in the colloquial vocabulary which are commonly supposed to be localized in their use ... for many more interesting items... the evidence is unconvincing: we have frequently allowed popular opinion a voice in a citation but ... it must remain opinion."

Moreover, a dialect dictionary of AusE, if it is ever attempted, will form another complement (as Wright's *EDD* did to the *OED*, Wentworth and the *DARE* to the *DAE* and *DA* etc.). Ramson rightly says (1988:145-6, information not in the introduction to the *AND*):

> The study of regional variation logically follows the establishment of the 'standard' vocabulary and a definitive study of SAusE will require an assessment of *AND*'s findings, the supplementation of these from specifically local sources, and the implementation of an oral survey ...

Further, the absence of other words is owing to their lack of printed attestation – or to the view that transparent formations modelled on productive patterns need no explanation: Thus, from the list of words in *-o* listed by Dabke (1976:45), *AND* includes *bottlo, milko, plonko* and *smoko*, but not *buggo, cheapo, druggo, dumbo* and *weirdo* (*MacqD* has *weirdo*, and the alternative forms *cheapie, druggie*).

As is natural for a variety in which new combinations make up so much of its particular flavour, compounds are generously included in *AND*. However, *AND* only very selectively indicates at the end of individual entries which combinations a word enters into as a second element. Although compounds in *-station* form an important clue to the understanding of the Australian way of life, and *back-, head-, heifer-, home-* and *out-station* have main entries devoted to them, there is nothing under *station* to guide the reader to these compounds.

As regards the individual entry, the arrangement of information and typographical legibility are excellent. Pronunciation (in IPA) and variant spellings are provided where necessary, as in words from Aboriginal languages. Usage labels (apart from frequent *obs.* and a few regional labels) are very cautiously applied; in particular, "labels like *coarse, colloq., derog., slang,* and *vulgar* which tend unnecessarily to categorize, have been omitted" (p. vii). Much thought has been devoted to etymologies, especially the problematic derivations from Aboriginal languages and British dialects; assignments are usually more confident than in Ramson (1966) – but it remains uncertain whether this is the result of scholarly progress or because there is less room for discussion in a dictionary. Justification for including a word is provided in cases where an item is "used elsewhere but recorded earliest in Australia". Historical documentation of individual words, combinations and specific meanings leaves nothing to be desired; the impressive "Select bibliography" (767-814) lists some 5,000 titles from which quotations have been drawn. Entries such as *Aboriginal/-e, bush, cocky, colonial, convict, corroboree* or *wowser* provide such a wealth of material that they should prove useful not only to the linguist, but also to the social historian – or the interested browser.

My review will have made it clear that is is difficult to point to any information lacking in *AND*. A second edition could perhaps include a greater proportion a) of words of regionally restricted use in Australia (rather than leave it to an independent dialect dictionary, which would be likely to be quite slim), b) of items from the spoken language (some words appear to be missing because they are either not recorded in written sources, or because they are too slangy, which would discredit them in a similar way), and c) of words some of whose meanings differ, however slightly, from BrE or other world varieties. (Any comparison with the more inclusive *MacqD* easily supplies a substantial number of possible additions in all three categories which – one assumes – must have been deliberately excluded). It is to be conceded that such an expansion, especially with regard to meanings, would have to be based on more international efforts of all the English-speaking nations. Finally, it is necessary to recognize that a dictionary of this type cannot do justice to one of the striking features of Australian lexis - the conflation of originally BrE with AmE lexical items, often with distinctive frequencies and stylistic marking.

Lexicographers, historical linguists and all who are interested in Australia will be grateful to Dr Ramson and his team who have produced, in the proper tradition of Dr Johnson, such a splendid piece of applied scholarship.

References
Dabke, Roswitha. 1976. *Morphology of Australian English*. München: Fink.
Ramson, W.S., Australian English. 1966. *An Historical Study of the Vocabulary*. Canberra: ANU Press.
---. 1988. "Some South Australian Words", In T.L. & Jill Burton, eds., *Lexicographical and Linguistic Studies*. Cambridge: Brewer, 145-50.

40 H.W. Orsman, ed., *The Dictionary of New Zealand English. A Dictionary of New Zealandisms on Historical Principles*. Auckland: OUP. xvi + 965pp.; from *IJL* 12 (1999), 182-3.

Orsman's monumental lexicographical account of NZE now completes a set of historical dictionaries of colonial Englishes – the Australian by Ramson (1988) and the South African by Silva (1996) preceded (or overtook) Orsman, who devoted some 40 years of his scholarly life to the project and which he completed almost singlehandedly: a beautiful illustration of what a dedicated scholar can achieve.

The 6,000 headword entries (with some 9,300 subentries) document the 150 years of the country's history and its emancipation, linguistically and otherwise. Arranged according to the successful Oxford pattern the headwords are followed by part-of-speech label, pronunciation in IPA where felt necessary (some 10% of the entries?), variants, etymologies (including cross-references to relevant entries in the *OED*, *EDD* and, most frequently, *AND*) definitions (including comprehensive encyclopedic information where appropriate) and lavish documentation by quotations, with at least one specimen per decade provided where available. The choice of this type of presentation was no question for a philologist like Harry Orsman, and it now provides excellent means for comparing several ENL varieties, old and new. The great distinguisher is of course NZE's wordhoard of Maori terms, for which letter *k*- unsurprisingly yields the richest haul. The documentation of these items often goes back to the first years of exploration or early settlement (1807-1820), many coming from travelogues and diaries, some still in manuscript or edited quite recently (cf. the sources quoted 933-65, a collection called a finding list since not all the texts have a quotation represented in the final form of the *DNZE*.)

Other layers outside the Maori component include survivals of BrE dialect, Americanisms dating from the first goldrush to recent media-influenced adoptions, and a particularly large component of items shared, or half-shared, with AusE. Survivals have always held a particular interest. However, two entries serve to illustrate the difficulties of proper documentation. *Messages* is an obvious Scotticism in the context of 'go shopping' (my former Oxford teacher Norman Davis remembered his grandmother using the term in New Zealand c1910). It must have come in with the mid-19th-century Scottish settlers – but is documented in *DNZE* only from 1950 on. For *skerrick* the *AND* has attestations from 1854 on – but *DNZE* only from 1960, which made Orsman add the cautionary note "The word is of much earlier use in New Zealand than its first recorded date." How are we to interpret that *dunnekin* 'outside privy' is recorded for 1837 and then not again before 1968, and that the much commoner *dunny* is attested only from 1941 onwards? Where written documentation is lacking, oral attestation will do (see *bugger-lugs*, where the earliest source, antedating the first written quotation by more than 70 years is quoted as "p.c. W.H.B. Orsman"). As in AusE, many of the items which are tentatively classified as deriving from BrE dialect on shaky evidence, proper equivalents not always having been established: *burl, dobbin, rort, sally-up, snig, snork, sook, sool* v. and *tin-kettle* v. are among the items I noted. The list includes exotic localisms (*spangweazling*) and total enigmas (*schnein* 'imitation metal', *scroggin* 'dried food etc.') .

As might be expected from settlement history, many early items are shared with AusE: *bonzer, chiack, cobber, crook, (fair) dinkum, fossick, new chum* etc. are all there – mostly with a delay of 4-30 years, but rarer slang terms like *snufflebuster* are also shared, and there are words which developed new historical relevance in NZ like *cockatoo*. Items or meanings shared with other varieties of English are often not easy to interpret sociohistorically – cf. NZE *rooster* (not *cock*) and *togs* shared with AmE, *slinter* shared with SAfE and *shagroon* (from IrE?).

Compounds are generously admitted, and rightly so, since they represent the major source of lexical innovation; many of these also illustrate a good deal of NZ history, especially in agriculture: compare the 20 compounds with *bullock* as their first element, or *cattle* (17), *cow* (32), *gold* (32) or the record-breaking *bush* compounds (some 200). Derivatives are again frequently shared with AusE as those in *-ie* (but a *dustie* 'dustman' is a *garbo*!); words in *-o* are found (*fleece-o, sexo, sheepo, smoko*), but they are less frequent than in AusE. In general, it is a pity that there was no room for a comprehensive comparison of the two vocabularies — what is shared (and which variety has the priority) and what is not, and what is the chronological development of this interrelationship? Morris (1898) did not think fit to distinguish between AusE and NZE, obviously because he thought most lexis was shared anyway, but today we would like to be better informed.

Among the items exclusive to NZE (apart from the Maori-derived vocabulary) we find a great deal of racy slang (*to be a sandwich short of a picnic, scarce as a frog's feather, thick as pigshit*) – but problems with documentation appear to have left some gaps: most of the items tested on NZ students in Gordon & Deverson (1998: 124) are not in, nor are expressions from estate dealers' jargon like *character* or *semicharacter mansion* and *handyman's delight* frequent in modern advertisements (E. Gordon, p.c.). Apart from items restricted to NZE words with a special relevance for the country's history are included; they are among the most attractive entries for browsers: *fence, flume, football, digger, Dominion, Empire City* and the 19th-century meanings of *civilization, colonize, Indian* etc.

Style labels are more sparingly used than might be expected; the most frequent are *Obs.* and *Hist.* However, in most cases, the definitions and the word histories make the status of the individual words clear. Occasionally, the language of the definitions is characteristically NZE, as it might well be: a *boil-up* is 'a brew of tea in a billy'.

The completion of the dictionary is not only a landmark in Orsman's life – it is a factual contribution to nation-building, documenting that NZE is not just another provincial dialect of BrE as many would have us believe (including New Zealanders!) nor a more or less legitimate offspring of the language of the Big Brother, Australia. The author is to be congratulated on completing and publishing in immaculate form a rich database and a mine of information on the smallest and southernmost settler variety of the world language.

References
Gordon, Elizabeth & Tony Deverson. 1998. *New Zealand English and English in New Zealand*. Auckland: New House Publishers.
Morris, Edward E. 1898. *Austral English. A Dictionary of Australasian Word, Phrases and Usages*. London; facs. ed. East Ardsley: S.R. Publishers, 1971.
Ramson, W.S. ed. 1988. *The Australian National Dictionary. A Dictionary of Australianisms on Historical Principles*. Melbourne: OUP.
Silva, Penny, ed. 1996. *Dictionary of South African English on Historical Principles*. Oxford: UP.

Reviews 1972-2002: A Bibliography

The following is a list of all my reviews published between 1972 and 2001 (with a few forthcoming, all marked '2002'); I have indicated those whose full text is reprinted in the preceding part of the book. For abbreviations of journals see p.i.

1) Abraham, Werner, ed., *Terminologie zur neueren Linguistik*, Tübingen, 1974, in: *Archiv* 215 (1978), 129-38.
2) Abrahams, Roger D. & John F. Szwed, eds., *After Africa*, New Haven & London, 1983, in: *EWW* 5 (1984), 150-1.
3) Adams, G.B., *The English Dialects of Ulster*, Holiwood, 1986, in: *EWW* 7 (1986), 342-3.
4) Adams, Karen L. & Daniel T. Brink, eds., *Perspectives on Official English. The Campaign for English as the Official Language of the USA*, Berlin, 1990, in: *EWW* 12 (1991), 327-8.
5) Adams, Valerie, *An Introduction to Modern English Word-Formation*, London, 1973, in: *IF* 80 (1975), 299-302.
6) Adamson, Sylvia, et al., eds., *Papers from the 5th International Conference on English Historical Linguistics*, Amsterdam, 1990, in: *EWW* 12 (1991), 143-4.
7) Adone, Dany & Ingo Plag, eds., *Creolization and Language Change*, Tübingen, 1994, in: *PBB* 118 (1996), 111-3.
8) Aertsen, Hendrik, *Play in Middle English. A Contribution to Word Field Theory*, Amsterdam, 1987, in: *Dutch Quarterly Review* 18 (1988), 330-2.
9) Afendras, Evangelos A. & Eddie C.Y. Kuo, eds., *Language and Society in Singapore*, Singapore, 1980, in: *EWW* 2 (1981), 132-3.
10) Aggarval, Narindar K., ed., *English in South Asia. A Bibliographical Survey of Resources*, Gurgaon, 1982, in: *EWW* 3 (1982), 271-2.
11) Agnihotri, Rama Kant, et al., *Tense in Indian English. A Sociolinguistic Perspective*, New Delhi, 1988, in: *EWW* 15 (1994), 168-9.
12) Agnihotri, Rama Kant & A.L. Khanna, eds., *Second Language Acquisition. Socio-Cultural and Linguistic Aspects of English in India*, New Delhi, 1994, in: *EWW* 16 (1995), 314-6.
13) Agnihotri, Rama Kant & A.L. Khanna, eds., *English Language Teaching in India. Issues and Innovations*, New Delhi, 1995, in: *EWW* 17 (1996), 148-9.
14) Agnihotri, Rama Kant & A.L. Khanna, *Problematizing English in India*, New Delhi, 1997, in: *EWW* 19 (1998), 149.
15) Algeo, John, ed., *English in North America* (CHEL 6), in: *EWW* (2002).
16) Alladina, Safder & Viv Edwards, eds., *Multilingualism in the British Isles*, 2 vols., London, 1991, in: *EWW* 12 (1991), 153-5.
17) Allen, H.B. & M.D. Linn, eds., *Dialect and Language Variation*, Orlando, 1986, in: *EWW* 8 (1987), 154-6.

18) Alleyne, Mervyn C., *Comparative Afro-American*, Ann Arbor, 1980, in: *IF* 88 (1983), 382-3.
19) Allsopp, Richard, *Dictionary of Caribbean English Usage*, Oxford, 1996, in: *EWW* 17 (1996), 289-96; repr. 155-60.
20) Ammon, Ulrich, ed., *Status and Function of Languages and Language Varieties*, Berlin, 1989, in: *EWW* 11 (1990), 141-3.
21) Ammon, Ulrich, *Die internationale Stellung der deutschen Sprache*, Berlin & New York, 1991, in: *Linguistics* 30 (1992), 660-3.
22) Ammon, Ulrich & Jenny Cheshire, eds., *Dialect and School in the European Countries*, Tübingen, 1989, in: *EWW* 11 (1990), 145-7.
23) Ammon, Ulrich, N. Dittmar & K.J. Mattheier, eds., *Sociolinguistics/Soziolinguistik*, Berlin, 1987-88, in: *EWW* 10 (1989), 339-44.
24) Ammon, Ulrich & Marlis Hellinger, eds., *Status Change of Languages*, Berlin, 1991, in: *EWW* 13 (1992), 322-5.
25) Ammon, Ulrich & Hartmut Kleineidam, eds., *Language Spread Policy*, 2 vols., Berlin, 1992 & 1994, in: *EWW* 15 (1994), 289-91.
26) Ammon, Ulrich, *et al.*, eds., *English Only? in Europe*, Tübingen, 1994, in: *EWW* 15 (1994), 293-4.
27) Ammon, Ulrich, *Ist Deutsch noch internationale Wissenschaftssprache?* Berlin, 1998, in *Linguistics* 37 (1999), 760-2.
28) Ammon, Ulrich, ed., *The Dominance of English as a Language of Science. Effects on Other Languages and Language Communities*, Berlin, in: *Sociolinguistics*. (2002)
29) Anderson, Peter, *A Structural Atlas of the English Dialects*, Beckenham, 1987, in: *ZDL* 56 (1989), 204-6.
30) Arends, Jacques, *et al.*, eds., *Pidgins and Creoles. An Introduction*, Amsterdam, 1995, in: *EWW* 16 (1995), 157-8.
31) Arends, Jacques, ed., *The Early Stages of Creolization*, (CCL 13), Amsterdam, 1995, in: *EWW* 18 (1997), 168-9.
32) Arthur, J.M., *Aboriginal English. A Cultural Study*, Melbourne, 1996, in: *EWW* 19, (1998), 145-6.
33) Auroux, Sylvain, E. H. F. Koerner, Hans-Josef Niederehe & Kees Verstegh, eds., *History of the Language Sciences/ Geschichte der Sprachwissenschaften/ Histoires des sciences du langage* (HSK 18). vol. 1, Berlin, 2000, in: *Linguistics* 39 (2001).
34) Avis, Walter S., *Essays and Articles*, Kingston, Ont., 1978, in: *EWW* 1 (1980), 156.
35) Avis, Walter S. & A.M. Kinloch, *Writings on Canadian English 1792 - 1975. An Annotated Bibliography*, Toronto, 1978, in: *EWW* 1 (1980), 157.
36) Ayto, John & John Simpson, *The Oxford Dictionary of Modern Slang*, Oxford, 1992, in: *EWW* 14 (1993), 151-2.

37) Bähr, Dieter, *Einführung ins Mittelenglische* (UTB 361), München, 1975, in: *Anglia* 95 (1977), 477-81.
38) Bailey, Guy, Natalie Maynor & Patricia Cukor-Avila, eds., *The Emergence of Black English. Text and Commentary*, Amsterdam & Philadelphia, 1991, in: *Linguistics* 30 (1992), 663-6.
39) Bailey, Richard W., ed., *Dictionaries of English*, Ann Arbor, 1987, in: *EWW* 9 (1988) 134-6.
40) Bailey, Richard W., *Images of English. A Cultural History of the Language*, Ann Arbor, 1991, in: *Anglia* 111 (1993), 464-6.
41) Baker, Colin, *Aspects of Bilingualism in Wales*, Clevedon, 1985, in: *EWW* 7 (1986), 341.
42) Baker, Donald C. & J.L. Murphy, introd., *The Digby Plays. Facsimiles of the Plays in Bodley MSS Digby 133 and e Museo 160*, Leeds, 1976, in: *Anglia* 105 (1987), 141-2; repr. 20-21.
43) Baker, Philip & Adrienne Bruyn, eds., *St Kitts and the Atlantic Creoles. The Texts of Samuel Augustus Matthews in Perspective*, London, 1998, in: *EWW* 20 (1998), 346-48.
44) Baldauf, R.B. & A. Luke, eds., *Language Planning and Education in Australasia and the South Pacific*, Clevedon, 1990, in: *EWW* 11 (1990), 324-5.
45) Bamgbose, Ayo, Ayo Banjo & Andrew Thomas, eds., *New Englishes. A West African Perspective*, Ibadan, 1995, in: *EWW* 19 (1998), 143-5.
46) Bammesberger, Alfred, ed., *Problems of Old English Lexicography. Studies in Memory of Angus Cameron*, Regensburg, 1985, in: *Lexicographica* 3 (1987), 253-5.
47) Barber, Charles, *Early Modern English*, London, 1976, in: *Anglia* 96 (1978), 174-80.
48) Barbour, Stephen & Cathie Carmichael, eds., *Language and Nationalism in Europe*. Oxford, 2000, in: *Sociolinguistica* 15 (2001), 120-4.
49) Barney, S.A., ed., *Word-Hoard. An Introduction to Old English Vocabulary*, New Haven, 1977, in: *Anglia* 96 (1978), 465-7.
50) Barnhart, Clarence L., et al., *The Barnhart Dictionary of New English Since 1963*; *The Second Barnhart Dictionary of New English*, Bronxville, N.Y., 1973; 1980, in: *EWW* 3 (1982), 127-8.
51) Barnhart, Robert K., *The Barnhart Dictionary of Etymology*, New York, 1988, in: *EWW* 11 (1990), 314-5.
52) Barnhart, Robert K., et al., eds., *Third Barnhart Dictionary of New English*, Bronx, N.Y., 1990, in: *EWW* 12 (1991), 151-2.
53) Baron, Dennis E., *Case Grammar and Diachronic English Syntax*, Janua linguarum, Series practica 233, The Hague, 1974, in: *IF* 81 (1976), 415-8.
54) Baron, Dennis E., *Grammar and Good Taste. Reforming the American Language*, New Haven, 1982, in: *EWW* 4 (1983), 327-8.

55) Baron, Dennis E., *The English-only Question*, New Haven, 1990, in: *EWW* 12 (1991), 329-30.
56) Barry, Michael V., *Aspects of English Dialects in Ireland*, Belfast, 1981, in: *EWW* 2 (1981), 285-6.
57) Bartelt, Guillermo, et al., eds., *Essays in Native American English*, San Antonio, 1982 in: *EWW* 4 (1983), 126.
58) Bartsch, Renate, *Sprachnormen: Theorie und Praxis*, Tübingen, 1985, in: *IF* 93 (1988), 255-7.
59) Bauer, Anton, *Das melanesische und chinesische Pidginenglisch. Linguistische Kriterien und Probleme*, Regensburg, 1974, in: *Archiv* 214 (1976), 405-8.
60) Bauer, Anton, *Das neomelanesische Englisch. Soziokulturelle Funktion und Entwicklung einer lingua franca*, Bern, 1975, in: *Archiv* 214 (1977), 405-8.
61) Bauer, Laurie, *Watching English Change. An Introduction to the Study of Linguistic Change in Standard Englishes in the 20th Century*, London, 1994, in: *EWW* 15 (1994), 299-301.
62) Baugh, Albert C. & Thomas Cable, *A History of the English Language*, 4th ed., London, 1993, in: *EWW* 15 (1994), 155-7.
63) Baumgardner, Robert, ed., *The English Language in Pakistan*, Karachi, 1993, in: *EWW* 15 (1994), 317-8.
64) Baumgardner, Robert, ed., *South Asian English. Structure, Use, and Users*, Urbana, 1996, in: *EWW* 18 (1997), 151-4.
65) Bautista, Ma. Lourdes S. *et al.*, eds., *Parangalcang Brother Andrew. Festschrift for Andrew Gonzalez on His Sixtieth Birthday*, Manila, 2000, in: *EWW* 22 (2001), 333-5.
66) Bayer, Jennifer M., *A Sociolinguistic Investigation of the English Spoken by the Anglo-Indians in Mysore City*, Mysore, 1986, in: *EWW* 9 (1988), 347-9.
67) Beadle, Richard & A.E.B. Owen, introd. *The Findern Manuscript, Cambridge University Library Ff. 1.6*, London, 1977, in: *Anglia* 105 (1987), 130-3; repr. 11-12.
68) Beal, Joan, *English Pronunciation in the Eighteenth Century. Thomas Spence's Grand Repository of the English Language*. Oxford, 1999, in: *ELL* 4 (2000), 125-33.
69) Beck, Heinrich, ed., *Germanische Rest- und Trümmersprachen*, Berlin, 1989, in: *Linguistics* 30 (1992), 1135-8.
70) Beeton, D.R. & Helen Dorner, *A Dictionary of English Usage in South Africa*, Cape Town, 1975, in: *Anglia* 99 (1981), 196-201; repr. 163-5.
71) Bell, A. & J. Holmes, eds., *New Zealand Ways of Speaking English*, Clevedon, 1990, in: *EWW* 12 (1991), 164-6.
72) Benson, David C. & Lynne S. Blanchfield. The Manuscripts of 'Piers Plowman': The B-Version. Cambridge, 1997, in: *Anglia* 119 (2001), 122-3.

73) Benson, Eugene & L.W. Conolly, eds., *Encyclopedia of Post-Colonial Literatures in English*, 2 vols., London, 1994, in: *EWW* 15 (1994), 315-7.

74) Benson, M., *et al.*, *Lexicographic Description of English/The BBI Combinatory Dictionary of English*, Amsterdam, 1986, in: *EWW* 8 (1987), 328-30.

75) Besch, Werner, *et al.*, eds., *Dialektologie. Ein Handbuch zur deutschen und allgemeinen Dialektforschung*, Berlin, 1984, in: *EWW* 6 (1985), 308-11; repr. 92-4.

76) Besch, Werner, O. Reichmann & S. Sonderegger, eds., *Sprachgeschichte. Ein Handbuch zur Geschichte der deutschen Sprache und ihrer Erforschung*, 2 vols., Berlin, 1984-86, in: *Word* 36 (1985), 266-9 (I); 38:3 (1987), 55-62 (II).

77) Besch, Werner, Anne Betten, Oskar Reichmann & Stefan Sonderegger, eds., *Sprachgeschichte. Ein Handbuch zur Geschichte der Deutschen Sprache und ihrer Erforschung*, 1. Teilband, Berlin, 1998 (2nd ed.), in: *Linguistics* 37 (1999), 566-8.

78) Besch, Werner, Anne Betten, Oskar Reichmann & Stefan Sonderegger, eds., *Sprachgeschichte. Ein Handbuch zur Geschichte der Deutschen Sprache und ihrer Erforschung*, 2nd edition, vol. 2. Berlin, 2000, in: *Linguistics* 39 (2001), 811-5.

79) Bevington, David, ed., *The Macro Plays. The Castle of Perseverance, Wisdom, Mankind. A Facsimile Edition with Facing Transcriptions*, New York/Washington, 1972, in: *Anglia* 105 (1987), 143; repr. 22.

80) Bex, Tony & Richard J. Watts, eds., *Standard English. The Widening Debate*, London, 1999, in *AAA* 26 (2001), 65-6.

81) Biber, Douglas, *Variation Across Speech and Writing*, Cambridge, 1988, in: *EWW* 10 (1989), 162-4.

82) Biber, Douglas & Edward Finegan, eds., *Sociolinguistic Perspectives on Register*, New York & Oxford, 1994, in: *JEngL* 24:3 (1996), 262-64.

83) Biber, Douglas, Stig Johansson, Geoffrey Leech, Susan Conrad & Edward Finegan, with a foreword by Randolph Quirk, *Longman Grammar of Spoken and Written English*, Harlow, 1999, in: *AAA* 25 (2000), 257-60.

84) Blake, N.F., *Selections from William Caxton*, Oxford, 1973, in: *Anglia* 92 (1974), 464-6.

85) Blake, N.F., *Non-standard Language in English Literature*, London, 1981, in: *EWW* 3 (1982), 124-5.

86) Blake, Norman Francis, ed., *1066-1476* (The Cambridge History of the English Language, II), Cambridge, 1992, in: *Anglia* 112 (1994), 130-5; repr. ; repr. 61-3.

87) Blake, Norman Francis, ed., *A History of the English Language*, Houndsmills, 1996, in: *AAA* 23 (1998), 118-9; repr. 55-6.

88) Blank, Claudia, ed., *Language and Civilization. A Concerted Profusion of Essays and Studies in Honour of Otto Hietsch*, Frankfurt, 1992, in: *EWW* 14 (1993), 317-9.

89) Bobda, Augustin Simo, *Aspects of Cameroon English Phonology*. Bern, 1994, in: *EWW* 17 (1996), 314-5.

90) Boffey, Julia & & A.S.G. Edwards, eds. *The Works of Geoffrey Chaucer and the Kingis Quair: A Facsimile of Bodleian Library, Oxford, MS Arch. Selden. B. 24. Ed.* Cambridge: Brewer, 1997, in: *Anglia* 119 (2001), 120-1; repr. 32-3.

91) Bolton, Kingsley & Helen Kwok, eds., *Sociolinguistics Today. International Perspectives*, London, 1991, in: *EWW* 13 (1992), 145-7.

92) Boretzky, Norbert, *Kreolsprachen, Substrate und Sprachwandel*, Wiesbaden, 1983, in: *Bulletin of the School of Oriental and African Studies* 2 (1984), 410-1.

93) Bourhis, Richard Y., ed., *French-English Language Issues in Canada*, Berlin, 1994, in: *EWW* 15 (1994), 306-7.

94) Bowden, Betsy, *Eighteenth-century Modernizations from the Canterbury Tales* (Chaucer Studies XVI), Woodbridge, 1991, in: *AAA* 20 (1995), 409-10.

95) Branford, Jean, *A Dictionary of South African English*, Cape Town, 1978, in: *Anglia* 99 (1981), 196-201; repr. 161-3.

96) Branford, Jean, *A Dictionary of South African English*, Cape Town, ²1980, in: *EWW* 1 (1980), 292.

97) Branford, Jean with William Branford, *A Dictionary of South African English*, Cape Town, ⁴1991, in: *EWW* 13 (1992), 166-7.

98) Branford, William, ed., *The South African Pocket Oxford Dictionary*, Cape Town, 1987, in: *EWW* 9 (1988), 143-4.

99) Braun, P., B. Schaeder & J. Volmert, eds., *Internationalismen. Studien zur interlingualen Lexikologie und Lexikographie*, Tübingen, 1990, in: *IJL* 5 (1992), 77-8.

100) Breitborde, Lawrence B., *Speaking and Social Identity. English in the Lives of Urban Africans* (Studies in Anthropological Linguistics 11), Berlin, 1997, in: *EWW* 19 (1999), 308-10.

101) Breuer, R. & R. Schöwerling, *Das Studium der Anglistik. Technik und Inhalte*, München, 1974, in: *Archiv* 213 (1976), 159-62 (together with H. Friedel).

102) Brewer, Derek S. & A.E.B. Owen, introd., *The Thornton Manuscript, Lincoln Cathedral MS 91.*, London, 1975, ²1977, in: *Anglia* 105 (1987), 128-30; repr. 9-11.

103) Bright, William, ed., *International Encyclopedia of Linguistics*, Oxford, 1992, in: *EWW* 14 (1993), 148-9.

104) "British linguistics in the 19th century", in: *Anglia* 117/4 (1999), 525-41; repr. 70-84.

105) Britton, J., et al., eds., *Teaching and Learning English Worldwide*, Clevedon, 1990, in: *EWW* 11 (1990), 308-9.

106) Brook, G.L., *The Language of Shakespeare*, London, 1976, in: *Anglia* 96 (1978), 174-80.

107) Brooks, Maureen & Joan Ritchie, *Words from the West. A Glossary of Western Australian Terms*, Melbourne, 1994, in: *EWW* 17 (1996), 316-7.

108) Brooks, Maureen & Joan Ritchie, *Tassie Terms. A Glossary of Tasmanian Words*, Melbourne, 1995, in: *EWW* 18 (1997), 167-8.

109) Brown, Adam, *Making Sense of Singapore English*, Singapore, 1992, in: *EWW* 14 (1993), 169-70.

110) Brown, Lesley, ed., *The New Shorter Oxford English Dictionary*, 2 vols., Oxford, 1993, in: *EWW* 15 (1994), 157-8.

111) Brumfit, C.J., ed., *English for International Communication*, Oxford, 1982, in: *EWW* 3 (1982), 266-7.

112) Buffet, A. & D. Laycock, *Speak Norfolk Today*, Norfolk Island, 1988, in: *EWW* 9 (1988), 352-3.

113) Burchfield, Robert W., *The English Language*, Oxford, 1985, in: *EWW* 6 (1985), 330-1.

114) Burchfield, Robert W., *The New Zealand Pocket Oxford Dictionary*, Auckland, 1986, in: *EWW* 8 (1987), 157-9.

115) Burchfield, Robert W., ed., *Studies in Lexicography*, Oxford, 1987, in: *EWW* 9 (1988), 136-7.

116) Burchfield, Robert W., *The Compact OED Supplement*, Oxford, 1987, in: *EWW* 9 (1988), 335-8.

117) Burchfield, Robert W., ed., *English in Britain and Overseas. Origins and Development* (CHEL 5), Cambridge, 1994, in: *Anglia* 113 (1995), 510-14.

118) Burchfield, Robert W., ed., *The New Fowler's Modern English Usage*, Oxford, 1996, in: *EWW* 18 (1997), 304-6.

119) Burgschmidt, Ernst & D. Götz, *Historische Linguistik: Englisch*, Tübingen, 1973, in: *Anglia* 92 (1974), 408-12.

120) Burton, Deirdre, *Dialogue and Discourse*, London, 1980, in: *EWW* 2 (1981), 276-7.

121) Burton, T.L. and J., eds., *Lexicographical and Linguistic Studies*, Cambridge, 1988, in: *EWW* 9 (1988), 351-2.

122) Busse, Ulrich, *Anglizismen im Duden*, Tübingen, 1993, in: *IJL* 8 (1995), 79-80.

123) Butler, Susan, ed., *The Macquarie Dictionary of New Words*, Macquarie University, 1990, in: *EWW* 12 (1991), 136-7.

124) Bynon, Theodora, *Historical Linguistics*, Cambridge, 1977 & *Historische Linguistik*, München, 1981, in: *Archiv* 220 (1983), 384-6.

125) Byrne, Frances & John Holm, eds., *Atlantic Meets Pacific. A Global View of Pidginization and Creolization*, Amsterdam & Philadelphia, 1993, in: *EWW* 14 (1993), 326-7.
126) Cairns, Craig, ed., *The History of Scottish Literature*, 4 vols., Aberdeen, 1987-88, in: *AAA* 15 (1990), 70-75.
127) Camden, Bill, *A Descriptive Dictionary Bislama to English*, Port Vila, 1977, in: *EWW* 5 (1984), 123-4.
128) Cameron, Deborah, *Verbal Hygiene*, London, 1995, in: *EWW* 16 (1995), 313-4.
129) Campbell, Lyle, *Historical Linguistics. An Introduction*, Edinburgh, 1998, in: *Anglia* 118 (2000), 267-9; repr. 53-4.
130) Cannon, Christopher. *The Making of Chaucer's English: A Study of Words*. Cambridge, 1998, in: *Anglia* 118 (2000), 270-2.
131) Cannon, Garland, *Historical Change and English Word-Formation*, New York, 1987, in: *EWW* 9 (1988), 334-5.
132) Carney, Edward, *A Survey of English Spelling*, London, 1994, in: *Linguistics* 32 (1994), 569-71.
133) Carrington, Lawrence D., *Literacy in the English speaking Caribbean*, Paris, 1981, in: *EWW* 4 (1983), 329-30.
134) Carrington, Lawrence D., ed., *Studies in Caribbean Language*, St. Augustine, 1984, in: *EWW* 6 (1985), 160-3.
135) Carrington, Lois, *et al.*, *Papers in Pidgin and Creole Linguistics*, No. 3, Canberra, 1983, in: *EWW* 6 (1985), 343-4.
136) Carstensen, Broder, fortgeführt von Ulrich Busse, *Anglizismen-Wörterbuch. Der Einfluß des Englischen auf den deutschen Wortschatz nach 1945*, Vol. 1, A-E, Berlin, 1993, in: *IJL* 8 (1995), 77-8.
137) Carstensen, Broder, fortgeführt von Ulrich Busse, *Anglizismen-Wörterbuch. Der Einfluß des Englischen auf den deutschen Wortschatz nach 1945*, Vols. 2 & 3, Berlin, 1995, in: *IJL* 12 (1999), 149-50.
138) Carver, Craig M., *American Regional Dialects. A Word Geography*, Ann Arbor, 1987, in: *ZDL* 56 (1989), 206-8.
139) Cassidy, Frederic G., ed., *Dictionary of American Regional English*, vols. 1 and 2, Cambridge, Mass., 1985 and 1991, in: *IF* 103 (1998), 318-21; repr. 143-6.
140) Cassidy, Frederic G. & Joan Houston Hall, eds., *Dictionary of American Regional English*, vol. 3, Cambridge, Mass., 1996, in: *IF* 103 (1998), 322-3; repr. 146-7.
141) Cassidy, Frederic G. & R.B. LePage, eds., *Dictionary of Jamaican English*, Cambridge, ²1980, in: *Anglia* 103 (1985), 157-65; repr. 148-51.
142) Cawley, A.C. & Martin Stevens, introd., *The Towneley Cycle. Facsimile of Huntington MS HM 1*, Leeds, 1976, in: *Anglia* 105 (1987), 140-1; repr. 19-20.

143) Charley, Dele, *Petikot Kohna; Fatmata*, Umeå, 1982, 1983, in: *EWW* 5 (1984), 317-8.
144) Charpentier, Jean-Michel, *Le Pidgin Bislama(n) et le multilinguisme aux Nouvelles-Hébrides*, Paris, 1979, in: *EWW* 5 (1984), 119-21.
145) Cheshire, Jenny, *et al.*, eds., *Dialect and Education: Some European Perspectives*, Clevedon, 1989, in: *EWW* 11 (1990), 143-5.
146) Cheshire, Jenny, ed., *English Around the World: Sociolinguistic Perspectives*, Cambridge, 1991, in: *AS* 67 (1992), 307-19.
147) Cheshire, Jenny & Peter Trudgill, eds. *The Sociolinguistics Reader*. London, 1998, in: *EWW* 118 (2000), 589-92.
148) Christian, Donna & Walt Wolfram, eds., *Dialects and Educational Equity*, Washington, D.C., 1979, in: *EWW* 2 (1981), 287-8.
149) Christie, William M., Jr., ed., *Current Progress in Historical Linguistics*, Amsterdam, 1976, in: *Anglia* 97 (1979), 179-82.
150) Clark, M. & O. Thyen, eds., *The Oxford Duden German Dictionary, German-English, English-German*, (1st ed. by W. Stolze-Stubenrecht & J.B. Sykes), Oxford, ^{2}1999, in: *IJL* 14 (2001), 137-9.
151) Clyne, Michael, ed., *Pluricentric Languages. Differing Norms in Differing Nations*, Berlin, 1992, in : *Linguistics* 30:6 (1992), 1132-5.
152) Cobarrubias, Juan & Joshua A. Fishman, eds., *Progress in Language Planning. International Perspectives*, Berlin, 1983, in: *EWW* 4 (1983), 121-2.
153) Collinge, N.E., *An Encyclopedia of Language*, London, 1990, in: *EWW* 14 (1993), 145-6.
154) Collins, Peter & David Blair, eds., *Australian English. The Language of a New Society*, St. Lucia, 1989, in: *EWW* 12 (1991), 309-13.
155) *Compact Oxford English Dictionary*, Oxford, ^{2}1991, in: *EWW* 13 (1992), 159-60.
156) *Concise Dictionary of Current English*, Oxford, ^{8}1990, in: *EWW* 11 (1990), 312-4.
157) Conklin, Nancy Faires & Margaret A. Lourie, *A Host of Tongues. Language Communities in the United States*, New York, 1983, in: *EWW* 7 (1986), 161-2.
158) Cook, Vivian, *Linguistics and Second Language Acquisition*, Basingstoke, 1993, in: *EWW* 16 (1995), 148-9.
159) Cooper, Helen, *The Canterbury Tales*. (Oxford Guides to Chaucer), Oxford, 1989, in: *AAA* 19 (1994), 142-5; repr. 43-4.
160) Corbett, John, *Written in the Language of the Scottish Nation*. A History of Literary Translation into Scots, Clevedon, 1999, in: *European English Messenger* VIII/2 (1999), 52-3; repr. 109-10.
161) Couillard, Xavier, *et al.*, *The Other Languages of England*, London, 1985, in: *EWW* 7 (1986), 155-6.

162) Coulmas, Florian, *Language and Economy*, Oxford, 1992, in: *EWW* 14 (1993), 310-11.
163) Coulmas, Florian, ed., *The Handbook of Sociolinguistics*, Oxford, 1997, in: *EWW* 18 (1997), 287-90.
164) Coupland, Nikolas, ed., *English in Wales*, Clevedon, 1989, in: *EWW* 11 (1990), 126-8.
165) Coupland, Nikolas & Adam Jaworski, eds., *Sociolinguistics. A Reader and Coursebook*, Basingstoke/New York, 1997, in: *EWW* 18 (1997), 301-2.
166) Craigie, William A. & James R. Hulbert, comps., *A Dictionary of American English on Historical Principles*, Chicago, ^{2}1978, in: *EWW* 2 (1981), 129.
167) Crawford, James, ed., *Language Loyalties. A Source Book on the Official English Controversy*, Chicago, 1992, in: *EWW* 14 (1993), 168-9.
168) Crewe, William, ed., *The English Language in Singapore*, Singapore, 1977, in: *EWW* 1 (1980), 157-8.
169) Crowley, Terry, *The Politics of Discourse. The Standard Language Question in British Cultural Debates*, Basingstoke, 1989, in: *EWW* 11 (1990), 149-51.
170) Crowley, Terry, *Beach-la-Mar to Bislama. The Emergence of a National Language in Vanuatu*, Oxford, 1990, in: *EWW* 12 (1991), 171-3.
171) Crowley, Terry, *An Illustrated Bislama-English and English-Bislama Dictionary*, Vila, Vanuatu, 1990, in: *Linguistics* 30 (1992), 648-50.
172) Crowley, Terry, *A New Bislama Dictionary*, Suva, Fiji, 1995, in: *EWW* 18 (1997), 335-6.
173) Crowley, Tony, *Proper English? Readings in Language, History and Cultural Identity*, London, 1991, in: *EWW* 13 (1992), 152-4.
174) Crowley, Tony, *Language in History. Theories and Texts*, London, 1996, in: *EWW* 17 (1996), 305.
175) Crowley, Tony, *The Politics of Language in Ireland, 1366-1922. A Sourcebook*. London, 2000, in: *AAA* 25 (2000), 261.
176) Crystal, David, *The Cambridge Encyclopedia of Language*, Cambridge, 1987, in: *EWW* 14 (1993), 141-4.
177) Crystal, David, *An Encyclopedic Dictionary of Language and Languages*, Oxford, 1992, in: *EWW* 14 (1993), 144-5.
178) Crystal, David, *The Cambridge Encyclopedia of the English Language*, Cambridge, 1995, in: *EWW* 16 (1995), 312-3.
179) Crystal, David, *The Cambridge Encyclopedia of Language*, 2nd edition, Cambridge, in: *EWW* 18 (1997), 306.
180) Crystal, David, *English as a Global Language*, Cambridge, 1997, in: *Anglia* 117:3 (1999), 417-8.
181) Cusack, Bridget, *Everyday English 1500-1700. A Reader*, Edinburgh, 1998, in: *Anglia* 118/3 (2000), 440-1.

182) Cypionka, Marion, *Französische "Pseudoanglizismen"*, Tübingen, 1994, in: *IJL* 9 (1996), 79-80.
183) Daichies, David, ed., *A Companion to Scottish Culture*, London, 1981, in: *EWW* 5 (1984), 311.
184) Dalgish, Gerald M., *A Dictionary of Africanisms*, Westport, Conn. & London, 1982, in: *EWW* 5 (1984), 318-20.
185) Dasgupta, Probal, *The Otherness of English. India's Auntie Tongue Syndrome*, New Delhi, 1993, in: *EWW* 16 (1995), 153.
186) Davis, Lawrence M., *English Dialectology: An Introduction*, Alabama, 1983, in: *EWW* 4 (1983), 317-9.
187) D'Costa, Jean & Barbara Lalla, eds., *Voices in Exile. Jamaican Texts of the 18th and 19th Centuries*, Tuscaloosa, 1989, in: *AS* 69 (1994), 187-91; repr. 116-9.
188) Delbridge, Arthur, ed., *The Macquarie Dictionary*, St. Leonards, 1981, in: *EWW* 5 (1984), 153-5.
189) Delbridge, Arthur, et al., eds., *The Macquarie Dictionary*. Second edition, Macquarie, 1991, in: *EWW* 13 (1992), 337-9.
190) *DEMEP. English Pronunciation 1500-1800*, Stockholm, 1976, in: *Anglia* 96 (1978), 474-6.
191) Denison, David, *English Historical Syntax*, London, 1993, in: *Linguistics* 32 (1994), 573-7; repr. 66-70.
192) Devitt, Amy J., *Standardizing Written English. Diffusion in the Case of Scotland, 1520-1659*, Cambridge, 1989, in: *AAA* 16 (1991), 103-4.
193) Devonish, Hubert, *Language and Liberation. Creole Language Politics in the Caribbean*, London, 1986, in: *EWW* 8 (1987), 316-9.
194) DeWolf, Gaelan Dodds, *Social and Regional Factors in Canadian English*, Toronto, 1992, in: *EWW* 14 (1993), 322-3.
195) *Dictionaries*, 1 (1979) - 5 (1983), in: *EWW* 5 (1984), 307-8.
196) Dil, A.S., ed., *Varieties of American English. Essays by Raven I. McDavid*, Stanford, 1980, in: *Archiv* 221 (1984), 346-8.
197) Dillard, J.L., ed., *Perspectives on American English*, Berlin, 1980, in: *AAA* 7 (1982), 216-8.
198) Dixon, R.M.W., et al., *Australian Aboriginal Words in English. Their Origin and Meaning*, Melbourne, 1990, in: *EWW* 13 (1992), 168-71.
199) Dobson, E.J., ed., *The English Text of the Ancrene Riwle, from BM Cotton MS, Cleopatra C VI*, EETS 267 (1972), in: *Anglia* 93 (1975), 322-5.
200) Dolan, T.P., ed., *The English of the Irish*, Dublin, 1990, in: *EWW* 11 (1990), 321-2.
201) Dolan, T.P. & Diarmaid Ó Muirithe, *The Dialect of Forth and Bargy, Co. Wexford, Ireland*, Blackrock, Co. Dublin, 1996, in: *EWW* 18 (1997), 166-7.
202) Donaldson, W., *The Language of the People. Scots Prose from the Victorian Revival*, Aberdeen, 1989, in: *EWW* 11 (1990), 317-9.

203) Drosdowski, Günter, general ed., *Duden. Das große Wörterbuch der deutschen Sprache*, 8 vols., 2nd ed., Mannheim, 1993-1995, in: *IJL* 10 (1997), 156-7.
204) *Duden - Das große Wörterbuch der deutschen Sprache*, 10 vols., Mannheim, 1999, in: *IJL* 13 (2000), 336-7.
205) Dürmüller, Urs & H. Utz, *Mittelenglisch. Eine Einführung*, Tübingen, 1974, in: *Anglia* 94 (1976), 456-62.
206) Dunger, Hermann, *Wörterbuch von Verdeutschungen entbehrlicher Fremdwörter. Engländerei in der deutschen Sprache*, [1882, 1909], Hildesheim, 1989, in: *IJL* 9 (1996), 161.
207) Duranti, Alessandro, *Linguistic Anthropology*, Cambridge, 1997, in: *EWW* 19 (1998), 142-3.
208) Dutton, Tom, *Queensland Canefields English of the Late Nineteenth Century*, Canberra, 1980, in: *EWW* 5 (1984), 156-7.
209) Dutton, Tom, *A New Course in Tok Pisin*, Canberra, 1985, in: *EWW* 8 (1987), 159.
210) Dutton, Tom, Malcolm Ross & Darrell Tryon, eds., *The Language Game. Papers in Memory of Donald C. Laycock*, Canberra, 1992, in: *EWW* 14 (1993), 316-7.
211) Eagleson, Robert D., *et al.*, *English and the Aboriginal Child*, Canberra, 1982, in: *EWW* 4 (1983), 330-1.
212) Edmondson, J.A., *et al.*, eds., *Development and Diversity. Language Variation across Time and Space. A Festschrift for Charles-James N. Bailey*, Dallas, 1990, in: *EWW* 12 (1991), 317-9.
213) Edwards, John, ed., *Language in Canada*, Cambridge, 1998, in: *EWW* 20 (1999), 176-8.
214) Edwards, Viv, *Language in Multiracial Classrooms*, London, 1983, in: *EWW* 4 (1983), 324-5.
215) Edwards, Viv, *et al.*, *The Grammar of English Dialect*, London, 1984, in: *EWW* 5 (1984), 308.
216) Edwards, Viv, *Language in a Black Community*, Clevedon, 1986, in: *EWW* 7 (1986), 339-40.
217) Eggington, William & Helen Wren, eds., *Language Policy. Dominant English, Pluralist Challenges*, Amsterdam & Canberra, 1997, in: *EWW* 19 (1998), 141-2.
218) Ehrlich, Eugene, *et al.*, comps., *Oxford American Dictionary*, New York & Oxford, 1980, in: *EWW* 2 (1981) 129-30.
219) *Englisch. Formen einer Weltsprache*, Bamberg, 1983, in: *EWW* 4 (1983), 321-2.
220) Enninger, Werner & Lilith M. Haynes, eds., *Studies in Language Ecology*, Wiesbaden, 1984, in: *EWW* 5 (1984), 299-300.

221) Escure, Geneviève, *Creole and Dialect Continua*, Amsterdam, 1997, in: *EWW* 18 (1997), 333-5.
222) Fasold, Ralph, *The Sociolinguistics of Society*, Oxford, 1984, in: *EWW* 8 (1987), 145-6.
223) Fasold, Ralph, *The Sociolinguistics of Language*, Oxford, 1990, in: *EWW* 11 (1990), 293-5.
224) Fennell, Barbara A., *A History of English. A Sociolinguistic Approach.* Oxford, 2001, in: *JEL* (2002).
225) Ferguson, Charles A. & Shirley Brice Heath, eds., *Language in the USA*, Cambridge, 1981, in: *AAA* 7 (1982), 216-8.
226) Fernández, Mauro, *Diglossia. A Comprehensive Bibliography 1960-1990*, Amsterdam, 1993, in: *EWW* 15 (1994), 153-4.
227) Filipović, Rudolf, *Anglicizmi u Hrvatskom ili Srpskom Jeziku: Porijeklo – Razvoj – Znacenje*, Zagreb, 1990, in: *IJL* 12 (1999), 152.
228) Filppula, Markku, *The Grammar of Irish English: Language in Hibernian Style*, London, 1999, in: *EWW* 21 (2000), 158-60.
229) Finegan, Edward, *Attitudes Towards English Usage*, New York, 1980, in: *EWW* 3 (1982), 125-6.
230) Fink, Hermann, *Von 'Kuh-Look' bis 'Fit for Fun': Anglizismen in der heutigen deutschen Allgemein- und Werbesprache*, Frankfurt, 1997, in: *Anglia* 116 (1998), 393-5.
231) Fink, Hermann, Liane Fijas & Danielle Schons, *Anglizismen in der Sprache der Neuen Bundesländer*, Frankfurt, 1997, in: *Anglia* 116 (1998), 393-5.
232) Fishman, Joshua A., et al., *The Spread of English. The Sociology of English as an Additional Language*, Rowley, Mass., 1977, in: *EWW* 1 (1980), 281-2.
233) Fishman, Joshua A., ed., *Advances in the Study of Societal Multilingualism*, The Hague, 1978, in: *EWW* 1 (1980), 254-6.
234) Fishman, Joshua A., ed., *Never Say Die!*, The Hague, 1981, in: *EWW* 3 (1982), 119-20.
235) Fishman, Joshua A., *Reversing Language Shift*, Clevedon, 1991, in: *EWW* 13 (1992), 147-9.
236) Fishman, Joshua A., Andrew W. Conrad & Alma Rubal-Lopez, eds., *Post-Imperial English. Status Change in Former British and American Colonies, 1940-1990*, Berlin, 1996, in: *Sociolinguistica* 11 (1997), 215-8.
237) Fisiak, Jacek, ed., *Contrastive Linguistics. Prospects and Problems*, Berlin, 1984, in: *EWW* 5 (1984), 305.
238) Fisiak, Jacek, ed., *Historical Dialectology: Regional and Social*, Berlin, 1988, in: *EWW* 10 (1989), 158-60.
239) Fisiak, Jacek, ed., *Historical Linguistics and Philology*, Berlin, 1990, in: *Anglia* 111 (1993), 118-9.

240) Fisiak, Jacek & Marcin Krygier, eds., *Advances in English Historical Linguistics*, Berlin, 1996, in: *Linguistics* 37 (1999), 770-3.
241) Flaitz, Jeffra, *The Ideology of English. French Perceptions of English as a World Language*, Berlin, 1988, in: *EWW* 10 (1989), 160-1.
242) Flaws, Margaret & Gregor Lamb, *The Orkney Dictionary*, Kirkwall, 1996, in: *EWW* 18 (1997), 320-1.
243) Fleith, Barbara, *Studien zur Überlieferungsgeschichte der lateinischen Legenda Aurea*, Bruxelles, 1991, in: *CG* 27 (1994), 64-6.
244) Fodor, István & Claude Hagège, eds., *Language Reform: History and Future*, vols. 4, 5, 6, Hamburg, 1989, 1990, 1994, in: *Linguistics* 33 (1995), 392-5.
245) Foley, Joseph, ed., *New Englishes. The Case of Singapore*, Singapore, 1988, in: *EWW* 10 (1989), 176-8.
246) Forster, Klaus, *A Pronouncing Dictionary of English Place-Names*, London, 1981, in: *EWW* 2 (1981), 284-5.
247) Fowler, David C., *John Trevisa*, Aldershot, 1993, in: *AAA* 19 (1994), 333-4.
248) Fox, Anthony, *Linguistic Reconstruction. An Introduction to Theory and Method*, Oxford, 1995, in: *ZAA*.
249) France, Peter, ed. *The Oxford Guide to Literature in English Translation*. Oxford, 2000, in: *AAA* 26 (2001), 67-70.
250) Francis, W.N., *Dialectology. An Introduction*, London, 1983, in: *EWW* 6 (1985), 329-30; repr. 94-5.
251) Frazer, Timothy C., ed., *"Heartland" English. Variation and Transition in the American Midwest*, Tuscaloosa, 1993, in: *EWW* 15 (1994), 143-5.
252) Fristedt, S.L., *The Wycliffe Bible. Part III: Relationships of Trevisa and the Medieval Spanish Bibles* (Stockholm Studies in English 28), Stockholm, 1973, in: *IF* 80 (1975), 297-9.
253) Fyle, C.N. & E.D. Jones, eds., *A Krio-English Dictionary*, Oxford, 1980, in: *Anglia* 102 (1984), 182-4.
254) García, Ofelia, et al., eds., *Focusschrift in Honor of Joshua A. Fishman*, 3 vols., Amsterdam, 1991, in: *EWW* 13 (1992), 149-52.
255) García, Ofelia & Joshua A. Fishman, eds., *The Multilingual Apple. Languages in New York City*, Berlin & New York, 1997, in: *EWW* 18 (1997), 325-6.
256) García, Ofelia & R. Otheguy, eds., *English Across Cultures*, Berlin, 1989, in: *EWW* 11 (1990), 117-21.
257) Gardt, Andreas, ed., *Nation und Sprache. Die Diskussion ihres Verhältnisses in Geschichte und Gegenwart*. Berlin, 2000, in: *Sociolinguistica* 15 (2001), 120-4.
258) Gazdar, Gerald, et al., comp., *A Bibliography of Contemporary Linguistic Research*, New York & London, 1978, in: *EWW* 1 (1980), 155-6.
259) Gburek, Hubert, *Der Wortschatz des Robert Mannyng of Brunne in Handlyng Synne*, Diss. Erlangen, 1977, in: *Archiv* 215 (1978), 398-9.

260) Geckeler, Horst, ed., *Strukturelle Bedeutungslehre*, Darmstadt, 1978, in: *Archiv* 217 (1980), 151-6.
261) Geeraerts, Dirk, *Diachronic Prototype Semantics: A Contribution to Historical Lexicology*, Oxford Studies in Lexicography and Lexicology, Oxford, 1997, in: *Linguistics* 36 (1998), 1023-5.
262) Gerzymisch-Arbogast, Heidrun, *Übersetzungswissenschaftliches Propädeutikum*, Tübingen, 1994, in: *Germanistik* 36 (1995), 40-1.
263) Gibbons, John, *Code-mixing and Code-choice*, Clevedon, 1987, in: *EWW* 8 (1987), 336-7.
264) Gilbert, Glenn G., ed., *Pidgin and Creole Languages*, Honolulu, 1987, in: *EWW* 9 (1988), 149-51.
265) Giles, Howard & Robert St. Clair, eds., *Language and Social Psychology*, Oxford, 1979, in: *EWW* 2 (1981), 275-6.
266) Giles, Howard & Bernard Saint-Jaques, eds., *Language and Ethnic Relations*, Oxford, 1979, in: *EWW* 2 (1981), 275.
267) Glowka, A. Wayne & Donald M. Lance, eds., *Language Variation in North American English. Research and Teaching*, New York, 1993, in: *EWW* 15 (1994), 285-8.
268) Goebl, Hans, Peter H. Nelde, Zdeněk Starý, Wolfgang Wölck, eds., *Kontaktlinguistik, Contact Linguistics, Linguistique de contact*, 2 Vols., Berlin & New York, 1996/1997, in: *Journal of Sociolinguistics* 1 (1998), 134-9; repr. 128-32.
269) Goetsch, Paul, *Presidential Rhetoric and Communication since F.D. Roosevelt. An Annotated Bibliography*, Tübingen, 1993, in: *EWW* 15 (1994), 164-7.
270) Goetsch, Paul & Gerd Hurm, eds., *The Fourth of July. Political Oratory and Literary Reactions 1776-1876*, Tübingen, 1992, in: *EWW* 15 (1994), 164-7.
271) Goetsch, Paul & Gerd Hurm, eds., *Die Rhetorik amerikanischer Präsidenten seit Franklin D. Roosevelt*, Tübingen, 1993, in: *EWW* 15 (1994), 164-7.
272) Gopinathan, S., et al., eds. *Language, Society and Education in Singapore*, Singapore, 1994, in: *EWW* 16 (1995), 143-6.
273) Gordon, Elizabeth & Tony Deverson, *New Zealand English*, Auckland, 1985, in: *EWW* 7 (1986), 349-50.
274) Gordon, Elizabeth & Tony Deverson, *New Zealand English and English in New Zealand*, Auckland, 1998, in: *EWW* 19 (1999), 316-7.
275) Gotti, Maurizio, *The Language of Thieves and Vagabonds. 17th and 18th Century Canting Lexicography in England*, Tübingen, 1999, in: *Linguistics* 38 (2000), 213-5.
276) Graddol, David, Dick Leith & Joan Swann, eds., *English History, Diversity and Change*, London, 1996, in: *EWW* 17 (1996), 303-4.

277) Graddol, David, *The Future of English? A Guide to Forecasting the popularity of the English Language in the 21th Century*, London, 1997, in: *EWW* 20 (1999), 171-2.
278) Graedler, Anne-Line & Stig Johansson, *Anglisismeordboka. Engelske lånord i norsk*, Oslo, 1997, in: *IJL* 12 (1999), 151.
279) Graham, John J., *The Shetland Dictionary*, Stornoway, 1979, in: *EWW* 1 (1980), 290-1.
280) Graham, William, *The Scots Word Book. English-Scots, Scots-English Vocabularies*, Edinburgh, ^{2}1978, in: *EWW* 1 (1980), 289-90.
281) Gramley, Stephan & Kurt Michael Pätzold, *Das moderne Englisch* (UTB 1359), Paderborn, 1985, in: *Der Fremdsprachliche Unterricht* 22, H. 92 (1988), 39.
282) Gramley, Stephan & Kurt-Michael Pätzold, *A Survey of Modern English*, London & New York, 1992, in: *EWW* 14 (1993), 159-61.
283) Gramley, Stephan, *The Vocabulary of World English*, London, 2001, in: *EWW* (2002).
284) Grant, William & D.D. Murison, eds., *The Compact Scottish National Dictionary*, Aberdeen, 1986, in: *EWW* 10 (1989), 164-6.
285) Green, Jonathan, *Newspeak. A Dictionary of Jargon*, London, 1983, in: *EWW* 4 (1983), 323-4.
286) Greenbaum, Sidney, ed., *Comparing English Worldwide. The International Corpus of English*, Oxford, in: *EWW* 17 (1996), 301-3.
287) Greenbaum, Sidney, et al., eds., *Studies in English Linguistics for Randolph Quirk*, London, 1979, in: *EWW* 2 (1981), 279-80.
288) Grote, David, *British English for American Readers. A Dictionary of the Language, Customs, and Places of British Life and Literature*, Westport, Conn., 1992, in: *EWW* 14 (1993), 166-7.
289) *Gudnius. Matiu, Mak, Luk, Jon (The Four Gospels in Solomon Islands Pijin)*, Honiara, 1988, in: *EWW* 11 (1990), 168-9.
290) Gunn, J.S. & B. Levy, *A Word History of Bushranging* and Langker, R., *Flash in New South Wales, 1788 - 1850*, Sydney, 1980, in: *EWW* 2 (1981), 134.
291) Gupta, Anthea Fraser, *The Step-tongue. Children's English in Singapore*, Clevedon, 1994, in: *EWW* 15 (1994), 318-9.
292) Guy, Gregory R. et al., eds., *Towards a Social Science of Language. Papers in Honor of William Labov*, 2 vols., Amsterdam & Philadelphia, 1997, in: *EWW* 18 (1997), 295-9.
293) Guy, J.B.M., *Handbook of Bichelamar - Manuel de Bichelamar*, Canberra, ^{2}1975, 1979, in: *EWW* 5 (1984), 121-3.
294) Haarmann, Harald, *Multilingualismus*, Tübingen, 1980, in: *EWW* 3 (1982), 116-7.
295) Häcker, Martina, *Adverbial Clauses in Scots. A Semantic-Syntactic Study*, Berlin, 1999, in: *Anglia* (2002).

296) Halford, Brigitte K., *Talk Units. The Structure of Spoken Canadian English*, Tübingen, 1996, in: *EWW* 18 (1997), 323.

297) Hancock, Ian F., ed., *Diversity and Development in English-related Creoles*, Ann Arbor, 1985, in: *IF* 94 (1989), 364-5.

298) Hands, Rachel, ed., *English Hawking and Hunting in the Boke of St. Albans. A Facsimile Edition of a2-f8 of the Boke of St. Albans (1486)*, Oxford English Monographs, London, 1975, in: *Anglia* 95 (1977), 236-8.

299) Hansen, Klaus, Uwe Carls & Peter Lucko, *Die Differenzierung des Englischen in nationale Varianten. Eine Einführung*. Berlin, 1996, in: *Anglistik* 8 (1997), 213.

300) Harlech-Jones, Brian, `You Taught Me Language'. The implementation of English as a medium of instruction in Namibia, Oxford, 1990, in: *EWW* 13 (1992), 335-6.

301) Harris, John, *Phonological Variation and Change. Studies in Hiberno-English*, Cambridge, 1985, in: *IF* 93 (1988), 354-7.

302) Harris, John, et al., eds., *Perspectives on the English Language in Ireland*, Dublin, 1986, in: *EWW* 7 (1986), 345-6.

303) Harris, Roy, ed., *British Linguistics in the 19th century*, 7 vols. London: Routledge/Thoemmes Press, 1993, in: *Anglia* 117 (1999), 525-41; repr. 70-5.

304) Harris, Roy, ed., *Language and Linguistics. Key 19th Century Journal Sources in Linguistics*. 4 vols. London: Routledge/Thoemmes Press, 1995, in: *Anglia* 117 (1999), 525-41; repr. 76-82.

305) Hartmann, Reinhard, ed., *The English Language in Europe*, Oxford, 1996, in: *EWW* 18 (1997), 157-8.

306) Hartmann, R.R.K., ed., *LEXeter '83. Proceedings*, Tübingen, 1984, in: *Archiv* 223 (1986), 381-4.

307) Haugen, Einar, et al., eds., *Minority Languages Today*, Edinburgh, 1981, in: *EWW* 3 (1982), 117-8.

308) Hausmann, Franz, ed., *Wörterbücher/Dictionaries/Dictionnaires*. I, Berlin, 1989, in: *Dictionaries* 14 (1992), 127-35.

309) Hausmann, Franz, et al., eds., *Wörterbücher. Dictionaries. Dictionnaires*, vol. 3, Berlin & New York, 1991, in: *Dictionaries* 15 (1993), 165-7.

310) Hawkins, J.M., *The Oxford Minidictionary*, Oxford, 1991, in: *EWW* 13 (1992), 159.

311) Hawkins, J.M. & R.E. Allen, *The Oxford Encyclopedic English Dictionary*, Oxford, 1991, in: *EWW* 13 (1992), 156-7.

312) Hawkins, R.E., *Common Indian Words in English*, Delhi, 1984, in: *EWW* 8 (1987), 334-5.

313) Hellinger, Marlis, *Englisch-orientierte Pidgin- und Kreolsprachen. Geschichte und sprachlicher Wandel*, Darmstadt, 1985, in: *EWW* 6 (1985), 341-2.

314) Hellinger, Marlis & Ulrich Ammon, eds., *Contrastive Sociolinguistics*, Berlin & New York, 1996, in: *EWW* 18 (1997), 155-7.
315) Henry, Avril, *Biblia Pauperum*, London, 1987, in: *AAA* 13 (1988), 203-4.
316) Henry, Avril, *The Mirour of Mans Saluacion*, London, 1986, in: *AAA* 13 (1988), 203-4.
317) Herberg, Dieter, Doris Steffen & Elke Tellenbach, *Schlüsselwörter der Wendezeit. Wörter-Buch zum öffentlichen Sprachgebrauch 1989/90*, Berlin, 1997, in: *Linguistics* 37 (1999), 759-60.
318) Herbert, Robert K., ed., *Language and Society in Africa. The Theory and Practice of Sociolinguistics*, Johannesburg, 1992, in: *EWW* 15 (1994), 312-3.
319) Hermerén, Lars, *English for Sale. A Study of the Language of Advertising*, Lund, 1999, in *ZDL* 68 (2001), 119-20.
320) Heringer, Hans Jürgen, *et al.*, eds., *Tendenzen der deutschen Gegenwartssprache*, Tübingen, 1994, in: *Linguistics* 33 (1995), 605-7.
321) Hesseling, Dirk Christiaan, *On the Origin and Formation of Creoles*, ed. and trs. T.L. Markey & P.T. Roberge, Ann Arbor, 1979, in: *EWW* 1 (1980), 159.
322) Hetherington, M.S., *The Beginnings of Old English Lexicography*, Spicewood, TX, 1980, in: *CG* 15:3 (1982), 157-8.
323) Hickey, Raymond & Stanisław Puppel, eds., *Language History and Linguistic Modelling. A Festschrift for Jacek Fisiak on his 60th Birthday*. 2 vols., Berlin, 1997, in: *EWW* 18 (1997), 308-9.
324) Highfield, Arnold & Albert Valdman, eds., *Historicity and Variation in Creole Studies*, New York, 1980, Ann Arbor, 1981, in: *EWW* 3 (1982), 262-5.
325) Hince, Bernadette, *The Antarctic Dictionary: A Complete Guide to Antarctic English*, Collingword, 2000, in: *EWW* (2002).
326) Hogg, Richard M., ed., *The Beginnings to 1066* (CHEL 1), Cambridge, 1992, in: *Anglia* 112 (1994), 130-5; repr. 58-60.
327) *Holi Baibul Kriol*, Canberra, 1984, in: *EWW* 7 (1986), 169.
328) Holloway, Joseph E. & Winifred K. Vass, *The African Heritage of American English*, Bloomington, 1993, in: *EWW* 15 (1994), 309-10.
329) Holm, John, ed., *Dictionary of Bahamian English*, in: *Anglia* 103 (1985), 157-65; repr. 151-5.
330) Holm, John, *Pidgins and Creoles*. 2 vols., Cambridge, 1988-89, in: *IF* 97 (1992), 312-4; repr. 113-6.
331) Holtus, Günter & E. Radtke, eds., *Sprachlicher Substandard*, Tübingen, 1986, in: *EWW* 8 (1987), 147-9.
332) Horvath, Barbara, *Variation in Australian English*, Cambridge, 1985, in: *EWW* 7 (1986), 140-3.
333) Hosali, Priya, *Nuances of English in India. What the Butler Really Said*, Pune, 1997, in: *EWW* 19 (1998), 149-50.

334) Hosali, Priya, *Butler English: Form and Function*. Delhi, 2000, in: *EWW* (2002).
335) Howatt, A.P.R., *A History of English Language Teaching*, Oxford, 1984, in: *EWW* 6 (1985), 331-3.
336) Hudson, Joyce, *Grammatical and Semantic Aspects of Fitzroy Valley Kriol*, Darwin, 1983, in: *EWW* 5 (1984), 155.
337) Hudson, R.A., *Sociolinguistics*, 2nd edition, Cambridge, 1996, in: *EWW* 18 (1997), 302-3.
338) Huber, Magnus, *Ghanaian Pidgin English* (VEAW G24). Amsterdam, 1999, in: *JPCL* (2001); repr. 119-21.
339) Hübler, Axel, *Einander verstehen. Englisch im Kontext internationaler Kommunikation*, Tübingen, 1985, in: *LSoc* 15 (1986), 439.
340) Huebner, Thom, *et al.*, *Solomon Islands Pijin*, Peace Corps Language Handbook Series, 4 vols., Brattleboro, 1979, in: *EWW* 5 (1984), 119.
341) Hüllen, Werner, ed., *Understanding Bilingualism*, Frankfurt & Bern, 1980, in: *EWW* 1 (1980), 286.
342) Hüllen, Werner, ed., *The World in a List of Words*, Tübingen, 1994, in: *IJL* 9 (1996), 161-3.
343) Hüllen, Werner, *English Dictionaries 800-1700. the Topical Tradition*, Oxford, 1999, in: *IJL* 14 (2001), 63-6; repr. 136-40.
344) Hughes, Joan, *Australian Words and their Origins*, Melbourne, 1989, in: *EWW* 13 (1992), 167-8.
345) Hymes, Dell, *Language in Education: Ethnolinguistic Essays*, Washington, D.C., 1980, in: *EWW* 2 (1981), 278.
346) Jabłonski, M., *Regularität und Variabilität in der Rezeption englischer Internationalismen im modernen Deutsch, Französisch und Polnisch*, Tübingen: Niemeyer, 1990, in: *IJL* 5 (1992), 77.
347) Janicki, Karol, *The Foreigner's Language*, Oxford, 1985, in: *EWW* 7 (1986), 336-7.
348) Jankofsky, Klaus P., ed., *The South English Legendary. A Critical Assessment*, Tübingen, 1992, in: *Mediävistik* 7 (1994), 478-80.
349) Johnson, Ellen, *Lexical Change and Variation in the Southeastern United States 1930-1990*, Tuscaloosa, 1996, in *JEngL* 26 (1998), 76-8.
350) Johnson, Sally & Ulrike Hanna Meinhof, eds., *Language and Masculinity*, Oxford, 1997, in: *EWW* 18 (1997), 303-4.
351) Johnson, Samuel, *A Dictionary of the English Language*, London, ʳ1983, in: *EWW* 5 (1984), 147-8.
352) Jones, Charles, ed., *A Treatise on the Provincial Dialect of Scotland by Sylvester Douglas*, Edinburgh, 1991, in: *EWW* 13 (1992), 163-4.
353) Jones, Charles, *A Language Suppressed. The Pronunciation of the Scots Language in the 18th Century*, Edinburgh, 1995, in: *Linguistics* 35 (1997), 429-30.

354) Jones, Charles, ed., *The Edinburgh History of the Scots Language*, Edinburgh, 1997, in: *Linguistics* 37 (1999), 358-64; repr. 103-8.
355) Jones, Eldred D., *et al.*, eds., *Reading and Writing Krio*, Stockholm, 1992, in: *EWW* 13 (1992), 331-2.
356) Jowitt, David, *Nigerian English Usage. An Introduction*, Ikeja, 1991, in: *EWW* 13 (1992), 333-5.
357) Joyce, P.W., *English as We Speak It in Ireland*, Dublin, ²1979, in: *EWW* 1 (1980), 291.
358) Jucker, Andreas H., *Social Stylistics. Syntactic Variation in British Newspapers*, Berlin, 1992, in: *EWW* 13 (1992), 320-2.
359) Jussawalla, Feroza F., *Family Quarrels. Towards a Criticism of Indian Writing in English*, New York, 1985, in: *EWW* 9 (1988), 349-51.
360) Kachru, Braj B., ed., *The Other Tongue: English Across Cultures*, Urbana, 1982, in: *LPLP* 8 (1984), 199-212.
361) Kachru, Braj B., *The Alchemy of English*, Oxford, 1986, in: *EWW* 7 (1986), 329-30.
362) Kachru, Braj B., ed., *The Other Tongue. English Across Cultures*, 2nd ed., Urbana, 1992, in: *EWW* 13 (1992), 325-7.
363) Kandiah, Thiru & John Kwan-Terry, eds., *English and Language Planning: A Southeast Asian Contribution*, Singapore, 1994, in: *EWW* 16 (1995), 154-5.
364) Kane, George & E. Talbot Donaldson, eds., *Piers Plowman: The B Version. Will's Vision of Piers Plowman, Do-Well, Do-Better and Do-Best*, London, 1975, in: *Archiv* 213 (1976), 396-9.
365) Kastovsky, Dieter, ed., *Historical English Syntax*, Berlin, 1991, in: *AAA* 17 (1992), 129-31.
366) Kastovsky, Dieter, ed., *Studies in Early Modern English*, Berlin & New York, 1994, in: *AAA* 20 (1995), 406-8.
367) Kastovsky, Dieter & Arthur Mettinger, eds. *Language Contact in the History of English*. Frankfurt/M., 2000, in: *AAA* 26 (2001), 215-9.
368) Kastovsky, Dieter & Arthur Mettinger, eds. *The History of English in a Social Context*. Berlin, 2000, in *AAA* 26 (2001), 215-9.
369) Kastovsky, Dieter & Aleksander Szwedek, eds., *Linguistics across Historical and Geographical Boundaries*, Berlin, 1986, in: *EWW* 7 (1986), 333-5.
370) Kellett, Arnold, *Basic Broad Yorkshire*, Otley, 1991, ²1992, in: *EWW* 18 (1997), 310-1.
371) Kellett, Arnold, *The Yorkshire Dictionary of Dialect, Tradition and Folklore*, Otley, 1994, in: *EWW* 18 (1997), 311.
372) Kellett, Arnold, trsl., *Ee By Gum, Lord! The Gospels in Broad Yorkshire*, Otley, 1996, in: *EWW* 18 (1997), 312.
373) Kellett, Arnold & Ian Dewhirst, eds., *A Century of Yorkshire Dialect*, Otley, 1997, in: *EWW* 19 (1998), 146-7.

374) Ker, N.R. introd., *The Winchester Malory. A Facsimile Edition*, Oxford, 1978, in: *Anglia* 105 (1987), 136-8; repr. 16-17.
375) Kerkhof, J., *Studies in the Language of Geoffrey Chaucer*, Leiden, ²1982, in: *AAA* 10 (1985), 279-80.
376) Kibbee, Douglas A., *For to Speke Frenche Trewely. The French Language in England, 1000-1600: Its Status, Description and Instruction*, Amsterdam, 1991, in: *AAA* 18 (1993), 134-5.
377) Kim, H.C., ed., *The Gospel of Nicodemus*, Toronto, 1972, 1973, in: *Archiv* 211 (1974), 426-7.
378) Kirk, John M., et al., eds., *Studies in Linguistic Geography. The Dialects of English in Britain and Ireland*, London, 1985, in: *ZDL* 55 (1988), 63-65.
379) Kirkpatrick, E.M., ed., *Chambers 20th Century Dictionary*, Edinburgh, 1983, in: *EWW* 5 (1984), 309-10.
380) Klegraf, Josef & D. Nehls, eds., *Essays on the English Language and Applied Linguistics (Nickel Festschrift)*, Heidelberg, 1988, in: *EWW* 10 (1989), 161-2.
381) Kloss, Heinz, *Die Entwicklung neuer germanischer Kultursprachen seit 1800*, Düsseldorf, ²1978, in: *EWW* 1 (1980), 153.
382) König, Ekkehard & Johan van der Auwera, eds., *The Germanic Languages*, London, 1994, in: *Linguistics*.
383) Korhammer, Michael (with the assistance of Karl Reichl & Hans Sauer), ed., *Words, Texts and Manuscripts (Gneuss Festschrift)*, Woodbridge, 1992, in: *AAA* 20 (1995), 404-5.
384) Koziol, Herbert, *Handbuch der englischen Wortbildungslehre*, Heidelberg, ²1972, in: *Archiv* 212 (1975), 169-73.
385) Kramer, Johannes, *English and Spanish in Gibraltar*, Hamburg, 1986, in: *EWW* 9 (1988), 142-3.
386) *Kriol Materials*, Darwin, 1979-81, in: *EWW* 3 (1982), 129-30.
387) Kropp Dakubu, M.E., ed., *English in Ghana*, Accra, 1997, in: *EWW* 19 (1998), 147-8.
388) Krygier, Marcin, *The Disintegration of the English Strong Verb System*, Frankfurt/M., 1994, in: *Linguistics* 33 (1995), 380-3.
389) Kujore, O., *English Usage. Some Notable Nigerian Variations*, Ibadan, 1985, in: *EWW* 11 (1990), 323-4.
390) Kunsmann, Peter & Ortwin Kuhn, eds., *Weltsprache English in Forschung und Lehre. Festschrift für Kurt Wächtler*, Berlin, 1981, in: *EWW* 2 (1981), 280-1.
391) Kynoch, Douglas, *A Doric Dictionary. Two-way Lexicon of North-East Scots. Doric~English, English~Doric*, Edinburgh, 1996, in: *EWW* 18 (1997), 162-3.
392) Labov, William, *Principles of Linguistic Change: Internal Factors*, Oxford, 1994, in: *JEngL* 25 (1997), 156-9; repr. 85-88.

393) Labov, William. 2001. *Principles of Linguistic Change. Social Factors.* Oxford, in: *EWW* 22 (2001), 326-30; repr. 88-92.
394) Labru, G.L., *Indian Newspaper English*, Delhi, 1984, in: *EWW* 9 (1988), 145-6.
395) Laforge, Lorne & Grant D. McConnell, eds., *Language Spread and Social Change. Dynamics and Measurement*, Saint-Foy, 1990, in: *EWW* 13 (1992), 143-5.
396) Laing, Margaret, *Catalogue of Sources for a Linguistic Atlas of Early Medieval English*, Cambridge, 1993, in: *Anglia* 113 (1995), 79-80.
397) Laing, Margaret & Keith Williamson, eds., *Speaking in our Tongues. Medieval Dialectology and Related Disciplines*, Cambridge, 1994, in: *JEngL*.
398) Lalla, Barbara & Jean D'Costa, *Language in Exile. Three Hundred Years of Jamaican Creole*, Tuscaloosa, 1990, in: *AS* 69 (1994), 187-91; repr. 116-9.
399) Lamb, Gregor, *Orkney Wordbook*, Birsay, Orkney, 1988, in: *EWW* 11 (1990), 320-1.
400) Lander, Steve & Ken Reah, eds., *Aspects of Linguistic Variation*, Sheffield, 1981, in: *EWW* 3 (1982), 120.
401) Lass, Roger, *The Shape of English*, London, 1987, in: *EWW* 9 (1988), 332-3.
402) Law, Vivien, *Wisdom, Authority and Grammar in the Seventh Century. Decoding Virgilius Maro Grammaticus*, Cambridge, 1995, in: *Archiv* 234 (1997), 223-4.
403) Lee, Ernest W., *Pride and Prejudice. The Status of Solomon Island Pijin*, Honiara, 1980, in: *EWW* 5 (1984), 118-9.
404) Leith, Dick, *A Social History of English*, London, 1983, in: *EWW* 4 (1983), 122-3.
405) Lewandowski, Theodor, *Linguistisches Wörterbuch* (UTB 200, 201, 300), Heidelberg, 1973, 1975, in: *Archiv* 215 (1978), 129-38.
406) *Lexicographica*, 1, Tübingen, 1985, in: *IF* 93 (1988), 272-3.
407) *Lexicology and Dialectology: Walter S. Avis in memoriam*, CIL 26 (1981), in: *EWW* 3 (1982), 271.
408) Lieberson, Stanley, *Language Diversity and Language Contact. Essays*, ed. Anwar S. Dil, Stanford, 1981, in: *EWW* 2 (1981), 279.
409) Lindberg, Conrad, ed., *The Earlier Version of the Wycliffe Bible. Volume 6: Baruch 3.20 - End of OT*, Stockholm, 1973, in: *Archiv* 213 (1976), 399-401.
410) Lindquist, Hans, et al., eds., *The Major Varieties of English. Papers from MAVEB 97*, Växjö, 1998, in: *EWW* 20 (1999), 173-4.
411) Lippi-Green, Rosina, *English with an Accent. Language, Ideology and Discrimination in the United States*, London & New York, 1997, in: *EWW* 18 (1997), 324-5.

412) Lockwood, W.B., *An Informal Introduction to English Etymology*, Montreux, London & Washington, 1995, in: *ZAA* 46 (1998), 177-8.
413) *Longman Dictionary of the English Language*, London, 1984, in: *EWW* 6 (1985), 339-40.
414) *Longman Dictionary of Contemporary English*, London, 1987, in: *EWW* 9 (1988), 138.
415) *Longman Dictionary of English Language and Culture*, Harlow, 1992, in: *EWW* 14 (1993), 319-20.
416) Lorimer, William Laughton, trs., *The New Testament in Scots*, Edinburgh, 1983, in: *EWW* 4 (1983), 325-6.
417) Lorimer, William Laughton, *New Testament in Scots. Portions waled frae...*, Glasgow, 1983, in: *EWW* 4 (1983), 326-7.
418) Lougheed, W.C., ed., *In Search of the Standard in Canadian English*, Kingston, Ont., 1986, in: *EWW* 9 (1988), 319-21.
419) Lougheed, W.C., *Writings on Canadian English 1976-1987. A Selective, Annotated Bibliography*, Kingston, Ont., 1989, in: *EWW* 11 (1990), 162.
420) Lüdtke, Helmut, ed., *Kommunikationstheoretische Grundlagen des Sprachwandels*, Berlin, 1981, in: *FLH* 3 (1982), 247-9.
421) Lumiansky, R.M. & David Mills, introd., *The Chester Mystery Cycle. A Facsimile of MS Bodley 175*, Leeds, 1973, in: *Anglia* 105 (1987), 138-140; repr. 18-19.
422) Lutz, William D., *The Cambridge Thesaurus of American English*, Cambridge, 1994, in: *EWW* 15 (1994), 308-9.
423) Lux, Friedemann, *Text, Situation, Textsorte*, Tübingen, 1981, in: *EWW* 3 (1982), 120-1.
424) Macafee, C.I., *Traditional Dialect in the Modern World. Some Studies in the Glasgow Vernacular*, Frankfurt/M., 1994, in: *Linguistics* 33 (1995), 383-5.
425) Macafee, C.I., ed., *A Concise Ulster Dictionary*, Oxford, 1996, in: *IJL* 10 (1997), 336-8; repr. 140-3.
426) Macafee, C.I. & Iseabail Macleod, eds., *The Nuttis Shell*, Aberdeen, 1987, in: *EWW* 9 (1988), 121-3.
427) McArthur, Tom, *The English Language as Used in Quebec*, Kingston, Ont., 1989, in: *EWW* 11 (1990), 163-4.
428) McArthur, Tom, ed., *The Oxford Companion to the English Language*, Oxford, 1992, in: *EWW* 14 (1993), 149-50.
429) McArthur, Tom, *The English Languages*, Cambridge, 1997, in: *Anglia* 117 (1999), 418-9.
430) McClure, J. Derrick, *et al.*, *The Scots Language. Planning for Modern Usage*, Edinburgh, 1980, in: *EWW* 1 (1980), 288-9.
431) McClure, J.Derrick, ed., *Scotland and the Lowland Tongue*, Aberdeen, 1983, in: *EWW* 4 (1983), 307-9.

432) McClure, J.Derrick & M.R.G. Spiller, eds., *Bryght Lanternis. Essays on the Language and Literature of Medieval and Renaissance Scotland*, Aberdeen, 1989, in: *EWW* 11 (1990), 161-2.

433) McConchie, R.W., *Lexicography and Physicke. The Record of Sixteenth-Century English Medical Terminology*, Oxford, 1997, in: *Linguistics* 36 (1998), 1021-3.

434) McCordick, David, ed., *Scottish Literature. An Anthology.* 2 vols., New York, 1996, in: *EWW* 18 (1997), 316-7.

435) McCormack, William C. & Stephen A. Wurm, eds., *Language and Society. Anthropological Issues*, The Hague, 1979, in: *EWW* 1 (1980), 285-6.

436) McCrum, Robert, *et al., The Story of English*, New and revised edition, London, 1992, in: *EWW* 14 (1993), 314-15.

437) McElhanon, K.A., ed., *Tok Pisin i go we?*, Papua New Guinea Linguistic Society, 1975, in: *EWW* 5 (1984), 113-5.

438) MacGillivray, Alan, ed., *Teachin Scottish Literature.* Curriculum and Classroom Applications, Edinburgh, 1997, in: *Scottish Language* (2002).

439) Machan, Tim William & Charles T. Scott, eds., *English in Its Social Contexts. Essays in Historical Sociolinguistics*, New York & Oxford, 1992, in: *EWW* 14 (1993), 155-7.

440) McIntosh, Angus, *et al., A Linguistic Atlas of Late Medieval English*, Oxford, 1986, in: *EWW* 9 (1988), 139-41.

441) McIntosh, Angus, *et al.*, eds., *Middle English Dialectology. Essays on Some Principles and Problems*, Aberdeen, 1988, in: *Anglia* 109 (1991), 112-4; repr. 49-52.

442) Mackey, William Frances & Jacob Ornstein, eds., *Sociolinguistic Studies in Language Contact*, The Hague, 1979, in: *EWW* 1 (1980), 154-5.

443) Macleod, Iseabail, *et al.*, eds., *The Pocket Scots Dictionary*, Aberdeen, 1988, in: *EWW* 10 (1989), 166-8.

444) Macleod, Iseabail, ed., *The Scots Thesaurus*, Aberdeen, 1990, in: *EWW* 12 (1991), 128-30.

445) Macleod, Iseabail & Pauline Cairns, eds., *The Concise English-Scots Dictionary*, Edinburgh, 1993, in: *EWW* 15 (1994), 159-61.

446) Macleod, Iseabail & Pauline Cairns, *The Scots School Dictionary. Scots-English, English-Scots*, Edinburgh, 1996, in: *EWW* 17 (1996), 310-11.

447) *Macquarie Dictionaries 1985-1990*, summary review, in: *EWW* 12 (1991), 130-7.

448) McSparran, Frances & P.R. Robinson, introd., *Cambridge University Library MS Ff. 2.38*, London, 1979, in: *Anglia* 105 (1987), 126-8; repr. 7-9.

449) McWhorter, John, ed., *Language Change and Language Contact in Pidgins and Creoles*, Amsterdam, 2001, in: *Sociolinguistica* (2002).

450) Malkiel, Yakov, *Etymology*, Cambridge, 1993, in: *Germanistik* 37 (1996), 382.

451) Malmkjaer, Kirsten, ed., *The Linguistics Encyclopedia*, London, 1991, in: *EWW* 14 (1993), 147.
452) Manczak-Wohlfeld, Elzbieta, *Angielskie Elementy Leksykalne w Jesyken Polskim*, Kraków, 1994, in: *IJL* 12 (1999), 151-2.
453) Marckwardt, Albert H., *American English*, rev. J.L. Dillard, New York, 1980, in: *EWW* 2 (1981), 130.
454) Mattheier, Klaus J., *Pragmatik und Soziologie der Dialekte*, Heidelberg, 1980, in: *EWW* 2 (1981), 128.
455) Mattheier, Klaus J. & Edgar Radtke, eds., *Standardisierung und Destandardisierung europäischer Nationalsprachen*, Frankfurt/M, 1997, in: *Linguistics* 37 (1999), 187-8.
456) Matthews, P.H., *Morphology. An Introduction to the Theory of Word-Structure*, Cambridge, 1974, in: *Archiv* 213 (1976), 144-6.
457) Maximova, Tamara V., *Slovar Anglizismov (50-90e gody xxv)*, (Dictionary of Anglicisms of the 1950s to 1990s), Volgograd, 1998, in: *IJL* 12 (1999), 152-3.
458) Mazzon, Gabriella, *Le Lingue Inglesi. Aspetti storici e geografici*, Roma, 1994, in: *EWW* 15 (1994), 294-5.
459) Melchers, Gunnel & Nils-Lennart Johannesson, eds., *Non-Standard Varieties of Language*, Stockholm, 1994, in: *EWW* 15 (1994), 303-4.
460) Meredith, Peter & Stanley J. Kahrl, introd., *The N-Town Plays. A Facsimile of British Library MS Cotton Vespasian D VIII*, Leeds, 1977, in: *Anglia* 105 (1987), 142-3; repr. 21-22.
461) Mesthrie, Rajend, *English in Language Shift*, Cambridge, 1992, in: *EWW* 14 (1993), 139-40.
462) Mesthrie, Rajend, ed., *Language and Social History. Studies in South African Sociolinguistics*, Cape Town & Johannesburg, 1995, in: *EWW* 18 (1997), 326-8.
463) Mesthrie, Rajend, et al., eds., *Introducing Sociolinguistics*, Edinburgh, 2000, in: *Sociolinguistica* (2002).
464) Metcalf, Allan & Luanne von Schneidemesser, *An Index by Region, Usage, and Etymology to the Dictionary of American Regional English, Vols. I and II*, Tuscaloosa, 1993, in: *EWW* 16 (1995), 150-1.
465) Mills, A.D., *A Dictionary of English Place-Names*, Oxford, 1991, in: *EWW* 13 (1992), 160-1.
466) Milroy, James, *Linguistic Variation and Change*, Oxford, 1992, in: *EWW* 13 (1992), 299-302.
467) Milroy, James and Lesley, *Authority in Language*, London, 1985, in: *EWW* 7 (1986), 151-2.
468) Milroy, James & Lesley, eds., *Real English. The Grammar of English Dialects in the British Isles*, London, 1993, in: *EWW* 15 (1994), 301-3.

469) Milroy, Lesley, *Observing and Analysing Natural Language*, Oxford, 1987, in: *EWW* 9 (1988), 119-21.
470) Mindt, Dieter, *An Empirical Grammar of the English Verb System*, Berlin, 2000, in: *AAA* 26 (2001), 221-24.
471) Minnis, A.J. & C. Brewer, eds., *Crux and Controversy in Middle English Textual Criticism*, Cambridge, 1992, in: *N&Q* 238 (1993), 235-6.
472) Moessner, Lilo & U. Schaefer, *Proseminar Mittelenglisch. Lehrbuch mit Texten, Grammatik und Übungen*, Darmstadt, 1974, in: *Anglia* 94 (1976), 456-62.
473) Montgomery, Michael, ed., *The Crucible of Carolina. Essays in the Development of Gullah Language and Culture*, Athens, Ga., 1994, in: *EWW* 16 (1995), 151-2.
474) Morgan, Marcyliena, ed., *Language and the Social Construction of Identity in Creole Situations*, Los Angeles, 1994, in: *EWW* 15 (1994), 310-1.
475) Moylan, Séamas, *The Language of Kilkenny*, Dublin, 1996, in: *EWW* 18 (1997), 321-3.
476) Mühlhäusler, Peter, *Growth and Structure of the Lexicon of New Guinea Pidgin*, Canberra, 1979, in: *EWW* 5 (1984), 111-3; repr. 124-6.
477) Mühlhäusler, Peter, *Pidgin and Creole Linguistics*, Oxford, 1986, in: *IF* 95 (1990), 377-9.
478) Mühlhäusler, Peter, *Linguistic Ecology*, London, 1996, in: *EWW* 17 (1996), 317-8.
479) Mühlhäusler, Peter, et al., *Papers in Pidgin and Creole Linguistics* 2, Canberra, 1979, in: *EWW* 5 (1984), 108-11.
480) Mufwene, Salikoko, ed., *Africanisms in Afro-American Language Varieties*, Athens, Ga. & London, 1993, in: *EWW* 15 (1994), 161-4.
481) Mufwene, Salikoko S., et al., eds. *African-American English. Structure, History and Use*. London, 1998, in *Anglia* 117 (1999), 267-8.
482) Mugglestone, Lynda, *'Talking Proper'. The Rise of Accent as Social Symbol*, Oxford, 1995, in: *Linguistics* 33 (1995), 1063-6.
483) Mugglestone, Lynda, ed. *Lexicography and the OED. Pioneers in the Untrodden Forest*. Oxford, 2000, in: *IJL* 14 (2001), 211-13.
484) Munske, Horst Haider, *Handbuch Friesisch*, in: *Sociolinguistica* (2002).
485) Munske, Horst Haider & Alan Kirkness, eds., *Eurolatein. Das griechische und lateinische Erbe in den europäischen Sprachen*, Tübingen, 1996, in: *PBB* 119 (1997), 487-90.
486) Murray, Thomas E., *The Language of St. Louis*, New York, 1986, in: *EWW* 8 (1987), 333-4.
487) Muysken, Pieter & N. Smith, eds., *Substrata versus Universals in Creole Genesis*, Amsterdam, 1986, in: *EWW* 8 (1987), 337-9.
488) Nabrings, Kirsten, *Sprachliche Varietäten*, Tübingen, 1981, in: *EWW* 2 (1981), 277-8.

489) Nehls, Dietrich, *Synchron-diachrone Untersuchungen zur Expanded Form im Englischen. Eine struktural-funktionale Analyse*, München, 1974, in: *Archiv* 213 (1976), 381-6.

490) Neumann-Holzschuh, Ingrid & Edgar W. Scheider, eds., *Degrees of Restructuring in Creole Languages*. Amsterdam, 2001, in: *Sociolinguistica* (2002).

491) Nevalainen, Terttu & Helena Raumolin-Brunberg, eds., *Sociolinguistics and Language History. Studies Based on the Corpus of Early English Correspondence*, Amsterdam & Atlanta, 1996, in: *Sociolinguistica* 10 (1996), 147-9.

492) Nevanlinna, S., ed., *The Northern Homily Cycle. The Expanded Version in MS Harley 4196 and Cotton Tiberius E vii*, Part I, Helsinki, 1972, in: *Anglia* 93 (1975), 233-6.

493) Newton, Gerald, ed., *Luxembourg and Lëtzebuergesch. Language and Communication at the Crossroads of Europe*, Oxford, 1996, in: *Linguistics* 35 (1997), 427-8.

494) Nichols, Lee, ed., *Conversation with African Writers*, Washington, D.C., 1981, in: *EWW* 3 (1982), 128-9.

495) Nickel, Gerhard & J.B. Stalker, eds., *Problems of Standardization and Linguistic Variation in Present-Day English*, Heidelberg 1986, in: *EWW* 9 (1988), 330-2.

496) Norton-Smith, John, introd., *Bodleian Library MS Fairfax 16*, London, 1979, in: *Anglia* 105 (1987), 133-5; repr. 14-15.

497) Noss, Richard B., ed., *Language Teaching Issues in Multilingual Environments in Southeast Asia*, Singapore, 1982, in: *EWW* 5 (1984), 152-3.

498) Noss, Richard B., ed., *Varieties of English in Southeast Asia*, Singapore, 1983, in: *EWW* 5 (1984), 143-6.

499) Oakland, John, *A Dictionary of British Institutions*, London, 1993, in: *EWW* 15 (1994), 159.

500) Ó Baoill, Donall P., ed., *Papers on Irish English*, Dublin, 1985, in: *EWW* 7 (1986), 344.

501) Olschansky, Heike, *Volksetymologie*, Tübingen, 1996, in: *IJL* 11 (1998), 159-61.

502) Ó Muirithe, Diarmaid, ed., *The English Language in Ireland*, Dublin, 1977, in: *EWW* 1 (1980), 156.

503) Ó Muirithe, Diarmaid, *A Dictionary of Anglo-Irish. Words and Phrases from Gaelic in the English of Ireland*, Blackrock, Co. Dublin, 1996, in: *EWW* 18 (1997), 164-6.

504) Ornstein-Galicia, Jacob, ed., *Form and Function in Chicano English*, Rowley, Mass., 1984, in: *EWW* 5 (1984), 312-3.

505) Orsman, Harry W., comp., *Heinemann New Zealand Dictionary*, Auckland, 1979, in: *EWW* 2 (1981), 134-5.

506) Orsman, Harry W., ed., *The Dictionary of New Zealand English. A Dictionary of New Zealandisms on Historical Principles*, Auckland, 1997, in: *IJL* 12 (1999), 182-3; repr. 171-3.

507) Orsman, Elizabeth & Harry, *The New Zealand Dictionary*, Auckland, 1994, in: *EWW* 16 (1995), 155-6.

508) *Oxford English Dictionary*, 2nd ed., Oxford, 1989, in: *EWW* 11 (1990), 310-2.

509) Ozolins, Uldis, *The Politics of Language in Australia*, Cambridge, 1993, in: *EWW* 14 (1993), 324-5.

510) Pakir, Anne, ed., *Words in a Cultural Context*, Singapore, 1992, in: *EWW* 14 (1993), 323-4.

511) Parakrama, Arjuna, *De-hegemonizing Language Standards. Learning from (Post)Colonial Englishes about 'English'*, Houndsmills, 1995, in: *EWW* 17 (1996), 149-50.

512) Parasher, S.V., *Indian English. Functions and Form*, New Delhi, 1991, in: *EWW* 15 (1994), 169-71.

513) Parkes, M.B. & Elizabeth Salter, introd., *Geoffrey Chaucer, Troilus and Criseyde. A facsimile of Corpus Christi College Cambridge MS 61*, Cambridge, 1978, in: *Anglia* 105 (1987), 135-6; repr. 15-16.

514) Partridge, Eric, *A Dictionary of Catch Phrases*, London, ʳ1983, in: *EWW* 4 (1983), 322-3.

515) Partridge, Eric, *A Dictionary of Slang and Unconventional English*, London, 1984, in: *EWW* 7 (1986), 152-3.

516) Partridge, Eric, *A Dictionary of Catch Phrases, British and American*, London, 1985, in: *EWW* 7 (1986), 154.

517) Pascasio, Emy M., ed., *The Filipino Bilingual*, Quezon City, 1977, in: *EWW* 2 (1981), 133-4.

518) Patrick, Peter L., *Urban Jamaican Creole. Variation in the Mesolect*, Amsterdam, 1999, in: *AAA* 25 (2000), 128-30.

519) Pattanayak, Debi Prasanna, ed., *Multilingualism in India*, Clevedon, 1990, in: *EWW* 12 (1991), 162-3.

520) Pearsall, Derek & I.C. Cunningham, introd., *The Auchinleck Manuscript, National Library of Scotland, Advocates' MS. 19.2.1.*, London, 1977, in: *Anglia* 105 (1987), 124-6; repr. 6-7.

521) Pearsall, Derek, ed., *Studies in the Vernon Manuscript*, Cambridge, 1990, in: *Anglia* 110 (1992), 486-9; repr. 33-6.

522) Pearsall, Derek, *The Life of Geoffrey Chaucer. A Critical Biography*, Oxford, 1992, in: *AAA* 19 (1994), 145-6.

523) Pearsall, Judy, ed., *The New Oxford Dictionary of English*, Oxford, 1998, in: *EWW* 20 (1999), 175-6.

524) Penhallurick, Robert, *Gowerland and Its Language*, Frankfurt, 1994, in: *EWW* 16 (1995), 149-50.

525) Pennycook, Alastair, *English and the Discourses of Colonialism*, London, 1998, in: *EWW* 20 (2002).

526) Penzl, Herbert, *Englisch. Eine Sprachgeschichte nach Texten von 350 bis 1992*, Bern, 1994, in: *Anglia* 114 (1996), 252-4.

527) Peters, P.H., *Frontiers of Style*, Macquarie University, 1990, in: *EWW* 12 (1991), 163-4.

528) Peters, Pam, *The Cambridge Australian English Style Guide*, Cambridge, 1995, in: *EWW* 16 (1995), 316-7.

529) Petti, A.G., *English Literary Hands from Chaucer to Dryden*, London, 1977, in: *Archiv* 215 (1978), 406-8.

530) Pfeffer, J. Allan & Garland Cannon, *German Loanwords in English. An Historical Dictionary*, Cambridge, 1994, in: *IJL* 9 (1996), 77-9.

531) Phillipps, K.C., *Language and Class in Victorian England*, Oxford, 1984, in: *EWW* 6 (1985), 333-4.

532) Phillipson, Robert, *Linguistic Imperialism*, Oxford, 1992, in: *Linguistics* 31 (1993), 417-20.

533) Picone, Michael D., *Anglicisms, Neologisms and Dynamic French*, Amsterdam, 1996, in: *IJL* 11 (1998), 242-4.

534) *Piers Plowman Concordance*: William Langland, *A Glossarial Concordance to The Vision of Piers Plowman*, ed. Tomonori Matsushita, in: *Anglia* (2002).

535) Pilch, Herbert, ed., *Orality and Literacy in Early Middle English* (ScriptOralia 83), Tübingen, 1996, in: *ZAA* 46 (1998), 178-9.

536) Pinsker, Hans, *Altenglisches Studienbuch*, Düsseldorf, 1976, in: *Archiv* 215 (1978), 156-9.

537) Platt, John, et al., *The New Englishes*, London, 1984, in: *LPLP* 9 (1985), 262-8.

538) Polomé, Edgar C., ed., *Research Guide on Language Change*, Berlin & New York, 1990, in: *Linguistics* 30 (1992), 445-8.

539) Porter, A.N., ed., *Atlas of British Overseas Expansion*, London, 1991, [2]1994, in: *EWW* 18 (1997), 309-10.

540) Pratt, T.K., ed., *Dictionary of Prince Edward Island English*, Toronto, 1988, in: *EWW* 10 (1989), 175-6.

541) Preston, D.R., *Perceptual Dialectology. Nonlinguists' Views of Areal Linguistics*, Dordrecht, 1989, in: *EWW* 11 (1990), 139-41.

542) Preston, Dennis R., ed., *American Dialect Research*, Amsterdam & Philadelphia, 1993, in: *Linguistics* 31 (1993), 985-8.

543) Preston, Dennis R., ed., *Handbook of Perceptual Dialectology*. vols. 1&2, Amsterdam/Philadelphia: Benjamins: 1999, in: *EWW* (2002).

544) Price, Glanville, *The Languages of Britain*, London, 1984, in: *EWW* 5 (1984), 287-90; repr. 99-101.

545) Pride, John B., ed., *Sociolinguistic Aspects of Language Learning and Teaching*, Oxford, 1979, in: *EWW* 1 (1980), 153-4.
546) Pride, John B., ed., *New Englishes*, Rowley, 1982, in: *LPLP* 8 (1984), 199-212.
547) Procter, Paul, ed., *Cambridge International Dictionary of English*, Cambridge, 1995, in: *EWW* 16 (1995), 147-8.
548) Pütz, Martin, ed., *Language Contact, Language Conflict*, Amsterdam, 1994, in: *EWW* 15 (1994), 298-9.
549) Pütz, Martin, ed., *Discrimination through Language in Africa? Perspectives on the Namibian Experience*, Berlin, 1995, in: *EWW* 17 (1996), 133-5.
550) Pütz, Martin, ed., *Language Choices. Conditions, constraints, and consequences*, Amsterdam & Philadelphia, 1997, in: *EWW* 18 (1997), 307-8.
551) Quirk, Randolph, *Style and Communication in the English Language*, London, 1982, in: *EWW* 4 (1983), 123-4.
552) Rahman, Tariq, *Pakistani English: The Linguistic Description of a Non-Native Variety of English*, Islamabad, 1990, in: *EWW* 12 (1991), 336-7.
553) Ramisch, Heinrich & Kenneth Wynne, eds., *Language in Time and Space. Studies in Honour of Wolfgang Viereck on the Occasion of his 60th Birthday*, Stuttgart, 1997, in *AAA* 23 (1998), 330-1.
554) Ramson, W.S., ed., *The Australian National Dictionary*, Melbourne, 1988, in: *EWW* 10 (1988), 145-9; repr. 168-71.
555) *Random House Dictionary*, 2nd ed., New York, 1987, in: *EWW* 9 (1988), 338-9.
556) Reichl, Karl, *Englische Sprachwissenschaft. Eine Bibliographie*, Berlin, 1993, in: *Archiv* 232 (1995), 162-3.
557) Reichl, Karl & Walter Sauer, *A Concordance to Six Middle English Tail-Rhyme Romances*, Part I, II, Frankfurt, 1993, in: *Anglia* 112 (1994), 524-5.
558) Reinecke, John E., et al., comp., *A Bibliography of Pidgin and Creole Languages*, Honolulu, 1975, in: *Archiv* 216 (1979), 377-9.
559) Reh, Mechthild & Bernd Heine, *Sprachpolitik in Afrika*, Hamburg, 1982, in: *EWW* 5 (1984), 315-7.
560) Richards, Jack C., ed., *New Varieties of English: Issues and Approaches*, Singapore, 1979, in: *EWW* 1 (1980), 282-3.
561) Richter, Michael, *Sprache und Gesellschaft im Mittelalter*, Stuttgart, 1979, in: *LPLP* 7 (1983), 99-101; *Archiv* 220 (1983), 147-8.
562) Rickford, John, ed., *A Festival of Guyanese Words*, Georgetown, ²1978, in: *EWW* 2 (1981), 131-2.
563) Rickford, John, ed., *Sociolinguistics and Pidgin-Creole Studies* (IJSL 71), Berlin, 1988, in: *EWW* 9 (1988), 324-7.

564) Rickford, John R. & Suzanne Romaine, eds., *Creole Genesis, Attitudes and Discourse. Studies Celebrating Charlene J. Sato*, Amsterdam, 2000, in *EWW* 22 (2001), 335-7.
565) Ricks, C. & L. Michaels, eds., *The State of the Language*, Berkeley, London, 1990, in: *EWW* 11 (1990), 307-8.
566) Riddy, Felicity, ed., *Regionalism in Late Medieval Manuscripts and Texts*, Cambridge, 1991, in: *N&Q* 238 (1993), 78-80.
567) Riemenschneider, Dieter, *Grundlagen zur Literatur in englischer Sprache: West- und Ostafrika*, München, 1983, in: *EWW* 4 (1983), 128-9.
568) Rigg, A.G., ed., *Editing Medieval Texts: English, French, and Latin Written in England*, New York, 1977, in: *Anglia* 98 (1980), 479-82.
569) Rissanen, Matti, et al., eds., *History of Englishes. New Methods and Interpretations in Historical Linguistics*, Berlin & New York, 1992, in: *EWW* 14 (1993), 164-6.
570) Rissanen, Matti, Merja Kytö & Minna Palander-Collin, eds., *Early English in the Computer Age: Explorations through the Helsinki Corpus*, Berlin & New York, 1993, in: *JEngL* 24 (1996), 71-3.
571) Roberts, Jane & Christian Kay, with Lynne Grundy, *A Thesaurus of Old English*, 2 vols., London, 1995, in: *Anglia* 116 (1998), 398-401; repr. 133-6.
572) Roberts, Peter A., *West Indians and Their Language*, Cambridge, 1988, in: *EWW* 9 (1988), 345-7.
573) Robertson, T.A. & John J. Graham, *Grammar and Usage of the Shetland Dialect*, Lerwick, 1991, in: *EWW* 13 (1992), 165.
574) Robinson, Mairi, ed., *The Concise Scots Dictionary*, Aberdeen, 1985, in: *EWW* 7 (1986), 157-9.
575) Rodríguez González, Felix, *Nuevo Diccionario de Anglicismos*, Madrid, 1997, in: *IJL* 12 (1999), 151.
576) Rodríguez Gonzáles, Felix, ed. *Spanish Loanwords in the English Language. A Tendency towards Hegemony Reversal.* Berlin, 1996, in: *IJL* 11 (1998), 65-6.
577) Rollinson, William, *The Cumbrian Dictionary of Dialect, Tradition and Folklore*, Otley, 1997, in: *EWW* 18 (1997), 312-3.
578) Romaine, Suzanne, ed., *Sociolinguistic Variation in Speech Communities*, London, 1982, in: *EWW* 3 (1982), 267-8.
579) Romaine, Suzanne, *Bilingualism*, Oxford, 1989, in: *EWW* 11 (1990), 148-9.
580) Romaine, Suzanne, ed., *Language in Australia*, Cambridge, 1991, in: *EWW* 13 (1992), 138-42.
581) Romaine, Suzanne, *Language, Education and Development. Urban and Rural Tok Pisin in Papua New Guinea*, Oxford, 1992, in: *Linguistics* 31 (1993), 408-11.

582) Romaine, Suzanne, *Language in Society. An Introduction to Sociolinguistics*, Oxford, 1994, in: *EWW* 16 (1995), 311-2.
583) Romaine, Suzanne, ed. *1779-1997*. (CHEL 4). Cambridge, 1998, in *Anglia* 117 (1999), 273-5; repr. 63-6.
584) Sabban, Annette, *Gälisch-englischer Sprachkontakt*, Heidelberg, 1982, in: *EWW* 5 (1984), 311-2.
585) Sankoff, Gillian, *The Social Life of Language*, Baltimore, 1980, in: *EWW* 5 (1984), 116-7.
586) Sandefur, John R., *Kriol of North Australia*, Darwin, 1986, in: *EWW* 9 (1988), 146-7.
587) Sandefur, John R., *An Australian Creole in the Northern Territory. A Description of Ngukurr-Bamyili Dialects (Part I)*; Darwin, 1979, in: *EWW* 1 (1980), 158.
588) Sandefur, John R. & J.L. Sandefur, *Beginnings of a Ngukurr-Bamyili Creole Dictionary*, Darwin, 1979, in: *EWW* 1 (1980), 158.
589) Sauer, Hans, *Nominalkomposita im Frühmittelenglischen. Mit Ausblicken auf die Geschichte der englischen Nominalkomposition*, Tübingen, 1992, in: *Anglia* 112 (1994), 140-3.
590) Saville-Troike, Muriel, *The Ethnography of Communication*, Oxford, 1982, in: *EWW* 3 (1982), 266.
591) Scaglione, Aldo, ed., *The Emergence of National Languages*, Ravenna, 1984, in: *EWW* 9 (1988), 130-2.
592) Schäfer, Jürgen, ed., *Bartholomaeus Anglicus. Batman vppon Bartholome His Booke De Proprietatibus Rerum 1582*, Hildesheim, 1976, in: *Archiv* 215 (1978), 399-400.
593) Schäfer, Jürgen, ed., *Commonwealth-Literatur*, Düsseldorf, 1981, in: *EWW* 4 (1983), 126-7.
594) Schäfer, Jürgen, *Early Modern English Lexicography*, Oxford, 1989, in: *AAA* 15 (1990), 176-8.
595) Scheffer, Johannes, *The Progressive in English*, Amsterdam, 1974, in: *Archiv* 213 (1976), 381-6.
596) Schiffman, Harold F., *Linguistic Culture and Language Policy*, London, 1996, in: *EWW* 17 (1996), 143-4.
597) Schmidt, A.V.C., ed., *William Langland. Piers Plowman: A Parallel-Text Edition of the A, B, C and Z Versions*, I: *Text*, Harlow, 1995, in: *Anglia* 115 (1997), 391-4; repr. 46-8.
598) Schmidt, A.V.C., ed., *William Langland. The Visions of Piers Plowman: A Critical Edition of the B-Text Based on Trinity College Cambridge MS B 15. 17.*, 2nd ed., London, 1995, in: *Anglia* 115 (1997), 391-4; repr. 48-9.
599) Schmidt, Lothar, ed., *Wortfeldforschung. Zur Geschichte und Theorie des sprachlichen Feldes*, Darmstadt, 1973, in: *Archiv* 217 (1980), 151-6.

600) Schmied, Josef J., *Englisch in Tansania*, Heidelberg, 1985, in: *LPLP* 10 (1986), 92-3.

601) Schmied, Josef, *English in Africa. An Introduction*, London, 1991, in: *Linguistics* 30 (1992), 1138-41.

602) Schmied, Josef, ed., *English in East and Central Africa*, 2, Bayreuth, 1992, in: *EWW* 13 (1992), 336-7.

603) Schneider, Edgar W., *Morphologische und syntaktische Variablen im amerikanischen Early Black English*, in: *ZDL* 52 (1985), 244-5.

604) Schopf, Alfred, ed., *Der englische Aspekt*, Darmstadt, 1974, in: *Archiv* 213 (1976), 381-6.

605) Schuchardt, Hugo, *Ethnography of Variation. Selected Writings on Pidgins and Creoles*, ed. and trs. T.L. Markey, Ann Arbor, 1980, in: *EWW* 1 (1980), 159.

606) Schuchardt, Hugo, *Pidgin and Creole Languages. Selected Essays*, ed. and trs. G.G. Gilbert, Cambridge, 1980, in: *EWW* 2 (1981), 136-7.

607) Schur, Norman W., *English English. A Descriptive Dictionary*, Essex, Conn., 1980, in: *EWW* 3 (1982), 127.

608) *Scottish Language. An Annual Review*, 1 (1982), 2 (1983), in: *EWW* 5 (1984), 309.

609) Sebba, Mark, *London Jamaican: Language Systems in Interaction*, Harlow, 1993, in: *EWW* 15 (1994), 305-6.

610) Sebba, Mark, *Contact Langages. Pidgins and Creoles*, Basingstoke, 1997, in: *EWW* 18 (1997), 332-3.

611) Sebeok, T.A., *Current Trends in Linguistics*, vol. 11, *Diachronic, Areal and Typological Linguistics*, The Hague, 1973, in: *Archiv* 214 (1977), 127-31.

612) Seymour, M.C., ed., *On the Properties of Things. John Trevisa's Translation of Bartholomaeus Anglicus De Proprietatibus Rerum, vol. I-II*, Oxford, 1975, in: *Archiv* 214 (1977), 138-41.

613) Seymour, M.C., *Sir John Mandeville*, Aldershot, 1993, in: *AAA* 19 (1994), 333-4.

614) Seymour, M.C., et al., *Bartholomaeus Anglicus and his Encyclopedia*, Aldershot, 1992, in: *AAA* 19 (1994), 334-5.

615) Shnukal, Anna, *Broken. An Introduction to the Creole Language of Torres Strait*, Canberra, 1988, in: *EWW* 12 (1991), 338-9.

616) Shopen, Timothy, ed., *Languages and Their Status*, Cambridge, Mass., 1979, in: *EWW* 1 (1980), 284-5.

617) Shopen, Timothy & Joseph M. Williams, eds., *Standards and Dialects in English*, Cambridge, Mass., 1980, in: *EWW* 2 (1981), 278.

618) Siegel, Jeff, *Language Contact in a Plantation Environment*, Cambridge, 1987, in: *EWW* 9 (1988), 147-8.

619) Sihler, Andrew L. *Language History. An Introduction*. Amsterdam, 2000, in *AAA* 26 (2001), 219-21.

620) Silva, Penny, ed., *A Dictionary of South African English*, Oxford, 1996, in: *IJL* 10 (1997), 330-5; repr. 165-8.
621) Simes, Gary, *A Dictionary of Australian Underworld Slang*, Melbourne, 1993, in: *EWW* 18 (1997), 331-2.
622) Simon-Vandenbergen, A.M., *The Grammar of Headlines in The Times 1870-1970*, Brussels, 1981, in: *EWW* 3 (1982), 122-3.
623) Simons, Linda & Hugh Young, *Pijin Blong Yumi. A Guide to Solomon Island Pijin*, Honiara, 1980, in: *EWW* 5 (1984), 118.
624) Simpson, David, *The Politics of American English*, New York, 1986, in: *EWW* 8 (1987), 156-7.
625) Singler, John Victor, *An Introduction to Liberian English*, East Lansing, 1981, in: *EWW* 6 (1985), 340-1.
626) Smith, Jeremy, *An Historical Study of English. Function, Form and Change*, London & New York, 1996, in: *AAA* 23 (1998), 118-9; repr. 56-7.
627) Smith, J.J., ed., *The English of Chaucer and His Contemporaries*, Aberdeen, 1988, in: *Anglia* 109 (1991), 114-6.
628) Smith, Larry E., ed., *English for Cross-Cultural Communication*, London, 1981, in: *LPLP* 7 (1983), 350-3.
629) Smith, Larry E., ed., *Readings in English as an International Language*, Oxford, 1983, in: *EWW* 4 (1983), 319-20.
630) Smith, Larry E., ed., *Discourse Across Cultures*, New York, 1987, in: *EWW* 9 (1988), 329-30.
631) Sörensen, Ilse, *Englisch im deutschen Wortschatz. Lehn- und Fremdwörter in der Umgangssprache*. Berlin, 1995, in: *IJL* 11 (1998), 164-6.
632) Sørensen, Knud, *A Dictionary of Anglicisms in Danish*. Copenhagen, 1997, in: *IJL* 12 (1999), 150.
633) Sorensen, Janet, *The Grammar of Empire in Eighteenth-Century British Writing*. Cambridge, 2000, in: *Anglia* (2002).
634) Sperk, Klaus, ed., *Medieval Saints' Legends*, Tübingen, 1970, in: *Anglia* 90 (1972), 507-10.
635) Sridhar, Kamal K., *English in Indian Bilingualism*, New Delhi, 1989, in: *EWW* 12 (1991), 334-6.
636) Stammerjohann, H., ed., *Handbuch der Linguistik*, München, 1975, in: *Archiv* 215 (1978), 129-38.
637) Standop, Ewald, *Englische Wörterbücher unter der Lupe*, Tübingen, 1975, in: *Archiv* 224 (1987), 141-3.
638) Stanforth, Anthony W., *Deutsche Einflüsse auf den englischen Wortschatz in Geschichte und Gegenwart*, Tübingen, 1996, in: *PBB* 119 (1997), 290-1.
639) Starnes, DeWitt T. & Gertrude E. Noyes, *The English Dictionary from Cawdrey to Johnson*, ed. Gabriele Stein, Amsterdam, 1991, in: *AAA* 18 (1993), 133-4.

640) Stein, Dieter, *The Semantics of Syntactic Change. Aspects of the Evolution of* do *in English*, Berlin & New York, 1990, in: *Linguistics* 30 (1992), 448-52.
641) Stein, Gabriele, *English Word-Formation over Two Centuries. In Honour of Hans Marchand on the Occasion of his Sixty-Fifth Birthday*, Tübingen, 1973, in: *IF* 80 (1975), 297-9.
642) Stein, Gabriele, *John Palsgrave as Renaissance Linguist*. Oxford, 1997, in: *IJL* 12 (1999), 77-9.
643) Steiner, Erich, *Die Entwicklung des Britischen Kontextualismus*, Heidelberg, 1983, in: *EWW* 4 (1983), 124.
644) Stemmler, Theo, *Die Liebesbriefe Heinrichs VIII und Anna Boleyn*, 1988, in: *AAA* 15 (1990), 69-70.
645) Stevenson, Patrick, ed., *The German Language and the Real World*, Oxford, 1995, in: *Linguistics* 37 (1999), 753-6.
646) Stevenson, Patrick, *The German Speaking World,* London, 1997, in: *Linguistics* 37 (1999), 756-7.
647) Stevenson, Patrick & Stephen Barbour, *Variation im Deutschen.* Soziolinguistische Perspektiven, Berlin, 1998, in: *Linguistics* 37 (1999), 757-8.
648) Stilz, Gerhard, *Grundlagen zur Literatur in englischer Sprache: Indien*, München, 1982, in: *EWW* 4 (1983), 127-8.
649) Story, G.M., W.J. Kirwin & J.D.A. Widdowson, *Dictionary of Newfoundland English*, Toronto, 1982, in: *EWW* 4 (1983), 114-5.
650) Strassner, Erich, *Deutsche Sprachkultur. Von der Barbarensprache zur Weltsprache*, Tübingen, 1995, in: *Linguistics* 34 (1996), 437-8.
651) Stubbs, Michael, *Language and Literacy. The Sociolinguistics of Reading and Writing*, London, 1980, in: *EWW* 2 (1981), 277.
652) Stubbs, Michael, *Educational Linguistics*, Oxford, 1986, in: *EWW* 7 (1986), 335-6.
653) Subbiondo, Joseph L., ed., *John Wilkins and 17th-Century British Linguistics*, Amsterdam, in: *Linguistics* 31 (1993), 584-6.
654) Sundby, Bertil, et al., *A Dictionary of English Normative Grammar, 1700-1800*, Amsterdam, 1991, in: *Anglia* 111 (1993), 469-72.
655) Sutcliffe, David & Ansel Wong, eds., *The Language of Black Experience*, Oxford, 1986, in: *EWW* 8 (1987), 149-51.
656) Tabbert, R., *Dictionary of Alaskan English*, Juneau, 1991, in: *EWW* 12 (1991), 330-1.
657) Tabouret-Keller, Andrée, et al., eds., *Vernacular Literacy, a Re-Evaluation*, Oxford, 1997, in *EWW* 19 (1999), 303-4.
658) Tamplin, R., ed., *Wynkyn de Worde's Gesta Romanorum*, Exeter, 1974, in: *Anglia* 94 (1976), 232-3.
659) Telling, Rudolf, *Französisch im deutschen Wortschatz. Lehn- und Fremdwörter aus acht Jahrhunderten*, 2nd ed., Berlin, 1988, in: *IJL* 11 (1998), 164-6.

660) Thomas, Alan R., ed., *Methods in Dialectology*, Clevedon, 1988, in: *EWW* 10 (1989), 155-8.
661) Thomas, Alan R., ed., *Issues and Methods in Dialectology*, Bangor, 1997, in: *EWW* 19 (1998), 151-3.
662) Thomason, Sarah Grey & Terence Kaufman, *Language Contact, Creolization, and Genetic Linguistics*, Berkeley, 1988, in: *IF* 97 (1992), 315-6; repr. 126-7.
663) Thomason, Sarah G., ed., *Contact Languages. A Wider Perspective*. Amsterdam, 2001, in: *Sociolinguistica* (2002).
664) Tieken-Boon van Ostade, Ingrid, ed., *Two Hundred Years of Lindley Murray*, Münster, 1996, in: *Linguistics*.
665) Todd, Loreto, et al., *Papers in Pidgin and Creole Linguistics* 1, Canberra, 1978, in: *EWW* 5 (1984), 108-11.
666) Todd, Loreto, ed., *Some Day Been Dey. West African Pidgin Folktales*, London, 1979, in: *EWW* 1 (1980), 157.
667) Todd, Loreto, *Modern Englishes. Pidgins and Creoles*, Oxford, 1984, in: *LPLP* 9 (1985), 262-8.
668) Todd, Loreto, *Words Apart. A Dictionary of Northern Ireland English*, Gerrards Cross, Bucks., 1990, in: *EWW* 12 (1991), 155-7.
669) Todorov, T. & O. Ducrot, *Enzyklopädisches Wörterbuch der Sprachwissenschaften*, Frankfurt, 1975, in: *Archiv* 215 (1978), 129-38.
670) Trask, R.L., *Historical Linguistics*, London, 1996, in: *AAA* 23 (1998), 119-20; repr. 57-8.
671) Traugott, Elisabeth Closs & Mary Louise Pratt, *Linguistics for Students of Literature*, New York, 1980, in: *EWW* 1 (1980), 288.
672) Tristram, Hildegard L.C., *How Celtic Is Standard English?* Sankt-Peterburg, 1999, in *ZCPh* (2002).
673) Tristram, Hildegard L.C., ed., *The Celtic Englishes II.* (Anglistische Forschungen 286), Heidelberg, 2000, in: *ZCPh* (2002).
674) Troy, J., *Australian Aboriginal Contact with the English Language in New South Wales 1788 to 1845*, Canberra, 1990, in: *EWW* 12 (1991), 167.
675) Truchot, Claude, *L'Anglais dans le monde contemporain*, Paris, 1990, in: *EWW* 12 (1991), 315-6.
676) Trudgill, Peter, ed., *Applied Sociolinguistics*, London, 1984, in: *EWW* 5 (1984), 297-8.
677) Trudgill, Peter, ed., *Language in the British Isles*, Cambridge, 1984, in: *EWW* 5 (1984), 283-90; repr. 95-9.
678) Trudgill, Peter, *On Dialect. Social and Geographical Perspectives*, Oxford, 1983, in: *ZDL* 52 (1985), 395-6.
679) Trudgill, Peter, *Dialects in Contact*, Oxford, 1986, in: *EWW* 8 (1987), 128-31; repr. 101-3.

680) Trudgill, Peter, *The Dialects of England*, Oxford, 1990, in: *EWW* 11 (1990), 316-7.
681) Trudgill, Peter & J.K. Chambers, eds., *Dialects of English. Studies in Grammatical Variation*, London, 1991, in: *EWW* 12 (1991), 325-7.
682) Tryon, Darrell T., *Bislama. An Introduction to the National Language of Vanuatu*, Canberra, 1987, in: *EWW* 10 (1989), 180-1.
683) Tulloch, Graham, *A History of the Scots Bible*, Aberdeen, 1989, in: *EWW* 11 (1990), 158-61; repr. 111-3.
684) Tulloch, Sara, *The Oxford Dictionary of New Words*, Oxford, 1991, in: *EWW* 13 (1992), 157-8.
685) Turner, G.W., et al., *The Australian Concise/Pocket/Little/Mini-Dictionary*, Melbourne, 1984-87, in: *EWW* 11 (1990), 165-8.
686) Upton, Clive & J.D.A. Widdowson, *An Atlas of English Dialects*, Oxford, 1996, in: *EWW* 17 (1996), 309-10.
687) Upton, Clive, David Parry & J.D.A. Widdowson, *Survey of English Dialects. The Dictionary and Grammar*, London, 1994, in: *Linguistics* 32 (1994), 571-3.
688) Upton, Clive, John Widdowson & Stewart Sanderson, *Word Maps: A Dialect Atlas of England*, Beckenham, 1987, in: *ZDL* 56 (1989), 204-6.
689) Urdang, Lawrence, *The Oxford Thesaurus, An A-Z Dictionary of Synonyms*, Oxford, 1991, in: *EWW* 13 (1992), 158-9.
690) Ureland, P. Sture, ed., *Sprachkontakte im Nordseegebiet. Standardsprache und Dialekte in mehrsprachigen Gebieten Europas. Sprachvariation und Sprachwandel. Kulturelle und sprachliche Minderheiten in Europa*, Tübingen, 1977, 1978, 1979, 1980, in: *EWW* 3 (1982), 118-9.
691) Ureland, P. Sture & G. Broderick, eds., *Language Contact in the British Isles*, Tübingen, 1991, in: *EWW* 12 (1991), 319-22.
692) Vachek, Josef, *Selected Writings in English and General Linguistics*, The Hague, 1976, in: *Archiv* 214 (1977), 394-5.
693) Valdman, Albert, ed., *Pidgin and Creole Linguistics*, Bloomington, 1977, in: *Anglia* 98 (1980), 474-9.
694) Van Leuvenstijn, J. & J. Berns, eds., *Dialect and Standard Language in the English, Dutch, German and Norwegian Language Areas*, Amsterdam, 1992, in: *EWW* 14 (1993), 157-9.
695) *A Variorum Edition of the Works of Geoffrey Chaucer, II:3, The Miller's Tale, II:9, The Nun's Priest's Tale, II:10, The Manciple's Tale*, in: *AAA* 11 (1986), 111-4; repr. 36-40.
696) Veltman, Calvin, *Language Shift in the United States*, Berlin, 1983, in: *IF* 90 (1985), 338-40.
697) Verhaar, John W.M., ed., *Melanesian Pidgin and Tok Pisin*, Proceedings of the First International Conference of Pidgins and Creoles in Melanesia, Amsterdam, 1990, in: *EWW* 12 (1991), 168-70.

698) *Vernon Manuscript. A Facsimile of Bodleian Library*, Oxford, MS. Eng. poet. a.1, ed. A.I. Doyle, Cambridge, 1987, in: *Anglia* 107 (1989), 520-3; repr. 30-1.

699) Viereck, Wolfgang, ed., *Sprachliches Handeln - Soziales Verhalten*, München, 1976, in: *EWW* 1 (1980) 283-4.

700) Viereck, Wolfgang, ed., *Studien zum Einfluß der englischen Sprache auf das Deutsche*, Tübingen, 1980, in: *EWW* 1 (1980), 287.

701) Viereck, Wolfgang, ed., *Dialect Structure and Classification. Proceedings of the International Congress of Dialectologists, Bamberg 1990*, Vol. 1, Stuttgart, 1993, in: *EWW* 14 (1993), 313-14.

702) Viereck, Wolfgang, ed., *Historical Dialectology and Linguistic Change. Linguistic Atlases and Dictionaries. Proceedings of the International Congress of Dialectologists, Bamberg 1990*, Vol. 2, Stuttgart, 1993, in: *EWW* 15 (1994), 154-5.

703) Viereck, Wolfgang, ed., *Regional Variation, Colloquial and Standard Languages. Proceedings of the International Congress of Dialectologists, Bamberg 1990*, Vol. 3, Stuttgart, 1994, in: *EWW* 15 (1994), 295-7.

704) Viereck, Wolfgang, ed., *Sociolinguistic Variation. Bilingualism, Multilingualism, Language Contact and Language Comparison. Dialect Use and Attitudes towards Linguistic Varieties. Proceedings of the International Congress of Dialectologists, Bamberg, 1990*, Vol. 4., Stuttgart, 1995, in: *EWW* 17 (1996), 139-40.

705) Viereck, Wolfgang & Wolf-Dietrich Bald, eds., *English in Contact with Other Languages. Studies in honour of Broder Carstensen on the occasion of his 60th birthday*, Budapest, 1986, in: *ZDL* 55 (1988), 76-8.

706) Wächtler, Kurt, *Geographie und Stratifikation der englischen Sprache*, Düsseldorf & Bern, 1977, in: *EWW* 1 (1980), 152-3.

707) Waddell, P. Hately, *The Psalms in Scots, 1871*, Aberdeen, 1987, in: *EWW* 9 (1988), 141-2.

708) Wallace, David, ed., *The Cambridge History of Medieval English Literature*, Cambridge, 1999, in *AAA* 25 (2000), 130-2.

709) Walker, Marshall, *Scottish Literature Since 1707*, Harlow, 1996, in: *EWW* 18 (1997), 317-8.

710) Wardhaugh, Ronald, *Languages in Competition*, Oxford, 1987, in: *EWW* 9 (1988), 132-4.

711) Warkentyne, Henry J., ed., *Methods V*, Victoria, 1985, in: *EWW* 8 (1987), 151-4.

712) Webb, Victor N., ed., *Language in South Africa*, Pretoria, 1995, in: *EWW* 16 (1995), 308-10.

713) Wells, John, *Accents of English*, 3 vols., Cambridge, 1982, in: *Anglia* 102 (1984), 176-8.

714) Welte, Werner, *Moderne Linguistik: Terminologie/Bibliographie*, München, 1974, in: *Archiv* 215 (1978), 129-38.

715) Wermser, Richard, *Statistische Studien zur Entwicklung des englischen Wortschatzes*, Bern, 1976, in: *Archiv* 216 (1979), 401-3.

716) Werner, Reinhold, ed., *Sprachkontakte*, Tübingen, 1980, in: *EWW* 3 (1982), 119.

717) Westhuizen, J.E. van, ed., *John Lydgate, The Life of Saint Alban and Saint Amphibal*, Leiden, 1974, in: *Anglia* 95 (1977), 234-6.

718) Wheeler, L.W., ed., *Ten Northeast Poets*, Aberdeen, 1985, in: *EWW* 8 (1987), 330-3.

719) Wilkes, G.A., *A Dictionary of Australian Colloquialisms*, 2nd ed., Sydney, 1985, in: *EWW* 11 (1990), 164-5.

720) Williams, Colin H., ed., *Language in Geographic Context*, Clevedon, 1988, in: *EWW* 11 (1990), 137-8.

721) Williams, Colin H., ed., *Linguistic Minorities, Society and Territory*, Clevedon, 1992, in: *EWW* 14 (1993), 161-4.

722) Williams, Colin H., *Called Unto Liberty! On Language and Nationalism*, Clevedon, 1994, in: *EWW* 15 (1994), 291-2.

723) Williams, Glyn, *Sociolinguistics. A Sociological Critique*, London, 1992, in: *EWW* 13 (1992), 317-20.

724) Williams, Ulla, *Die Elsässische "Legenda aurea" Band III. Die lexikalische Überlieferungsvarianz, Register, Indices*, Tübingen, 1990, in: *CG* 26 (1993), 279-80.

725) Williams-Krapp, Ulla and Werner, & Konrad Kunze, eds., *Die Elsässische Legenda Aurea*, 1 & 2, Tübingen, 1980, 1983, in: *AUMLA* 62 (1984), 253-5.

726) Williams-Krapp, Werner, *Die deutschen und niederländischen Legendare des Mittelalters. Studien zu ihrer Überlieferungs-, Text- und Wirkungsgeschichte*, Tübingen, 1986, in: *CG* 23 (1990), 175-7.

727) Willinsky, John, *Empire of Words. The Reign of the OED*, Princeton, 1994, in: *Linguistics* 33 (1995), 1194-6.

728) Wilson, E., *A Descriptive Index of the English Lyrics in John of Grimestone's Preaching Book*, Oxford, 1973, in: *Anglia* 93 (1975), 511-2.

729) Windeatt, Barry A., ed., *Geoffrey Chaucer, Troilus and Criseyde*, London, 1984, in: *AAA* 10 (1985), 280-2; repr. 40-3.

730) Windeatt, Barry A., *Troilus and Criseyde*. (Oxford Guides to Chaucer), Oxford, 1992, in: *AAA* 19 (1994), 142-5; repr. 44-6.

731) Winterbottom, M., ed., *Three Lives of English Saints*, Toronto Medieval Latin Texts, 1 and 2, Toronto, 1972, 1973, in: *Archiv* 211 (1974), 426-7.

732) Wolf, Hans-Georg, *English in Cameroon*. Berlin, 2001, in: *Sociolinguistica* (2002).

733) Wolf, Helmut, *Sir Francis Kynastons Übersetzung von Chaucers 'Troilus and Criseyde'*, Frankfurt, 1997, in: *Anglia* 116 (1998), 539-41.
734) Wolff, Dieter, *Grundzüge der diachronischen Morphologie des Englischen*, Anglistische Arbeitshefte 7, Tübingen, 1975, in: *IF* 81 (1976), 411-5.
735) Wolff, Friedrich & Otto Wittstock, *Latein und Griechisch im deutschen Wortschatz. Lehn- und Fremdwörter*, 6th ed., Berlin, 1990, in: *IJL* 11 (1998), 164-6.
736) Wood, Richard E., ed., *National Language Planning and Treatment*, Word 30 (1979), in: *EWW* 2 (1981), 127-8.
737) Woolford, Ellen B., *Aspects of Tok Pisin Grammar*, Canberra, 1979, in: *EWW* 5 (1984), 115-6.
738) Woolford, Ellen B. & William Washabaugh, eds., *The Social Context of Creolization*, Ann Arbor, 1983, in: *IF* 90 (1985), 340-1.
739) Wright, Laura, ed., *The Development of Standard English, 1300-1800. Theories, Descriptions, Conflicts*. Cambridge, 2000, in: *Linguistics* 39 (2001), 832-5.
740) Wurm, Stephen A., ed., *Language, Culture, Society and the Modern World*, Canberra, 1976, ²1979, in: *EWW* 5 (1984), 104-6.
741) Wurm, Stephen A., ed., *New Guinea and Neighboring Areas: A Sociolinguistic Laboratory*, The Hague, 1979, in: *EWW* 5 (1984), 106-8.
742) Wurm, Stephen A. & P. Mühlhäusler, eds., *Handbook of Tok Pisin*, Canberra, 1985, in: *EWW* 7 (1986), 147-50; repr. 121-4.
743) Yang, W., *Anglizismen im Deutschen. Am Beispiel des Nachrichtenmagazins DER SPIEGEL*, (Reihe Germanistische Linguistik 106), Tübingen, 1990, in: *IJL* 5 (1992), 78-9.
744) Young, Douglas, ed., *How do We Ensure Access to English in a Post-Apartheid Southern Africa?*, Cape Town, 1993, in: *EWW* 15 (1994), 314-5.
745) Yule, Henry & A.C. Burnell, *Hobson-Jobson. A Glossary of Colloquial Anglo-Indian Words and Phrases*, London, ʳ1985, in: *EWW* 7 (1986), 164-5.
746) Zgusta, Ladislav, ed., *Theory and Method in Lexicography*, Columbia, S.C., 1979, in: *EWW* 1 (1980), 154.

Appendix

747) Gieszinger, Sabine, *The History of Advertising Language. The Advertisements in the Times from 1788 to 1996*, Frankfurt am Main, 2001, in: *Anglia* (2002).
748) Singh, Ishtla, *Pidgins and Creoles, An Introduction*, London, 2000, in: *Sociolingistica* (2002).

Index of persons

The index lists authors of books reviewed in the first section, including contributors to collections; a few major authors forming the topic of discussions are also listed. In the alphabetical survey of my reviews authors are indexed only if they come second in a team (these references are to numbers, such as B705, and not to pages).

Aarsleff, Hans 72, 84
Abbott, E.A. 78
Abrahams, Roger, D. 117, 119
Aelfric 137
Aitken, A.J. 96, 108
Alexander, J.J.G. 4, 27
Alford, Henry 77, 83
Algeo, John 64, 147
Allsopp, Richard 155-61
Alston, R.C. 70, 76, 84
Ammon, Ulrich B314
Angus, William 78, 83, 108
Anttila, Raymo 59
Avis, Walter S. 168, B407
Awbery, G.M. 97
Bailey, Charles-James N. B212
Bailey, Richard W. 66
Bain, Alexander 77-79, 83
Baker, Donald C. 4, 20, 21, 27, 36, 178
Bald, Wolf-Dietrich B705
Bammesberger, Alfred 59, 178
Banjo, Ayo B45
Barbour, Stephen B647
Barnes, Michael 72, 98
Barry, Michael V. 97
Bartholomaeus Anglicus B592, 612, 614
Barthos, G.A. 17, 27
Bartlett, John 77
Bauer, Laurie 108
Baugh, Albert C. 58, 62, 63, 108, 130, 179, 201
Baynes, T.S. 78
Beadle, Richard 3, 11, 12, 22, 179
Beale, Joan 105
Beattie, James 70

Becker, Karl Ferdinand 70
Beeton, D.R. 161, 164-5
Benskin, Michael 4, 25, 27, 28
Benson, David C. 179
Benson, Eugene 179
Benson, Larry D. 44
Benson, M. 179
Berkeley, George 81
Berns, J. B694
Besch, Werner 92-4
Betten, Anne B77, 78
Bevington, David 4, 19, 22, 27, 180
Biber, Douglas, 69, 180
Blair, David B154
Blake, Norman F. 34, 36-38, 40, 55, 56, 58, 61, 62
Blanchfield, Lynne S. B71
Bliss, Alan J. 7, 96, 150, 155
Bloomfield, Leonard 74
Boccaccio, Giovanni 41-43, 45
Boethius 16, 32, 41
Boffey, Julia 27, 32
Boleyn, Anna B644
Bonheim, Helmut 3
Bopp, 70-72, 79, 80, 83
Bradley, Henry 72, 78
Branford, Jean 155, 161-4, 165, 167-8
Branford, W.R.G. 161, 165, 167-8
Brewer, Charlotte 49
Brewer, Derek 3, 9, 10, 13, 24-26, 29, 32, 33, 36, 40, 41, 46, B471
Brown, T.J. 27
Brusendorff, A.A. 12, 14, 27
Bruyn, Adrienne B43
Burnell, A.C. B745

Burnley, David 62
Burrow, John 34-36
Bynon, Theodora 54, 57, 58
Cable, Thomas 58, 63, 108
Cameron, Angus B46
Campbell, Lyle 53, 54, 79, 81, 83, 128, 130
Cannon, Garland B530
Carls, Uwe B299
Carmichael, Cathie B48
Carstensen, Broder B705
Carver, Craig M., 144, 147
Cassidy, F.G. 118-9, 143-55, 160
Cawley, A.C. 3, 20, 27, 183
Caxton, William 13, 16, 17, 27, 28, 56, 62, B84
Chambers, J.K. B681
Chaucer, Geoffrey 3, 6, 8, 11-16, 23, 24, 26-29, 31-33, 36, 37, 39-46, 49, 51, 52, 62, 180, 183, 184, 195, 203, 204, 209, 212, 214, B375, 513, 522, 627, 729, 730, 733
Cheshire, Jenny B22
Clanvowe, Sir John 32
Clark, Cecily 60, 62
Clement, David 97
Coates, Richard 64
Coleridge 77, 79
Conolly, L.W. B72
Conrad, Andrew W. B232, 236
Conrad, Susan B83
Cooper, Helen 43-45
Corbett, John 109-10
Cordes, Gerhard 93
Craigie, Sir William 168
Craik, G.L. 77
Crowley, Terry 118-9
Crystal, David 66
Cukor-Avila, Patricia B38
Cunningham, I.C. 3, 7, B520
Darwin, Charles 71, 75, 81, 83, 89
Darwin, G.H. 82

Dasent, G.W. 77
Davis, Alfred 14-16, 28
Davis, Norman 4, 14-16, 22, 28, 94, 172
Dayley, Jon P. 155
D'Costa, Jean 116-9, B398
Delbridge, Arthur 169
Denison, David 64, 66-69
De Quincey, Thomas 76
de Saussure, Ferdinand 74
Deverson, Tony 173, B274
Devitt, Amy J. 108, 110
Dewhirst, Ian B373
de Worde, Wynkyn B658
Dieth, Eugen 92
Dil, Anwar S. B408
Dillard, J.L. B453
Dittmar, Norbert B23
Donaldson, E. Talbot 4, 28, 46, 47, 49, B364
Dorner, Helen 161, 164-5
Dornseiff, Franz 139
Douglas, Sylvester B352
Douglas-Cowie, Ellen 96
Doyle, A.I. 3, 6, 13, 26, 27, 29-31, 33, 34, B698
Dryden, John 46
Dutton, Tom 121-2
Eccles, Mark 22
Edwards, A.S.G. 32, 35, 96
Edwards, J. 98
Edwards, Viv 97
Edwards, Walter 149
Eggers, Hans 140
Ellis, Alexander J. 65, 76, 78, 83, 97
Finegan, Edward 65, 69, B83
Fischer, Olga 61, 67
Fishman, Joshua A. B152, 254
Fisiak, Jacek B323
Fitch, J.G. 77
Foster, A.F. & M.E. 77
Fowler, Henry W. B118
Francis, W. Nelson 92, 94-5

Freeman, E.A. 77, 78, 82, 83
Fries, Udo 44, 59, 63
Furnivall, F.J. 14, 20, 22, 28
Fyle, C. 155
Garnett, Richard 76
Gibson, M.T. 4, 27
Gilbert, G.G. B606
Galliéron, Jules 95
Gimson, A.C. 96
Gneuss, Helmut 3, B383
Godden, Malcolm 60
Goebl, Hans 128-32
Görlach, Manfred 6, 7, 28, 29, 31, 34, 48, 54, 55, 58, 63, 64, 66, 70, 76, 84, 103, 104, 107, 108, 110, 113, 127, 140, 142, 143, 147, 156, 161
Götz, Dieter B119
Gonzalez, Andrew B65
Gordon, Elizabeth 173
Gower, John 24, 32, 42, 46, 51, 52
Graham, John J. B573
Gray, Douglas 4, 28
Greg, W.W. 18, 28, 48
Grimm, Jacob 72, 73, 83
Grose, Francis 76
Guddat-Figge, Gisela 4, 12, 28
Hagège, Claude B244
Hall, Clark 133
Hall, Joan H. 143
Hall, Louis B. 27
Hallig, Rudolf 129
Hammond, E.P. 14, 28
Hancock, I.F. 98, 121
Hands, Rachel 23, 28, 70, 73-76, 83, 96, 117
Harris, John 96, 119
Harris, Kate 11, 12, 25, 28
Harris, Roy 70
Haugen, Einar 101
Haynes, Lilith B220
Hazlitt, William 76
Heath, Shirley Brice B225

Heffernan, Thomas J. 34
Heine, Bernd B559
Hellinga, Lotte 17, 28
Hellinger, Marlis B24
Henry VIII B644
Herzog, Marvin 85, 88
Hietsch, Otto B88
Hilton, W. 10
Hinman, Charleton 23
Hirshberg, Jeffrey 155
Hoccleve, Thomas 32
Hoenigswald, Henry M. 59
Hogg, Richard M. 58, 59, 63
Holm, John 151-5, 160, B125
Holmes, Janet B70
Huber, Magnus 119-21
Hudson, Anne 3, 23, 27, 28
Hüllen, Werner 136-40
Hulbert, James R. B166
Humboldt, Wilhelm von 80
Hunt, Richard William 27
Hurm, Gerd B270, 271
Hussey, S.S. 34
Isidor (of Sevilla) 137
James I 32-3
Jamieson 76, 105, 109
Jespersen, Otto 72
Johannesson, Nils-Lennart B459
Johanson, Stig B83
Johnson, Samuel 76, 77, 83, 171, B351, 639
Johnston, Paul 104, 105-6
Jones, Charles 103-8, 110
Jones, Eldred 155, B253
Jupp, James 108
Käsmann, Hans 3
Kaiser, Rolf 50
Kahrl, Stanley J. 4, 21, B460
Kane, George 4, 28, 46-49
Kastovsky, Dieter 59, 127
Kaufman, Terence 126-7, B662
Kay, Christian 133-6, 139, 140, B571

Keiser, George E. 28
Ker, N.R. 3-5, 16, 17, 28, 32
Kerkhof, Jelle 44
Kibbee, Douglas A. 62, 63
Kinloch, A.M. B35
Kirkness, Alan B485
Kirwin, W.J. B649
Kleineidam, Hartmut B25
Kniezsa, Veronika 104
Kolb, Eduard 92
Krygier, Marcin B240
Kuhn, Ortwin B390
Kunze, Konrad B725
Kurath, Hans 92
Kwan-Terry, John B363
Kwok, Helen B89
Kynaston, Sir Francis B733
Labov, William 85-92
Laing, Margaret 25, 27, 49-51
Lalla, Barbara 116-9
Lamb, Gregor B242
Lancashire, Ian 18-20, 27, 28
Lane, John 44
Langland, William 3, 24, 42, 46-49, 51, 52, B364, 597, 598
Lass, Roger 29, 61, 62
Layamon 62
Laycock, Donald C. 121-2, B210
Leech, Geoffrey B83
Lehmann, W. 88
Leith, Dick 101, B276
Le Page, R.B. 118-9
Levy, B. B290
Lewis, M.G. 34, 116
Lightfoot, David N. 66, 68
Locke, John 72, 79, 83, 138
Lockwood, W.B. 101
Loomis, L.H. 6, 7, 28
Lorimer, W.L. 109-11
Lowth, Robert 70
Lucko, Peter B299
Luke, A. B44

Lumiansky, R.M. 3, 18, 19, 22, 28, 40
Lydgate, John 14, 24, 32, B717
Macafee, C.I. 104-5, 106, 140-3
McClure, J.D. 108
McConnell, Grant D. B395
McDavid, Raven I. Jr. B196
McIntosh, Angus 4, 10, 25, 27, 28, 49-51, 61, 63, 127
Macleod, Iseabail B426
MacMahon, Michael K.C. 65
McSparran, Frances 3, 6-8, 26, 31
Madden, R.R. 10, 116
Mätzner, Eduard A. 70
Malkiel, Y. 88
Malory, Sir Thomas 3, 16, 17, 27, 28, B374
Mandeville, Sir John B613
Manly, I.M. 13, 28
Mannyng, Robert, of Brunne B259
Marchand, Hans B641
Markey, T.L. B321, 605
Marsh, George Perkins 72
Marx, C.W. 34, 35
Mason, Charles Peter 78
Mathews, Mitford M. 168
Mattheier, K.J. B23
Maynor, Natalie B38
Meale, Carol M. 35
Mehl, Dieter 35
Meredith, Peter 4, 21, 22, 28
Mesthrie, Rajend 168
Metcalf, Allan 147
Meurman-Solin, Anneli 103, 108
Michaels, Leonard B565
Mills, David 3, 18, 19, 22, 28, B421
Milroy, James 95
Milroy, Leslie B467, 468
Mirk, John 50
Mitchell, Bruce 59, 66
Möhn, Dieter 93
Moessner, Lilo 104
Monboddo, James Burnett, Lord 70

Montgomery, Michael 106
Morell, John Daniel 78
Morris, Edward E. 160, 173
Mossé, Fernand 68
Mühlhäusler, Peter 115, 121-6, B742
Müller, Friedrich Max 71-74, 77-83, 126
Müller, Ulrich 4, 28
Mugglestone, Lynda 66
Murison, D.D. B284
Murphy, J.L. 4, 20, 21, 27, 178
Murray, Alexander 70, 71, 74, 76, 79, 82, 83, 87, 111
Murray, H.G. 116
Murray, Lindley B664
Mustanoja, Tauno F. 61, 63, 66
Nehls, Dietrich 68, 69, B380
Nelde, Peter H. 128-32
Newman, John Henry 78, 83
Nickel, Gerhard 68, B380
Nicodemus B377
Nicol, Henry 78
Niles, Norma 117, 119
Norton-Smith, John 3, 14, 15
Noyes, Gertrude E. 140, B639
Oakeshott, Walter 16, 17, 28
Ó Baoill, Dónall P. 106
Ó Doghartaigh, Cathair 97
Onions, C.T. 17
Ornstein, Jacob B442
Orsman, H.W. 171-3
Owen, A.E.B. 3, 10-12
Pace, George B. 14-16, 28
Pätzold, Kurt-Michael B281, 282
Palsgrave, John B642
Parkes, M.B. 3, 4, 6, 13, 15, 16, 26-28, 42
Parry, David B687
Pearsall, Derek 3, 4, 6, 7, 15, 23, 25-29, 33, 36-40, 46, 47, 49
Pettman, Charles 161
Pickering, O.S. 3

Pitman, Isaac 78, 83
Pollard, A.W. 20
Pott, August Friedrich 72, 83
Pratt, Mary Louise B671
Pratt, R.A. 38, 41
Price, Glanville 95, 99-101
Priestley, Joseph 70
Puppel, Stanisław B323
Putschke, Wolfgang 92-4
Quirk, Randolph B287
Radtke, Edgar B331, 455
Raumolin-Brunberg, Helena B491
Ramson, W.S. 165, 168-71, 173
Ray, John 161
Reah, Ken B400
Reichl, Karl 35, 36
Reichmann, Oskar B76, 77, 78
Reid, Euan 97
Richardson 71, 76, 77, 83
Rickert, Edith 13, 28
Rickford, John R. 117, 119
Rigg, A.G. 4, 27-29, 46-49
Ritchie, Joan B107
Roberge, P.T. B321
Roberts, Jane 133-6, 139, 140
Robbins, Rossell Hope 11, 14, 27, 29, 31
Robinson, P.M. 3, 4, 8, 9, 14, 29, 31, 34, 42-44
Robinson, P.R. B448
Rogers, Henry 76
Roget, Peter Mark 136, 138, 140
Rolle, Richard 10, 51
Romaine, Suzanne 63-6, 101, B564
Root, R.K. 15, 29, 41-43
Ross, Malcolm B210
Ross, Thomas W. 36, 37, 39, 121
Rowland, Beryl 31
Rubal-Lopez, Alma B236
Ruggiers, Paul G. 13, 32, 36, 39, 40
Russell, George 4, 46, 49
Saint-Jacques, Bernard B266

St. Clair, Robert B265
Salter, Elizabeth 3, 15, B513
Samuels, M.L. 3, 4, 6, 13, 25, 27, 28, 29, 44, 49-52, 56, 58, 139, 140
Sanderson, Stewart B688
Sato, Charlene J. B564
Sauer, Walter B557
Schäfer, Jürgen 140
Schaefer, Ursula B472
Schleicher, August 70, 72
Schmidt, A.V.C. 46-48, 126
Schneider, Edgar W. 117, 119, B490
Schöwerling, R. B101
Schuchardt, Hugo 126
Scott, Charles T. B439
Scott, M. 116
Scott, Sir Walter 107, 113
Seeley, J.R. 78
Shakespeare, William 23, 36, 56, 78, 109
Shuken, Cynthia 97
Silva, Penny 165-8, 173
Simpson, John B36
Skeat, Walter W. 46, 52
Smith, Jeremy J. 49, 51, 52, 56-58, 81, 112, 113
Smith, N. 121, B487
Smith, W.W. 112
Sonderegger, Stefan B76, 77, 78
Spector, Stephen 21
Speght, Thomas 38
Speitel, Hans 92
Spence, Thomas B68
Spurgeon, Caroline C.F. 36, 40
Stalker, J.B. B495
Stanley, Eric G. 4, 28
Starnes, DeWitt T. 140
Starý, Zdeněk 128-32
Stein, Dieter 68, 139, 140
Stein, Gabriele 140, B639
Stern, Karen 9, 10, 27, 29
Stevens, John 29

Stevens, Martin 3, 11, 20, 32
Stewart, Dugald 71, 74, 81, 83, 114
Strite, Victor L. 60, 63
Sutcliffe, David 97
Swann, Joan B276
Sweet, Henry 65, 71, 72, 75, 82, 83
Szwedck, Aleksander B369
Thomas, Alan 97
Thomas, Andrew B45
Thomason, Sarah Grey 126-7
Thompson, John J. 9, 10, 26, 27, 29, 35, 36
Thornton, Robert 3, 5, 8-11, 13, 25-27, 29, 31, 36, 51
Thyen, O. B150
Todd, Henry John 76, 77
Tooke, Horne 70, 74, 79-81, 83
Toon, Thomas E. 60
Trask, R.L. 57-8
Traugott, Elizabeth 59
Trench, Richard Chenevix 70-72, 74, 77, 83
Trevisa, John B247, 252, 612
Trudgill, Peter 95-9, 101-3
Tryon, Darrell B210
Tulloch, Graham 105, 106, 111-3
Turville-Petre, Thorlac 34
Tylor, E.B. 78
Tyrwhitt, Thomas 14, 29, 38
Usk, Thomas 43, 46
Utz, H. B205
Valdman, Albert B324
van der Auwera, Johan B382
van der Leek, F. 67
Vass, Winifred K. B328
Viereck, Wolfgang B553
Vinaver, Eugène 16, 17
Virgilius Maro B382
Visser, F. Th. 66, 67
von Schneidemesser, Luanne B464

Wächtler, Kurt B390
Wakelin, Martyn 50, 94, 96, 97
Washabaugh, William B738
Watson, A.G. 28
Watts, Richard J. B80
Webster 76, 77, 83
Wedgwood 77, 81
Wehrle, Hugo 140
Weinreich, Uriel 88
Wells, J.C. 96
Wenker, Georg 95
Wentworth, Harold 143, 147
Widdowson, J.D.A. B649, 687, 688
Whitney, William Dwight 71, 73, 74, 79, 82, 83
Wiegand, Herbert Ernst 92-4

Wilkes, G.A. 169
Wilkins, John 138, B653
Williams, Jeffrey P. 119
Williamson, Keith B397
Windeatt, Barry A. 4, 15, 24, 27, 29, 32, 33, 40-46
Winer, Lise 119
Wiseman, Nicholas 71, 75
Wolfram, Walt B148
Wong, Ansel B655
Wordsworth, William 47
Wren, Helen B217
Wright, Joseph 18, 76, 97, 143, 145, 170
Wurm, Stephen A. 121
Wycliffe, John, 50, B409
Young, Hugh B623

Index of topics

AAVE (=BEV) 117-8, B480, 481, 603
Aboriginal English B32, 198, 211, 674
accent B411, 482, 713
accessibility of texts 5
adaptive translation 4
advertising B319
Africa B318, 494, 549, 559, 567, 601, 602
Africanisms B184, 328, 480
Afrikaans 166
Afro-American B18
Alaska B6456
album 12
American English B196, 197, 251, 267, 328, 441, 422, 453, 464, 473, 480, 486, 603, 624
analogy 53
Ancrene Riwle 23, B199
anglicisms B122, 136, 137, 182, 227, 230, 231, 278, 346, 452, 457, 533, 575, 631, 632, 743
anglicization 104
Anglo-Norman 100
Angloromani 98, 100, 126
Anglo-Saxon history 59
Antarctic B325
antiquarians 18
anthology B434
anthropology B435
apartheid 162, B744
applied linguistics 76
appropriateness 46
aspect 68, B604
Atlantic Creoles B43
atlas B29, 396, 440, 539, 686, 688
attitudes B229, 564
Australia 106, 168-71, B32, 44, 107, 108, 123, 154, 188, 189, 198, 208,

211, 290, 327, 332, 336, 509, 528, 529, 554, 580, 586, 587, 588, 615, 621, 674, 685, 719
author's original text 38-9, 42
authority B467
auxiliaries 68
Bahamas 151-5, B329
Barbados 117, 156
Belize B221
Beowulf 16, 23
best manuscript 46, 47
Bible 24, 109, 111-3, B289, 315, 327, 372, 377, 409, 416, 417, 683
bibliographical information 9, 10, 15, B10, 35, 396, 419, 556, 558, 714
bibliophile 4
bilingualism B41, 93, 341, 517, 579, 635
biography B522
Bislama B127 144, 171, 172, 293, 682
Black English B38, 214, 216, 655
book, medieval 4
Book of St. Albans B298
booklet 7, 8, 12, 14, 20
bookshop theory 6, 14, 34
borrowing 53
British English B288, 677, 691
British Isles B16
Butler, E. B333, 334
Cambridge HEL 58-66
Cameroon B89, 666, 732
Canada B34, 35, 93, 194, 213, 296, 407, 418, 419, 427, 540
cant B275
Caribbean 155-61, B2, 18, 19, 133, 134, 193, 572
case grammar B53
catch phrases B514, 516
Celtic 96-7, 99-100, B544, 672, 673
chain shifts 86
Chancery English 56
change from above/below 87

Chaucer B37, 130
Chaucer, *Book of the Duchess* 15
  Canterbury Tales 13, 23, 36-40, 53-4, B94, 159
  Equatorie 51
  Legend of Good Women 15, 32
  Minor Poems 14-5, 32-3
  Parliament of Fowls 15, 32
  Troilus and Criseyde 15-6, 24, 32, 40-3, 44-6
Chaucer Variorum 11, 13, 23, 27, 36-40, B695
Chester Cycle 18, 22, B421
Chicano B504
Chinese Pidgin B59
code-mixing B263
codicology 5, 25, 26, 30, 33, 42
collation 12
collector's taste 5, 6, 8, 9, 25, 26
colloquialisms B719
colonialism B525, 539
Commonwealth literature B593
communication B420, 551, 590, 628, 630
comparative linguistics 53, 59, 72-3, 75, 79-80, B248
compilation 21, 25, 30, 33-4
complementization 67
compounds B589
concordance B434, 557
conduct books 83, B482
contact 101-3, 126-7, 128-32, B268
contrastive linguistics B237
conversation B494
copyists 12
copy text 17
corpus linguistics B470, 491, 570
correctness 56
creoles 113-9, B30, 92, 135, 208, 221, 264, 297, 314, 321, 324, 330, 398, 474, 477, 487, 518, 558, 563, 564, 605, 606, 610, 615, 665, 667, 693

creolization 126-7, B7, 31, 125, 490, 662, 738
critical editions 18-9, 23, 26, 46
cultural history B40
Cumbria B577
Danish B632
DARE 143-8, B464
dead languages B544
dialect 9-10, 18, 25, 26, 35, 57, 76, 96-7, 101-3, 104-5, 141-2, 144-5, 149-50, B3, 17, 29, 56, 145, 148, 201, 205, 370, 371, 372, 373, 454,. 468, 577, 617, 680, 681, 686, 694
dialectology 87, 92-5, 111, 152, B186, 196, 238, 250, 349, 378, 553, 611, 660, 661, 678, 679, 687, 688, 701, 702, 703, 704, 711, 720
dialectology, ME 49-52, B396, 397, 407, 441, 541, 542, 543, 566
dialogue B121
dictionaries 133-73, B19, 50, 51, 52, 95, 96, 97, 98, 107, 108, 110, 113, 114, 116, 123, 127, 136, 137, 139, 140, 141, 150, 155, 156, 166, 171, 172, 184, 188, 189, 203, 204, 206, 218, 242, 246, 253, 259, 278, 279, 280, 284, 288, 310, 311, 312, 325, 329, 351, 371, 379, 391, 399, 413, 414, 422, 425, 443, 444, 445, 446, 447, 452, 457, 464, 465, 483, 503, 505, 514, 515, 516, 523, 531, 540, 547, 554, 555, 574, 577, 588, 607, 620, 621, 631, 632, 649, 656, 668, 684, 685, 719, 745
Digby Plays 20-1
diglossia B226
discourse B121
discrimination B411, 549
divergence 57
do 640
dominance of English B28, 217
Doric B391

draft version 42, 46, 52
drama, ME 18-22, B421
Dutch B694, 726
Early Modern English B47, 181, 190, 366, 594
ecology B220, 478
economy B162
education B145, 148, 211, 272, 438, 581, 652
EETS 16, 18, 20-1, 24
editorialization 37
editorial procedure 38
emendation 47
Elizabethan English 56
ELT B13, 105, 335
encyclopedia B103, 153, 176, 177, 178, 179, 405, 428, 451, 499, 636, 669, 714
English historical syntax 66-70, B640
English language survey B281, 282
English only B4, 26, 55
English studies B101
ethnicity 90, B266
ethnolinguistics B345, 590, 605
etymology 77, 159, B51, 412, 450
expanded form/progressive B489, 595
facsimiles 3-33, B374, 448, 460, 513, 529, 698
festschriften 4, B65, 88, 210, 212, 287, 292, 323, 369, 380, 383, 390, 407, 426, 553, 641, 705
Fiji B618
final *-e* 51
fit technique 49
folk etymology B501
folklore B577
folk tales B666
foreigner's language B347
French B93, 182, 241, 376, 533, 561, 568, 659
Frisian B484
functional analysis 56, 88-9

future of English B277
Gaelic 97, 99-100, B503, 584
gender 90, 350
genetic relations 54, 126-7, B662
genre 45
German 92, B21, 27, 76, 77, 78, 122, 135, 136, 150, 203, 204, 206, 257, 317, 320, 454, 530, 631, 638, 645, 646, 647, 650, 694, 700, 724, 725, 726, 735
Germanic B74, 381, 382
Gesta Romanorum B658
Ghana 119-21 = B338, B387
Gibraltar B385
Gowerland B524
Glasgow B424
grammar 77, B215, 228, 402, 468, 573, 681
grammaticalization 54
graphemics 49
Greek B735
Great Vowel Shift 86
Grimm's law 73
Gullah B473
Guyana B562
halbsprache 110
handbook B163, 354
handwriting 16, 19, 24, 30, B529
headlines B622
heteronyms 156
historical linguistics 49-52, 53-84, B6, 76, 77, 78, 124, 129, 149, 192, 238, 239, 240, 352, 353, 354, 365, 366, 367, 388, 439, 659, 611, 619, 670
historical syntax B191, 365, 469
historiography of linguistics 70-84, B33, 303, 304, 402, 643, 653, 664
history of English 55-6, 127, B62, 87, 113, 115, 119, 174, 224, 276, 326, 401, 404, 436, 526, 583, 626
identity B474
ideology B411

imitations 44
imperialism B532
India B11-14, 66, 185, 312, 333, 334, 359, 360, 361, 362, 394, 461, 511, 512, 519, 635, 648, 745
Indo-European 53, 74
indulgence 17
inflexion 67, 104
internal factors of change 85-8
International Corpus of English B286
international language B21, 27
inventory of ME scribes 49
Ireland 96-8, 140, B56, 175, 200, 201, 228, 301, 302, 357, 475, 500, 502, 503
Jamaican 97, 116-9, 148-51, 156, B141, 187, 398, 518, 609
jargon B285
journals B406, 608, 743
Kilkenny B475
King of Tars 35
Kingis Quair 32
koinéization 102
Krio B143, 253, 354
Kriol B327, 336, 386, 586, 587, 588
language acquisition B12, 158, 291
language change, theories 54, B7, 61, 392, 393, 418, 449, 538
language contact B367, 376, 385, 395, 408, 427, 442, 449, 462, 548, 584, 609, 610, 618, 662, 663, 679, 690, 691, 700, 705, 716
language conflict B548
language death B234, 235
language in society B100, 157, 213, 222, 233, 272
language loyalty B167
language planning B44, 152, 244, 363, 430, 437, 736
language policy B193, 217
language shift B461, 696
language spread B25, 39, 232, 395, 532

language teaching 76-8, B497, 545
Late ModE literary language 65, B633
Late ModE onomastics 64, B654
Late ModE phonology 65, B654
Late ModE syntax 64
Late ModE usage 65
Late ModE vocabulary 64
Late Modern English 56
Lateran Council, Fourth 8
Latin 100, B374, 485, 568, 733, 735
Legenda Aurea B243, 724, 725
letters B491, 644
lexical change 57, B131, 317, 349, 715
lexicography 76, 78, 133-73, B39, 73, 99, 115, 195, 275, 306, 308, 309, 342, 343, 344, 407, 433, 483, 594, 637, 639, 642, 746
lexis 104-5, B283, 510
Liberia B625
linguistic anthropology B207
linguistic change, principles 85-94, B92
linguistic classification 53
linguistic evolution 56
linguistic nationalism B48, 257, 722
linguistic prehistory 54, 58
linguistic science 71-3
linguistic variables 86
literacy B133, 354, 535, 651, 657
literary critics 23, 44, B494
literature/literary language 107, B85, 249, 359, 434, 438, 531, 567, 593, 708, 709, 718
loanwords B99, 485, 530, 576, 638, 659
Lollards 24
London 25, 57, 61, B609
Luxemburg B493
lyrics 35-6
Macro Plays 4, 22, 23
Malvern Hills 52
manuscripts B383, 566
  Auchinleck 3, 5-7, B520
  B.L. Caligula A II 8

B.L. Cotton Tiberius
B.L. Cotton Vespasian D. VIII 4, 21-2, B460
B.L. Harley 4196 B492
Bodley 175 3, 18-9
Bodley 959 50
Bodley Digby 133 & e Museo 160 4, 20-1
Bodley Fairfax 16 8, 14-5, 33, B496
Bodley Hatton 96 50
Cambridge CCC 61 3, 15-6, 41, B513
Cambridge Trinity B15-17, B598
Cambridge UL Ff. 2.38 3, 7-9, 31, E vii B492
Ellesmere 13, 51
Findern 3, 8, 11-3
Hengwrt 13, 36, 51
Huntington HM 1 3, 19-20
Thornton 3, 8, 9-11
Vernon 29-31, 33-6, B521, 698
Winchester Malory 3, 16-7
Simeon 30, 31
Manx 100
medieval studies B383, 440, 535, 561
Medieval Drama Facsimile Series 18, B460
Mennonite 92
mergers 86-7
mesolect B518
metre 39
Middle English B86, 205, 472, 568, 589, 627
ME dialectology 61
ME literary language 62
ME literature B708
ME morphology 61
ME onomastics 62
ME poetry 728
ME phonology 61
ME semantics 61
ME syntax 61
minority languages B157, 160, 690, 727

mischsprache 25, 26, 33, 50
mixed language 102, 126-7, 129
morphology (*cf.* word-formation) B456, 734
Morte Arture 10
multilingualism B144, 233, 255, 493, 497, 519, 561, 712
mystics 24
N-Town Plays 21-2, B460
Namibia B300, 549
national languages B591, 736
Native American English B57
Neogrammarians 85, 87
New English B50, 52
New Englishes B45, 245
Newfoundland B649
New Guinea 121-7, B59, 60
newspapers B358, 394
new words B123, 684
New York B255
New Zealand 171-3, B70, 114, 274, 507
Nigeria B356, 389
non-cycle plays 22
non-standard B85, 331, 459
norms B58, 151
North America B15
Northern Homily Cycle 34, B492
notional structure 134
official English B4, 167
Old English B326, 536, 571
OED B483, 508, 727
OE dialects 60
OE lexicography B46, 322
OE literary language 60
OE morphology 59
OE onomastics 60
OE phonology 59
OE semantics 59
OE syntax 59
OE style 60
OE thesaurus 133-6
OE vocabulary B49

OE word-formation 60
onomasiology 133-40
onomastics B246, 465
orality B535
origin of language 81
Orkney B242, 399
Owl and Nightingale 16
Pacific B44, 741
Pakistan B63, 552
palaeographer 4, 23, 24
parallel-text edition 46-8
passive 67-8
patronage 16
Pearl 16
Pennsylvania Dutch 92
Philippines B65, 517
philological research 4, 23, 31, 49, 54, 78
philosophy of language 81
phonetics/phonology 86, 93, 104-5, 114, 150, B68, 89, 190, 246, 301
photography 7, 11, 19, 29, 30
Pictish 99
pidgins 113-27, B30, B59, 60, 125, 135, 264, 314, 330, 403, 449, 477, 479, 558, 605, 606
Piers Plowman 364, 534, 597, 598
placenames B246, 465
plantation B618
play B8
pluricentric B151
policies B509, 559, 596, 624
Polish B452
postcolonial B72, 511
post-imperial English B236
pragmatics B454
prehistory 99
prescriptivism B654
preservation 5
Prick of Conscience 34, 50
Prince Edward Island B540
proper English B173, 482

protolanguage 71
psalms B707
punctuation 43
Quare of Ielusy 32
Quebec B427
Queen's English 83
questionnaire 144
reader B147, 165
real language B468
recension 4, 38
reception 44, 46
reconstruction 53, 57
recording B417
register B81, 82
relative clauses B215
religious poems 6, 33-6
religious prose B316
Renaissance B432, 433
reprint series 70
research possibilities 26, B258, 267, 538, 542
rhetoric 46, B269, 271
romances 6, 7, 9, 35, B557
Russian B457
S-shaped curve 86
saints' legends B634, 717, 726, 731
St Katherine 7
St Kitts B43
St Louis B486
St Margaret 7
Scandinavian 60, 100, 127
Scotification 32
Scotland 96, 98, B183, 352, 584
Scots 50, 96, 100, 103-8, 109-10, B160, 192, 202, 280, 284, 295, 352, 353, 354, 391, 416, 417, 424, 425, 426, 430, 431, 432, 443, 444, 445, 446, 574, 608, 683, 707, 709, 718
Scottish literature B126, 160
Scottish Troy Book 51
scribal profiles 49
semantic change 54, 72, 74, B261

semantic field B599
semantics 114, B8, 260, 261
Shakespeare's language B106
Shetland B279, 573
Singapore B9, 109, 168, 245, 272, 291, 363, 510
slang B36, 290, 515, 621
social factors of change 88-92, B376, 393, 404
social networks 90
social psychology B265
social variables 86
sociolinguistics 85-92, 94, B9, 23, 91, 146, 147, 163, 165, 185, 194, 223, 292, 318, 337, 358, 393, 395, 424, 439, 442, 454, 461, 462, 463, 482, 531, 545, 563, 578, 582, 585, 597, 646, 647, 651, 676, 699, 723
sociology of literature 7, 16, 25, 26
Solomon Islands B289, 340, 403, 623
sound change 53, 57, 73, 88, 91
sources 37-8, 41-2, 45
sourcebook B167, 169, 173, 174, 175, 181, 187
South Africa 161-8, B95, 96, 97, 98, 461, 462, 620, 712, 744
South Asia B10, 64
South East Asia B363, 497, 498
South English Legendary 34, B348
Spanish B385, 575, 576
speculation 71-74
speech community 89, B578
spelling 51-2, 57, 104, B132
spelling reform 76, 78
spoken English B81, 83, 296
Standard English/language 55, B61, 80, 169, 173, 418, 617, 672, 694, 739d
standardization 103, 124, B192, 381, 455, 495, 511, 591
state of English B565
status B20, 21, 24, 376, 403, 616
stemma 42

structural changes 55
style 46, B528, 529, 551
substrate B92, 487
Sydney B332
syntax 104-5, 114-5, 122, 295, B358
syntactic change 54, 57
Tanzania B600
tense 68
terminology B1, 433
textbooks 43-6, 53-4, 55-8, 453, 463, 472, 536, 579, 582, 671
text editions B364, 377, 409, 568, 597, 598
text types B81, 82, 423
textual apparatus 39
textual commentary 38, 42-3
textual criticism 38, 45, B471
textual relationship 25
textual transmission 4, 8, 14, 24, 26, 38, 42, 51, B364
textual variants 39-41
thesaurus B444, 571, 689
Thopas, Sir 6, 7
Times B622
Tok Pisin 121-7, B209, 435, 437, 476, 477, 479, 581, 697, 737, 738, 740, 741, 742
Torres Strait B615
Towneley Cycle 19-20
transcription 22
translation 109-10, B160, 249, 262, 416, 612, 733
Troilus B513, 729, 730
Ulster 106, 140-3, B3, 425, 668

uniformitarian principle 85
universals 74, B587
urban dialects 97
USA B4, 138, 139, 140, 157, 166, 196, 225, 251, 288, 349, 411, 696
usage 164-5, B19, 54, 118, 229, 356, 389
variation B17, 81, 82, 212, 400, 466, 488, 495, 706
verb morphology B388
verb phrase 67
verb system B470
verbal hygiene B128
Victorian 531
Wales B41, 164, 524
watermarks 12
Welsh 97, 100, B721, 722
Weltbild 134
West Africa 119-21, B45, 100
Wexford B201
working facsimile 29, 33
word formation B5, 131, 384, 641d
word geography 50, B688
word order 67
world English 79, B111, 115, 146, 180, 219, 236, 241, 256, 299, 306, 339, 390, 410, 429, 458, 537, 546, 560, 628, 629, 630, 675
world languages B710
writing B81, 192, 692a
written ME 49
Yiddish 93
York Play 22
Yorkshire 340, 371, 372, 373